The Triple Bond

*This book
pays tribute to
Arthur Colby Sprague,
whose pioneering work in
Shakespearean stage history and
theatre research has
contributed to a
new perspective
in dramatic
criticism.*

Edited by JOSEPH G. PRICE

The Triple Bond

Plays, Mainly Shakespearean, in Performance

The Pennsylvania State University Press
University Park and London

Library of Congress Cataloging in Publication Data

Main entry under title:

The triple bond.

Published as tribute to A. C. Sprague.
"Bibliography of Arthur Colby Sprague": p. 281.
1. Shakespeare, William, 1564–1616—Dramatic produc-
tion—Addresses, essays, lectures. 2. Shakespeare,
William, 1564–1616—Stage history—Addresses, essays,
lectures. 3. Sprague, Arthur Colby, 1895–
I. Price, Joseph G., ed. II. Sprague, Arthur
Colby, 1895–
PR3091.T74   822.3'3   74–15140
ISBN 0–271–01177–9

Designed by Andrew Vargo

Printed in the United States of America

Contents

Contributors   vii
Preface   ix

PART I

The Playwright and Interpretation

Stanley Wells	The Academic and the Theatre 3
Kenneth Muir	The Critic, the Director, and Liberty of Interpreting 20
M. St. Clare Byrne	Dramatic Intention and Theatrical Realization 30
M. C. Bradbrook	The Triple Bond: Audience, Actors, Author in the Elizabethan Playhouse 50

PART II

The Playwright and Audience

Clifford Leech	Shakespeare's Songs and the Double Response 73
Anne Barton	The King Disguised: Shakespeare's *Henry V* and the Comical History 92
Frances Shirley	Shakespeare's Use of Oaths 118
J. C. Trewin	In the Margin 137

Contents

PART III

The Playwright and Performance

Jane Williamson	The Duke and Isabella on the Modern Stage 149
Lois Potter	Realism Versus Nightmare: Problems of Staging *The Duchess of Malfi* 170
Jeanne T. Newlin	The Darkened Stage: J. P. Kemble and *Troilus and Cressida* 190
Robert Hamilton Ball	*The Taming of the Shrew*—with "Additional Dialogue"? 203

PART IV

The Playwright and Theatre

Nevill Coghill	*Macbeth* at the Globe, 1606–1616 (?): Three Questions 223
Alan S. Downer	Heavenly Mingle: *Antony and Cleopatra* as a Dramatic Experience 240
Rudolf Stamm	The Alphabet of Speechless Complaint 255
Sybil Rosenfeld	Hubert Herkomer's Theatrical Theories and Practice and the New Stagecraft 274

Helen D. Willard	Bibliography of Arthur Colby Sprague 281

Notes 285
Index of Plays 305
General Index 309

Contributors

Robert Hamilton Ball Professor Emeritus of English, Queens College, The City University of New York

Anne Barton Fellow of New College and University Lecturer in English, University of Oxford

Muriel C. Bradbrook Professor of English and Mistress of Girton College, Cambridge University

Muriel St. Clare Byrne Theatre historian and critic, London

Nevill Coghill Professor of English, Oxford University

Alan S. Downer Late Professor of English, Princeton University

Clifford Leech Professor of English, University College, University of Toronto

Kenneth Muir Professor Emeritus of English Literature, University of Liverpool; Editor of *Shakespeare Survey*

Jeanne T. Newlin Curator, Harvard Theatre Collection, Harvard University

Lois Potter Lecturer in English, University of Leicester

Joseph G. Price Professor of English, The Pennsylvania State University

Sybil Rosenfeld Joint editor, *Theatre Notebook*, London

Frances Shirley Professor of English, Wheaton College, Massachusetts

Rudolf Stamm Professor of English, Basel University

J. C. Trewin Drama critic, London and Birmingham

Stanley Wells Reader in English and Fellow, The Shakespeare Institute, University of Birmingham

Helen D. Willard Cambridge, Massachusetts (Curator, Harvard Theatre Collection, 1960–72)

Jane Williamson Associate Professor of English, University of Missouri, St. Louis

Preface

As M.C. Bradbrook entitles her essay, a play is a "triple bond," an art completed in the interaction of author, actors, and audience. Scholars have not always accepted this. With few exceptions, critics in the nineteenth and early twentieth centuries regarded the play as a literary work to be divorced from the theatre with its damaging compromises. As with poetry and fiction, they analyzed dramatic artistry by isolating elements: characterization, plot, theme, moral philosophy, diction, rhetoric, imagery, poetics, and later symbol, archetype, and myth. The Renaissance playwright, in particular, was thought to have composed dramatic poems unless he was a mere theatrical hack. The giants—Marlowe, Shakespeare, Jonson, Webster—were hampered by a primitive theatre which dictated distortions because of the physical stage, the inadequacies of actors, the crude taste of groundlings. In recent times, however, our critical focus has been expanded to see the play as a communal art, one in which authorial intention is realized fully only in production with the benefit of visual and aural support. Today, the dramatic text, whether classical or modern, is studied as a script to be vitalized in the theatre.

For this critical shift in perspective, especially with respect to Renaissance drama, we owe much to Arthur Colby Sprague. As the authority on Shakespeare's plays in performance, he has enriched our understanding by describing the experience of drama in the theatre without sacrificing the literary analysis of the text. Throughout this book, his influence is recorded directly or indirectly. We, his colleagues and students, hope that our contributions will be a fulfillment to him.

For the general reader, the volume moves beyond tribute to an extension of Professor Sprague's work, a demonstration of our dependence on theatrical production for full understanding of the play. In Renaissance drama, this perspective has been shared by increasing numbers of critics. It has dominated recent conferences such as the

Preface

World Shakespeare Conference at Vancouver in 1971, the International Shakespeare Conference at Stratford-upon-Avon in 1972, and the Shakespeare Association meeting in Washington, D.C., in 1973. It has been the stimulus to much recent scholarship, including recreations of Shakespeare the theatre professional that have been devised by Anne Righter (Barton) in *Shakespeare and the Idea of the Play* (1962), Bernard Beckerman in *Shakespeare at the Globe* (1962), Nevill Coghill in *Shakespeare's Professional Skills* (1964), M.C. Bradbrook in *Shakespeare the Craftsman* (1969), and Clifford Leech in *The Dramatist's Experience* (1970). Much practical criticism has evolved from the study of plays in contemporary performance and from the evidence of their stage histories.[1]

I need not elaborate on this new direction in Shakespearean criticism, for the essays that follow demonstrate its history, validity, and value. The contributors, distinguished by their knowledge of both text and stage, establish principles for and limits to theatrical interpretation. Their focus is on the dramatist's conception as it is realized in the theatre. Their evidence ranges from Elizabethan conventions and performances to modern productions. It involves all sorts of interpreters: adapters and directors, actors and designers, scholars and reviewers, a film scriptwriter and composer. Refreshingly, the record of the past often is vivified by the theatrical experience of the contributor. Where E.M.W. Tillyard was forced to admit in his critical study of *All's Well that Ends Well*, "Fail the play does, when read: but who of its judges have seen it acted? Not I at any rate," the scholar in this volume corroborates theory (and delights the reader) with his own notes as theatre-goer.

Part I of the book deals with interpretative principles in a communal art form. Examining early conditions of the theatre which militated against the serious study of Shakespeare and subsequent conditions in the classroom which replaced the classics with Shakespeare for linguistic and rhetorical study, Stanley Wells maps out a meeting ground for academic critic and theatre professional. Kenneth Muir, sifting through theatrical practices, discusses the kind of interpretation legitimate to critic and director. After demonstrating that dramatic intention always extends beyond the words of the text, M. St. Clare Byrne cites twentieth-century productions of Elizabethan drama. Her major illustration is *Henry VIII*, where principles of interpretation shed light on both textual problems and performance. How the practices of Renaissance drama established principles for a social art such as the theatre is described by M.C. Bradbrook; she recreates the milieu in which "the actors' roles became increasingly interpretative, that of the audience differentiated, while in certain kinds of play the author acquired independent status."

The second section is concerned with Shakespeare's response to and manipulation of his audience as evidence of its role in his creative imagination. Objecting to admiration of Shakespeare's songs as splendid lyrical ornaments, Clifford Leech argues that the dramatist intends and evokes irony by juxtaposing the sentiment of the song with a jarring stage picture, particularly in *The Two Gentlemen of Verona* and *Cymbeline*. After a comprehensive survey of the disguised king in Elizabethan tradition and convention, Anne Barton shows us how Shakespeare's sense of his audience influenced the composition of *Henry V*. By frustrating its expectations, he achieves startling effects. On the other hand, Frances Shirley demonstrates how Shakespeare triggers anticipated responses through the connotations of familiar oaths and colloquialisms. Even the experienced reader of plays falls short of Shakespeare's visual conceptions. J.C. Trewin, as an audience of one, tells charmingly how the characters in the margins of the texts have assumed life for him on stage.

Part III considers the play in performance, interpreted and modified by director, actor, and now screenwriter. It includes theatrical interpretations of *Measure for Measure*, *The Duchess of Malfi*, and *Troilus and Cressida*, three difficult Renaissance plays, yet now, before modern audiences, enjoying their greatest popularity. Jane Williamson explores the characterizations of the Duke and Isabella as they have been acted from 1950 to 1972. Lois Potter writes of the director's dilemma in reconciling or choosing between convention and realism as he sorts out Webster's intention in *The Duchess*. If *Troilus* has been produced frequently in recent decades, no manager dared Shakespeare's play in the eighteenth and nineteenth centuries. In "The Darkened Stage," Jeanne T. Newlin analyzes the alterations worked out by John Philip Kemble for a production which never reached the stage. In an early instance of Shakespeare on film, Robert Ball discusses the scriptwriter for the 1929 Pickford-Fairbanks film, *The Taming of the Shrew*.

The elaborate stage descriptions and directions by modern dramatists for printed editions confirm the ever-present anxiety of the playwright for the theatre in which his play is produced. We now recognize the shaping influence of the Elizabethan theatre. In Part IV, Nevill Coghill suggests the extent of that influence by posing three questions concerning the staging of *Macbeth* at the Globe. Among the pleasant debts I incurred in preparing this book, perhaps the most fortunate is owed to Mrs. Alan Downer, who discovered an unpublished manuscript of her late husband. Alan Downer was a student, colleague, and close friend of Arthur Colby Sprague. His essay, which sets the composition of *Antony and Cleopatra* in the theatrical conditions of its time, exemplifies the critical spirit of this volume. Rudolf Stamm writes about Shakespeare's struggle to coordinate his poetical and his theatrical means of expression, especially in that most difficult of dramatic situations, the speechless communication of Lavinia in *Titus Andronicus*. As the final link in the social art, the stage designer and his craft are discussed by Sybil Rosenfeld; her example is Hubert Herkomer, who contributed to the late nineteenth-century revolution in scene design and theatrical construction.

These essays along with the bibliography at the end of this volume provide sufficient testimony to Professor Sprague's leadership and exacting scholarship in Shakespearean stage history. Another quality, no less significant to his students and colleagues, deserves note. In the days when male graduate students were still something of an oddity in the Bryn Mawr English Department, I began doctoral studies there in a climate where traditions, customs, and rules for survival were passed along the halls of the women's residence houses. Without this guidance, naively I chose my three courses for the year. It was not until early December that whispered warnings caught up with me; I had embarked on a near suicidal course. I had enrolled with the department's "three B's," a fearsome trio for their scholarly and critical demands—the Beard, the Bird, and the Bard. The Beard was Stephen Joseph Herben, manneredly forbidding but wonderfully warm-hearted, a medievalist whose own treasure hoard, unearthed in his Scandinavian digs, quickened the text. The Bird, according to a typically undergraduate caricature for his features, was Samuel Chew, whose breadth of literary knowledge swept me back and forth between the sixteenth and nineteenth centuries as his personality defined for me the term gentleman-scholar. The Bard, of course, was the Shakespearean, Arthur Colby Sprague. His interest in theatrical history and his insistence on scholarly precision were well known. But what he shared with his colleagues was an unusual critical perception, a soundness and wisdom that characterized the textual approach of the "three B's." I could not have had a more fruitful year in learning the tools of explication.

Through this critical sensitivity, Professor Sprague has wedded the roles of literary and theatrical critic. Both roles have been guided by a single principle, one enunciated by his mentor, George Lyman Kittredge. In an introductory essay to Kittredge's *Sixteen Plays of Shake-*

speare (an edition which he completed after Kittredge's death), Professor Sprague writes, "To Kittredge the function of the interpretative critic was clear. It was to seek Shakespeare's meaning and intention—to seek it with devotion and self-abnegation, for the disciple was never to 'mistake himself for the master.' " In an article on William Poel, Professor Sprague extends the criterion to the stage, "As with the criticism of great plays, so with their representation: a sensitive regard for the author's intention is ever to be preferred to mere impressionism or virtuosity." He has corrected impressionism and objected to virtuosity in both literary theory and theatrical practices. Who will disagree with his characterization of Falstaff in argument against Morgann, Bradley, Dover Wilson, and with reluctance Kittredge? We can only admire his rejection of distracting stage business, even when it is as enticing as Hamlet's theft of Claudius's sword in the prayer scene. We are brought back to authorial intention when he writes against fad: "I refer to what Goneril and Regan say about their father's attendant knights in *King Lear*: that they are a crew of dangerous ruffians, a desperate train. Sometimes in the study, and lately on the stage, their word, the word of these monstrous women, has been taken against the King's. . . . Against these assertions is, however, the strongest sort of dramatic evidence." The whole question of Brutus as tragic hero is put into perspective for me as I read of the quarrel scene, "When we like Brutus least and feel we know him best. . . ." Theatrical experience elucidates style: in explaining the effect of hearing a line from a familiar play seemingly for the first time in the theatre, he chooses Desdemona's line at the dropping of the handkerchief ("I am very sorry that you are not well") to comment upon the "ease . . . with which Shakespeare achieved a transition from one level of expression to another." How many of us are brought up short in our reading of *Othello*: "At the end of the scene a point is made which is likely to escape any but the most attentive of readers: Iago gets the promotion he desired. On the stage, the importance of this has been brought out in various ways"? In a question of authorship and structure, he writes of the masque in *Cymbeline*: "I would make one point in its favour, a point which, perhaps, has not been made before. This is the difference in our attitude towards the play's denouement when, in performance, the vision is included. The presence of the supernatural makes acceptable what otherwise we condemn for its excess of coincidence, the too perfect solving of difficulty—an art no longer concealing art."

Unlike the typical specialist, Professor Sprague has made his work serve the universal interest in Shakespeare. He has admired the scope of Dr. Johnson: "And as in much of Johnson's best criticism the appeal is to life as it is lived by us, to human experience which admits of no such simplification [the rigid segregation of tragedy from comedy]." In his own view, "I would not subscribe even to the idea that such-and-such a work of Shakespeare's is a play about appearance and reality; order and disorder. It may be about order and disorder, or appearance and reality, or both; but it is also a play, once more, about life as it is lived, about men and their passions and aspirations, their nobility and littleness."[2]

Almost thirty years later, we can do no better than echo Granville-Barker's assessment of Arthur Colby Sprague, "His critical judgment is usually excellent; and the reader could only benefit by more of it."[3]

I am grateful to Dr. Jeanne T. Newlin, Curator, Harvard Theatre Collection, for permission to use the Angus McBean photographs of productions and for supplying the following illustrations:

Edmund Kean as Richard III, del. I.R. Cruikshank, sculpt. G. Cruikshank, 1814.

"A Minute & Correct View of the Inside of the New Theatre Covent Garden." Del. G. Argenzio, sculpt. Heideldorf, 1810.

An English country performance, perhaps Macbeth. Sepia aquatint by J. Wright after W.R. Pyne, 1788.

The title page of William Alabaster's *Roxanna*, 1632.

State College, Pa.   Joseph G. Price

I
The
Playwright
and
Interpretation

The Academic and the Theatre

Stanley Wells

There was a time—a pre-Sprague era—when the worlds of the study and the stage seemed to be separated by an almost unbridgeable chasm. This essay is an attempt to sketch some of the changing aspects of the relationship between academic study and theatrical presentation of Shakespeare's plays with reference to productions in England and especially Stratford-upon-Avon.

One reason for the division is that before state subsidy of the theatre became an accepted aspect of English society, Shakespeare's plays were generally performed in conditions governed largely by commercial considerations, alleviated occasionally by a measure of private patronage such as that given by Sir Barry Jackson at the Birmingham Repertory Theatre. The plays belonged to the popular theatre. In some ways this was healthy, but it meant that the ways in which the plays were presented were shaped by the demands and conventions of such a theatre, in the ways Professor Sprague described in his essay "Shakespeare and Melodrama."[1] It meant that the less popular plays were neglected, and that those that were played were often seriously abbreviated and rearranged to conform to the theatrical fashions of the time. They were regarded largely as vehicles for the display of the talents of virtuoso performers, and visual spectacle often was emphasized at the expense of other qualities more germane to the plays themselves. To recognize Shakespeare within a theatrical tradition that has ceased to exist we need only recall Dickens's account, in *Great Expectations*, of Mr. Wopsle's exertions in the role of Hamlet, or his essay describing the fit-up theatre in which actors paid to enact roles of their choice.

In the Patent theatres, too, Shakespeare's plays formed an important part of the staple repertory—or at least certain plays did, especially those that provided star roles for leading actors. The theatre of, at any rate, the period from Garrick to Macready was predominantly an actors' theatre, in which the audience included a high proportion

3

of connoisseurs of acting with a detailed knowledge of a limited range of plays. They were comparatively little interested in ensemble-playing, or in overall interpretation. This meant that those who wished to study Shakespeare seriously were almost forced to do so on the page rather than on the stage, either because certain plays could not be seen at all or because those that were seen were acted in heavily adapted versions. Lamb, Hazlitt, Leigh Hunt, and others might and did protest at the violence done to the plays; but the theatre was slow to change its ways.

When the theatre eventually did change, it was in a manner that we are bound to associate with the spread of popular education. There was an earnestness about Samuel Phelps's suburban audiences at Sadler's Wells—"reverent" is Henry Morley's repeated word for them—and Charles Kean's at the Princess's Theatre which reflects changing social conditions. The difference between Edmund Kean and his son Charles epitomizes at a personal level the difference be-tween the theatre of the Regency and that of mid-Victorian England: Edmund of uncertain parentage and informal education, the fre-quent center of scandal, often disabled by drink, but at his best a brilliantly exciting star actor; Charles educated at Eton, later a Fel-low of the Society of Antiquaries, carrying his interests as an anti-quarian into the setting and costuming of his productions, for which the enormous programmes were full of carefully footnoted back-ground information, but as an actor, it would seem, careful and yet generally uninspired, though he could promote performances of well-disciplined group-playing.

As vehicles for star performers in the popular theatre, some of Shakespeare's plays retained their popularity for a long time. Irving, Tree, Benson, and Wolfit were to some degree maintainers of the tradition, as, to some extent, Laurence Olivier is. As long as some actors are better than others, the tradition will never disappear, but recently, especially at Stratford, there has been an increased emphasis on ensemble-playing.

If the spread of popular education did something to lift the status of Shakespeare's plays above the general level of repertory pieces, it did not altogether work to bridge the gap between study and stage. During the nineteenth century, works of English literature, especially Shakespeare's plays, came to supplant the Greek and Roman classics as the basis of a literary education, and in the process the methods by which the authors of classical antiquity had been studied came to be applied—not always appropriately—to the English authors who took their place. Anyone familiar with the Pitt Press editions of Shakespeare prepared by A.W. Verity during the 1890s and later will remember how strongly they emphasize philology, the derivation of words, the discussion of prosody using classical terminology, analysis of syntax as if it were that of a dead language, linguistic and literary features at the expense of dramatic ones. In their way they are excellent editions, but they show scarcely any awareness of the plays as theatrical creations. Since many of those who wrote about the plays in the early years of the twentieth century were the product of this educational system, and also were themselves involved with it, it is understandable that they tended to take an untheatrical standpoint.

Though the use of Shakespeare's plays as instruments of education had little to do with the tradition of their popular presentation, it has worked in favor of their recognition as theatrical classics, to be treated with a degree of reverence, a fitting basis for the repertory of a subsidized, noncommercial theatre. At the present time, most school children undergoing secondary education are expected to know several Shakespeare plays, often in some detail; and there are far more school children than there used to be. For this reason alone, performances of the plays in texts not too remote from those studied in schools are—once the desirability that pupils see performances of the plays they are studying is granted—a practical necessity and, if not a commercial proposition, at least obviously deserving of educational subsidy.

One influence that has affected the manner in which performances are given in England originated in events of the scholarly amateur theatre during the last quarter of the nineteenth century. It is scarcely possible to overestimate the importance of William Poel's work with the Elizabethan Stage Society, which changed the course of Shakespeare production and has had a profound, though less easily traceable, effect on Shakespeare scholarship and criticism. One important point about it is its opening of the way for the evolution of a style or styles of production that make it possible to present Shakespeare's plays without severe textual alteration. Though he was no textual purist, Poel strongly influenced the establishment of the principle that it is possible and desirable to present Elizabethan and Jacobean plays in conditions adapted to the plays, rather than (as was usual up to his time) adapting the plays to the theatrical conditions.

More recently, other educated men with strongly developed historical and literary senses, and some who also had an ability to commit their views to print, have worked in the theatre: one thinks of Harley Granville-Barker, Barry Jackson, Nevill Coghill, and George Rylands. It is significant that a good deal of their practical work is associated with amateur and subsidized theatre. It appealed, initially at least, to select audiences; only slowly has their influence made itself felt on the professional stage. These men, and others like them, have gradually helped to bring about a change in the theatrical presentation of Shakespeare that has made it much more possible than it once was for the academically minded spectator to feel that he can study the plays even while seeing them performed. Increased awareness of historical considerations in performances of plays has helped to elevate them from warhorses of the popular theatre into works that deserve the most careful treatment in the intellectual theatre. And this theatre—which developed along with the changes in style of Shakespeare production and is inextricably linked to them—is not an actors' but a directors' theatre, with an emphasis on ensemble work, on the play as a total work of art, to be produced with equal care for all its parts. This development has its dangers, since directors are as capable as actors of indulging their virtuosity at the expense of the play. But at its best, it makes for a fuller concentration on the total experience of the play, and thus gives more scope to historical considerations than a theatre devoted principally to the display of virtuosity in acting.

The spread of education among theatre audiences has been paralleled by an increase of formal, advanced education among theatre people themselves. Actors who are university graduates, and graduates in English literature, are not uncommon, though many present-day actors went straight into the theatre or a drama school at the age of sixteen or eighteen. But a degree in English seems in danger of becoming a required qualification for directing a Shakespeare play, at any rate at Stratford-upon-Avon. The present artistic director, Trevor Nunn, and his predecessor, Peter Hall, both read English at Cambridge. The two previous directors, Anthony Quayle and Glen Byam Shaw, on the other hand, both went straight into the theatre from their public schools. Peter Brook, who has been associated with Stratford for over twenty years, was at Oxford. John Barton, who has been directing at Stratford since 1960, is an old Etonian who also went to Cambridge, did graduate work in English, and was for several years Dean of King's College. Terry Hands, who has been with the Royal Shakespeare Company since 1966, is a graduate in English and Drama of the University of Birmingham. All this reflects a lowering of the barrier between the academic world and that of the professional theatre and suggests a strong influence of the older universities on that theatre. Both Oxford and Cambridge have so well developed a tradition of amateur theatricals that they have

6

served virtually as academies of the higher dramatic art—or at any rate of the art of the higher drama; and Nevill Coghill at Oxford and, still more, George Rylands at Cambridge have exerted a strong though usually informal influence on professional Shakespeare production since the 1930s. Of course, there are still good Shakespeare directors who have not undergone a university training; but inevitably they are affected by the environment in which they work. It might be suggested that the products of a literary education are presenting Shakespeare's plays to audiences increasingly composed of those who themselves have received, or are receiving, such an education. Presentation of Shakespeare's plays on television, which might reach a majority audience, poses special problems for which no generally successful solutions seem yet to have been found.

I have been considering some factors that have resulted in Shakespeare's plays belonging no more to the mainstream of the popular theatre but predominantly to the subsidized theatre. It is difficult to produce statistical evidence, but a glance at the tables in J.C. Trewin's *Shakespeare on the English Stage: 1900–1964*[2] is enough to suggest what seems certainly true, that commercial managements have become increasingly reluctant to finance the production of a Shakespeare play, with the result that most English Shakespeare productions are given under the umbrella of the Arts Council. The plays have been pushed by economic pressures into a highbrow status. On the rare occasions when they are produced by a commercial management it is usually with an eye to audiences of school parties wishing to see the plays they are studying for their examinations, a factor that tends to induce conservatism in production methods and in the handling of texts. Whereas the great actor-managers at the turn of the century found in Shakespeare's plays a large part of their staple diet, for the great actors of today the performance of a Shakespearean role is a luxury, indulged in to the detriment of their bank balances and in defiance of the tax men.

Up to about 1960, the Shakespeare Memorial Theatre, as it then was called, had a serious London rival in the Old Vic Company, which included in its repertory a high proportion of Shakespeare productions. But with the fading of the Old Vic into the National Theatre, whose repertory has included comparatively few Shakespeare plays, the Royal Shakespeare Company has become the principal purveyor of Shakespeare's plays to the English nation. Its position in this respect has been strengthened by its acquisition of a London home and by the development of a policy that has turned that home into, among other things, a showcase for the company's most successful Stratford productions. The economics of the situation seem to be that there is a guaranteed audience for most Shakespeare plays at Stratford, but that only the better-reviewed productions—Hobson's choice, as it were—will sell in London.

This dominance of the Royal Shakespeare Company has been easily accepted by other companies. The only other company regularly presenting Shakespeare in London has been the subsidized one in Regent's Park. The Prospect Players, also directed by a Cambridge graduate, and also heavily subsidized, have worked mainly in the provinces. In London, the National Theatre has shown a comparative lack of interest in Shakespeare, in spite of its opening production of *Hamlet* (1963) and its memorable *Othello* (1964). This may seem surprising considering that the theatre is directed by one of the greatest of all Shakespeare actors. Perhaps Lord Olivier has felt that the world of Shakespeare production is passing out of the hands of the old pros like himself into those of the young dons. The National Theatre's *As You Like It* (1967)—a consciously experimental production—was directed by Clifford Williams (not a university graduate), who till then had been associated rather with the Royal Shakespeare Company. Frank Dunlop, who was the Associate Director of their *Love's Labour's Lost* (1968), read English at University College, London. In *The Merchant of Venice* (1970), Olivier allowed himself to be directed by one of Cambridge's most brilliant and successful postwar graduates, Dr. Jonathan Miller. The other most important subsidized company of recent years has been the Chichester Company, which also has included only a small number of Shakespeare's plays in a generally classical repertory.

How does this situation affect the ways in which plays are presented? Most basically, it is influencing attitudes to the text. Here we have had, and are having, a quiet revolution. Again, its roots can be traced far back, as far as the protests against theatre versions that were already being made in the eighteenth century, such as those by Theophilus Cibber against Garrick. Much later, William Poel is important, mainly because, as I have suggested, he showed the way toward the development of production methods in which the employment of full texts was practical. Still more important has been Harley Granville-Barker, who in both practice and precept encouraged directors to think afresh before altering the text, and to alter it as little as possible. Symptomatic of the changing attitude is the disappearance of the acting edition. For over 200 years the presenta-

8

tion of major Shakespeare revivals at the London theatres was regularly accompanied by the issue of a text of the play as acted. And from the time of Bell's theatre edition, published in the 1770s, there have been available series of editions which reflect current practice in the major theatres and thus influence it in minor ones. Editions such as Cumberland's and Lacy's, which were based on London productions, were used in provincial theatres—a practice that no doubt was particularly convenient at a time when star actors from London were liable to descend upon the provincial theatres with very little time for the resident company to prepare itself. (Even in this century there is a story of an old actor who, invited to perform Kent in *King Lear* at a provincial theatre, wrote back accepting and saying "Usual moves, I suppose?") The Henry Irving Shakespeare, which appeared in 1888, marking omissions made or recommended, is a nineteenth-century parallel to Bell. The practice of issuing acting texts simultaneously with the production seems to have died out. When it did so I do not know. Granville-Barker did it for his three Savoy Theatre productions in 1912 and 1914, giving full texts of the plays but marking the few lines that he omitted in performance. I know of nothing systematic later than this. Yet the recent volume *The Wars of the Roses*,[3] John Barton's adaptation of some of the history plays, is in the same line of succession, and acting editions not related to specific productions continue to appear from the firm of Samuel French, which is a descendant of Lacy's, under the supervision of George Skillan.

But professional directors and actors now seem to work directly from academically prepared editions. For a long time the New Temple was popular, mainly, I suppose, because of its handy size. For working purposes actors need the text, preferably with no notes on the page, and with a good margin. Nowadays the most commonly used editions in England appear to be the New Penguin, the Signet, and the New Cambridge. The choice is sometimes reasoned, sometimes not. The selection of a working text is of slight but not negligible importance. Conventions of presentation, modernization, punctuation, and so on, vary from one edition to another, and all have their influence on the way lines are spoken. The guiding hand, of course, is the director's, and it may be hoped he has consulted a number of different editions and in a sense imposed his own editorial conventions, discussing with his actors the scansion of difficult lines, for instance, so that they sound trippingly on the tongue. But it is surprising how often actors within a single production are inconsistent about such matters as the pronunciation of names, with the result that we hear "*Bull*-ingbroke," "*Boll*-ingbroke," and "*Bow*-lingbroke" within a single evening, and even "Petru*ckio*" as well as "Petru*chio*." I have even heard actors conscientiously, if misguidedly, trying to say "y'are," with a hiccough in the middle, or " 'a," when they would have been well advised to adopt any easy modern colloquial way of saying "you're" or "he." This is the result of a failure to understand a printing convention and possibly an editor's failure to explain the convention. Punctuation, of course, can affect sense. I think and hope that the New Penguin edition, which is appearing under the general editorship of T.J.B. Spencer, will be the only complete edition so far consistently to print correctly the Elizabethanisms "look how," "look when," "look where," and so on—meaning "however," "whenever," "wherever"—without intermediate punctuation, as if "look" were exclamatory. But neither this nor the provision of notes explaining the construction is necessarily enough to persuade actors to say, for instance, "Look what I speak, or do, or think to do/ you still are crossing it" (*The Taming of the Shrew*, IV.iii.195) rather than, in defiance of grammar, "Look! What I speak. . . ."

Of course, working from a fully academically prepared text by no means implies use of the full text. Omission of lines, sometimes in large numbers, is common, and the order of scenes is occasionally rearranged. But directors are far less likely than formerly to follow traditional cuts and rearrangements, far more likely to experiment with the inclusion of passages once traditionally cut. They are more likely to start from a full text, omitting passages, when they do so, for their own reasons rather than simply following custom. Often we hear lines that have traditionally been omitted; sometimes we are denied lines that we are accustomed to hear.

In its attitudes toward the text the theatre, then, has come to reflect academic influence. On the whole, this influence has encouraged the view that Shakespeare's plays are unified poetic-dramatic structures easily damaged by the removal of a part. Critics and scholars have defended the authenticity of once suspect episodes such as the final scene of *The Two Gentlemen of Verona*, and the vision scene in *Cymbeline*, and even the Hecate scenes in *Macbeth*; and they have found artistic justification for the King's Evil scene in *Macbeth* and the clown scenes in *Othello*. At least some directors, whether obediently or just experimentally, have included these scenes in their productions. But the world of Shakespeare studies does not present a united front. Academic influence can result in textual disintegration as well as rehabilitation. It is paradoxical that the Shakespeare director with the highest academic qualifications in English literature is the one who has been most free in his handling of texts. In his excellent productions of many of the comedies John Barton has taken no more liberties than the next man. But in *The Wars of the Roses,* in which he subtracted 6000 lines and added about 1400 to the three parts of *Henry VI* and *Richard III,* turning four plays into three, he made one of the most drastic revisions of Shakespeare since the time of the Restoration, and with *When Thou Art King* (not published, but often performed by the mainly touring Theatregoround division of the Royal Shakespeare Company) he is in the long line of those who have conflated the later history plays; but unlike most of them, he has read, and uses, *The Famous Victories of Henry V* and the Chronicles. His attitude toward *Henry VI* in *The Wars of the Roses* reflects that of the disintegrationists. He has written: "The long period during which I have lived with the texts, in the rehearsal room, and in performance, leaves me increasingly doubtful whether the *Henry VI*'s are wholly by Shakespeare. More crucially, I believe that the form in which they have come down to us in the Folio represents the adaptation and partial revision of some earlier texts (whose nature and authorship we can only guess at) undertaken by Shakespeare to make them part of a cycle which was completed by his *Richard III.*"[4] John Barton's introduction to the printed text of *The Wars of the Roses* is a very interesting contribution to the study of the ethics of adaptation. It amply shows how academic influence has helped to create adaptations no less extreme than those made on grounds purely of theatrical effectiveness.

I referred earlier to the antiquarian pursuits of Charles Kean, whose productions represent a climax in the presentation of Shakespeare with inordinate care for archaeological authenticity in settings, costumes, properties, and so on. Kean was a theatrical pedant. Not only did he take care to be precise about necessary details, which seems excusable and perhaps even desirable; he overlaid the plays with irrelevancies which the audience could appreciate only after reading the programme notes. Similar tendencies may be discerned in modern productions. At the end of a recent *Merchant of Venice,* for instance, after the last words had been spoken and the happy couples were grouped with Antonio at the back of the stage, a moan as of the soughing of cattle was heard. The figures on stage were jolted out of their cheerfulness and assumed expressions of melancholy wariness. The lights faded. Most members of the audience assumed it was an instance of the fashionable directorial dolefulness, a warning to anyone naive enough to think that the comedy really ended happily. There was some speculation. The sound might have been derived from the famous breaking of the string at the end of *The Cherry Orchard*. Someone thought it was the music of the spheres, and was cross because the same director had not let this music sound in *Pericles*, and now here it was cropping up in the most unseemly circumstances. Finally, in a public talk, the director let it be known that the sound was not purely symbolic but was that of the shofar, an instrument sounded to mark the end of the Jewish Day of Atonement. Of course it is only fair to the director to say that the sound could make an effect without being recognized; but it is also fair to the audience to say that the sound was representational, and that very few members of the audience could be expected to have the knowledge to know what it represented, and thus to respond fully to its potential suggestiveness. A Charles Kean-type footnote in the programme seemed to be called for.

This is a tiny example of a kind of directorial academicism. I want to turn now to the difficult area of the relationship between academic work on Shakespeare and the presentation of the plays. This is not always direct or obvious. The Shakespeare scholar who never goes to the theatre is a common butt (although perhaps he is only a phantom), but some types of research carried out independently of theatrical considerations can nevertheless make a contribution to the theatre. Scholarly investigations into linguistic evidence such as may be provided by Warwickshire parish archives can produce results that are pertinent to theatre performers and that can easily be transmitted to both actors and audiences. Textual investigations pursued in laboratory conditions, perhaps with the aid of collating machines, may seem far from the footlights, but they can affect theatre texts.

It is indisputable that any kind of academic activity about Shakespeare that implies an overall response to the play rather than being simply an investigation of a small part of it calls for a full awareness of the play as something made for the theatre. Then there may be a real interplay between criticism and performance. As John Barton says in the Introduction to which I have referred, the director of a play is "engaged in an act of critical interpretation analogous to that undertaken by the literary critic in his study."[5] Sometimes it is difficult to tell whether an interpretative point is academic or theatrical. I think of a detail in *The Two Gentlemen of Verona* in Gareth Morgan's Theatregoround production (1969). The text was illuminated by the vocal emphasis the actor playing the Duke gave to two words. Having discovered Valentine's plot to make his way secretly to

Silvia's room, the Duke seizes the letter Valentine has written and reads it (III.i.140). The actor, Derek Smith, said:

My thought do harbour with *my* Silvia nightly,

giving to "my" an emphasis conveying indignation that Valentine should be so presumptuous as to claim Silvia as his. Then, in the last act, when the Duke forgives Valentine and admits his right to Silvia, the actor again emphasized the pronoun:

Thou art a gentleman, and well derived.
Take thou *thy* Silvia, for thou hast deserved her.
(V.iv.147–48)

His good-humored way of saying "thy" here, with a twinkle in his eyes, cast our minds back to his earlier refusal to admit Valentine's possession of Silvia, and so enriched our sense of the changing relationships among the characters of the play. Thus the actor made a point that might have been made, but so far as I know has not been made, by an academic critic. A point of a similar kind was made by Judi Dench in John Barton's production of *Twelfth Night* by a mere catch in the voice as she spoke a particular word:

I am all the daughters of my father's house,
And all the *brothers* too. . . .
(II.iv.119–20)

The speaking of "brothers" in a way that conveyed a sudden recollection of her real brother took us movingly from the fictional situation of Viola speaking equivocally to conceal her own disguise, to the reality of the situation in which she genuinely believed she had lost her brother.

Larger interpretative ideas, too, may be used in, and emerge from, performance. Criticism has made much of the imagery of blood and darkness in *Macbeth*. It is possible for a designer to underline this imagery in his color schemes—as Peter Hall did at Stratford in 1967, using a great, blood-red carpet—without our feeling that he must have read Wilson Knight first. It is natural to consider to what extent a producer is wise to attempt to objectify perceptions obtained from a study of the text, and especially the "subtext," whether he has arrived at them as the result of his own study or of reading criticism.

It is worth observing that Shakespeare sometimes makes theatrical capital out of the neutrality of setting which we suppose to have been normal in his own theatre. Perhaps the most obvious play to illustrate

13

this is *The Tempest*, in which, as has often been remarked, characters are to some extent delineated by the irreconcilable discrepancies in their reactions to, and descriptions of, features of the island. Upon Adrian the air breathes most sweetly; upon Antonio, as if it were perfumed by a fen. To Gonzalo the grass looks lush, lusty, and green; to Antonio, it is tawny. A director who makes any one of the characters demonstrably right takes the risk of spoiling Shakespeare's point.

This may suggest that it is sometimes best to let the actors work upon our imaginations in the simplest possible way, without the addition of theatrical devices aimed at "bringing out" selected features of the text. When one thing is "brought out," another is in danger of being obscured; explicitness may mean simplification, a denial of complexity which becomes a form of falsification. I suspect a rather bad example in Peter Brook's famous production of *A Midsummer Night's Dream* (1970). He perceived correspondences between Oberon and Theseus, Titania and Hippolyta. But to have them played by the same performers seemed to me to reduce the play's suggestiveness rather than to enhance it. Again, it is good for the producer to be aware of the play's concern with reality and illusion, and of the fact that this is specially important in the final episodes, and that at times the actors can be seen through their stage personae. But to underline this perception by having the final speeches addressed to the audience with homiletic solemnity seemed to me a denial of Shakespeare's delicacy of touch.

Much worse examples could easily be found of productions in which a director has thrown his play off balance by an overearnest attempt to underline undeniable significances. There is a danger that a producer will decide that a play is "about" something. Critics, of course, do the same. Criticism can oversimplify just as crudely as ill-judged direction. The director's position is particularly difficult because we expect from him a balanced interpretation. The academic critic can write about a "theme" of a play—mercy in *Measure for Measure*, perhaps—while acknowledging that he is exploring only one facet. But we could scarcely afford a production of *Measure for Measure* with special reference to mercy, followed by another with special reference to justice, and yet another stressing relationships among characters of the main plot and the subplot. The producer must try to realize as much of the play as possible; and to do this he may be well advised to simplify rather than elaborate.

Nevertheless, the potential expressive power of optional additions, of symbolical theatrical devices, is undeniable. Sometimes a director can achieve interesting visual realization of hints carried by verbal

imagery in a way that seems unobtrusive and satisfying. Trevor
Nunn's 1970 production of *Hamlet*, for example, made some interesting links between properties and text. The closet scene was, for
once, not a bedroom scene. The Queen was seated at a dressing table,
on which stood a looking-glass which Hamlet picked up when he
said "You go not till I set you up a glass / Where you may see the
inmost part of you" (III.iv.19–20). Also on the table were the two
pictures of old Hamlet and Claudius. Furniture and properties were
economically used, and the dressing table seemed appropriate in
view of the cosmetics imagery. But dominant among the imagery
picked up for visual effect was the ecclesiastical. On the whole, this
was visually a sparse production. Perhaps the scene most fully realized in visual terms was act III, scene i, though even this had only
a long pew to the audience's right of the forestage, with a curtained
confessional further back at the left. A bar or two of church music
was heard at the beginning and end of the scene. Ophelia entered
carrying a prayer book and knelt, facing the audience, to an unseen
altar before sitting on the pew. The King's lines

> O 'tis too true.
> How smart a lash that speech doth give my conscience.
> The harlot's cheek, beautied with plastering art,
> Is not more ugly to the thing that helps it
> Than is my deed to my most painted word
>   (III.i.50–53)

were spoken as if before the altar, and at the end of the speech he
crossed himself, perhaps a little perfunctorily. There was a sense of
formal acknowledgment of guilt rather than true feeling, and his
hypocrisy was underlined by the fact that Polonius and he concealed
themselves one in each box of the confessional. Hamlet entered and
knelt to the altar. A crucifix hung from his neck, and he crossed himself before speaking "To be or not to be," which he began as a
hushed, prayerful meditation. He became excited as he progressed.
Ophelia looked up from her book and became obviously aware of him.
We did not know whether she was supposed to be able to hear him
or not. At the end of the soliloquy Hamlet stood before noticing
Ophelia. The word "orisons"—"Nymph, in thy orisons / Be all my sins
remembered"—gained in meaning from the setting. I wondered
whether it was ironically significant that later, when the King really
tries to pray, he did so kneeling on the players' stage.

Thus far the visual objectification of hints in the scene's language
seemed justifiable, a reinforcement of points in the text which did

15

not throw the scene off balance. Later developments of the same motif were less acceptable. When Hamlet appeared before the praying King he was wearing monkish robes, again with a cross hanging from his neck. The main reason for the robes seemed to be to make a point in a later scene (IV.iii), also played in an ecclesiastical setting, where the King says that he has sent to seek Hamlet and to find the body of Polonius. A cross was prominent in the middle of the stage. A band of monks chanting and tolling hand bells opened the scene. When Hamlet entered he was still wearing his monkish robes. As the monks left the stage he joined them, and was for a moment undistinguishable from them. But he was hauled out, stripped of his robes, and stood almost naked, his arms held outstretched by his captors, while the King brutally punched him, as if to get from Hamlet the information he wanted. With the cross on the stage, it was difficult not to feel that we were meant to associate Hamlet with Christ.

I do not suggest that Trevor Nunn's methods in this production were the direct result of his reading of academic criticism. But the episodes I have described have affinities with critical writing, his handling of act III, scene i resembling a sensible study of verbal nuance, his handling of the scene in which he had Hamlet beaten up resembling rather a strained interpretative imposition on the text.

An interpretative device that may have been derived from academic criticism, but that seemed to me to be sensitively handled in an independent and effective but unstrained manner, was John Barton's use in *Twelfth Night* (1969) of sounds of the sea and sea birds, associated with certain visual effects. The basic setting was a wicker construction, receding to the back of the stage, which could be made semitransparent by the variations of lighting. These were used to suggest the wonder of a romance story, and they were associated with sounds of the beating of waves and the cries of sea birds. This aural and visual effect was used at various points in the action, including Viola's first entry, when we hear of Sebastian's supposed death, the point in the play when Viola strongly suspects that Sebastian is alive:

> He named Sebastian . . .
>
>   O, if it prove,
> Tempests are kind, and salt waves fresh in love
>
>   (III.iv.413–18)

and for Sebastian's apparent resurrection. There is no need to suggest that John Barton was here directly influenced by Wilson Knight's views about the symbolic significance of sea imagery, but it seems fair to suppose that he was working within the same frame of reference, and I found his devices an entirely acceptable complement to the text.

In this essay on the relationship between scholarly and theatrical activity I am concerned partly to find a justification for the academic in terms of the theatre. On the whole, I suppose, Shakespeare scholars adopt a take-it-or-leave-it attitude. They give lectures, write books, publish articles in the learned journals, and leave it to the theatre people to take notice of them or not, as they please. Of course, they are indispensable. The plays have to be edited. The theatre people must use edited texts; and in the process it is very difficult for them to avoid picking up something from the annotations with which the texts are besprinkled. Scholars can provide information about allusions, paraphrases of difficult passages, and the like. Critics can suggest interpretative views of the plays. And some directors and actors take the trouble to read widely among academic criticism of the plays they are working on. This is not necessarily a good thing. For example, the academic critic often isolates parts of a play in order to pursue analytical studies. He may be studying language patterns, or recurrent ideas, or something of the kind. He may not claim to be doing anything more than isolating one aspect of a complex whole, but there is a danger that a director will be overinfluenced by this and produce a distorted interpretation. That which is subtly expressed on the printed page may emerge rather crudely when transferred into stage terms. Examples might be provided by psychologically based studies of plays such as *Hamlet* and *Coriolanus*. It is possible to write about the Oedipus complex in terms that do not seem too remote from *Hamlet*, but a producer who is overimpressed with the notion may bring it too close to the surface of the play and thus destroy subtlety and suggestiveness, replacing complexity by overexplicitness.

Academic critics rarely write in terms that give precise recommendations for performance. To the layman this may seem surprising, and he is liable to suggest that "constructive criticism" is desirable, that since we so often dislike what we see in the theatre we ought to say how we should like to see the plays presented. This sounds plausible, but I do not feel that the critic can lay down any rules for performance. Producers and actors discover how they want to interpret a play as they rehearse it. The physique and personality of individual actors, the size of the theatre in which the performance is to be given, the amount of money available for costumes and sets—factors such as these help to mold the interpretation as it is being created, and cannot be allowed for in the study. Admittedly some of the most respected Shakespeare criticism of the century is in Granville-Barker's *Prefaces*, which do face up to the practicalities of production. But Granville-Barker was a rare case: not an academic by training, but a man of the practical theatre, though one with strong scholarly instincts and academic leanings. No one has succeeded as well as he in bridging the gap.

But perhaps academics ought to be bolder in offering advice to the theatre. Perhaps they might at least begin to define the areas where help might be given. A commentary on a play such as is provided in most editions can offer consideration of the needs of the theatres, can point to features of style and structure that ought to be realized in performance. The commentator is likely to be of more help to the director than to the actor. He can suggest overall lines of interpretation, and he can help with the meaning of individual passages of the text. What he cannot do is solve the problems of the actor trying to find points of contact between his personality and that of the character he is trying to portray. This is an intensely personal business, and the performer needs complete freedom in the means by which he grows imaginatively into his role. Some actors construct imaginary off-stage lives for their characters. Sometimes they imagine incidents that are supposed to happen between one scene and another. Sometimes they build a character on the basis of someone they know. I have heard an actor say that when he was playing the Fool in *King Lear*, he found it useful to study the behavior of monkeys in the zoo. (He played the Fool very well, all the same.) All these are entirely legitimate methods. Anything is legitimate that helps to provide effects that are in tone with the play. Sometimes the actor's grappling with a role results in a remarkable sense of identification, so that aspects of his personality seem to be fused with those inherent in the words the character speaks, giving a sense of someone beyond the ordinary. This is creative acting; this is where the actor makes his personal contribution, which cannot be planned by either critic or director. And if in the process the actor has imagined for the character an off-stage life entirely without warrant in the text—one that would set academic critics howling with derision—that is entirely his business.

I am content to think of the academic as someone to whom theatre people can turn for information and advice, but who is not necessarily any further involved; as an observer and appraiser, one who scrutinizes carefully and responds sympathetically but judiciously rather than throwing himself into the whirlpool. I am content to regard him as a guardian of standards rather than one who realizes them in performance; as a suggester of ideas rather than a layer-down of rules. He should respect the fact that the practically interpretative faculty is an art in its own right, one whose results we sometimes deplore but more frequently delight in. Academics and theatre people are both servants of Shakespeare. They should pursue their separate tasks with respect and considerateness to one another, and always with fidelity to the immense and varied possibilities that lie within a Shakespeare text.

The Critic,
the Director, and Liberty of
Interpreting

Kenneth Muir

At the World Shakespeare Congress held at Vancouver in August 1971, there was a certain tension apparent between those members who approached the plays as theatrical scripts and those who regarded them as primarily works of literature. Most of the participants in the Theatre Colloquium assumed that it was the right—and even the duty—of theatre directors to impose their own interpretations on the plays, that it was necessary to make certain adjustments to fit the plays for a modern stage, and that it was legitimate to adapt them so that they would speak more directly to a modern audience. If challenged, nearly everyone would have agreed with Kittredge: "It has been my experience that in any given instance Shakespeare is pretty certain to be right." Yet when it was suggested that we should always ask of an adaptation "Does it improve on the original?" this was regarded as unfair. An attempt to give what was called a "'true-to-score" performance of two scenes from *Troilus* satisfied neither party. The actors, who were not very experienced, had the impossible task of playing the scenes out of context before a difficult audience. The experiment did not prove the desirability of sticking to the text, since the performance was flat. Nor did it prove the desirability of adaptation; only the failure of great actors to make the scenes come alive could have done that.

Oddly enough, the one occasion when the conference seemed unanimous was the standing ovation given to Grigori Kozintsev's film of *King Lear*. This was an adaptation and some of the alterations would have outraged purists in the theatre: for example, the hovel and the farmhouse scenes were run together, as in many nineteenth-century productions; Lear addressed the poor naked wretches who were sheltering from the storm; Cordelia and the King of France were married in Latin; Edgar tied two sticks together to make a cross to place on his father's grave; and at the end the Fool survived to play a few mournful notes on a pipe as the victims of invasion began to rebuild their devastated dwellings. Yet these points did not offend the audience. This was partly because it was recognized that a film should not be a record of a stage performance—like Olivier's *Othello* —but should re-create the spirit of the play in another medium. To Kozintsev, quite legitimately, the plight of the poor naked wretches was a central theme of the play and this was brought home to us by dozens of touches. He was also influenced by Maxwell's remark— which he since disclaimed—that *King Lear* was a Christian play in a pagan setting. This was suggested by the relics of Christianity in a country which had apparently relapsed into paganism. The visual impact of the film was overwhelming and one is never likely to see a better Lear or as good a Cordelia or Fool. The audience was devastated but uplifted.

The Peter Brook stage production had fewer cuts and, it could be argued, was more faithful to the text, but the overall effect was one of distortion. For Brook, following Jan Kott, was determined to make *King Lear* as much like *End Game* as possible. He also wished to show its affinities with the Theatre of Cruelty. For this reason he ended the last scene of act III with Regan shrinking from her wounded husband. He omitted the significant last lines which bring out the unnaturalness of Cornwall and Regan. The surviving servants discuss the horrible events we have just witnessed:

Second Serv.   I'll never care what wickedness I do
If this man come to good.
Third Serv.   If *she* live long,
And in the end meet the old course of death,
Women will all turn monsters.
Second Serv.   Let's follow the old Earl, and get the Bedlam
To lead him where he would: his roguish madness
Allows itself to any thing.
Third Serv.   Go thou; I'll fetch some flax and whites of egg
To apply to his bleeding face. Now, heaven help
him!

(III.vii.98–106)

By their cuts ye shall know them! By omitting these lines Peter Brook played down the humanity, love, and compassion which is called forth by the opposing evil. The evil and cruelty are made to seem the natural characteristics of man, and man's humanity to man is made to seem exceptional and unnatural. Gloucester's cry

21

The Playwright and Interpretation

As flies to wanton boys are we to the gods:
They kill us for their sport

(IV.i.36–37)

becomes, as it was to some nineteenth-century critics, the central statement of the play. To regard *King Lear* as a contribution to the Theatre of the Absurd is itself an absurd distortion, as disastrous as Tate's happy ending. Kott is an influential critic, Brecht is a major dramatist, and Brook at his best is a great director—but their combined influence has not been a happy one. The contrast between the acceptance of the Kozintsev film and the rejection of many stage adaptations was not, therefore, due entirely to the difference of media.

One of the recurring themes at the Vancouver Congress was the legitimacy of divergent interpretations of all Shakespeare's plays. As Professor John Russell Brown said, "The text of *Twelfth Night* can suggest a Viola who is pert, lyrical, practical, courageous or helpless. Shakespeare's words support all these interpretations." Perhaps—but some of these would be more supportable than others. No one considering the play as a whole could reasonably describe Viola as helpless.

The liberty of interpretation, claimed by Lascelles Abercrombie, is wide, but not limitless. It is possible to depict Shylock as a comic villain or as a tragic villain—but not as a tragic hero. Duke Vincentio can be depicted as a busybody or as a symbol of divine providence; Isabella can be depicted as saintly or puritanical. Maria can be depicted as young or as an old maid clutching at her last chance of marriage. Katherine can be a problem child or a forerunner of the women's liberation movement. Othello can be presented as Coleridge and Pushkin saw him or (almost) as Leavis sees him. Iago can be motivated by the devil's hatred of goodness or by an entirely human envy and jealousy. Hamlet can be shown as suffering from over-reflective intellectualism, melancholia, doubts about the morality of revenge. He may even be given an Oedipus complex, though one gets rather tired of seeing the closet scene turned into a bedroom scene and hopes that the Hamlet who demonstrated his wish to return to the womb by hiding in the actors' trunk will have few followers. There have even been some reputable critics who argued that it was Hamlet's duty *not* to kill Claudius.

The aberrations of critics are corrected by their fellows, but almost all the aberrations of directors may be traced to some critical heresy promulgated by a reputable critic. The idea, for example, that Portia cheated over the caskets; the view that much of *Henry VI* was not by Shakespeare; the theory that Lear and Cordelia were incestuously attracted, as Freud imagined; the idea that *A Midsummer Night's Dream* was a black comedy and Hippolyta the most lascivious of Shakespeare's women; the moral superiority of Claudius to his nephew—all these heresies have influenced productions of the plays. It seems certain that a Stratford Titania was made to pronounce "dewberries" as "dewber-eyes" (to rhyme with *thighs*) because Dover Wilson and De La Mare thought that the rhymed verse of the play was so bad that Shakespeare could not have written it at any stage of his career—but they were referring to the verse of the lovers, not Titania's.

Even the best critics have sometimes had a baleful influence on the actors. Until Coleridge wrote about the way Hamlet's tendency to think inhibited his ability to act, no one had regarded the play as puzzling. Now the actor playing the part has to walk as delicately as Agag. Is he going to agree with Coleridge and show that Hamlet's delay is caused by his losing the power of action in the energy of resolve? Or with Goethe who compared Hamlet to an oak tree planted in a costly vase, a pure and moral nature without the strength of nerve which makes the hero? Or is Hamlet the caddish egotist depicted by Madariaga and Rebecca West, who is able to kill Claudius only when his own life is threatened? Or is he the pacifist depicted by Middleton Murray and Roy Walker? Or the immature neurotic depicted by L.C. Knights? Or should he be regarded as a patient of Dr. Timothy Bright or of Dr. Freud? An actor has to choose among these and scores of other interpretations; and, whichever he chooses, most of the critics and half his audience will complain that he has wrongly chosen.

Sometimes, on the other hand, critics have prepared the way for successful productions. *Measure for Measure,* until comparatively recently, was generally disliked. Coleridge said it was the only one of Shakespeare's plays he disliked. When Mrs. Siddons played Isabella in 1811, a reviewer called it "the most offensive play in the English language," and even as late as 1935 it was said that the play insulted the respectability of the people of Melton Mowbray. Except in such backwoods, the tide began to turn in 1930 when Wilson Knight published his defense of the play. This was followed by a performance at Sadler's Wells—with Charles Laughton as Angelo and Flora Robson as Isabella—which earned the praise of T.S. Eliot. Since the war it has been revived several times at Stratford-upon-Avon, always with success. It was not merely that the critics had prepared the way for successful productions; the climate of the age had changed and the frankness of the dialogue no longer seemed obscene. The same thing may be said about *Troilus and Cressida*, which was generally regarded as unactable. Bernard Shaw astonished the New Shakspere Society by proclaiming that Cressida was "most enchanting" and Shakespeare's "first real woman"; but when Edith Evans played the part of Cressida before the First World War, the critic of *The Times* said it was impossible to arrange the play for the stage. In 1923 the same critic declared that much of the play was bound to be dull. But the play was received enthusiastically at Cambridge before an audience of veterans who found that the mood of the play chimed with their own. Wilson Knight—himself a veteran —wrote an enthusiastic essay on the play, and he was followed by Theodore Spencer, Derek Traversi, and others. The play has been revived frequently in the last twenty-five years; its success is due not to the fact that Shakespeare is our contemporary but because, after a lapse of three centuries, its theme has become relevant. It was, indeed, always relevant; but its truths were as unpalatable to the Victorians as they had been to the Romantics or to their neoclassical predecessors.

Although a successful stage production has often been preceded by a critical reassessment, the reverse has sometimes been true. It used to be assumed that *Titus Andronicus* showed either that Shakespeare had prostituted his talents to please the groundlings or that he had added only a few touches to a play by some lesser dramatist. The possibility of reviving the play was not seriously considered, but Peter Brook's production in 1955 proved to be an outstanding success, not merely in the horrific parts. Artaud had demanded a theatre which would have the function of a sacrificial rite, which would bring about "the exteriorization of latent cruelty," which would "evacuate those feelings which are normally exposed in more destructive ways in the name of patriotism, religion or love," and which would use the language of incantation. All this the Peter Brook production accomplished; more successfully, indeed, than any plays written after Artaud's manifesto.

Another play which succeeded on the stage before it was generally recognized by the critics was *Love's Labour's Lost*. Dr. Johnson thought it was unworthy of Shakespeare; Sir Edmund Chambers spoke of "impenetrable memorials of vanished humour"; and even Granville-Barker remarked: "Here is a fashionable play; now, by three hundred years, out of fashion. Nor did it ever, one supposes, make a very wide appeal." Soon after these words were written the play was revived at the Old Vic in a production directed by Tyrone

Guthrie. I have seldom heard so continuous a sound of thoughtful laughter—of laughter mingled with surprise that we had not realized what a good comedy it was. John Dover Wilson confessed that it was Guthrie's production which revealed to him that the play was a first-rate comedy, "so full of fun, of *permanent* wit, of brilliant and entrancing situation, that you hardly noticed the faded jesting and allusion, as you sat spell-bound and drank it all in."

It is plain that critics have learned from stage performances almost as often as directors have learned from critics, and that, despite the aberrations of both parties, they can still learn from each other. Yet some tension is inevitable, and it is symbolized by Lamb's confrontation with the Garrick monument, on which the actor was ranked with the poet:

Shakespeare and Garrick like twin-stars shall shine.

Shakespeare's tragedies, Lamb retorted, cannot be acted. They are too huge for the stage, which inevitably vulgarizes them. Lamb, indeed, had never seen a performance of one of Shakespeare's tragedies. He had seen only Tate's *King Lear* or Garrick's *Romeo and Juliet*. In Shakespeare's play, the lovers do not exchange a word in the Capulet vault. Garrick makes Juliet awaken from her trance before the death of Romeo, who absentmindedly forgets he has swallowed poison and addresses fifty lines of pedestrian blank verse to his unfortunate bride. Garrick's version of *The Winter's Tale* was even more deplorable. He remedied Shakespeare's violation of the unities of place and time by beginning the play when Perdita was of marriageable age and by giving a retrospective account of earlier events. He retained the scene in which Hermione's statue comes to life, despite Mrs. Lennox's criticisms of it; but he ruined its dramatic effect by inserting some lines of his own composition:

Leon.   Hark! hark! she speaks—
O pipe, through sixteen winters dumb! then deem'd
Harsh as the raven's note; now musical
As nature's song, tun'd to th'according spheres.

Herm.   Before this swelling flood o'erbear our reason,
Let purer thoughts, unmixed with earth's alloy,
Flame up to heaven, and for its mercy shown
Bow we our knees together.

Leon.   Oh! if penitence
Have power to cleanse the foul sin-spotted soul,
Leontes' tears have washed away all his guilt.

> If thanks unfeigned be all that you require,
> Most bounteous Gods, for happiness like mine
> Read in my heart, your mercy's not in vain.

Herm. This firstling duty paid, let transport loose
My lord, my king, —there's distance in those names,—
My husband!

Leon.   O my Hermione!—have I deserved
That tender name?

Herm.   No more; by all that's past
Forgot in this enfolding, and forgiven.

Leon. Thou, matchless saint!—Thou paragon of virtue!

Shakespeare had not allowed Hermione to address a single word to Leontes. He knew, as Garrick did not, when silence is golden. In view of the changes made by Garrick, his claim in the prologue

> 'Tis my chief wish, my joy, my only plan
> To lose no drop of that immortal man!

appears to be self-delusion or impudence, as fatuous as Tate's boast that he had polished the rough stones of Shakespeare's *King Lear*.

During the nineteenth century the versions of Shakespeare's plays which could be seen in the theatre were closer to the originals than those of the eighteenth century had been: the view of the romantic critics began to have some effect. But there were still many cuts and alterations and even in the present century Wolfit made the same cuts in *Cymbeline* which Irving had made half a century earlier. As a result, despite Wolfit's virtuoso performance as Iachimo, much of the last act was unintelligible. It was because of his memories of the Irving production that Shaw was induced to write a new fifth act for the play, although, on rereading the original, Shaw confessed that it was superior to his own version. The actor-managers who improved on Shakespeare, although they spoke reverentially of his genius, really believed that he was a very incompetent dramatist. By the end of the century, however, increased knowledge of the Elizabethan stage made it apparent that Shakespeare could hardly be described as incompetent; the productions of William Poel, odd as they often were, showed that the plays were more interesting to watch the closer the staging was to that of the Globe; the criticism by Bernard Shaw, especially his declaration that the score was more important than the libretto and his denunciation of cutting, gradually won acceptance, and, in the present century, the work of Harley Granville-Barker both as director and as writer of prefaces gradually reformed the method of staging Shakespeare's plays.

Kenneth Muir

It is difficult to compare productions separated by half a century but it is certain that productions at the Old Vic in the 1920s and early 1930s were remarkably faithful to the text. There were hardly any cuts, no gimmicks, the settings were entirely unobtrusive, and the verse was spoken as verse. Not all the acting was first-rate, but there have been few performances in recent years to match the Rosalind of Edith Evans or the Othello of Ion Swinley. This kind of "true-to-score" performance was carried over to the West End, so that it was possible to see the Gielgud-Olivier-Ashcroft *Romeo and Juliet*, Jean Forbes-Robertson's unforgettable Viola and the Gielgud *Richard II*. Such productions made the style of the older touring companies seem impossibly stagy and artificial.

After the Second World War we moved into a director's theatre, each director anxious to impose a new interpretation on each play. They do not realize that for many members of each audience it is their first experience of the play in the theatre and, to judge from conversation in the foyer, they are righteously indignant at the liberties taken by the directors. Portia's "quality of mercy" speech may be staled by repetition, but there is no excuse for relieving the supposed boredom of the audience by making the Duke play with a yo-yo. There is no reason why Shakespeare's plays should not be performed in modern dress, but a modern dress production of *The Merchant of Venice* is a mistake because we cannot forget Belsen and Dachau; and to dress *Much Ado about Nothing* in the costumes of nineteenth-century Italy means that there will be a clash between the words and the behavior of the characters. One can see the point in havng a Watteau setting for *Love's Labour's Lost*, but the point was ultimately confusing.

Such mistakes are comparatively trivial; the ones that really matter are those whose cuts and alterations impose a meaning on the play that runs counter to any sane interpretation. It was perfectly justifiable for Gordon Bottomley to make Goneril the heroine of *his* play and to make Cordelia a spoiled brat; but it is illegitimate to pretend that this was Shakespeare's intention. It is possible to make Troilus into a tragic hero or a fool; it is not possible, without altering the text, to make him into an Italianate roué.

It is not surprising, therefore, that Noel Annan in *The Cambridge Journal* (1950) should complain of the way in which "the clear meaning of the lines is repeatedly sacrificed" and the "ideas of the producer are everything." He pleaded for less egotism, more reverence, less by-play, more seriousness, less naturalism, more of the grand style. The things of which Annan complains reveal that many directors of today have reverted to the views of the actor-managers of the last century: first, that Shakespeare was a great poet with a unique understanding of human nature, but that his plays need to be altered to be palatable to a modern audience; and second, that his published texts are scripts that should be revised for the greater glory of actor-manager then and of director now.

Some alterations can be shown to be disastrous, as we can all see with regard to Dryden's, Davenant's, and Garrick's. In Margaret Webster's production of *The Merchant of Venice* at the Stratford Memorial Theatre, Bassanio's account of Portia in the first scene was accompanied by soft music and the appearance behind a gauze curtain of Portia feeding a caged canary. Even worse was a *Twelfth Night* at the Liverpool Playhouse in which the first two scenes were transposed. Viola appeared on board ship talking to the Captain who had rescued her. On the cyclorama was projected a film of the coast of Yugoslavia, so that the ship appeared to be moving; as the scene ended, the ship berthed in the harbor of Dubrovnik. The audience, I confess, loudly applauded. But they had not heard a word of the dialogue since they were engrossed by the film. In any case the words were drowned by the chorus of sailors below decks, singing sea shanteys. This, presumably, is what is meant by "Shakespeare without tears." There is so much going on that we are bored by the poetry.

As mentioned previously, several speakers at the Vancouver conference emphasized that there were many legitimate interpretations of one of Shakespeare's plays, and different critics and different generations are naturally attracted by one rather than another. It is proper for a critic to stress one aspect of a play, which he feels has been neglected; and it is natural that the director should assume the same freedom. Often this is quite justifiable. But all the same the ideal production, like the ideal criticism, would keep the options open. Just as the written text of the play means different things to different readers, so the play in the theatre should not be strait-jacketed to fit one director's point of view. We should come out of the theatre not arguing about the director, but arguing about the play. Any good production of *Measure for Measure* would necessarily present us with the possibility that Duke Vincentio was a symbol of divine providence, or an earthly ruler who was God's steward, or a puppet-master, or a busybody. It is not the business of the director to choose one of these and exclude the others. Shakespeare left the character ambiguous, and the ambiguity should be retained.

This might seem to restrict the rightful freedom of a director in an epoch when he has greater power than ever before. But the kind of production we have been advocating requires not less ability on the part of the director but more and it requires too qualities of modesty and self-denial which are inevitably rare.

Most directors have learned one vital lesson, the necessity of speed and the simplicity of staging which contributes to speed. We also have the right to expect that the verse should be spoken as verse, and this lesson too has been generally learned. It has not, however, been generally accepted that there should be no major cuts. As Shaw remarked, no one thinks of cutting two bars from a Beethoven symphony: "The moment you admit that the producer's business is to improve Shakespeare by cutting out everything that he himself would not have written, and everything that he thinks the audience will either not like or not understand, and everything that does not make prosaic sense, you are launched on a slope on which there is no stopping until you reach the abyss."

Finally, we should not attempt to think of Shakespeare as our contemporary; he was not, although one can sympathize with Jan Kott's wish to establish the relevance of his plays to the present age. There may be analogies between the Trojan War and Vietnam, but no director should dress the Greeks as G.I.s. We may appreciate more the testing of Macduff by Malcolm because we know what life under a dictatorship is like, but Macbeth does not really resemble Hitler. Shakespeare remains relevant not for such superficial and transitory accidents but because he gives a picture of human behavior which has remained more or less satisfactory for three and a half centuries. The relevance of Kozintsev's film of *King Lear* was everywhere apparent—and it was achieved by essential faithfulness to the spirit of Shakespeare's play.

Dramatic Intention and Theatrical Realization

M. St. Clare Byrne

To the modern heresy that it is impossible to know what the author meant there is only one answer: You may be right, but it never hurt anyone to make the necessary mental effort to try and find out. The idea that you cannot know Shakespeare's intention in a play unless you can re-create within yourself the mind and the experience of a man of his time and join the audience at The Globe is specious nonsense. Are we to put ourselves into Jeffrey's editorial chair at *The Edinburgh Review* to help us to know Wordsworth's intention and understand *The Lyrical Ballads* and *The Excursion*, or refer to Lockhart and Croker and *The Quarterly* for an understanding of the intention of Keats? Have we already forgotten the critical howls which greeted *Ghosts*, and the very mixed reception given to the original production of *The Family Reunion*? With which contemporary audience group and its response must posterity align itself for an understanding of the intentions of John Whiting's *Saints Day*? The solid disapproval of the contemporary critics, or the infinitely more sympathetic response to both the author's intention and the power of the work which came from writers, theatre people, and certain sections of the general audience? It can be an even chance whether the contemporary ear or posterity's is the better attuned to the overtones; we are not always on time with the receptivity of our response to intention and our understanding of technique and methods which are strange to us. Admittedly we shall come much nearer to a just perception of a classic author's intention the more we know of the ideas he accepted as commonplaces which now mean nothing to us; and the more we know of the social pattern and the background of life implicit in his writing, and of the theatrical conditions for which he wrote, the more consistent and credible will our interpretation of a play become. It is also true that the full potential of a genuine work of art is not known even to its creator, still less to any other individual, because the potential is the sum of every single reaction to that work

30

M. St. Clare Byrne

throughout its existence. As T.S. Eliot said, "In all poetry there should be more than the author himself is aware of," and "The great play will affect different people differently: it will be capable of innumerable interpretations, and it will have a fresh meaning for every generation."[1] Nevertheless, if you cannot catch enough of the author's meaning, whether he is a classic or a contemporary, to be able to say what you think he is writing about and then to check the apparent intention by examining the structure of his work, you are in no position to enjoy it intelligently yourself, still less to attempt to interpret it to others.

If you set up as critic the first question the ordinary person wants you to answer is elementary but vital: What is the play about? There are many definitions and descriptions of the function of criticism, but the Plain Man's instinct to ask some intermediary who talks the same language as the Author to interpret the latter's intentions goes to the root of the matter, and however much comment on goodness or badness he may add later the intermediary's first business is to bridge the gap between Expression and Impression[2] and help the recipient—reader or audience—to understand what the author has to say. The good critic is himself the ideal recipient, the perfect audience on whom nothing is lost.

Lascelles Abercrombie's reminder that "the existence of a work of art is completed by the recipient's *attention* to what the author says to him"[3] may be a commonplace of critical theory, but too often one must seek far for its practice. This is especially true in the approach to drama where the chief need is always for brainwork more fundamentally receptive to the attempt to discover the author's intention while remaining attentive to the crucial distinction yet vital relationship between dramatic intention and theatrical effect. It is necessary for study and stage alike to keep the theatre's traditional handling of any classic drama continually under review, and we need clearer recognition of the fact that all intermediaries between the author and the recipient are substantially in the position of critic. They must, therefore, when concerned in that completion of the work of art which we call "the play produced," discriminate sharply between their proper critical-interpretative faculty and function and the critical-creative ability allied thereto which can lead them to wrest a play or any of its parts quite from the author's meaning, whether by cutting or any other form of adaptation, or even fundamental misapprehension.

One does not have to be a creative artist to read a poem or look at a picture without the help of an intermediary to interpret, but the playwright's work, like the composer's, needs executants for its proper completion, and it is arguable—and now generally maintained—that the dramatic artist's intention is not fully realized without the participation of an audience. The actors and the producer are as much critical intermediaries as the professed critic: what the audience receives is the author's intention as understood by them and communicated through the art of acting. The critic as interpreter—as distinct from the writer of notices—also practices an art; and the more he studies the work of these other intermediaries and recognizes the creative factor common to them all, the more clearly will this ideal recipient distinguish between what I have called the critical-creative impulse and the critical-interpretative. The former is less rare because it asks the less disciplined mind and springs from that more spontaneous and fecund responsiveness to which the temptation to seize upon the possibilities the author suggests, without considered reference to the manifest intention of the whole work, can be as irresistible as it is unconscious. The perception of what one would like to do with a subject oneself can be so instantaneous as to be virtually unnoticed by the conscious mind, which then applies to the author's concept aesthetic judgments of "good" and "bad" based on and biased by devices and desires of its own heart. As T.S. Eliot remarks, "The critic must have a very highly developed sense of fact"; and the fact which is the play is not raw material upon which actors and producers and critics may work their creative will. Pure interpretation, the absolute giving-up of one's perceptive powers to the author, the acceptance of what he does as intentional and deliberate, is so rare that many people find it difficult to understand that there is any difference between an objective report of what a writer says and does in his play and what a producer or an actor or critic thinks about these facts, and the way, consequently, in which he colors them in his interpretation.[4] Yet the measure of the faithfulness with which the mind applies itself to the first of these processes is the measure of the validity of the second.

When he prints his poem the poet makes what he wants to say directly available, however little or however much the varying individual apprehension makes of it. The critic may take a different view of it on different occasions, but the difference is in himself; the poem remains constant. Not so with the playwright: the executants and the audience are at once his special occupational risk and the main source of his compulsive strength. They are his risk in that their interaction, from performance to performance, and therefore the total effect of his play, is incalculable. Thus the critic, apart from the possible difference in mood in his own approach, is faced on different occasions by a different sum total of objective statement. They are a strength, in that they can simplify and therefore "plug" intention: the executants' massed, unanimous, directed intention, with its power to gather up into acceptance the mass feeling of an audience, has an immediate compulsion in it which the written word by itself cannot command. Yet even this extra source of strength for communicating or underlining meaning may involve for the playwright a counterbalancing risk.

Reciprocal excitement, generated between stage and auditorium, will affect the critic, if he is a good audience-man and properly responsive to the happy condition known as "having the audience with you" and, provided it is dramatic intention that is thus emphasized, all is indeed well for the author and his play. But it is not well at all when, as so often happens, a successful theatrical effect is a deliberately contrived substitute for the original intention which the theatre has either disliked or failed to recognize. We have all seen, at one time or another, the damage which can thus be done to a play, and the unfortunate, almost hypnotic, authority such an illegitimate effect can continue to exercise, once it has been successfully put across as a good bit of theatre.

Now it is as useless to argue that the author is always right as that the theatre always knows best—he isn't, and it doesn't. But because the play produced is conditional on the existence of the play as text there are certain basic assumptions by which all intermediaries between the text and its audience should be governed in their approach to the play. It is the first right of a play to be considered as a play—neither as a good play nor a bad play, neither as a piece of literature nor as raw material for the theatre, but simply as a specimen of this particular kind of work which depends for its artistic completion and substantial existence on the response and understanding of actors, producer, and audience to the suggestions of the dramatist.

A reading cannot be a substitute for stage realization, but anyone who has watched a play grow, develop, come to life or die on its feet in rehearsal, and knows that nothing save performance gives us its full measure, knows also that performance may equally fail to do justice to the writer's intentions. When, for example, apparent faults of construction obtrude themselves—an obvious *scène a faire* missed, dramatic tension let down at a critical moment, a legitimate theatrical opportunity ignored—he will not label these as faults but will register them as effects and impressions, and he will not say "These are bad" but will investigate the particular intention that lies behind them and ask "Why?" Modesty and humor should tell him that the author probably knows his own business at least as well as his critics —probably better—that he understands what effects he is creating, has deliberate intention in what he does, and believes it is properly calculated for realization on the stage.

Anyone approaching a play in this manner will use the term "intention" both in the general and in the particular sense, to convey first an overall impression of statement, or "what the author means," and then to say what any specific portion of the action is and does and how it functions as a part of the total impression. "Effect" is a term which also has to do double duty, and in the initial process, when the play is read by actor, producer, or student, the two terms together are the equivalent of what Vernon Lee calls "Expression and Impression," which "mean merely the Writer and the Reader."[5] In the theatre, however, "effect"—or, more precisely, "theatrical effect"— means more than impression, because it has to include the idea of how it is handled on the stage and therefore the further impression— factual, circumstantial, emotional, but not necessarily identical— which it makes on the audience. In the ideal performance that everyone aims at, the circuit completes itself, and the impulse transmitted by the author's intention to producer and actors is received by the audience as an effect which links them to that intention. When this process goes wrong it is not always easy to locate the fault, especially in the case of a new play seen for the first time. With a classic, however, where he has both his text and his accumulated experience of the play in the theatre to help him, the genuine critic of drama should be able to recognize when the receptivity of the executants has been insufficiently sensitive, so that the fault results either from misunderstanding or deliberate misrepresentation of the effect intended.

Receptivity is in itself difficult for both readers and audiences. The dramatic form demands a certain technical alertness that conflicts with the Wordsworthian "wise passiveness" and the quiet listening mind that the reader of poems learns to cultivate. The theatre generates its own proper excitement, is stimulating and provocative of thought, question and answer, and discussion. To sustain throughout the passive role of listener, letting the play soak in, with a minimum of comment either to oneself or others, becomes more difficult the more we cultivate a quick sensitivity to the successive impressions made on us. But in general we do better justice to the total impression the more we can refrain, during the process of assimilation, from letting too much crystallize too soon. An impression received can become an opinion formed almost without our noticing the change, once we start pinning it down with the precision imparted by words. Nevertheless, in the listener's approach, as in all the practical words. of theatrical interpretation, there is an inherent categorical imperative to "jump to it," which we disregard at our peril. The responses of theatre people, quite properly, tend to be ultrasensitive and rapid, and unless there is a certain immediacy of apprehension in their preliminary attack we are probably right to diagnose in the play some failure of specific dramatic power—as often as not, either a lack of substance to be apprehended or else a plethora which cannot be contained within the limitations of the dramatic form. A sufficiency of theatrical power, fully exploited by brilliant production, may convert either type into a stage success; the London theatre is rarely without current specimens of both kinds.

This quick, instinctive response, essential to the executant in the theatre, is not, however, peculiar to him; it is to some degree shared by all who "interpret," on whatever level, and every experience of a play in the theatre should help the listener to develop this faculty within himself. It is the intuitive leap—something positive, and therefore apparently opposed to the passive attitude, but not in fact opposed to it if we remember the proper qualification of *wise* passiveness, which has nothing whatever in common with the spongy, mechanical absorption that does not know whether it has the radio on or off, and is equally removed from the tangential self-assertion that only "listens" insofar as is necessary for scoring debating points. It is the moment of discovery which is the beginning of exploration, when we begin to be aware of what we are looking for and to reach out toward it with the author. When a production, like a ship, has "found" itself and come together completely, the whole of the play is implicit in every part, but to receive it as explicit statement the audience must listen for the duration of the performance, accumulating impressions, following suggestions, giving a full response of feeling, and holding intellectual and aesthetic judgments in suspense until the statement has been made. And we should remember that, while we are giving perhaps two and a half hours—and, it is to be hoped, some quiet afterthoughts—to an evaluation of this statement, it has taken the executants weeks of work and thought to achieve this crystallizing, this expression of what we must accept as the author's intention, unless, of course, certain inadequacies in the rendering, together with our own knowledge of the text, indicate that intention has been lost sight of or distorted. In such a case we owe it to play and players to ask how and why and also to remind ourselves, if it is a first performance, that it can sometimes take a week of playing to an audience before a production really comes together, whether it is a new play or a revival.

The modern reluctance to bother about the author's intentions springs from various causes. Allowance for two respectable reasons has already been made: it may be true that often we cannot *know* the truth about specific details, and it is always true that, in the case of a great work of art, the total sum of "meaning" is more than the specific "intentions" of the author at the time of writing. The real trouble springs partly from mental and imaginative laziness, which finds genuine and sustained receptivity difficult, partly from the undisciplined creative-critical approach with premature rule-of-thumb aesthetic judgments of "good" and "bad" and its consequent instinctive desire to re-handle the author's material, and partly from the unwillingness of stage and study to pay enough attention, at once analytical and synthetic, to the fact of dramatic structure and the unavoidable inferences to be drawn from them. If you accept the aesthetic fact of dramatic structure itself you accept the idea that each part fulfills some specific function—that is, you accept intention.

The dramatist cannot make his text absolutely foolproof any more than any other kind of writer can, but if he cares for the integrity of his writing he will himself give to it all the fundamental critical brainwork of which he is capable, to check the clarity and the consistency of his own expression of intention. He must try to write so that the actor in his characterization will be one hundred percent right by the instinctive and emotional approach—the intuitive leap—rather than correct as a result of cerebration. His relationship with his producer is similar: the producer may with reason complain that the text is incompletely and insufficiently dramatized if, for example, the author, by his placing or wording and preparation for it, has given the entry of a character without making it clear whether he means it to be "an entrance," or the unemphatic "*enter-so-and-so.*" If the latter, he must make it obvious to producer and actor that the overriding demand of dramatic intention requires the unemphasized, because unless this is a positive requirement it is uneconomical—even against nature—to waste an effective theatric moment. "They have their exits and their entrances." Similarly, the action is incompletely dramatized if the author, by the arrangement of his ideas, the structure of an argument, and the rhythm of his dialogue, does not make it plain where inevitable moves or movement—as distinct from individual spontaneous movement—ought to occur. If he does not deal honestly in this matter he has only himself to thank when he finds his scene—especially in comedy—victimized by the arbitrary or the purely theatrical move, which is used for the sake of relief, for variety in the stage picture, to keep the audience's attention during discussions, and, by physical action, to make them feel something important or decisive has been said when in fact it has not. It is the playwright's business to understand not only the relationships between words, thought, and movement but also the relative values of words and movement at a given moment, and he must be able to "see" just when a developing tension in the action or an argument has reached the point where it can be resolved either by movement or regrouping alone, or a move plus dialogue, or words only. If he does not himself discriminate between the organic dramatic move and the arbitrary theatrical move, he must not be surprised if he has the latter imposed upon him.

Slovenly work on the part of the dramatist has been to some extent encouraged by a certain modern theatre cant which says, in effect, leave all matters of theatrical realization to the theatre; in its more tiresome manifestations this same cant launches periodic attacks on what it calls "author's stage directions." It is easy to see how such an attack began, as a natural and inevitable reaction against the exuberant asides of Barrie, the meticulous realization of detail in Bernard Shaw, and the imaginative excursions, spatial and temporal, of Granville-Barker. These delights, we are told, are "quite from the purpose of playing"—"trespasses upon the domain of the novel: redundancies: evidence of incomplete dramatization." Actually, they are nothing of the kind: they are simply evidence of the superabundant vitality of these dramatists, who were all masters of theatrical craft and of the art of writing. That these directions contain grace notes, and even superfluities such as descriptions of the physical appearance of the characters, need trouble no one, and will certainly aid the genuinely receptive mind that likes to get everything possible from the author. No producer is bound by Shaw's descriptions of the doctors who gather to congratulate Ridgeon on his knighthood, any more than they are bound by the text's description of Hamlet as "fat and scant of breath"; and no producer need be anything but grateful for these notes, unless he lacks the essential qualification of receptivity and wants to substitute the second-hand creativeness for the critical-interpretative faculty.

It is not surprising that this particular theatre snobbism is often accepted by young and inexperienced writers, who are naturally anxious to avoid imputations of a "literary" taint, and who find the attack led by men of distinction like Gordon Craig and Ashley Dukes.[6] Essential directions for entrances and exits are allowed, and there is some indication of the actions of individuals. According to Ashley Dukes, however, "Authors should be content if they see the minds of their characters and little more"; if they were to visualize their scenes and personages as completely as they pretend in their stage directions, they would be "a very great nuisance in the theatre," as neither would ever come up to their expectations, and they would be "continually occupied with matters of detail that lie properly within the director's province."[7]

This kind of lazy man's playwriting is sometimes advocated as the proper thing because there are only essential stage directions in Shakespeare and the early dramatists. Having picked up the parrot-cry that he and his contemporaries and successors were real men of the theatre, the deduction then follows that what was good enough for Shakespeare ought to be good enough for us—regardless of the fact that he wrote for a nonscenic stage and was further involved in the business of staging as author, sharer, and actor. But in these actual "matters of detail that lie properly within the director's province," who is to delimit the proper spheres of author and producer? Is there a hard and fast line to be drawn? Are there any principles, or even any general rules? And is it true that some of the proof of Shakespeare's genuine-man-of-the-theatre status lies in the absence from his texts of these author's stage directions against which the young are so solemnly warned? There are no elaborate descriptions of the physical appearance of his personages, nothing to tell their precise ages, nor yet, in many instances, their relative ages; there are no bothersome requirements in the way of costume, nothing to "worry" the producer—no pauses or silences indicated at what he considers the "wrong" moments, no nonsense about *slowly, laughing, irritably, rising to his feet, moving restlessly about, seated, opens book and reads,* and other "impertinences."

Or so it may seem—until the text pulls us up with precise indications of, say, the ages of Juliet or Miranda, the relative heights of Hermia and Helena; the pauses, accelerations, silences dictated by the structure of the line and the choice and juxtaposition of words, and the movements, or immobility, clearly inevitable from emotional or intellectual content or structure; until, in fact, a piece of production that misses some obvious detail, which we take for granted in reading because it is written into the text, reminds us that these things can be overlooked, or even deliberately ignored by producers or actors.[8] Tradition, too, can get between the artist's perception and the author's intention. It took a Mrs. Siddons to put down Lady Macbeth's candle for the sleepwalking scene; her predecessors had clung to it throughout, in spite of what is written into the text. Even Sheridan, author and man of the theatre, genuinely feared that by disregarding tradition and following the author's intention Mrs. Siddons would wreck the performance. But his disapproval of the candle innovation was mild in comparison to the general howl of sentimental dismay which in 1951 greeted Alec Guinness when his Hamlet gave us the authentic bearded young men of Elizabethan portraiture, like Essex or Southampton, instead of trying to put across the vivid, forceful, brutal vigor of "plucks off my beard and blows it in my face" with a smooth chin.[9]

The fallibility of the interpreters and receivers of a work of dramatic art and the failure of the artist to communicate his intention in all its fullness contribute to the eternal fascination of a classic. "We shall go / Always a little further," as we hope, at each new interpretation, always prepared for the fresh approach to reveal what our predecessors have missed. But even when Shakespeare has written in the theatrical realization of his intention by the very texture of his verse, its tone and inflection, pause and pace, and by the choice, weight, and juxtaposition of words, it does not necessarily secure recognition. Productions of *Macbeth* too often provide examples of this. In the "Tomorrow and tomorrow and tomorrow" passage, some actors take—or are persuaded to take—their cue from the end of the speech, and from the start will strut and fret, striding the stage like any poor player. But if ever a line called in its syllabic structure and pointing for the immobility of despair it is this. The words are stones, dropped one after another to plumb the bottomless depths of the well of emptiness and futility into which Macbeth gazes. The rhythmic implication should freeze the speaker to the stoniness of Keats's fallen Saturn.

The most astonishing example, however, can be the treatment of act III, scene iv—that awful moment of lowest ebb of life and purpose and ambition, when the guests have withdrawn from the banquet and left Macbeth and his Lady alone together. The pause in the middle of the line

The secret'st man of blood. // What is the night?

and the incredible flat weariness of Lady Macbeth's reply,

Almost at odds with morning, which is which.//

together with the break in the thought and the pause before Macbeth's

39

How sayest thou that Macduff denies his person
At our great bidding?

all combine to communicate with indescribable power the feeling of
that death-hour of the night, at about three or four in the morning,
when the vitality of the world itself seems to go out with the tide. To
the normally sensitive ear it is the crucial break, the caesura in the
line of the play, the turning point in the whole action. Yet I have
known it cut altogether, and it is only rarely well realized in performance. From that moment the countermovement begins, with
Macbeth's

For mine own good
All causes shall give way.

But unless this structural pause is marked, as the verse marks it, so
that the last assertion of Lady Macbeth's dominance of spirit which
we have just witnessed in the banquet scene is finally overthrown
here, and unless her despairing "Nought's had, all's spent," of act III,
scene ii is thus echoed in the rhythm of her "Almost at odds with
morning," we miss the economical but brilliant dramatization of the
process of her collapse, so that the final transition from the self-
command and resourcefulness of act III, scene iv to the "mind dis-
eased" and broken spirit of the sleepwalking scene becomes too
violent. The author has provided the hints; we need only observe
them. Equally, as she is drained of her very quality of life by the
flattened rhythm of her lines, so in the resurgence of vigor in Macbeth's last two speeches does the flood tide of evil begin to flow
again, but for him alone. The whole passage is central and crucial,
yet even when it is not cut down to a few lines, I have heard and seen
its emotional values entirely wrecked, first by insensitive handling of
the rhythm and then by a final brisk walk upstage, hand-in-hand,
heads up, regal mantles flowing behind them, as for a triumphal exit.
We may agree that there should be no need of stage directions for
such a passage because tone and time are completely written in;
nevertheless, an adequate rendering of it—and therefore, presumably, adequate understanding of meaning and function—are the
exception.[10]

"Judge by results," wrote Lascelles Abercrombie, "by any results
that may come of living in the art of the play and attending to everything it consists of."[11] Producer, actor, designer, critic, and audience
are identified as recipients of the author's intention; but what the
individual auditor receives is the experience of life which the author
intends to impart, as transmitted through the refracting glass of this

orchestrated and collective response of the executants, however close that interpretation may be and however little it is modified, as a happening, by total audience response. Just as the sensitivity of an ear for great poetry is cultivated by continually submitting oneself to the experience, so all these recipients of drama, in their varying degrees of expertise and instinctive creativity, are conditioned in their response to the author's intention by standards and associative values derived from their accumulated theatre experience. Consciously or unconsciously, they refer scenes, situations, and characters to theatrical predecessors and cognates known to them. A scene for which there is no precedent, or where the effect achieved does not square with the expectation aroused by its label, inevitably attracts comparative evaluation, and the author's handling of it is instinctively referred, especially, but not exclusively, by professional intermediaries, to similar emotional and visual effects, whereas ideally it should lodge and germinate in the mind in its own particularity.

It was an experience of this kind with the trial scene in Shakespeare's *Henry VIII* which originally alerted me to the danger of "good" and "bad" evaluation-by-comparison, which results when cognates of class A set standards for specimen X. Examining Spedding's contention that it was a companion picture to Hermione's trial in *The Winter's Tale*, finding this supposed resemblance superficial and misleading, and then comparing the scene with the trials in *The Merchant of Venice* and *The White Devil*, I realized that whereas these three could reasonably be compared and classified as effect A, the *Henry VIII* trial had nothing in common with them and had to be taken as X, the unknown quantity.[12] Every theatrical effect legitimately obtained by these others was flatly contradicted by the effects of the Blackfriars trial, which was entirely unrelated to them in my own experience of the play in both the theatre and the study. However the scene is cut or staged, theatrically it "flops" when Queen Katharine, after her impassioned and moving appeal to Henry, leaves the court as magnificently as she entered it, so that the only character who speaks the language of emotion is removed at l. 133, and the remaining 108 lines, if not savagely cut or even entirely omitted in performance, are devoted to an historical and academic statement of the King's case, in which the emotional temperature drops to zero. It flops, that is, *if*, as in the other three plays, we look for a terrific personal conflict packed with theatrical excitement, the clash of opposed personalities, the scoring of points, suspense and its resolutions, surprises and all the devices of dramatic tension which constitute normal audience expectation.[13] But because the scene does not end on Katharine's exit, if we have any real belief in our author, whoever he may have been, we must credit him with that intention in what he does and must not say "This is bad," because we have been cheated of the popular fare for which we crave—"the same again, but longer and louder." What we must as is "*Why?*"

If we ask the right questions, we get the right answers. The remaining 108 lines set forth the author's theme explicitly. This is the play's intention—what the play is about—namely, the Tudor succession, realized by an Elizabethan, who had lived through the struggle and the last phases as "something understood": understood in terms of the price paid for it in blood and tears and what, by 1613, it had meant to a man born into the Elizabethan greatness, who had also lived through the disillusionment and the fears and scruples that had shaken his own generation in the last years of the great Queen's reign and the first years of her successor's, of which *Lear, Timon*, and *Troilus and Cressida* give us the measure. This achievement is the substance of Cranmer's prophetic vision at the conclusion, which in Tyrone Guthrie's 1949 Stratford production could be described as the writer's "gravely beautiful valediction over the age that had bred him," spoken in the spirit in which it was written.[14] Though even in this, the best production I have seen,[15] the completeness of the author's final intention was frustrated by the omission of the concluding tribute to James I.

Grasp the answer to this crucial question of theme and the treatment of the story and its several episodes becomes clear. This author is not writing another chronicle history; there is no distance of centuries or epochs between him and the story, nor is he in any doubt, having digested the whole of Holinshed's 180 double-columned pages, that he needs just four episodes to carry that theme. To suggest, as so many critics have done, that the play consists of "a number of unrelated scenes"[16] is to ignore the dramatist's intention. This is no haphazard dip into the Holinshed lucky-bag; it is the selectivity of a brilliant mind, in which genuine historical insight is balanced by an equally sure dramatic instinct and is theatrically "realized" in the arrangement of the episodes and the unity given to the whole by the sustained, consistent angle of vision from which they are all viewed, until we reach the last act and its triumphant conclusion. He has selected three main historical episodes and the semiapocryphal Cranmer-Gardiner scenes, all leading up to the birth of Elizabeth as the climax of the action and the theme it carries. The critical-creative impulse to rewrite the author's play according to one's own ideas must be resisted.[17] Structurally his action-plot is simply the removal of obstacles, enabling the theme or idea-plot to be brought to a successful issue. Its three tragic episodes are the destruction of Buckingham, who threatens the Tudor succession, the divorce and death of Katharine, who has failed to ensure it with a male heir, and the destruction of Wolsey, who threatens the Anne Boleyn marriage, culminating in the showpiece of the coronation scene which in theatrical realization must outdo the trial scene as spectacle and in its own day undoubtedly did so. The necessary anticlimactic movement between the coronation and the climax of the birth of Elizabeth is the Cranmer-Gardiner episode, which in the theatre suffers from a bad tradition and tends to be either cut or clowned, but has a genuine thematic value if honestly handled, in spite of Speddings's assertion that these scenes "are utterly irrelevant to the business of the play" and have "poetically no value but the reverse." The real "business of the play" is the Tudor succession, and as Henry must now be more fully, personally, traditionally, and sympathetically established for the conclusion of the action, so that the affirmation of the theme includes the individual as well as the idea, he is shown in the familiar "bluff King Hal" guise in which, as one might say, contemporary playgoers knew him by heart. Gardiner, by his association with Wolsey, has been identified with the negation of the theme; Cranmer, by his support of the divorce, with its affirmation; and Henry now takes the center of the stage in true kingly style—a *deus ex machina*, commanding reconciliation and resolving the theme in a concord:

> As I have made ye one, lords, one remain,
> So I grow stronger, you more honour gain.
> (V.iii.181–82)

It is, once more, the old national moral emphasized by Shakespeare in the whole series of the history plays—in unity and concord at home lies true strength.[18] Theme and action unite as Henry stands forth at his most effective—the Tudor purpose, the national purpose, incarnate in the person of the Tudor monarch, at this moment fully, plainly, and explicitly symbolic of the force he represents.

Not only does the Cranmer episode resolve all discords on the symbolic plane, in preparation for the triumphant conclusion, thereby entirely justifying its position in the play, but its treatment also has a definite tonal value in the action plot. It introduces a romantic note to bridge the gap between the realistic level of the preceding scenes and the raised, emotional, visionary level of the conclusion. As action, it is an episode in the older and more theatrical manner, with the romantic touches of the monarch's talismanic ring and the rescue of

43

the virtuous minister by the all-seeing, all-powerful, righteous and just ruler, as which, for the only time in the play, Henry at last appears. He never speaks better, more royally, or to more purpose than in these four speeches. It is a simple yet subtle transition, effectively carrying us over by its vigor from Katharine's death to the final rejoicing, and thus fulfilling its proper anticlimactic function. I have never been able to understand how the theatre can bring itself to ignore so completely the natural movement of the play, as it does when it omits this episode in its entirety, and goes—as in Irving's and Tree's versions—straight from Katharine's death to Elizabeth's christening. If both are to be played for their true value, a pause, a breathing space between them, is essential.[19] The recoil after crisis and before climax is so written into all normal Elizabethan play structure, and is so essential for the full effect of the conclusion, that indecent haste of this kind argues an irresponsibility to the dramatic material and a lack of attention to what the author has to say, which destroy confidence in the dramatic integrity of the producer's approach. The idea that the scenes of *Henry VIII* are "unrelated" is in fact promoted when the theatre treats them in this fashion.

Recognizing that the theatrically popular trial scene of the time is here treated realistically and deliberately avoids the dramatic tension of conflict, we must accept intention. This author is discarding the theatrical convention for something nearer to life, for historical fact and for realism, not only in structure but also in style, which is something quite other than the percentages of "'ems" and "thems" and tricks of phrasing. He is vitally concerned with angle of vision and consistency of tone and purpose—a fusing of style and structure which make us realize that the writer's cast of mind is individual, unique. As he says in his Prologue, "All is true." On the stage you can launch one emotional force against another and the exhilaration of conflict with another human being carries you on; you can sweep aside lawyers with their Latin and legal jargon and the spirit does not submit to the inexorable processes of law and reason. In life, as the author of *Henry VIII* insists, it is not like that. Emotion and human feeling spend themselves in vain against the impersonality of the process that has trapped its human victims; and you cannot fight a personal duel, sustained on both sides by personal hate, when no one will meet you as such an opposer. Katharine appeals to her husband in eloquent and moving words—to meet only silence. Her appeal is personal, but Henry is no longer a person, and the law and the Church, speaking as one, deal briefly, courteously, firmly with her request for delay. As far as they are concerned, the human values

44

for which she pleads do not exist. She is up against the process, the machine, the rocklike wall-face of law itself. Passion hurls itself unavailingly against the dispassionate, as in a Galsworthy trial scene: "Is this relevant, Mr. Frome?" asks the judge.

> William Falder, you have been given fair trial . . . throughout the trial your counsel was in reality making an appeal for mercy. . . . And this plea of his, which in the end amounted to a passionate appeal, he based, in effect, on an indictment of the march of Justice. . . . *The Law is what it is*—a majestic edifice, sheltering all of us, each stone of which rests on another. I am concerned only in its administration.

It is the equivalent of a deliberately nonemotional statement of the reasons that must decide an issue against all the personal sympathies of the audience, as when the judge sums up against Falder in *Justice*, or when Shaw's Inquisitor puts the case against Joan of Arc. We do this kind of thing well today, perhaps better, and our prose medium is more suited to lengthy monologues which explain the precise reasons, intellectual or customary, laudable or reprehensible, sound or sophistical, that account for behavior and for the course of the action we are witnessing. The function of such speeches is to strike a balance between our emotional and intellectual responses to the writer's purpose and our understanding of it. The Elizabethan writer, I fancy, reckoned to deal with little beyond the emotional reactions; the Jacobean began to wrestle with the intellectual statement and the response to it, as in Ford's long exposition of honor in *The Broken Heart* (III.i). The exposition of Henry's scruples of conscience is skillfully handled, for its date, and it is likely to have held a contemporary audience, although it fails to hold a modern one, but there is no reason why it should have been less successful in its own day than our equivalent attempts.

This particular investigation of dramatic intention and theatrical effect, which I have summarized very briefly, had a further consequence that I did not anticipate. Being totally uncommitted over the divided authorship issue I had intended simply to give the pros and cons and leave the reader to make up his own mind;[20] and I am still as skeptical as I was then about the stylistic arguments used by literary critics to distribute portions of Elizabethan plays, even among known collaborators.[21] But the approach to the play itself, accepting the author's effects as intended, convinced me that *Henry VIII* was indubitably Shakespeare's, and further converted both Dr. A.W. Pollard and Professor Caroline Spurgeon to this view. I also found, six months later, that Professor Wilson Knight, in his own production of the play, had anticipated some of my arguments and come unequivocally to the same conclusion.[22] Since then, Professor R.A. Foakes, in his admirable introduction to the 1957 New Arden edition, has given us the most judicious and perceptive editorial account of the play, *considered as a play*, and of the authorship problem, that I know.[23] I think the basic resemblance between my 1935 essay and his appreciation, which is as balanced as it is brilliant, together with the fact that he ends it as I did mine, suggests that modern criticism has been steadily advancing along the right lines, even as modern productions since Guthrie's in 1949 have dealt with the play as a play, not simply as a vehicle for actors.

Professor Foakes concludes that perhaps the play should be thought of as "the last innovation of a mind forever exploring; and if the history of its supposed deficiencies can be forgotten, then the conception of the play may be allowed its full originality, as a felicitous new solution to problems posed by the nature of the material with which Shakespeare's last plays deal."[24] My conclusion in 1935, before the Guthrie production, was that the real play, which has been buried for too long beneath its own effective scenes and the authorship controversy, should prove, if properly produced, a rational entertainment for intelligent people. The mind that conceived this dramatic experiment was very evidently that of an experienced man of the theatre. You must know all about "theatre" before you can afford to reject it for the sake of the theatre. This 1613 experiment with fresh dramatic values reminds me of that daring and tremendous experiment which is the last twenty minutes of *A Doll's House*. Ibsen, in 1879, aged fifty, had behind him the experience of preparing the productions of 145 typical well-made plays of his day, and had himself written *the* model of all such, two years previously, in his *Pillars of Society*. When the tarantella ends, all the situations, tricks, and methods of the well-made play are hustled off the stage, and the real drama begins. Similarly, the mind that conceives *Henry VIII* decides that physical action, heroes, conflict, romantic poetry, and all the rest of the Elizabethan stock-in-trade are to be hustled off his stage for the sake of a sober and truthful play, a great theme, and a closer touch with reality. The author does not successfully anticipate Ibsen's experiment, which made the discussion of ideas the dominant interest in modern European drama for nearly half a century. But the future toward which this 1613 experiment was reaching out is the future that was Ibsen, the great poet-dramatist of two and a half centuries later.

M. St. Clare Byrne

For our identification parade, therefore, we have found a mind. Is it recognizable or not? Are we in touch with the kind of mentality we may legitimately associate with the forty-nine-year-old Shakespeare?

The Shakespeare we all know and admire was an original genius. He refused to go on writing the same play over again. He had an extremely practical conception of the business of playwriting, but at the same time found scope in the writing of plays for the exercising of a very daring mind. It is perhaps a commonplace to say that he was always experimenting with dramatic methods—more particularly toward the end of his career. But it cannot too often be reaffirmed that this delight in experiment is always the characteristic of the great and original mind, and not of the merely popular writer. Sir Edmund Chambers finds "the reversion to the epic chronicle at the very end of Shakespeare's career is odd."[25] But surely there is nothing odd in the spectacle of an original mind discovering that there is still something new and exciting to be done with the old material, which it has used so often, although never before in this particular way. What I find odd is the idea that a popular writer like Fletcher, who has discovered the formula that everyone wants, who never otherwise touches this particular kind of play, and never employs methods comparable to those we have been analyzing, should, at the height of his success and popularity, revert to an outmoded type. Oddest of all is what can only be described as the basic improbability that there should be any failure of the full and accepted theatrical effect if Fletcher is concerned in the writing of a scene. It is axiomatic that his situations will hold, whereas the whole trouble with *Henry VIII* starts from the fact that the situations do not hold, in the old, easy, normal, accepted theatrical way, because something quite different from the normal theatrical effect is what the author intended.

If we seek to identify a mind, surely the mind which, around 1602, took a grimly realistic attitude to the romantic *Troilus and Cressida* story and to the heroic-epic treatment of war is a more likely guess than the mind which habitually exploited the tragicomedy formula and allowed the audience both to have its cake and eat it. Surely the mind which had already between 1600 and 1604 expressed its dissatisfaction with the romantic formulae that serve as plots for *All's Well* and *Measure for Measure* is more likely to turn toward realism in tone and attack than the specialist in the exploitation of emotionalism? Not for Fletcher the poetry that might be squeezed from the "pure crude fact" of the chronicle history: the melodrama and the excitement of the end of Bonduca and her daughters, yes; but not the sober quietude and poignancy of the death of Katharine:

Remember me
In all humility unto his highness:
Say his long trouble now is passing
Out of this world.

(IV.ii.160–63)

Shakespeare was only fifty-two when he died. Had he lived on and continued to write plays it is possible that he would have made the one experiment which none of the Jacobean writers had the vitality to attempt. Having presumably said what he had to say about life, and seeing what was happening to blank verse, he could have turned his energies to the development of English prose for dramatic purposes. There is no doubt that the Shakespeare of the histories and the middle comedies, around 1600, was finding prose a more suitable medium for some of the material he was handling.[26] The tragedies had yet to be written, and for them he would create their own astounding blank verse; for dramatic purposes there has been no further development since that creation. But it is not a vain imagining that, had he eventually turned to the "realistic" manner, as the writer of *Henry VIII* does, he might have put his mind to the problem which occupied the mature Ibsen, who in 1883 criticized the "immense injury" done by verse to the art of the theatre: "I myself, for the last seven or eight years, have hardly written a single verse, but have cultivated exclusively the incomparably more difficult art of poetic creation in the plain unvarnished speech of reality."

As a true poet Ibsen had set himself the task of writing poetry without the aid of the high style, of which Shakespeare had proved himself a rare master. There is none of the high style in *Henry VIII*, though time and again we hear the authentic accents of poetry. To put it at its lowest, if we accept *Henry VIII* as Shakespeare's, we are committing ourselves to no more than saying that it is an unexpected and daring experiment in a new kind and a new style, and a much better and more original experiment than was *Cymbeline*. It is not the work of "a tired mind," but the work of a great mind tired of the theatrical convention in which it has been working. "Shakespeare is not content with perfection of achievement at any stage of his career; he must always go on to a stage beyond."[27] The stage beyond is not necessarily the stage better, but it enlarges the boundaries, thrusts into unexplored territory, carries the dramatic adventure a step further, even if no one follows up the experiment for a couple of centuries. For those who feel that nothing of vital importance happened to drama

48

between Shakespeare and Ibsen, *Henry VIII*, as his last play, may perhaps acquire a new significance.

How fully his own audience was always "with" him we know in general terms only. Just how far away the perception of succeeding centuries could drift we know from the adaptations and recorded mutilations of his text and the perversities of interpretation that still from time to time afflict us in performance; and we have had to wait for our own century to catch up with his intentions, not only in *Henry VIII* but in *Troilus and Cressida, Measure for Measure, All's Well, Antony and Cleopatra*, and *Love's Labour's Lost. Henry VIII's* critical and theatrical history provides an outstanding example of the failure of literary criticism and stage production to give proper consideration to the facts of dramatic intention, as expressed in structure and style; but the succession theme was pinpointed in 1918, and the case for Shakespeare as sole author was supported by Marjorie Nicolson and Baldwin Maxwell in 1922 and 1923, by Peter Alexander in 1930, and by Professor Wilson Knight in 1936. With the New Arden edition, and finally with Professor Sprague's 1964 account of "the play in performance" in his happily timed quadricentenary studies of Shakespeare's *Histories*, I believe that this remarkable play, for so long, as he says, "badly treated on the stage and rather worse in the study,"[28] has been definitively rehabilitated by the investigation of "what the author meant." But concentration on intention is still erratic, and when at this moment of writing we are confronted with a naked Desdemona, in defiance of three explicit author's stage directions about her smock or shift for her nightly wearing, progress, perhaps, "seems here no painful inch to gain." Slow it has been, but "e pur si muove"; and all who know the work of the scholar to whom this volume pays tribute will recognize that the two sections of this essay are simply footnotes to the principles and practice which have, throughout, determined his own approach to drama, the theatre, and the play in performance, and have also done so much to inspire and guide students of the drama, and especially of Shakespeare, to listen to what the author says, to see straight and recognize and respect intention.

The Triple Bond:
Audience, Actors, Author in the
Elizabethan Playhouse

M. C. Bradbrook

Arthur Colby Sprague's contribution to the history of Shakespearean performance established the significance of its ever-varying interpretation, in the spirit of Ezra Pound's definition—"The medium of drama is not words, but persons moving about on a stage using words." However, today's open stage makes it possible to extend this definition to "persons moving about on a stage using words, and responding, while eliciting a reciprocal response from an audience around the stage."

The variety of buildings that served as Elizabethan playhouses, the social constitution, size, and customary manners of the audience made up one part of that "two hours' traffic of the stage," to which Shakespeare, more than anyone else, gave unity. The audience was part of the performance.

"Poetry is a deed" as Tarlton and the Epilogue to *Cambises* (1561) proclaim.[1] The oral art and the scenic display by which actors and audience participated in an *event*, in the city streets, the game place, or the hall were supported by music and other "activities" and in the earlier sixteenth century had been directed toward a common function or shared task—worship and religious observance, welcomes, triumphs, civic installation; seasonal rites of spring, harvest, winter solstice; weddings and natal feasts; vassals' tributes to a lord or lady —or, contrariwise, flouting, social mockery, and scorn, directed toward a common enemy.

Any relationship, social or personal, depends on both parties maintaining roles that are mutually acceptable and recognized; the alteration of any one role will change or disrupt the relationship, and thereby change also the nature of the events in which it is embodied. Sharing a task is a sure way to stabilize personal relations—whether bringing up children or cooking a meal, whether customary or contractual. During the sixteenth century, as I shall show below, the relation of actors to audience moved from the customary to the contractual. The actors' role became increasingly interpretative, that of the audience differentiated, while in certain kinds of play the author acquired independent status.

At the beginning of Elizabeth's reign, the guildhall of a London church might serve as a stage for players one week and for a wedding feast the next.[2] In 1565 two inns began staging fencers' prizes—as we know from records of the Masters of Fence—which implies some kind of auditorium;[3] the Bull and the Bell Savage later became well known as players' inns. Another, the Bell, kept a stock of theatrical properties for hire.[4] An atmosphere of holiday and revelry was proper to inns. Along with the appearance of the great Theatre of Shoreditch in 1576, an actor belonging to the Earl of Warwick's Men erected a small playing place in the garden of his house at Newington Butts, which, enjoying pleasant and reputable surroundings, survived to be used by Oxford's Men and, in 1592, Lord Strange's Men (who reopened there after a plague season with two of Shakespeare's plays).[5] This little suburban playhouse, which was left standing till 1597, may represent the casual playing, which dwindled and almost vanished by the end of the century. There were probably similar haunts in such villages as Islington to the north. The playing place came in all shapes and sizes.

Within the City of London, the Inns of Court maintained varied traditions of revelry at Christmas, which might have significant political implications; the production of *Gorboduc* in 1569 was part of Robert Dudley's campaign for favor.[6] They also offered a training in public speaking, which began with the study of drama at the grammar schools. Thomas Kyd attended the Merchant Taylors' School; he may have performed on that occasion in 1574 when the Livery protested that they were kept out of the best places to see the school play because an admission charge had brought too many of the general public.

The singing children of St. Paul's may have presented their plays to so select an audience as to constitute a kind of club;[7] they were suppressed in 1590 for commenting too directly on ecclesiastical politics. The Theatre of the Hall was theatre of privilege; but on that account it was vulnerable when authority frowned. The earliest surviving secular play, given between intervals of feasting in the hall of Cardinal Morton at Lambeth, could be prolonged only "when my lord shall so devyse," but

It is the mynde and intent
Of me and my company to content
The least that stondeth here
(Prologue, Part 2, *Fulgens and Lucres*, 1497)

Accordingly, a debate was "interlaced" with clowning from actors "planted" in the audience.

One of the plays at St. Paul's specifies the dilemma of the actors by the mid-sixteenth century:

The proverb is, how many men, so many minds . . .
No play, no party can all alike content.
The grave divine calls for divinity,
The civil servant for philosophy,
The courtier craves some rare sound history,
The baser sort for knacks of plesantry.
(Prologue, *Contention between Liberality and Prodigality*, 1565)

One of the readiest ways to unite a small group is to join in mockery of a common enemy. From the time when Wolsey was lampooned at the Inns of Court to 1624, when Spain was mocked in the record success of the Elizabethan stage, Middleton's *Game at Chess* (1624), libel ranged from indirect "glancing" to open mimicry in the victim's own apparel. It was calculated to attract and hold an audience, perhaps all the more since the savage penalties incurred turned it into a sort of Russian roulette.

Conversely, celebration of good fellowship might provide positive incentive to the social art of playing, strengthening collective identity. This was especially developed in London. (But here also the contractual element appeared when the new theatres imposed a fixed, regular price to see plays, which thereby became "wares" for sale—"show business.") In *The Book of Sir Thomas More* (1590) Tudor household players of "My Lord Cardinal" are shown offering their services to More at his Sheriff's feast. He is prepared to help them out with improvising, but their entertainment is of little more significance than "background music" would be today. Although they are rather prematurely cut short, the customary reward is given, in spite of a dishonest servant's attempt to pocket a share. This play, itself the product of five hands, and fated never to reach the boards at all, shows that a lively sense of their own history animated the players of Shakespeare's day, even as part of a great Londoner's life story. The merry jests of More persist after the final tragic turn of Fortune's wheel (the cause of his death is naturally unexplained and he remains a popular hero).

Extemporal jesting continued on the public stages, chiefly in the afterpieces of the clowns. Harvey accused Spenser in jest of casting him as a clown and setting him on a "painted stage" as an object of mirth; Nashe thought his pleading would make more sport than "old *Mother Bombey*" did at Paul's.[8] Extemporal jesting could easily turn into a scolding match and so demanded skillful handling of the audience by the clown. Fighting among the audience was the chief civic risk at plays.

In the 1580s Lyly and the first play of Peele, *The Arraignement of Paris* (1581), were presented by the Children of the Chapel at court and in the Blackfriars Hall theatre. Centering on compliment to the Queen, the action is directed to the one Lady, who herself becomes the chief actor when the golden apple is delivered into her hands. Here Peele was relying on a commonplace—the same triumph over the three goddesses was depicted by Hans Eworth in the picture now at Windsor, and it might have formed part of any triumphal entry to London or any public pageant. The legend of the Queen absorbed older religious symbols and classical grandeur or pastoral familiarity with equal ease, so that all Lyly's plays were offerings of this kind.

Whenever the Queen was seated on the stage (being of greater interest to the spectators than the show, even if she were not its subject) audience and players would become united in the common rite of homage. The public theatres, lacking such a focus, more slowly built up popular forms, evolving under workshop conditions. Shifting relations of actors and audience were stabilized by the growing power of dramatic poetry—poetry as communal action, words with a subtext. Forms ultimately derived from particular combinations of actors and poets, working in certain playing places; to these the classical names of "tragedy" and "comedy" became attached, as the classical name "theatre" had become attached to the game place or playing place. These were conventions but "a convention has a history, it changes in time and in response to social pressures of various kinds."[9] They were not prescriptive.

The plays survive only in haphazard, confused, sometimes nonsensical printed texts, of indirect relation to what must have been the original compositions of Peele, Greene, and Marlowe. The oral nature of the art meant that, to the public and the actors, "the book" was susceptible to variation. Moreover, collaboration between a group of writers (as between groups of actors) was accepted; so little was the author's identity a part of the tradition that Kyd's name does not appear on the title page of *The Spanish Tragedy*, nor Marlowe's on *Tamburlaine*, nor Peele's on a number of his plays.

"What is a comonty?" asks Christopher Sly, "Is it a Christmas gambold or a tumbling trick?" To which the answer comes: "It is a kind of history." *The Love of King David and Fair Bethsabe with the Tragedy of Absalom* (1587) includes a comic drunken act (for Uriah), some delicate songs, a spectacular death for Absalom; the chorus then offers a third "discourse," but what follows is not at all what they promise:

> Now since the story lends us other store
> To make a third discourse of David's life . . .
> Here end we this, and what wants here to please
> We will supply with triple willingness.

This looks forward to the epilogue to *Selimus* (1592):

> If this first part, Gentles, do like you well,
> The second part shall greater murthers tell.

Like a minstrel, he is offering another "fitte." *King Edward I* (1591) includes some chronicle material with some from popular ballads. It attacks the common enemy, in the person of the wicked Spanish Queen, and exalts London. Comedy provides the King's clever judgment against his Queen, the flailing match between the Friar and the Potter; Tragedy, the murder by the Spanish Queen of London's Lady Mayoress—by tying her to a chair and giving her a serpent to suckle—followed by the spectacular sinking of Queen Eleanor into the earth and her emergence at Potter's Hithe. These "activities" achieve the same kind of unity as the street pageants which Peele, like his father before him, devised. All the marvels are familiar and traditional marvels, all the characters are animated images, and their "discourse" more resembles proclamation than dialogue. What is being communally enacted is the solidarity or unity of the "mere English"; even where the material is not so popular and customary it takes on the coloring. The atrocities are no more blood-chilling than beatings in a popular farce are supposed to hurt the victim. This is in a very direct sense a play world, all the more so since London or Respublica no longer appears as a character but is represented by the audience. So the English chronicle history emerged in its festive form—it had several others.

Confused as he is, the seeds of development lie with Peele rather than in the entirely well-planned *True Chronicle History of King Leir*

M.C. Bradbrook

(1590), which is indeed, in conventional terms of planning, more rationally motivated than Shakespeare's tragedy.

Form and identity came to the popular stages at the end of the 1580s with those two tragic masterpieces, *Tamburlaine* and *The Spanish Tragedy*. Both were imitated and affectionately parodied for years; they remained models into Jacobean times. "Tragedy" was loosely used in the playhouse to mean "death scene"; a death speech was the big finale for any actor, demanding complete identification. Marlowe's combination of intellectual fire and primitive violence satisfied all tastes; his professed contempt for "jigging veins of rhyming mother wits" was justified by his own superb achievement. Kyd's play is set in an entirely evil and treacherous court, where the one just man is himself finally driven to treachery and gratuitous crime. There was no need of direct contemporary reference to this Evil Kingdom, the equivalent of the nightmare kingdom of Shakespeare's *Richard III*. All the actions are linked; an intricate pattern of interlocked betrayals and counterminings effectively cuts out spontaneous death, such as that of the poisoner in *Selimus*, who, offered the fatal cup by one of his destined victims, drinks it off farcically with the reflection:

> Faith, I am old as well as Bajazet
> And care not much to end my life with him.

The Spanish Tragedy is self-conscious about dramatic form—witness the superb play-within-the-play that concludes it. Nashe in an early pamphlet proved plays to be "a rare exercise of virtue" and no mere pastime, since "for the most part . . . borrowed out of our English Chronicles" they revive the past so it lives again. Thus "brave Talbot the terror of the French" revives and dies on the stage, "embalmed by the tears of ten thousand spectators, at least"—at several times, Nashe prudently and hastily adds (*Pierce Penilesse* [1592]; *Works* [I: 212]). But these "tragedies" succeeded as independent dramatic events.

Whether or not, as F.P. Wilson suggested, Shakespeare's are the first English history plays, he alone evolved an interpretation of the course of history continuous with the old craft cycles.[10] A providential pattern linked events, so that prefiguration implanted the events of that day within the still living past. Richard of Gloucester stabs Henry VI with a direct recollection of the role of the Prophet in the older cycles:

> Die, prophet, in thy speech,
> For this, among the rest, was I ordained.
>   (V.vi.57–58)

55

Richard is nevertheless always conscious of himself as an actor—Edward Hall has the common people compare the King's "games" to stage plays.[11] In *3 Henry VI* (1591) a series of great death scenes pile up on each other; the prologue of Rutland's murder leads to the grand death scene of Richard of York, with its ritual of contempt and the tremendous lament that excited Greene's envy. This is followed by the death of his enemy Clifford, Clifford's by the death of the Prince of Wales, so that when finally King Henry VI greets his murderer, Gloucester, with the line

> What scene of death hath Roscius now to act?
> (V.vi.10)

the audience's expectation must have been gratified by this acknowledgment of the climax.

Yet Shakespeare was also uncomfortably aware that an audience might fail to respond sympathetically; in *King John*, the citizens of Angiers mock the combatants ranged below:

> As in a theatre, whence they gape and point
> At your industrious scenes and acts of death
> (II.i.375–76)

And before many years had passed, the set death scene of older plays was parodied, in its proclamatory discursiveness, by the death of Pyramus:

> Now am I dead,
> Now am I fled,
> My soul is in the sky.
> Tongue, lose thy light,
> Moon, take thy flight,   [*exit Moonshine*]
> Now die, die, die, die, die.
> (V.i.306–11)

Death in a very different key concludes *Summer's Last Will and Testament*, which in the late autumn of 1592, when all public theatres were closed because of the plague, was given for the Archbishop of Canterbury "on the tilestones" of his palace at Croydon. This is "no play but a show"—consciously nostalgic and at the same time critically balanced between lyric and paradox, jest and lament. The pageantry and speeches are controlled by two figures—Will Summers, the Jester of Henry VIII's court, who opens with what appears to be extemporal jesting, who constantly breaks the illusion to mock players and audience with ever-varying fluency; and the silent or almost silent figure of the dying King Summer, the "beautiful and death-struck year," supported on the shoulders of his two heirs, Autumn and Winter. The procession of the seasons is embodied in traditional rustic ceremonies—harvest games, dancing, dubbing of knights with the blackjack, intermingled with cosmic figures like Sol and Orion the Hunter, with scholarly paradoxes, and a mock sermon or two such as Nashe might have used in his college plays at Cambridge. The medley is bound together by the audience and the players being almost indistinguishable; it sustains the feeling of an impromptu sport rising out of the company's after-supper jests and songs. (This element of the play can be revived if it is performed in the right surroundings, for instance, in a college hall.) It is directed toward the Archbishop himself by his tenants and servants; in the words of the prologue, "No man pleaseth all; we seek to please one." Archbishop Whitgift was said to love mock debates with his household of young clerks; but almost the entire company might at some point have moved from the audience into the play group and back again. The circling of time and seasons, planets and feasts, ends with the arrival of the savage and poet-hating Winter and his sons, a miserly Christmas and a hostile January (or "back-winter"). Summer, having called all his household to account, bequeaths the remnant of his good days to "Eliza, that most sacred dame." The concluding songs, which are litanies, lead out from the play world to the plague-stricken city beyond the rustic safety of Croydon, whence the Archbishop had come, with his train, and sojourners who may have included Nashe himself:

Adieu, farewell, earth's bliss,
This world uncertain is . . .
Lord, have mercy upon us . . .

Autumn hath all the summer's fruitful treasure,
Gone is our sport, fled is poor Croydon's pleasure . . .
London doth mourn, Lambeth is quite forlorn,
Trades cry woe worth that ever they were born . . .
From winter, plague and pestilence, Good Lord, deliver us. . . .

Yet this household "show"—a nostalgic revival of old hospitality—is modernized by the built-in satire of the jester Will Summers, who breaks the illusion, comments and mocks, mines and countermines with his jests; for though he is also a ghost from a departed kingdom, like Yorick, he is very much a professional player. Nashe, throughout

57

his writings, sustained a jester's role—the semidramatic style of his pamphlets belongs with the games of Tarlton and Kemp, though crossed with the learning of which he was so proud. It has a Shakespearean copiousness and natural abundance, a mixture of sophistication and the natural and direct ease of common life.

Nashe raises the language of customary festive sports toward art; he does not achieve "a pleasant comedy" for the *public* playhouse. Indeed, his public comedy, *The Isle of Dogs* (1597), was so far from pleasant that it caused a general closing of theatres, drove him to take refuge in Yarmouth, and gave his young collaborator, Ben Jonson, a first taste of a situation that in future years was to recur quite frequently. This play contained too much of the invective traditional in the privileged theatre of the Hall. Even at Cambridge Nashe had got into trouble for playing the "Knave of Clubs" in the scurrilous *Terminus et Non Terminus.*

There is something of the perpetual undergraduate about Nashe. It was by combining novelty with "the whole complex of metaphors relating man's life to the cycle of days and seasons . . . metaphors already just *there* for everybody"[12] that the folk elements are caught up and preserved in his show.

Love's Labour's Lost (1594), perhaps written also in some country house, ends similarly with a dark death-shadow falling, and a final contest between winter and spring, the owl and the cuckoo. In the self-consciousness of its linguistic art, it could have originated for a private audience (and some of its private jokes remain incomprehensible), but it is also a true play, shaped to needs of the public stages; the contrast with Nashe is powerful. For Shakespeare, the different levels of playing had by now themselves become the subject of banter, in a more sophisticated yet more humane spirit than Will Summers's jest. It is not to be expected that the King of Navarre should make a good player, but the shew of the nine Worthies was a loyal offering from the tenantry, and "to dash it like a Christmas comedy" merits the rebuke—"This is not generous, not gentle, not humble" (V.ii.629). Later, that more assured performer, Signior Cesario, defended himself in advance, saying "Good beauties, let me sustain no scorn; I am very comptible, even to the least sinister usage" (*Twelfth Night*, I.v.174–76), but he refused to be deflected from delivering the speech which had asked such pains in the study—"and 'tis poetical."

Parody or burlesque is the surest measure of social change, and Shakespeare in both comedy and history not only developed a sense of form but displayed an easy, masterful ability to toy and play with different sorts of dramatic experience, to project it in plays-within-the-play, or to frame a comedy with an induction. Such ability to separate levels comes only with professional engagement—for "perfect use worketh mastery" while Art without Exercise is as barren as Nature without Art.[13] In a play where he reached out to break and re-mold tradition—a play almost at the frontiers of drama—Shakespeare later defined the basis of his own art, under the image of a triumphant Entry, made under the flashing steel of a raised portcullis. A noble civic welcome for a hero (which itself is a form of new creation of the "deed" such as Nashe had envisaged for Talbot at the playhouse) unites with images of applause and the reverberation of a lofty speech, as if for a "well-grac'd actor":

> No man is the lord of anything,
> Though in and of him there be much consisting,
> Till he communicate his parts to others;
> Nor doth he of himself know them for aught
> Till he behold them form'd in th'applause
> Where they're extended; who, like an arch reverberate
> The voice again; or like a gate of steel
> Fronting the sun, receives and renders back
> His figure and his heat.
> (*Troilus and Cressida*, III.iii.115–23)

With this may be compared the "barbaric" treatment of the defected Richard as if he were an actor to be "scowled" on with "contempt" and pelted with rubbish (*Richard II*, V.ii.23–36) as he follows the victorious Bolingbroke into London.

Since the significance of Shakespeare's idea of the play has been fully developed by Anne Righter (Barton),[14] I shall not now expatiate on it; I would suggest, however, that the varieties of audience for which he wrote, the versatility of his approach, may be to some extent disguised by the dignity of the First Folio, with its tripartite plan of Comedies, Histories, and Tragedies. Sometimes perhaps Shakespeare was able to call on a troupe of choristers; at other times he may have had to adapt a play for the Inns of Court or the Court itself; he may have penned pageant speeches, or given other additions than those surviving in *Sir Thomas More*—the additions for *The Spanish Tragedy* have sometimes been claimed for him. Hamlet calls for a play "extempore"—which seems to mean without rehearsal, for later he objects to clowns extemporizing. His own court entertainment, *The Murder of Gonzago*—a wedding offering from the heir apparent to the reigning sovereigns—was staged in the Great Hall where later Claudio sets up another show—a Royal Palace. In the *Sonnets*, there is a lament against the need to wear the motley and "gore my own thoughts"; another sonnet protests against the shame of "public means" to earn a livelihood.

The usual target for general mockery was not Shakespeare, but Anthony Mundy, a pageant writer to the City, who was ready to write plays, to make them, and to act (and whose share in *Sir Thomas More* brought him once in collaboration with Shakespeare). His *John a Kent and John a Cumber*, once part of the same volume as *Sir Thomas More*—which can be dated 1590[15]—shows a country troup of tenants led by one Thomas Turnop, who present various shows at a noble wedding. They give a pageant in honor of the bridegrooms, a serenade to the noble brides, and in a Morris flout and jest at one of the two rival magicians, dressing him in a fool's coat; but the plot recoils so that they inflict mockery on their own ally. These country players discuss their own acting programme, and though little more than clowns, they serve to show how country sports were seen by one who himself was to be depicted in much the same way seven years later by the young Ben Jonson. By this time visits to provincial towns by actors almost ceased.[16] In *The Case is Altered* (1597) Antonio Balladino, "pageant poet to the City of Milan," defends extemporizing: "No matter for the pen, the plot shall carry it." Then another character praises the fencing matches of "Utopia," which are played in the public theatres where "Plays, too, both Tragedy and Comedy [are] set forth with as much state as can be imagined." Being asked "And how are their plays, as ours are, extemporal?" he denies it: "O no, all premeditated things, and some of them very good, i'faith" (II.vii.35–36). A more lengthy and embittered satire both of Mundy and of a hastily assembled troupe of tradesmen players was given by the young John Marston in his first play, *Histriomastix* (1599), as part of the Christmas revels of the Middle Temple.[17] The pot-poet Post Haste (to his many other occupations Mundy added that of pursuivant) assembles them in an inn (by now no place for regular players):

> For we can all sing and say
> And so with practice soon may learn to play
> Belch. True, could our action answer your extempore.
> (I.i.)

This company runs from one patron to another, with a few old plays such as *Mother Gurton's Needle, a tragedy,* and give such a shabby performance before an Italian lord that they are dismissed as "trash."

The parody of professional forms was by now taken up by gentlemen amateurs—though this particular parody is set in a very old-fashioned pageant morality framework, organized to show the revolution of time and seasons in their social and political aspect, culminating in the triumph of Queen Elizabeth, patroness of the Seven Liberal Arts. The effect therefore is itself near to Nashe's ritual abuse of his enemies, though much sharper; and the end of Mundy's unlucky troupe is to be impressed for military service—"Look up and play the Tamburlaine," cry their tormentors, "Now we are the sharers and you are the hired men." The subject of the theatre became increasingly an analysis of theatrical life and the theatrical experience itself. Social relations were analyzed by analyzing plays.

The much discussed question of whether Elizabethan acting was by modern standards conventional or naturalistic may be put in a different way: Did the poets succeed in giving the players a language which allowed the development of sympathetic audience-identification, which replaced "discourse" and proclamation by the subtler form of introjective and projective art? The audience had taken this attitude when at *Henry VI* they lamented "brave Talbot, the terror of the French"; but in the English histories a tragical series was succeeded by a comical group. In 1599 Shakespeare's company put on *A Warning for Fair Women* where the Induction presents a debate between Comedy, History, and Tragedy, with Tragedy protesting to Comedy and History:

> 'Tis you have kept the theatre so long
> Painted in playbills upon every post,
> Whilst I am scorned of the multitude.

Variety was still a prime demand of the public stages, however; the inclusiveness of Shakespeare's comical histories culminates in *Henry IV*.

About this time, possibly for the Children of St. Paul's, someone, possibly Rowley, rewrote an old play of *Wily Beguiled*. At first the stage bill proclaims that the play is to be *Speculum*—that is, some grave moral—but after various adjurations from the Prologue—

> For shame, come forth; your audience stays so long
> their eyes grow dim with expectation

—*Speculum* is whisked away and *Wily Beguiled* appears in its place. So in more complex change King Henry V appears at his coronation as his father's true heir,

> With his spirits sadly I survive
> To mock the expectation of the world.
> (*2 Henry IV*, V.ii.125–26)

The keyed-up spirits of the playhouse are suggested by the Choruses to *Henry V*, where those in the audience are urged to "work their thoughts" like a glowing forge. This apology is not so much intended to decry the players as to compliment the audience, who themselves supply the living re-embodiment of Henry's London: "Now sits Expectation in the air" (Prologue to act II, l. 8) not only for Agincourt but for the triumphant return of the Earl of Essex from Ireland—an expectation that was to be sadly mocked in the event. When his faction hired the players to put on *Richard II* on the eve of the Essex rising, they were offering a mirror for deposition of the sovereign; the Queen asserted it had been played "forty times" in streets and houses.

Whatever the reason, at the end of the century the English history play suffered a sudden and almost total eclipse. It had been the main means of transferring to the Elizabethan stage that providential linking of past and present, which enlarged the dramatic experience into something like a social ritual and which had been the shaping force of the older craft cycles, thus uniting it with a new professional dramatic art. But customary tradition was giving way to contract and a mood of critical questioning informed both tragedy and comedy.

The reopening of Theatres of the Hall in London in 1599–1600 by St. Paul's and the Chapel Boys meant that identification between audience and author replaced identification between audience and players. The "little apes" could be admired for their precocious ability—but as Heywood noted later, they were used as a screen for satiric abuse directed at the City in general and also at particular individuals. St. Paul's was restarted with the financial backing of the Earl of Derby and later attracted William Percy; it may have been run much more as a club, with a nominal admission charge for "choice selected influence."[18] In Marston's induction the little players came on before *Antonio and Mellida* and criticized their own performance in a preview of their own technique. One has a stock part, which another characterizes "Rampum, scampum mount tufty Tamburlaine"—no boy could hope to rival Alleyn. Another uses euphuistic balance for his apology, and is maliciously twitted for it "Whoop, in the oldcut?" The peculiar mixture of violence and self-righteousness which made his verse satires so vulnerable gives way in Marston's plays to a greater uncertainty, a kind of protective prickliness; arrogance is tempered with apprehension. Fashions veered quickly; even in 1601 Marston was objecting to overconfidence and "bubling wit" in his audience at Paul's—the "best seal of wit is wit's distrust"—and yet

Music and Poetry were first approv'd
By common sense; that which pleased most
Held most allowed pass . . . rules of art
Were shap'd to pleasure, not pleasure to your rules
(Induction to *What You Will*, 1601)

He numbers up all the species of play, by this time well established, but concludes this one is "perfectly neither, but even What you Will" —a disclaimer of the accepted modes which became increasingly fashionable. They include "Comedy, Tragedy, Pastoral, Moral, Nocturnal and History." Marston's address to his audience varied from self-deprecation to defiance, but was always more or less one of discomfort.

Ben Jonson, who moved from the public to the private theatres and back again, and whose "humours" set the fashion, adopted every kind of attitude to his audience—but he never ignored it. In *The Case is Altered* he had objected to the pretensions of the vulgar:

But the sport is at a new play, to observe the way and variety of opinion . . . a confused mixture of judgment, poured out in the throng there, as ridiculous as laughter itself. One says he likes not the writing, another likes not the plot, another not the playing; and sometimes a fellow that comes not there past once in five years, at a parliament time, or so, will be as deep mired in censuring as the best. (II.vii.40–48)

He ended a play for the Chapel Boys with a flat defiance "By God, 'tis good, and if you like't, you may"—yet at other times he wooed his audience, bullied it, praised the judicious element, or defied the lot. Wit consists of "scourging" folly and for this he assumes attentive auditors. The "gull" who affected judgment became a figure of fun not only for Jonson but for his enemy Dekker, who drew such a figure in *The Gull's Horn Book*, displaying himself on stage as if he were the Lord of the troupe and leaving ostentatiously with a derogatory exit line.

The epilogue to *Epicoene* (1609), written for another troupe of boys, is more accommodating, at the expense of other authors (one consequence of the authors' new prominence was this public quarreling):

> Of old the art of making plays
> Was to content the people; and their praise
> Was to the poet money, wine and bays.
> But in this age, a sect of writers are
> That only for particular likings care,
> And will taste nothing that is popular,
> With such we neither mingle brains, nor breasts:
> Our wishes, like to those make public feasts,
> Are not to please the cook's taste, but the guests'.

Jonson recognized eventually that the contractual part of the bargain must be respected; on several occasions he drew up mock conditions with the audience which allowed "censure" to be related to the price of seats—he was particularly severe on judgments exercised by the penny stinkards in the public playhouse. He wrote inductions with such characters as Tattle, Expectation, Mirth, and Curiosity (*The Staple of News*, 1626)—the last coming to see "whose clothes are best penned, whatever the part be; which actor has the best leg and foot; what king plays without cuffs and his queen without gloves; who rides post in stockings and dances in boots." He also wrote inductions for ideal spectators and in his last play (*The Magnetic Lady*, 1633) makes one judge say "We come here to behold plays as they are made, and fitted for us; not . . . as we were to mould every scene anew. That were a mere plastic or potter's ambition, most unbecoming the name of a gentleman" (chorus after act IV). But his bitterest contests were to rise over precedence in the composition of Court masques, where in one case he shows a poet in a debate with a cook, describing himself as "a kind of Christmas ingine; one that is used, at least once a year, for a trifling instrument of wit or so."

Shakespeare's response to his larger audience was at once more sensitive and less obtrusive. In the "problem plays" he tested and sometimes disclaimed old conventions. *Henry V* and *Troilus and Cressida* display opposite sides of one coin—the bright and dark aspects of war; the general view that the second was written for a private audience has recently been challenged.[19] On the other hand, *The Merry Wives of Windsor*, if it were really produced at speed for a Court performance, also achieved a popular success.[20] *Hamlet* "represents an enormous effort to move forward to the heroism of the individual, without abandoning the older social and religious framework of external action";[21] this came at least in part from the challenge and stimulus of the theatre itself, including the rival playhouses. In *King Lear* the archaic splendors of the King and Fool are joined to the bravura role of Poor Tom, described on the title page of the Quarto as a "sullen and assumed humour."

Because of Shakespeare's sophisticated treatment of the conventional and the popular, his company dominated the public theatre. As we might expect, the company now reached out to the best of the new in the private playhouses. Eventually, it absorbed their themes, their playwrights, and finally the Blackfriars playhouse itself.

If, as a song of the time put it, "Grief and joy and hope and fear / Play their pageants everywhere," those of the children's theatres were more self-consciously literary. The prologue to Marston's *Antonio's Revenge* (1600), the promised sequel to *Antonio and Mellida*, dismisses anyone afraid to see "what men were, and are" and demands a mood, sensitive, emotional, and introverted. This mood is nearer to Henryson's

> Ane doolie sesoun to ane cairful dyte
> Suld correspond and be equivalent
> Richt as it wes when I began to wryte
> This tragedie

than it is to the opening scene of *Hamlet*. It begins:

> The rawish dank of clumsie winter ramps
> The fluent summer's vein; and drizzling sleet
> Chilleth the wan bleak cheek of the numb'd earth,
> While snarling blasts nibble the juiceless leaves
> From the nak'd shuddering branch. . . .

In the private theatres, tragedy was not fully dramatic (the best was Chapman's). When Marston turned to the black comedy of *The Malcontent*, Shakespeare's company thought it worth appropriating (and Marston seems to have cooperated). The "select" audience, aggressively superior and even anti-social in some moods, supplied a better seedbed for City comedy, whose themes were cheating and the power game among London citizens and in the London underworld. This kind of comedy soon evolved its own conventions.[22] Even here, however, the masterpieces—such as *The Alchemist*—belonged to the men's playhouses.

The exclusiveness of the select audiences becomes most entertainingly explicit in Beaumont's burlesque, *The Knight of the Burning Pestle* (1607). The theme is obsolete theatrical demands put forward by a good citizen and his wife who somehow stray into the private playhouse. There they behave as if they were at a City Feast in Sheriff More's day, and in perfect good nature they take over the show, assigning the leading part to their 'prentice. The kind of play they are expecting is a mixture of impossibly heroic adventure interlaced with direct presentation from scenes of city life; the sting lies in the fact that it is a fairly close parody of a recent success, *The Four 'Prentices of London*, which had enthralled a city audience at the Red Bull.

Unlike the upstart gallant, who misbehaves in the theatre, the Citizen and his Wife are engaging characters. Like Bottom, the Weaver, they want everything to be put into the play, and, also like Bottom, they enjoy a big death scene:

> *Citizen's Wife:* Now, good husband, let him come out and die.
> *Citizen:* He shall, Nell. Ralph, come away quickly and die, boy!

Entering promptly "with a forked arrow through his head," Ralph dies at great length with extracts from *The Spanish Tragedy* to help him out. But it is significant of the limitations of the select audience that this burlesque did not succeed on the stage (although it may have given Ben Jonson ideas for some of his later inductions). Ben Jonson's more critical scrutiny of society withdrew the audience from the "game" of comedy, imposing on them a measure of detachment. It may be that a measure of detachment also enabled him to fill out his crowded canvases with such a full picture of society. His comic world was meant to be looked at and not lived in; in the subhuman zoo of *Volpone*, the animals may be observed as if they were caged.

Though he abandoned the peremptory tone of his earliest comical satire, Jonson remained always present in his work. According to Dekker, after a play he would come on stage "to exchange courtesies and compliments with the gallants in the Lord's Room" (*Satiromastix*, V.ii.305).

Jonson's affiliations with the older drama were with "morals teaching education" rather than with the civic pageantry that Marlowe and Shakespeare drew on. It is significant that Aubrey reported he "was never a good actor, but an excellent instructor"—especially, it might be hazarded, of the boys. He expected his plays to be judged by "those Comic Laws / Which I, your Master first did teach the age," and which he expected pupils like Dick Brome "to observe." When accused of writing only one play a year, he retorted " 'Tis true. I would that they could not say that I did that" (Prologue to *Poetaster*).

Only in his Court masques does he introduce playfully and with freedom old customs, rural sports; only here could he escape the need for judgment not only to be applied, but to be seen to be applied. Masques became the one cohesive social rite as audiences grew more diversified; for the ten years following Shakespeare's death, Ben Jonson too had withdrawn from the public stage, writing only for the Court.

In the best of the public theatres, playwrights achieved something like the feat of conducting an orchestra as they wove together the variety of demands that a mixed audience exacted. Some were theatrical, some purely social. In the Prologue to *No Wit, No Help, Like a Woman's* (1613), Middleton runs through a "naming of parts" which implies that everyone accepted an obvious diversity.[23] Education was not one of the objects:

> How is't possible to suffice
> So many ears, so many eyes?
> Some in wit and some in shows
> Take delight, and some in clothes.
> Some for mirth they chiefly come,
> Some for passion—for both, some;
> Some for lascivious meetings, that's their arrant;
> Some to detract, and ignorance their warrant.
> How is't possible to please
> Opinions toss'd on such wild seas?
> Yet I doubt not, if attention
> Seize you above, and apprehension
> You below, to take things quickly,
> We shall both make ye sad, and tickle ye.

Middleton's favorite solution was the multiple or composite plot. Shakespeare's experiments continued throughout the group of his latest plays, although in modern times an underlying recurrence of certain themes has tended to mask their differences. They belong to quite different theatrical species, yet each could be given in diverse surroundings. The appeals to the audience in *Pericles* are deliberately archaic; it became a great popular success, yet was also acted at Court. *Cymbeline* is far more courtly in tone and complex in plot; it includes one purely spectacular triumph which is poetically a blank (the descent of Jove's eagle) but which could not easily be cut. *The*

Winter's Tale, like *Pericles*, drew snorts from Ben Jonson, but its two halves are beautifully balanced. *The Tempest* bears many marks of a courtly masque, yet it combines old romances and a recent adventure from the Virginian voyages. Shakespeare, equally with Marston, might have disclaimed the usual definitions and subtitled all his later plays "What You Will."

Webster, to judge from the Address to the Reader prefixed to *The White Devil* (1612), cherished some rather simple-minded hankering for a Nuntius and Chorus, yet he knew that in the theatre, "the breath that comes from the uncapable multitude" would forbid them. Although the season had corresponded with his tragic theme, this had in his case proved disastrous "since it was acted in so dull a time of winter, presented in so open and black a theatre, that it wanted (that which is the only grace and setting-out of tragedy) a full and understanding auditory."

Yet in this play, and still more in *The Duchess of Malfi* (1614), which appears to have succeeded rather better (Burbage took the lead), Webster himself "plays over the whole gamut between firm convention and firm realism"—but "the balance is held by poetic means."[24] Shakespeare had combined his memories of naive early romances with a lifetime's experience of the stage's variety; the "impure art of John Webster" achieved at its greatest a similar balance. This represents the recovery (or continuity) of popular traditions, along with a great deal taken from the "black comedy" of the private theatres, which itself had been based on rejecting popular forms. It is a feat of synthesis.

The fourth act of *The Duchess of Malfi*, as Inga-Stina Ekeblad (Ewbank) has so brilliantly shown,[25] presents her death scene as beginning with an anti-masque of madmen drawing on the folk tradition which inflicted social insults on a socially rejected bridal. This folk game in its popular form could be savage and primitive as the game with which Margaret of Anjou humiliates Richard, Duke of York, before killing him, in *3 Henry VI*. Here simulation of some of the forms of legal execution follow, adding evil magic to gruesome mockery.

The music which accompanies this "device" is sophisticated in its discords; the songs are not folk songs. The gifts presented to the bride and chief spectator, who is to be the chief actor, include a shroud and a crucifix; and the art of the Duchess's death is an art of performance. With a macabre social jest she addresses both her murderers and the theatre at once:

M.C. Bradbrook

I'ld fain put off my last woman's-fault:
I'll not be tedious to you.

For Webster, however, there was a second audience to be reckoned with, for he looked forward to readers, publishing his text "with divers things printed that the length of the play would not bear in the presentment," and thereby asserting his independence as an author, in the manner characteristic of Ben Jonson.

If the conditions determining the splitting and cohesion of society are among those reflected in drama, the significance of the madman's role on the Jacobean stage—one both split from society and split within his own identity—concentrates the tremendous effort needed to mirror and reflect back those conflicts, "like a gate of steel / Fronting the sun." It is unlikely that *The Duchess of Malfi* could have been accepted or acceptably produced except by the company in whose repertory stood "kind Lear" and "the grieved Moor." The supreme figures of this kind are Poor Tom and Lear's Fool (both added by Shakespeare to the original story). They are close enough to the audience to indulge in direct address—Poor Tom's momentary removal of his mask would hardly be playable today. But here perhaps for the Elizabethans, the triple bond was asserted in its darkest, most chthonic aspect.

The masque at Court had replaced the Street Theatres or Royal Entries or rural Welcomes. Monarchs themselves played in masques but shut away from their subjects. Charles I positively refused a Royal Entry to London, and the City pageants, half-built, had to be dismantled. The citizens developed their own pageantry, the Lord Mayor's Show, a real street theatre. It still survives today, the last of the old social rituals, which has suddenly become relevant again. Street theatre can still be found in the City of London.

II
The
Playwright
and
Audience

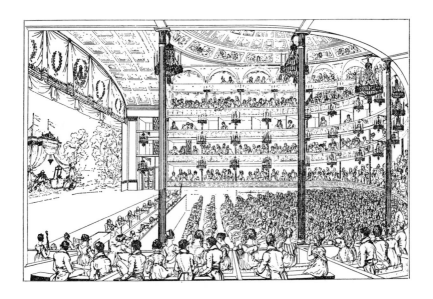

Shakespeare's Songs
and the
Double Response

Clifford Leech

It is especially appropriate, in contributing to a collective tribute to
Arthur Colby Sprague, that I should draw upon a recent experience
in the theatre. In 1970 *Cymbeline* was acted at Stratford, Ontario,
and as I was watching I grew conscious anew of the deliberateness
of Shakespeare's manner of composition. What we were offered was
in some ways a brilliant performance, in some ways a wrong-headed
one. That does not much matter: performances of Shakespeare, like
critical essays or books on his plays, can give us sudden insights even
as they manifest their inadequacy. On this occasion the lyric "Hark,
hark, the lark" was intentionally ill performed: Cloten, for once
intelligent (for he was otherwise presented as a boor throughout,
which, as I shall later argue, is surely wrong), was made to rebuke
his musicians for presenting a totally inadequate rendition of the
aubade with which he wished to forward his suit for Imogen's love.
I was affronted by the director's indifference to the lyric's splendor
and complexity, but, as so often in the theatre, I was made to think
anew of the strangeness with which Shakespeare made use of song.
If this, as is commonly recognized, is a splendid lyric, then at first
sight its use in Cloten's wooing of Imogen is puzzling. It can make
one think back to a similar incongruity in a much earlier play, the use
of "Who is Silvia?" in *The Two Gentlemen of Verona* for the wooing
of Silvia, nominally on Thurio's behalf, but with Proteus as master of
ceremonies, himself hoping to be the successful wooer, himself a
traitor to his friend Valentine, Silvia's accepted lover, and to his own
earlier love Julia. In both instances there seems a major irony: fine
poetry is used for a base purpose. We might say, like Lytton Strachey
writing on Shakespeare's last plays, that this playwright could not
hold back from writing fine poetry in any circumstances, even when
he was "half bored to death."[1] But that seems an inadequate explanation. Rather, I think, we should see the use of splendid lyrics in
dubious circumstances, in *Cymbeline* and elsewhere, as constituting

73

one of Shakespeare's ironic uses of his gift. He shrugs over his own craft; he places the lyric in an elaborate context; he realizes that great or splendid writing is itself a rather absurd thing; he is a poet who sees the absurdity of poetry[2] and the tawdry uses to which it may be put. We may remember his sonnets, where he both asserts the "immortality" that celebration in poetry may bring to the person celebrated and admits the frequent extravagance of the sonneteer's mode, as when in Sonnet 130 he burlesques the kind of praise that a poet customarily offers to his mistress. In the two plays I have mentioned he works in a different way: the lyrics are glorious (both of them later set by Schubert), but they are ironically placed. To see the irony properly, we must consider a group of scenes in which the lyric occupies a focal position.

To begin with the earlier of the two, *The Two Gentlemen of Verona* is one of Shakespeare's earliest plays, perhaps the first of his comedies.[3] To see what the dramatist has done in his use of "Who is Silvia?" we must consider the action from the last scene of act III to the second scene of act IV. In the first scene of this group, the Duke talks with Thurio, his daughter's wooer whom he favors, and with Proteus, who loves Silvia, who has, for the time being, abandoned his love for Julia, and who has engineered the banishment of Valentine, whom Silvia loves, by betraying to the Duke his planned elopement with Silvia. The Duke enlists Proteus's help in Thurio's wooing, and Proteus urges that poetry should be put to use in this:

> *Pro.*   But you, Sir Thurio, are not sharp enough.
> You must lay lime, to tangle her desires
> By wailful sonnets, whose composed rhymes
> Should be full-fraught with serviceable vows.
>
> *Duke.*   Ay, much is the force of heaven-bred poesy.
>
> *Pro.*   Say that upon the altar of her beauty
> You sacrifice your tears, your sighs, your heart.
> Write till your ink be dry; and with your tears
> Moist it again; and frame some feeling line
> That may discover such integrity.
> For Orpheus' lute was strung with poets' sinews,
> Whose golden touch could soften steel and stones,
> Make tigers tame, and huge leviathans
> Forsake unsounded deeps to dance on sands.
> After your dire-lamenting elegies,
> Visit by night your lady's chamber-window
> With some sweet consort; to their instruments

Tune a deploring dump: the dead night's silence
Will well become such sweet complaining grievance.
This, or else nothing, will inherit her.

Duke. This discipline shows thou hast been in love.

(III.ii.67–87)[4]

This is manifest mockery of love poetry, indicating how it can be deliberately used in a wooing, however unsatisfactory the lover. The Duke's last line is unconsciously ironic. Proteus's advice does not show he has been in love: it merely shows he is aware of the usual mode of making advances. He is himself an unfaithful lover, and he is deceiving both the Duke and Thurio here. He knows that girls like verses addressed to them, as of course they do. He intends that Silvia shall be moved, but he wants her to be moved on his behalf, not Thurio's. The Duke and Thurio are indeed deceived: Thurio declares he will get "some gentlemen, well skill'd in music," and declares too that he has "a sonnet that will serve the turn." Where he got it from is neither here nor there: it is surely not meant to be seen as his own composition. So the scene ends with this determination to use poetry in Thurio's wooing of Silvia, although we hear nothing more of the suggestion that he should send love poems before following them up with a serenade.

The first scene of act IV takes us to a new locality, where Valentine meets some outlaws and, fantastically enough, because of his skill in languages is accepted as their new leader; the ludicrousness of this puts all that follows out of the range of common expectation. We are ready to take only half-seriously, at most, what is given us in the rest of the play. Yet the next scene is perhaps the most moving of all the scenes in *The Two Gentlemen of Verona*. Shakespeare was here already adept in combining absurdity with a full sense of the anguish of a particular character. First Proteus enters, admitting that he has been false to Valentine and Julia and now plans to be false to Thurio, wooing Silvia only apparently on Thurio's behalf. When Thurio and the musicians enter, they get ready for the serenade. But on another part of the stage the forsaken Julia (now in boy's clothes) enters with the Host of the inn where she has taken lodging, and she will watch Proteus's wooing of another woman. The musicians play, and a song is sung. It has been argued that this song "had its origin" in "caricature of the conventional sonnet,"[5] but it is difficult to see any trace of caricature here. Rather, it exalts the lady beyond what any woman is entitled to, but at the same time embodies what we feel when, in our youngest years, we have the experience of loving; a song

75

provided merely to "serve the turn" may thus, ironically, seem appropriate to the expression of genuine feeling. We may note the falling-away in the last line of each stanza, a lapsing into a quasi-silence that a lover must always feel compelled upon him:

> Who is Silvia? What is she
> That all our swains commend her?
> Holy, fair, and wise is she,
> The heaven such grace did lend her,
>   That she might admired be.
>
> Is she kind as she is fair?
> For beauty lives with kindness.
> Love doth to her eyes repair,
> To help him of his blindness;
>   And, being help'd, inhabits there.
>
> Then to Silvia let us sing,
> That Silvia is excelling;
> She excels each mortal thing
> Upon the dull earth dwelling.
>   To her let us garlands bring.
>   (IV.ii.38–52)

Yet Julia is there, and listening. The girl is of course in a distressed state, but she tries to pull herself together by inquiring after Launce and then has to listen when Silvia appears and, first rebuking Proteus for his infidelity to Valentine and to Julia, nevertheless agrees to let Proteus have a picture of herself. The scene ends with the Host waking from sleep, for " 'tis almost day," but Julia comments only on the length of the night she has endured:

> it hath been the longest night
> That e'er I watch'd, and the most heaviest.
>   (IV.ii.135–36)

Even so, the end tells us that day is coming, that the sun's light will put an end to this episode at least and, by symbolic suggestion, to the whole nightmare that Julia is going through. Song, at the heart of the night, has been ironically used, has been juxtaposed and contrasted with the simple fact of an old love that will not be denied. Shakespeare prepared for this in the earlier scene where the faithless Proteus celebrates the power of poetry and the Duke gives his doddering approval of its employment.

Cymbeline, a much more complicated play, also presents a famous lyric placed within the context of a group of scenes. Of course we do not have to postulate a different background for each scene: scene followed scene without any appreciable break, and in this instance we have not even a conceivable interval between acts; the Folio text has act divisions, for what that is worth, but the stretch of action we are concerned with lies wholly within act II, extending from scene ii to scene iv. And we have extraordinary complexity here. Once again the wooing-lyric, this time an *aubade*, is a major Shakespearean song. And its purpose is to forward the repellent Cloten's wooing of Imogen, as "Who is Silvia?" was in effect intended for Proteus's wooing of Silvia. To make the irony fully plain, consider what immediately precedes.

Imogen reads herself to sleep in act II, scene ii, not knowing that Iachimo is concealed in the trunk that has been brought into her bedroom. We may be surprised at her choice of book: it is Ovid's story of the rape of Philomel, appropriate enough for what follows in the scene, but strange reading for this particular girl—a matter that must be returned to. Most of our current experts on Shakespeare's stage will have us believe that Imogen in her bed and Iachimo in his trunk are carried onto the stage;[6] we may still wonder if Imogen was not in some kind of "discovery space" and if Iachimo, on emerging from the trunk, did not at first advance onto the main stage as he talked of her and her chamber's embellishments. It might be effective if Imogen were kept remote here and Iachimo moved back and forth as he commented on what he saw. In any event, his comparison of himself with Tarquin as he approached Lucrece's bed is important: here there is to be no physical rape, but there is indeed a strong sense of illicit intimacy. As so often elsewhere, Shakespeare recalls what he has previously written, but with a difference. And if, as editors have suggested, up to and including those of the New Arden and New Cambridge editions, the scene ends with the drawing of a curtain or the closing of a door, we have a stronger sense of the woman and her would-be seducer being finally shut in together. Innocent as she is, the two of them do, after a fashion, share the night. We cannot blame a modern director if he feels the scene should begin in a "discovery space" and end there. But Imogen, no longer visible after Iachimo's withdrawal into the trunk—whether because a curtain has been drawn or a door closed, or because both bed and trunk have been carried off—is now greeted by Cloten with his *aubade*. The first word we have of him in this scene concerns his having once more lost a game; he is, after all, a loser throughout. But he will not accept the label—he goes on trying. He uses musicians and a song, as Proteus did, but, unlike Proteus, he is not himself the singer. Song can exist for him only at second-hand. In rough and bawdy prose he exhorts his hired deputies:

> I would this music would come: I am advised to give her
> music a-mornings, they say it will penetrate.
> [*Enter musicians*]
> Come on, tune: if you can penetrate her with your fingering,
> so: we'll try with tongue too ...
>
> (II.iii.11–15)

Then follows the famous lyric:

> Hark, hark, the lark at heaven's gate sings,
>   and Phoebus gins arise,
> His steeds to water at those springs
>   on chalic'd flowers that lies;
> And winking Mary-buds begin to ope their golden eyes;
> With every thing that pretty is, my lady sweet arise:
>   Arise, arise!
>
> (II.iii.20–26)

We can hardly miss the sexual element here when we are told that Phoebus's steeds will "water at those springs / on chalic'd flowers that lies," and "chalic'd" may link the eroticism with the Eucharist. Moreover, we are bound to remember, if we have the text before us (and Shakespeare, in his innermost concern with his writing, surely did imagine something of the sort, disregarding the playgoer's simpler memory), that Iachimo in the previous scene talked of "the crimson drops / I' th' bottom of a cowslip," which he compared with the "mole cinque-spotted" on Imogen's left breast. In this instance there is an interesting inversion: the flower's "chalice" is related to the girl's breast; the idea of concavity is insisted on throughout the song.

That Shakespeare could dream of making such a connection between a phrase here and a phrase there, in different scenes, may seem a strange suggestion in view of his apparent indifference, except perhaps in the case of *Hamlet*, to the publication of his plays, but I have argued elsewhere that a dramatist has in mind two audiences, that of the theatre where his play will probably be acted, and that of an ideal theatre which can never exist. Sometimes the one will dominate, sometimes the other, but a major play can be written only when both audiences are held in mind. The practical and the impossible are kept in solution, whether or not the playwright thinks of making his play available for reading.[7] An analogous situation can be seen in the writing of nondramatic poetry: we are aware that some complexities in what we write are unlikely to be apparent to an actual reader—there may even be private references which no one, or perhaps only one, could possibly grasp; yet we imagine an ideal reader who might follow us into all the nooks and crannies of our composition. So it becomes possible to link Phoebus's watering of his steeds "at those springs / on chalic'd flowers that lies" with Iachimo's reference to "the crimson drops / I' th' bottom of a cowslip," and the "crimson" not only deepens the eroticism but, if I am right about the reverberations of "chalic'd," links the erotic with Christ's blood.

In any event, Iachimo cannot be far away from our minds as we watch Cloten's behavior here. The boor and the small Machiavel have both wanted to have their way with Imogen. Ironically, the Machiavel contents himself with mental rape, while the boor presses on. Cloten's wooing, through a poem obviously beyond his own capability, is linked with Iachimo's brooding over Imogen's sleeping body, and the splendor of the poem is in counterpoint to the condition of mind of the two would-be ravishers. The lark heralds the coming of day that, at the play's end, will be dominated by the figure of Imogen, despite Iachimo, despite Cloten. The poem's splendor is appropriate to the girl, because of her beauty and her gentleness; yet it is also in counterpoint to the coldness that accompanies her affection for her husband, which perhaps in her own way she compensated for by reading in bed the story of Philomel's rape. At the end of act II Posthumus speaks of this coldness:

> Me of my lawful pleasure she restrain'd,
> And pray'd me oft forbearance: did it with
> A pudency so rosy, the sweet view on't
> Might well have warm'd old Saturn; that I thought her
> As chaste as unsunn'd snow.
>
> (II.iv.161–65)

This woman, so aloof yet loving, is wooed by two gross men in addition to her careful husband.

The *aubade* over, Cloten shows his inability to know whether it is good or bad. He is concerned only with whether it will "penetrate," a bawdy word used for the third time in this scene:

> So get you gone: if this penetrate, I will consider your
> music the better. . . .
>
> (II.iii.27–28)

79

It is a foolish trick of the stage to justify him by making the musicians inadequate. Then Cymbeline and the Queen enter, and Cymbeline talks to Cloten in a way similar to that used by the Duke to Thurio in *The Two Gentlemen of Verona*, assuring him that the absent loved one will be forgotten soon and then the new suit will surely prosper. Next a messenger announces the arrival of Caius Lucius, ambassador from Rome; Cymbeline praises him as "A worthy fellow," and the affairs of love we have been concerned with are brought up against the affairs of the kingdom. Here, more clearly than in *The Two Gentlemen of Verona*, the love-business tends to be put in its place. The fate of Britain is now in question. Nevertheless, Cymbeline and the Queen leave Cloten to pursue his wooing.

Like Silvia in *The Two Gentlemen*, Imogen comes out to her un-welcome wooer, but she does not, like Silvia, even while rebuking Proteus, agree to let him have a portrait of her: it is in tune with the general character of this later play that the aggressive wooer is al-together beyond a token of sympathy. Imogen says that the "mean'st garment" of Posthumus is dearer to her than "all the hairs above thee, / Were they all made such men"—that is, men like Cloten. This carries its special irony, for later she will assume that Cloten's body in Posthumus's clothes is indeed Posthumus. At the moment she speaks in terms of high contempt, yet the scene remains complicated: Cloten here speaks throughout in blank verse, so different from the clumsy prose he has used before, and he speaks, both here and occasionally later, with such an eloquence, an involuted kind of language, and an authority, that it is difficult to reconcile him with the boor who has previously complained about his losses in gaming and who is com-mented on for his reluctance to change his shirt. This, for example, is how he can rebuke Imogen:

> You sin against
> Obedience, which you owe your father; for
> The contract which you pretend with that base wretch,
> One bred of alms, and foster'd with cold dishes,
> With scraps o' th' court, it is no contract, none;
> And though it be allow'd in meaner parties
> (Yet who than he more mean?) to knit their souls
> (On whom there is no more dependency
> But brats and beggary) in self-figur'd knot,
> Yet you are curb'd from that enlargement, by
> The consequence o' th' crown, and must not foil

The precious note of it; with a base slave,
A hilding or a livery, a squire's cloth,
A pantler; not so eminent.
(II.iii.112–25)

These are repulsive, but not contemptible, words. Cloten is here a figure of fear. Certainly he relapses into boorishness in the last twenty lines of the scene, blustering with threats, saying "I will inform your father." At the same time we get to know that Imogen has missed the bracelet that Iachimo took from her as part of his evidence. We, thus reminded of the mental rape, are made to bring Cloten and Iachimo into yet closer relation: the two aggressions directed on Imogen—the one purely mental, the other potentially grossly physical; the one temporarily successful, the other always a grotesque failure—are simultaneously contrasted and associated. There is an irony in that Iachimo's nonphysical attempt will cause Imogen the greater anguish. In a sense (for her the most important sense) she has escaped from Iachimo; but Cloten, despite his occasional eloquence, will not be content with mental rape: he will be a threat of violence until he is decapitated by Imogen's brother in the Welsh mountains; he is a creature of the corrupt court who will be overcome only when far away from it. For the moment there is a strong threat in his declaration at the end of the scene that "I'll be reveng'd."

Yet we must recognize how large a problem Shakespeare has set his actor here. In *The Two Gentlemen of Verona* Proteus was a faithless wooer, agonized over his treachery, trying to persuade himself that it was right to pursue his new love and ultimately recognizing that he should return to the old one; that he could in the end come to goodness suggests a measure of uniformity in the character. But Cloten is simultaneously a figure of grotesque fun, mocked by his own servants, a figure of fear, whom Imogen not merely rebukes but detests, feeling the deepest sexual repulsion from him, and a young man capable of eloquence in rebuking Imogen and in defying the Roman threat. At Stratford, Ontario, in 1970, he was played as a figure of grotesque fun throughout, so that his rebuke of the Romans and Imogen's fear of him seemed quite out of relation to the man we saw. Perhaps Shakespeare here demanded too much: he had often presented two-or-more-sided figures—Othello so noble, so primitive, so unable to live up to his own idea of himself as a sacrificing priest; Hamlet so courteous and so brutal—but here he wants us to see the coexistence of the boor, the threat, and the patriot. We can indeed imagine all

81

this being acceptable in a novel. Dostoievsky has examples of characters so complicated. But on the stage the actor is tied, after all, to a single appearance throughout the play. I do not know how Cloten should be acted; I doubt whether the figure in its full many-sidedness can be satisfactorily acted.

It is appropriate that Cloten's "I'll be reveng'd" should be followed by the scene where Iachimo brings to Posthumus his "evidence" of Imogen's infidelity. But Iachimo does not enter at once: at first we hear from Philario and Posthumus of the crisis in Roman-British relations; the love affair is again put within a larger context. Then Iachimo comes, bringing his recollections of Imogen's chamber:

> First, her bedchamber,
> (Where I confess I slept not, but profess
> Had that was well worth watching) it was hang'd
> With tapestry of silk and silver, the story
> Proud Cleopatra, when she met her Roman,
> And Cydnus swell'd above the banks, or for
> The press of boats, or pride.
>
> (II.iv.66–72)

This, of course, is yet another example of Shakespeare's recalling of his previous work, and there is a special irony here: no woman could be more unlike Cleopatra than Imogen is, yet we have to remember that Imogen read Ovid in bed—the cold girl could be preoccupied with violent sexuality. Notably, too, Iachimo had not mentioned this while he was actually in Imogen's chamber; the Cleopatra hanging must have been truly there, though not necessarily shown on stage, for Posthumus's memory is invoked. Shakespeare has avoided simple repetition, yet he has in retrospect associated Imogen with the "lass unparallel'd" of a previous play: her coldness, which Posthumus will refer to later, is here made a more complex thing. But Iachimo proceeds further on the adornments of Imogen's chamber:

> The chimney
> Is south the chamber, and the chimney-piece,
> Chaste Dian, bathing: never saw I figures
> So likely to report themselves; the cutter
> Was as another Nature, dumb; outwent her,
> Motion and breath left out. . . .
> The roof o' th' chamber
> With golden cherubins is fretted. Her andirons
> (I had forgot them) were two winking Cupids

Of silver, each on one foot standing, nicely
Depending on their brands.
(II.iv.80–85, 87–91)

The purity, the coldness, of the girl exists in a setting of high eroticism. The purity is not merely stressed, it is questioned, almost tarnished, by this setting which Posthumus is made to remember. In this scene, moreover, Posthumus is altogether too easily convinced, as his friend Philario repeatedly tells him. He is immediately ready to believe Iachimo simply because Iachimo swears he has enjoyed Imogen. Quickly he declares "She has been colted by him," using a brutal word that he finds release in when he is ready to accept Iachimo's pretences. He echoes Othello in his wish to tear his wife "limb-meal." And finally he comes out on the stage alone, accusing all women, including his mother, as Troilus did, believing that Iachimo perhaps

spoke not, but

Like a full-acorn'd boar, a German one,
Cried "Oh" and mounted; found no opposition
But what he look'd for should oppose and she
Should from encounter guard.
(II.iv.167–71)

Here he degenerates into the total skepticism of fidelity that Leontes exhibits in *The Winter's Tale*: "no barricado for a belly." But Posthumus's tirade becomes ludicrous when he threatens that he will write satires against women. Satire is here put in its place, as lyrical poetry was earlier. Poor Posthumus—indeed, poor Imogen to have put her faith in this man. He will of course repent, will win his forgiving lady again. Shaw in *Cymbeline Refinished* made Imogen rebuke him strongly before once more taking him to her love. But, as Shakespeare wrote the play, we have three men—Iachimo, Cloten, Posthumus—all avid for aggression or revenge, and one woman, the objective they all aim at, cold but firmly choosing and forgiving. It is a painful situation, and at the heart of it is the splendid "Hark, hark, the lark": the suggestion of dawn and its healing, which for Julia in *The Two Gentlemen of Verona* was also a token of relief, is manifest in the ethereal yet erotic song that the grotesque Cloten offered as an *aubade* in his wooing of this remote girl. Thornton Wilder in *The Bridge of San Luis Rey* mentioned that any grief, any pain, is to some extent assuaged with the coming of dawn.[8]

There is irony, too, in the use of song at the end of act III of

83

Measure for Measure. The Duke, having persuaded Isabella—so easily—to let Mariana take her place in bed with Angelo, has a more than twenty-line speech of gnomic couplets asserting the rightness of his plan to defeat Angelo in this surely dubious fashion. Then act IV begins with a boy singing in Mariana's presence:

> Take, o take those lips away
>> that so sweetly were forsworn,
> And those eyes, the break of day
>> lights that do mislead the morn:
> But my kisses bring again,
>>> bring again;
> Seals of love, but seal'd in vain,
>>>> seal'd in vain.
> (IV.i.1–6)

Again there is a suggestion of dawn, but this time it is a false dawn: the light in the lover's eyes does not immediately herald the day-spring. It appears that directors are frightened by this song: in 1969 at Stratford, Ontario, in an otherwise brilliant production,[9] it was deliberately sung off-key and its words made unintelligible. Mariana is, it appears, longing for the man who has deserted her, even though she believes the seals of love have been sealed in vain. Not surprisingly, therefore, she quickly agrees to take Isabella's place in bed with Angelo, expecting in that way to win him at last. It is indeed a painful situation: Isabella has no more difficulty in persuading Mariana to get into Angelo's bed than she had in persuading herself to accept the Duke's plan after having rejected Angelo's bargain to let Claudio go free if she would let Angelo have his will with her. An irony is provided in that Claudio would not have escaped even if Isabella had gone to Angelo's bed, and so the Duke's plan does not work. Yet, amazingly, a song comes in the midst of this action. It is erotic enough; it invites the love-making that Mariana has been deprived of; it makes her the readier to accept the bed-trick that surely, except in the most simply comic or deliberately painful writing (as in Arthur Schnitzler's *Casanovas Heimfahrt*, where the dreadfulness is explicit), we must be affronted by. Mariana in this play must be taken as a simple and sensual creature and, as an ally of Isabella and the Duke, must cast her special light on them. The sensual strain in the play is made fully apparent, here as so often, in Shakespeare's use of song.

Yet what if Isabella had accepted Angelo's bargain? The best comment on that is provided in a passage in Ilya Ehrenburg's novel *The Love of Jeanne Ney*, where a young woman in a similar situation agrees to the bargain; the dreadfulness of the acquiescence at least equals the dreadfulness of Isabella's refusal. There is no escape from the dilemma that Shakespeare offers for our consideration.

I am not claiming that his use of song always has the special kind of counterpoint or irony that has been illustrated so far. The song which is a prelude to Bassanio's choice in *The Merchant of Venice* may conceivably give him a hint in the rhymes to "lead"; but, like John Russell Brown, the New Arden editor, we can hardly be sure of that[10] and in any event the effect would be different from that noted above. Yet in one way or another we often feel that Shakespeare's songs provide a variant on the general current of the action. Each song is splendid in its own being, but it may be used by Proteus for his dishonest wooing of Silvia, by Cloten in his aggression against Imogen, by Mariana, through the singing boy, to indicate her frustrated but continuing desire for Angelo. In *Twelfth Night* the Duke apologizes for wanting his "passion" to be relieved by an "old and antic song." He relates it, and himself, to the simplicity of the women from whom he has heard it, and asserts his sense of refuge in the past when he declares:

> it is old and plain:
> The spinsters and the knitters in the sun,
> And the free maids that weave their thread with bones
> Do use to chant it: it is silly sooth,
> And dallies with the innocence of love,
> Like the old age.
>
> (II.iv.44–49)[11]

It is a different kind of song from any we have noted yet. Highly accomplished, it illustrates a luxuriating in lovesickness: when a lover declares he is "slain," as the singer does here, he is manifestly in advance of the event. Feste gives the Duke what he wants, as the musicians at the beginning of the play had fed their master's melancholy. The irony is to be different again in the song with which the play ends, where Feste addresses the audience and reminds them of the contrast between the entertainment they have been witnessing and the world of the wind and the rain in which they live outside the theatre. Yet the manifest exaggeration of "Come away, come away, death" has a further irony in that it is immediately followed by Viola's near-admission of her love for Orsino and his failure to understand her: her story of the death through love of her surely imaginary sister is superficially fitting for juxtaposition with the song of lovesickness, but it brings us to something real, Viola's love for Orsino, which stands in contrast to the old song with its easy exaggeration.

Finally I want to return to *Cymbeline* and to look, in its context, at a song that is spoken, not sung. We have reached the Welsh mountains, where Imogen in her male disguise has been welcomed by Belarius and her unknown brothers Guiderius and Arviragus. But then Cloten comes in Posthumus's clothes, threatening that his rival's head shall be cut off "within this hour." This is one of the play's smaller ironies: it is Cloten's severed head that we shall soon see. He speaks prose here, reverting to the clownishness that was his characteristic mode when he first appeared in the play, though it was discarded, we have seen, on certain later occasions. As he goes off, looking for Imogen and Posthumus, Imogen enters with her brothers and Belarius, and they leave her for a day's hunting because she is sick. She remarks that she will take the drug that Pisanio has left her. There is a double irony here, for we know that the Queen has given it to Pisanio, believing it to be poison though pretending it is a cordial, while the Doctor has made it clear to us that it is harmless. Consequently we are aware that Imogen is not dead when the drug operates on her. When she retires into the cave, Cloten reappears, and surprisingly is recognized by Belarius, who last saw him twenty years before, when Cloten must have been the youngest of boys. The implausibility is in line with many another such in this play, where Shakespeare seems so often to want to go beyond the credible while at the same time exploring a genuine human anguish. Guiderius asks to be left alone with the intruder: again rather surprisingly, he is allowed this privilege. So after some exchange of abuse he and his unknown stepbrother exeunt fighting. Soon he returns, presenting Cloten's head to Belarius and Arviragus. Then there is apparently a second death: Arviragus goes into the cave to help the sick "Fidele" and returns with what he thinks is her dead body. There is interesting comment on these deaths of the noble and the ignoble. In the midst of their mourning for "Fidele" Belarius reminds the two boys of Cloten:

> He was a queen's son, boys,
> And though he came our enemy, remember
> He was paid for that: though mean and mighty, rotting
> Together, have one dust, yet reverence

(That angel of the world) doth make distinction
Of place 'tween high, and low. Our foe was princely,
And though you took his life, as being our foe,
Yet bury him, as a prince.

(IV.ii.244–41)

Guiderius brushes this aside, expressing the idea of the equality of
all human creatures in death:

> Pray you, fetch him hither,
> Thersites' body is as good as Ajax',
> When neither are alive.

(IV.ii.251–53)

This is indeed the kind of cry we should expect over the death of
someone loved. Yet in the last plays in general, notably in *The Winter's Tale*, there is strong emphasis on the notion of "degree," Leontes,
for example, holding back from the full reproach that he thinks his
wife deserves:

> Lest barbarism, making me the precedent,
> Should a like language use to all degrees,
> And mannerly distinguishment leave out
> Betwixt the prince and beggar.

(II.i.84–87)

In act IV of that play there is a good deal of irony when Perdita, angry at her future father-in-law's arrogance, claims that the sun shines
on all alike yet shows a noticeable condescension in her attitude to the
simple girls of the countryside: she feels she is the princess she actually is. As so often, Shakespeare holds ideas here in tension with
each other. We should do wrong to claim him as a democrat, but, as
Guiderius's words indicate in *Cymbeline*, he was at one with perceptive men of the seventeenth century in recognizing that all dust
is the same.

The dirge for "Fidele" is spoken by the two boys while Belarius
goes to bring Cloten's body; it is spoken simply for her, the apparently dead boy-girl, so its words about "Golden lads and girls" are
fully appropriate. But, as we know she is not dead, there is an irony
additional to that which depends on the mourners' mistake about
her sex. Moreover, the dirge is spoken, not sung. Arviragus has suggested they should "sing him to th' ground" even though "our voices /
Have got the mannish crack," but Guiderius says bluntly:

I cannot sing: I'll weep, and word it with thee;
For notes of sorrow out of tune are worse
Than priests and fanes that lie.

(IV.ii.240–42)

J.M. Nosworthy, the New Arden editor, has suggested that our text "represents a stage in the company's history when the breaking of an actor's voice made the substitution of the spoken . . . word a temporary necessity."[12] But the New Cambridge editor, J.C. Maxwell, surely rightly argues that "the princes' parts are conceived throughout for adult actors";[13] after all, the boys were to do major things in the coming battle. The choice of speaking, the rejection of song in its proper sense, gives us yet another variant on Shakespeare's use of the inserted lyric. "Fidele," we know, is not dead. We need something different from the usual, therefore, in the "dirge" sung over the body. Moreover, it is all the sadder because denied the accompaniment of music, for the merely spoken word has its special austerity and authority. This can be linked to Guiderius's reference, already quoted, to the pretenses of religion's high and pretentious manner of utterance ("priests and fanes that lie"): there is a kind of intellectual puritanism in this use of the simply speaking voice. And the simple enunciation of the death theme here is in remarkable counterpoint to the fantastic incidents that have led up to it.

Near the end of Thomas Mann's *Dr. Faustus* the composer Leverkühn summons to his Bavarian retreat some thirty of his friends and acquaintances, promising to give them "some idea of his just finished choral symphonic work," *The Lamentation of Dr. Faustus*. But he never gets to the piano. In what is meant to be a prelude to the music, he tells them, with anguish, of the price he has paid for his eminence as a composer, the damnation, as he sees it, he has incurred. It is a long and frightening speech, and some of the small audience leave as he is making it. His life-long friend, Serenus Zeitblom, the schoolmaster-narrator of the novel, listens in terror and compassion, and records how he longed for the spoken words to stop and the music to begin. There some relief might come, and in his narrative he comments on "the bareness and baldness of unmediated revelation." Not that Leverkühn's words are disordered, except occasionally in articulation (and which of us has not noted that in ourselves from time to time?), for the speech is deliberate, fashioned, appropriately couched in archaic diction, recalling that earlier time when men's minds were powerfully hospitable to the idea of demonic visitation. But the words without music bring the auditors directly up against

88

the simple fact of the speaker's condition. They force a confrontation with the terrible, while music, with its sensuality—even at its bleakest, it has that consolation to offer—can mitigate the terrible. We may remember how Wordsworth in the 1800 preface to the *Lyrical Ballads* spoke of rhyme and meter as mitigating the distress of a painful story.[14] Even more so does music itself: hence in Alban Berg's *Wozzeck*, we can get a pleasurable excitement which Büchner's play refuses us; hence it is that Feste's singing epilogue in *Twelfth Night* gives us a kind of benediction;[15] and how could we endure with any sort of equanimity, *Der Rosenkavalier* without its music? But Thomas Mann's words in *Dr. Faustus* constitute, I believe, a major comment on an aesthetic fact:

> Never had I felt more strongly the advantage that music, which says nothing and everything, has over the unequivocal word; yes, the saving irresponsibility of all art compared with the bareness and baldness of unmediated revelation.[16]

Yet it is not so simple as that: the deliberateness of Leverkühn's words indicate the use of "art," but an art that provides a less immediate consolation than music does. This less immediate consolation is what, at the most, we have normally to accept, and thus the dirge for "Fidele" in *Cymbeline* gives us an extra turn of the screw.

The first two stanzas of the lyric eloquently enunciate its theme:

> Gui. Fear no more the heat o' th' sun,
>   Nor the furious winter's rages,
> Thou thy worldly task hast done,
>   Home art gone and ta'en thy wages.
> Golden lads and girls all must,
> As chimney-sweepers, come to dust.
>
> Arv. Fear no more the frown o' th' great,
>   Thou art past the tyrant's stroke,
> Care no more to clothe and eat,
>   To thee the reed is as the oak:
> The sceptre, learning, physic, must
> All follow this and come to dust.
>   (IV.ii.258–69)

The insistence on ultimate equality is strong here, as in Guiderius's earlier matching of the dead Thersites with the dead Ajax; all the dead are free from hardship and duty and the tyrant's threat; for all of them there is no distinction in nature, no substance in renown or the holding of a scepter. Underlining this, Belarius returns with Cloten's headless body, which he lays down beside "Fidele." Then he strews flowers on them both. There is something very moving in this "Thersites" lying by this "Ajax"—not the dim-witted Ajax of Shakespeare's own *Troilus and Cressida*, written some years before, but the Ajax of antiquity, an anguished hero. In death, or apparent death, the two are brought together, as they could not be in life. When they are left alone on the stage, they come even closer. Imogen awakens and thinks the headless body, dressed in Posthumus's clothes, is truly the body of her husband. She thinks Pisanio is to blame, and her immediate assumption of this faithful servant's guilt palliates a little the easy deception that Posthumus let himself fall into. Her mistake about the body is grotesque—surely Shakespeare is having a measure of fun with the disguise convention he had used so freely throughout his career. But this is a play where he persistently carries the long-established methods of his stage up to and beyond their normal limits. Yet it is not a mere burlesque: Imogen's mistake leads her to embrace, after his death, the body of the man she abhorred. Cloten has his posthumous—the pun is hardly to be avoided —triumph. "O my lord! my lord!" she cries, and all men are lords in death. "How happy are the dead!" said someone whose name I do not remember. When the Roman Lucius enters and takes her into his protection, she asks for permission to bury the body; Cloten's last rites are given to him, mistakenly, by the girl he wished to violate. Did Shakespeare here consciously make a variant on Antigone's crucial action? Cloten was, after a fashion, Imogen's brother.

    Professor G.R. Hibbard has drawn my attention to an earlier use of the spoken dirge, in Marston's *Antonio's Revenge*:

> *Ant.* Wilt sing a Dirge boy?
> *Pan.* No, no song: twill be vile out of tune.
> *Alb.* Indeed he's hoarse: the poore boyes voice is crackt.
> *Pa.* Why cuz? why shold it not be hoarce & crackt,
> When all the strings of natures symphony
> Are crackt & iar? why should his voice keepe tune,
> When ther's no musick in the breast of man?
> Ile say an honest antick rime I haue;
> (Helpe me good sorrow-mates to giue him graue.)
>
> *[They all helpe to carie Feliche to his graue.]*
>
> Death, exile, plaints, and woe,
> Are but mans lackies, not his foe.

No mortall scapes from fortunes warre,
Without a wound, at least a scarre.
Many haue led these to the graue:
But all shall followe, none shall saue.
Bloode of my youth, rot and consume,
Virtue, in dirt, doth life assume:
With this ould sawe, close vp this dust;
Thrice blessed man that dyeth iust.

      (Malone Society Reprints, ll.1781–1801)

It seems likely that Shakespeare had this in mind when he wrote the *Cymbeline* dirge.

 It would be profitable to consider many of Shakespeare's other songs in close relation to their contexts. In perhaps every instance we do Shakespeare an injustice when we abstract a song from its particular position in the play where it finds its proper place.

The King Disguised
Shakespeare's Henry V and the
Comical History

Anne Barton

In the worst moment of the French campaign, when the night before Agincourt finds the English army reduced, dispirited, and ailing, "even as men wrack'd upon a sand, that look to be wash'd off the next tide" (IV.i.97–98), Henry V pays two quite different visits to his despondent troops. Although the first of them, made in his own person as king, is not enacted, the Chorus testifies eloquently to its success:

> every wretch, pining and pale before,
> Beholding him, plucks comfort from his looks.
> A largess universal like the sun
> His liberal eye doth give to every one,
> Thawing cold fear, that mean and gentle all,
> Behold, as may unworthiness define,
> A little touch of Harry in the night.
> (IV.41–47)

Later, in the first scene of act IV, Henry borrows a cloak from Sir Thomas Erpingham, conceals his royal identity, and ventures alone among soldiers no longer able to recognize him as their king. His fortunes in this second sally are altogether less prosperous. Thorny and disquieting from the start, his conversation with Williams, Court, and Bates ends in an open quarrel. Moreover, it provokes Henry's only soliloquy in the play: a bitter examination of kingship itself and of the irremovable barriers isolating the monarch from a world of private men.

Shakespeare may well have remembered from Holinshed, or from *The First English Life of Henry V*, that the historical Henry "daylie and nightlie in his owne person visited the watches, orders and stacions of everie part of his hoast."[1] Nowhere, however, is it suggested that he ever did so incognito. Geoffrey Bullough has argued that when Shakespeare made Henry muffle himself in Erpingham's cloak he was thinking of a passage from Tacitus's *Annals* in which Germanicus disguises himself on the eve of a battle in order to assess the morale of the Roman legions.[2] Germanicus, however, lurks outside his soldiers' tents as a mere eavesdropper; he never attempts a personal encounter. Although the passage cannot be discounted entirely as a source for Henry's disguise, its importance has surely been overestimated. For those Elizabethans who watched *Henry V* in the new Globe theatre in 1599, the king's behavior before Agincourt would have had analogues far more striking and immediate. There is a surprising number of disguised kings to be found in those English history plays which have survived from the period 1587–1600. A few of these princes are driven to dissemble their identity for a time out of political necessity, as Marlowe's Edward II does after the triumph of Young Mortimer and Queen Isabella, or Shakespeare's Henry VI in the last part of the trilogy, when he rashly steals across the border into England "disguised, with a prayerbook," only to be recognized despite this precaution by the two Keepers and haled away to the Tower. A larger and more interesting group is composed of kings who, like Shakespeare's Henry V, adopt disguise as a caprice, for reasons that are fundamentally exploratory and quixotic.

Toward the end of *George a Greene, the Pinner of Wakefield* (?Robert Greene, c. 1590), an unspecified King Edward of England decides to "make a merrie journey for a moneth"[3] along with his friend King James of Scotland, for the purpose of meeting the folk hero George a Greene, a loyal pinner in the north country who has been instrumental in putting down a rebellion against the Crown. The two monarchs travel on foot and in disguise. At the town of Bradford they yield meekly to the insolent demands of the locals, trailing their staves in order to pass without argument through the town. George a Greene, disgusted by such pusillanimity, berates the two kings soundly for cowardice and forces them to hold up their staves. King Edward gains a vivid and somewhat disconcerting idea of the character and temper of his subject before the revelation of his royal identity puts an end to the game. All is forgiven. George is offered a knighthood, which he politely refuses, preferring to remain an English yeoman. Edward unites him with Bettris, his love, over-riding the snobbish objections of her father, and the play ends harmoniously with a feast at which King Edward, King James, George a Greene, Robin Hood and Maid Marian, and all the shoemakers of Bradford sit side by side as friends and good companions.

Peele's *Edward I* (c. 1591) also associates the king in disguise with the Robin Hood stories. Lluellen, the rebellious Prince of Wales, his mistress Elinor, and his friend Rice ap Meredith have taken to the greenwood in the company of a friar, "to live and die together like Chamber-Britaines, Robin Hood, Little John, Frier Tucke, and Maide Marrian."[4] King Edward, intrigued to learn of this little society, decides to pay it a secret visit, disguised, and accompanied only by Lluellen's brother, Sir David of Brecknock:

> as I am a Gentleman,
> Ile have one merrie flirt with little John,
> And Robin Hood, and his Maide Marian.
> Be thou my counsell and my companie,
> And thou maist Englands resolution see.
>
> (x.1548–52)

In the forest, Edward adjudicates in a dispute between two rogues who have tried to cozen one another, agrees with Lluellen that his purse will belong to whichever man can overcome the other in a fair fight, and (exactly as his prototype Richard Coeur de Lion had done in the ballads) sends "Robin Hood" sprawling. The exigencies of Peele's plot made it impossible for this forest scene to end with reconciliation and pardon in the ballad tradition. Lluellen, rebellious to the end, is killed in battle later in the play. It is remarkable, however, how close this personal encounter between the outlaw and the king he cannot recognize—in both senses of that word—has come to healing the breach between them. When "Longshanks" has gone, his identity disclosed, Lluellen admits ruefully that "his courage is like to the Lion, and were it not that rule and soveraigntie set us at jarre, I could love and honour the man for his valour" (xii.1917–19).

The two anonymous plays *Fair Em* (c. 1590) and *The True Chronicle History of King Leir* (c. 1590) both present kings who disguise themselves in the cause of love. William the Conqueror, in *Fair Em*, falls in love with a picture of Blanch, Princess of Denmark, and travels to see her in her father's court under the name of Sir Robert of Windsor. Finding the lady less glamorous in reality than she seemed in her portrait, he tries to elope with Mariana, a lady promised to his friend and traveling companion, the Marquis of Lubeck. Mariana, however, not only surmounts the temptation to abandon Lubeck for a crown but contrives to substitute a masked and love-sick Blanch for herself at the rendezvous appointed. William, who discovers the fraud on arrival in England, is understandably put out but decides that although Blanch is not Mariana she is nonetheless

94

tolerable, and certainly preferable to war with Denmark. At the end of the play, William marries Blanch and, at the same time, restores Godard the supposed miller to his rightful place in society and bestows his daughter Em upon Valingford, the suitor who best deserves her.

In *King Leir*, the Gallian king comes to England disguised as a pilgrim, in order to determine which is the best and most marriageable of Leir's three daughters. He meets Cordella after her disgrace, finds her fair and good, and pretends that he has been sent as an ambassador by his royal master to make her the Gallian queen. Cordella, who has most perspicaciously fallen in love with the humble palmer himself, spurns this splendid offer and bids him "cease for thy King, seeke for thy selfe to woo."[5] After this gratifying proof that Cordella loves the man and not the monarch, the palmer reveals his identity and the two are married immediately and return to France. Disguise, however, remains a feature of their court. In scene xxiv, the Gallian king and queen mingle with their subjects in the guise of country folk and, thus obscured, discover and are reconciled with the wretched Leir and his counsellor Perillus on the seacoast of Brittany.

Finally, *The First Part of King Edward IV*, a play written by Thomas Heywood before 1599, presents two quite separate royal disguises. Edward conceals his identity when he goes into Lombard Street for the first time to lay amorous siege to Mistress Shore. More relevant to *Henry V*, however, is his encounter with John Hobs the tanner. The king, hunting incognito at Drayton Basset, becomes separated from his queen and courtiers. Hobs, meeting him in the forest, suspects him at first for a thief ("How these roysters swarm in the country, now the King is so near"[6]), but is persuaded at length that Edward is a minor hanger-on at court: in fact, the king's butler. Under this delusion, he prattles on merrily about the two kings of England, Edward at court and the deposed Henry VI in the Tower. Edward, slyly anxious to know how he is regarded by this outspoken subject, receives some disconcertingly frank answers to the questions he puts. The commons of England, according to Hobs, love King Edward

as poor folk love holidays, glad to have them now and then; but to have them come too often will undo them. So, to see the King now and then 'tis comfort; but every day would beggar us; and I may say to thee, we fear we shall be troubled to lend him money; for we doubt he's but needy.

Even more improbable in its light-hearted political inconsequence is Edward's amused acceptance of the tanner's shifting loyalties. "Shall I say my conscience?" he inquires cunningly. "I think Harry is the true king."

> *Hobs.* Art advised of that? Harry's of the old house of Lancaster; and that progenity do I love.
>
> *King.* And thou dost not hate the house of York?
>
> *Hobs.* Why, no; for I am just akin to Sutton Windmill; I can grind which way soe'er the wind blow. If it be Harry, I can say, "Well fare, Lancaster." If it be Edward, I can sing, "York, York, for my money."

Basically, as it turns out, Hobs approves of King Edward for reasons that have nothing to do with his government of the realm: "He's a frank franion, a merry companion, and loves a wench well." To his way of thinking, the king ought not to encourage patents and monopolies, but Hobs is willing to believe that Edward does so out of ignorance, because he has been misled by greedy counsellors and because he cannot see for himself how the system operates. As subject and king converse, Edward's respect for this "honest true tanner" and for his powers of observation grows. Hobs, for his part, comes to like the supposed butler so well that he invites him home to his cottage for dinner and the night. The tanner has a pretty daughter and there is even some talk of a match, although Hobs would like his prospective son-in-law to have a steadier profession, not one of these fly-by-night court posts. Not until daybreak does Edward tear himself away from the tanner's hospitality to return to London and the troubles of a kingdom in revolt. Again, the meeting between subject and king in disguise has generated harmony, good fellowship, and mutual understanding.

In all these English histories—and there must have been many more plays like them, now lost—the king's disguise demands to be seen as a romantic gesture. Edward IV, William the Conqueror, Edward I, the Gallian king, or the brace of monarchs in *George a Greene*, all conceal their identities in much the spirit of Haroun al Raschid, the caliph of *The Arabian Nights* who liked to walk the streets of Baghdad incognito, in search of the marvellous and the strange. Moreover, the people they meet come from the world of balladry and legend. Robin Hood and Maid Marian, the folk-hero George a

Greene, the miller and his daughter, thieves and outlaws, the beggar-maid destined to become a queen, or the tanner of Tamworth: all were characters nurtured in the popular imagination. Maurice Keen, in *The Outlaws of Medieval Legend*, describes the informal meeting of commoner and king as the wish-dream of a peasantry harried and perplexed by a new class of officials, an impersonal bureaucracy against which the ordinary man seemed to have no redress:

> They only knew that the King was the ultimate repository of a law whose justice they acknowledged, and they saw treason against him as a betrayal of their allegiance to God himself. If they could only get past his corrupt officers, whose abuse of the trust reposed in them amounted to treason in itself, and bring their case before the King, they believed that right would be done. Their unshakeable faith in the King's own justice was the most tragic of the misconceptions of the medieval peasantry, and the ballad-makers and their audiences shared it to the full.[7]

In the ballads, king and unsuspecting subject meet time after time and discover unanimity of opinion and mutual respect. Richard Coeur de Lion banquets in Sherwood Forest on stolen venison, forgives Robin Hood and his men, and confounds the sheriff of Nottingham. Henry II so enjoys the rough but generous hospitality of the miller of Mansfield that he makes him a knight and gives him a royal license to keep the forest of Sherwood. Other ballads describe the meeting of Edward I and the reeve, King Alfred and the shepherd, Edward IV and the tanner, Henry VIII and the cobbler, James I and the tinker, William III and the forester, and many similar encounters.

That conversations of this sort represent a fantasy, the "misconception," as Keen terms it, of a victimized agrarian class, is obvious. They derive from attitudes far removed from anything which the hard-headed citizens of Elizabeth's London actually believed. Yet the old roots ran deep. This type of ballad not only survived through Jacobean and Caroline times: the idea behind it remained oddly resonant and haunting. Real Tudor monarchs sometimes played at enacting it. Henry VIII, as Hall tells us, graciously allowed himself to be "waylaid" and dragged off to a reconstruction of Coeur de Lion's feast with Robin Hood, Maid Marian, and their fellows.[8] Queen Elizabeth, walking in Wanstead gardens, suddenly found herself confronting a group of supposed country folk: "Though they knew not her estate, yet something there was which made them startle aside and gaze upon her."[9] Cunningly, Philip Sidney proceeded to involve the queen in a dispute between a shepherd and a forester for possession of the Lady of May, requesting her, after she had heard the rustic arguments of both sides, to award the lady to the suitor she considered most deserving. Traces of this kind of situation can be seen as well in some of the masques at court, but it was in the drama proper that the idea of the king's personal engagement with his subjects and their problems flowered and was most fully exploited.

There are a few Elizabethan plays in which the king manages to mingle with his subjects freely and dispense justice without resorting to disguise. At the end of Dekker's *The Shoemaker's Holiday*, Henry V in his own person sweeps away the snobbery of his officers and nobles:

> Dost thou not know that love respects no blood,
> Cares not for difference of birth or state?
> The maid is young, well born, fair, virtuous,
> A worthy bride for any gentleman.[10]

As benevolent *deus ex machina*, he joins the hands of Rose, the citizen's daughter, and Lacy, nephew to the Earl of Lincoln. Annihilating objections based upon wealth or class, he acts from principles of perfect equity as soon as he examines the case himself, just as the medieval minstrels had always believed he would. Yet even Dekker's Henry, in a play which could scarcely be described as realistic, worries about the constraints and inhibitions which his declared royal presence may impose on London's madcap mayor, Simon Eyre, at the Shrove Tuesday banquet where these events take place. Most Elizabethan dramatists seem to have accepted the idea that disguise was an essential prerequisite for the ease and success of the meeting between private man and king. Only if the king's identity was concealed could there be natural conversation, frankness, and a sense of rapport. It is the fundamental premise of all these plays that the king, rightly considered, is but a man, and a remarkably understanding man at that. If only, they seem to suggest, king and commoner could talk together in this way, without formality or embarrassment, how many problems would be solved, how many popular grievances redressed. Humanity and humor, an easy cameraderie: these qualities, usually obscured by ceremony, distance, and that hierarchy of officials standing between the monarch and his people, emerge clearly as soon as he steps down from his throne to speak, for a little while, as a private man.

When Shakespeare sent Henry V to converse incognito with Williams, Court, and Bates on the night before Agincourt, he was surely influenced by plays like these far more than by any distant memory of how Germanicus had behaved in the war against Arminius. Generically, Shakespeare's disguised king belongs with Peele's Edward I, Heywood's Edward IV, or the accommodating monarchs of *George a Greene*. Yet the *Henry V* episode is unique. By 1599, the king who freely chooses disguise had become the hallmark of a particular kind of play. Polonius almost certainly would have defined the mode (quite shrewdly) as the "comical-historical." *Henry V*, however, is not a comical history. Far more ironic and complicated than the plays which belong properly to that genre, it introduces the time-worn and popular dramatic motif of the king disguised into its fourth act in order to question, not to celebrate, a folk convention. In itself, the gesture could be relied upon to generate certain clearly defined emotional expectations in an Elizabethan audience powerfully conditioned by both a ballad and a stage tradition. Shakespeare built upon this fact. He used Henry's disguise to summon up the memory of a wistful, naive attitude toward history and the relationship of subject and king which this play rejects as attractive but untrue: a nostalgic but false romanticism.

As the royal captain of a ruined band, a sun-god radiating his beams indiscriminately upon the soldiers among whom he walks, Henry is effective, as the Chorus makes plain. Throughout this play, the relation between the Chorus's unequivocal celebration of Henry and his war in France and the complicated, ambiguous, and sometimes flatly contradictory scenes which these speeches are made to introduce is productive of irony and double focus. This duality of attitude is particularly striking in act IV, where the Chorus's epic account of the king dispensing comfort to his troops in his own person leads directly into that altogether more dubious scene in which Henry visits the army a second time, disguised, in the manner of a ballad king. Once he has obliterated his identity, Henry falls into a series of nonencounters, meetings in which the difficulty of establishing understanding between subject and king is stressed, not the encouraging effect of "a little touch of Harry in the night" (IV.47).

It is true that Ancient Pistol, the first man Henry faces, is scarcely capable of rational discourse. Pistol lives in a wholly private world, a heightened and extravagant realm where everything appears twice life size. His overcharged style of speech, filled with contempt for Fortune, exotic geography, and resounding proper names, derives from Marlowe and from those lesser dramatists who imitated Marlowe. Pistol's language is a tissue of play scraps. In his own mind, as

Leslie Hotson has pointed out, he is Tamburlaine.[11] "As good a gentleman as the emperor" (IV.i.42), he appears blatantly literary, a mere stage king, as soon as he confronts Henry. Linguistically, Shakespeare's early histories had been intermittently Marlovian. Here, at the end of his Elizabethan cycle, he effectively laid the ghost of Tamburlaine as a hero, making it impossible for him to be taken seriously again until the Restoration. By deliberately weighing Pistol's egotism, his histrionics, against the workaday prose of the true king, he indicated the distance between one kind of theatrical fantasy and fact.

Perhaps because he fears recognition by his captains, Henry makes no attempt to speak to Fluellen and Gower. He waits in silence until the entry of Williams, Court, and Bates: three ordinary soldiers for whom the king has always been an unapproachable and distant figure. This encounter is, of course, the mirror image of all those scenes in plays like *George a Greene* or *Edward IV* in which the king and his humble subject reach a frank and mutual accord. Here, nothing of the kind occurs. Instead, Henry finds himself embroiled in a tough and increasingly embarrassing argument. He is rhetorically dexterous, and he succeeds in convincing the soldiers that the king cannot be held responsible for the particular state of soul of those individuals who die in his wars. The other question raised by Williams, that of the goodness of the king's cause in itself, his heavy reckoning at that latter day when he must confront the subjects who have been mutilated and have died for him in a war that perhaps was unjust, Henry simply evades. Here, as in the play as a whole, it is left standing, unresolved.

Even worse, Henry discovers with a sense of shock that his soothing account of the king as "but a man, as I am" (IV.i.101–2), sensitive to the disapprobation or approval of his humblest subject, is treated as flatly absurd. For Williams, the gulf between commoner and king is unbridgeable. A man "may as well go about to turn the sun to ice with fanning in his face with a peacock's feather" as expect his "poor and private displeasure" to influence the behavior of a monarch (IV.i.194–99). This shaft strikes home, exposing the speciousness of Henry's pretense that he can really be the friend and brother of these soldiers, as well as their king. The conversation ends in a quarrel, a failure to arrive at understanding which contradicts the romantic, ballad tradition. Left alone, Henry meditates acrimoniously on the pains of sovereignty, the doubtful worth of the "ceremony" that divides the king from a world of private men without providing him with any adequate compensation for his isolation and his crippling weight of responsibility.

Subsequently, after Agincourt has been won, Williams learns that it was the king himself whom he offended and with whom he has promised to fight. Like the outlaws of medieval legend, Williams meets not only with pardon but with royal largesse. He receives his glove again filled with golden crowns by Henry's bounty. Yet this gift, unlike its archetypes in the ballads and in Elizabethan comical histories, seems strangely irrelevant. Consciously anachronistic, it provides not the ghost of an answer to the questions raised during this particular encounter between common man and king disguised. Is the king's cause just? If not, what measure of guilt does he incur for requiring men to die for anything but the strict necessity of their country? Can the opinions and judgments of private men influence the sovereign on his throne? Henry is generous to Williams, but it is a dismissive generosity which places the subject firmly in an inferior position and silences his voice. The two men do not sit down at table together to any common feast, in the manner of Dekker's Henry V or Heywood's Edward IV. Indeed, Williams himself seems to be aware that the answer represented by the glove full of crowns is inadequate. He never thanks Henry for the present, accepting it without a word and turning, in the next instant, to repudiate the shilling offered him by Fluellen: "I will none of your money" (IV. viii.70). That gift he can dare to refuse. Even his plea for pardon is filled with suppressed anger and resentment:

> Your majesty came not like yourself: you appeared to me but as a common man; witness the night, your garments, your lowliness; and what your highness suffered under that shape, I beseech you, take it for your own fault, and not mine. (IV.viii.51–56)

Henry V is a play concerned to force upon its audience a creative participation far more active than usual. The Chorus urges an unceasing visualization, bright pictures in the mind, of horses, ships under sail, silken banners, or the engines of siege warfare. Within the play itself, Shakespeare suggests without indicating priority a multiplicity of possible responses to every character and event. Celebration and denigration, heroism and irony exist uneasily side by side. The Chorus may regard England's despoliation of France as a species of sacred obligation. Elsewhere, the attitude is far less clearcut. Always in the background there hovers a disconcerting memory of Canterbury and Ely in the opening scene, busily fomenting the war in France to divert attention from the temporal wealth of the Church. Behind that lurks Henry IV's deathbed advice to his son to "busy giddy minds with foreign quarrels" (*2 Henry IV*, IV.v.213–14) in the hope that the shaky legitimacy of Lancastrian rule might thus escape scrutiny. Among Shakespeare's other histories, only *Henry VIII* is so deliberately ambiguous, so overtly a puzzle in which the audience is left to forge its own interpretation of action and characters with only minimal guidance from a dramatist apparently determined to stress the equivalence of mutually exclusive views of a particular complex of historical event.

In both *Henry V* and *Henry VIII*, the fact that the mind and heart of the king are essentially opaque, that his true thoughts and feelings remain veiled behind a series of royal poses—as those of Richard II, Richard III, King John, Henry VI, or even Henry IV do not—contributes to the difficulty of assessment. Even Henry's soliloquy before Agincourt is strangely externalized and formal, in no sense a revelation of the private workings of a mind. Neither here nor anywhere else in the play is the whole truth about the king's personal decision to invade France disclosed. This reticence is not accidental. Henry is, by secular standards, an extraordinarily successful example of the God-man incarnate. The conception of kingship in this play derives not from the relaxed and essentially personal tradition of the ballads but from a complicated, inherently tragic Tudor doctrine of the king's two bodies.[12] Shakespeare had previously dealt with the violence of divorce or incompatibility between the twin natures of the king. Henry V, by contrast, has achieved a union of body natural and body politic difficult to flaw. Yet the price he pays for his subordination of the indivdual to the office is heavy, in personal terms. There is loss as well as gain in the gulf that now divides Henry from his old associates Bardolph and Pistol, from a world of private men in which he alone speaks out of a double nature. Hal's sudden unavailability as a person, his retreat into an oddly declamatory series of stances, reflects neither his own nor Shakespeare's weakness. It is simply a measure of the signal effectiveness of this man's incarnation as king.

In many respects *Henry V* is a success story. Agincourt, at least from one angle, is a splendor. Within its own limited sphere the rhetoric of the Chorus rings true. Henry himself can be described as an "ideal" sovereign, God's gift to an England weary of rebellion, usurpation, and civil war. At the same time, it is not easy for any mere mortal to support the psychological and moral burden of a double self. At a number of points in the play, particularly in situations which seem to demand an essentially personal response, the strain involved in maintaining such a constant ventriloquism becomes obvious. Even when Henry tries temporarily to obliterate one half of his identity, as he does in the scene with Williams, Court, and Bates, he finds it impossible to produce a natural and unforced imitation of a private man. Richard II, ironically enough, had experienced similar difficulties after his deposition. In Henry's case, the suppression of one side of his nature is only momentary, the product of whim rather than political defeat. Nevertheless, his awkwardness with the soldiers points to the irrevocability of that mystic marriage of king and man accomplished in the ceremony of coronation. Only death can dissolve this union.

Meanwhile, the king must contrive to deal with a world of single-natured individuals from which he himself stands conspicuously apart. Henry cannot have personal friends as other men do. There is a sense in which the rejection of Falstaff at the end of *2 Henry IV* leads directly on to the rejection of the traitor Scroop in the second act of *Henry V*. Precisely because Scroop is someone Henry has imagined was bound to him as a man by private ties of affection and liking, his treason is far more painful than the more neutral betrayal of Cambridge and Grey. With the latter he deals in an efficient, almost perfunctory fashion. Only Scroop evokes a long and suddenly emotional remonstrance in which Henry effectively bids farewell to the possibility of personal relationship. Significantly, this scene at Southampton is placed between the two episodes in London dealing with the death of Falstaff. The epic voyage to France is thus preceded by three scenes dealing not merely with the death of former friends but with the final severance of the new king's remaining personal ties. Thereafter in the play, he will use the term "friend" in a special sense.

Not by accident, Henry abruptly abandons the royal "we" when he turns to accuse Scroop. In act I he had spoken almost entirely from this corporate position, allowing himself only infrequently to be jolted into an adventurer's "I." The Southampton scene is also one which insists throughout upon the double nature of the king and makes that nature grammatically clear through his habitual use of a plural first person. Cambridge and Grey, it seems, have conspired to kill "us" (II.ii.85–91): "But O, / What shall *I* say to thee, Lord Scroop?" (II.ii.93–94). In his long, passionate speech to this false friend "that knew'st the very bottom of my soul" (II.ii.97), Henry grieves more as man than as king. Not until the moment comes for sentencing all three conspirators does he regain his balance, discriminating calmly between the offense intended to his body natural and his body politic:

> Touching our person seek we no revenge;
> But we our kingdom's safety must so tender,
> Whose ruin you have sought, that to her laws
> We do deliver you. Get you therefore hence,
> Poor miserable wretches, to your death.
>
> (II.ii.174–78)

The voice here is impersonal, speaking from behind the mask of kingship, deliberately avoiding the first person singular of individual response.

Once arrived in France, Henry refers to himself far more often as "I" or "me" than he does as "we" or "us," at least up to the council of Troyes in the fifth act. As leader of an English host stranded in a foreign country and in a position of increasing danger, Henry finds it not only possible but necessary to simplify his royalty to some extent. After much painful marching in the rain-drenched field, he can describe himself as a soldier, "a name that in my thoughts becomes me best" (III.iii.5–6). In this role he achieves a measure of escape from the royal impersonality demanded under more ordinary and formal circumstances. When he warns the governor of Harfleur of the horrors that lie in store for his city if it fails to capitulate, when he exchanges badinage with Fluellen, or celebrates honor in the Crispin day speech in terms that Hotspur would have understood, he is playing a part—much as Prince Hal had done in the tavern scenes of the *Henry IV* plays or among the alien but imitable chivalries of Shrewsbury. In this context, the infrequent appearances of the royal "we" in acts III and IV become purposeful and striking reminders of the ineluctable reality of the king's twin nature—a nature temporarily obscured by the adventurer's pose appropriate to the French campaign.

Gravely, Henry reminds Williams that "it was ourself thou didst abuse," before he dismisses him with pardon and reward (IV.viii.48). When his old associate Bardolph is summarily executed for robbing a church, Fluellen informs the king and, describing the dead man's face in terms so vivid that there can be no possible mistake, inquires somewhat tactlessly: "If your majesty know the man" (III.vi.96–101). Henry's stiff reply to this appeal to his memory of a time before his coronation is more than a politic evasion: "We would have all such offenders so cut off." His sudden use here of the first person plural of majesty, occurring as it does in a scene where even the French herald Montjoy is addressed by Henry as "I," constitutes the real answer to Fluellen's question. As a twin-natured being, the king is stripped not only of personal friends but also of a private past. To recognize Bardolph, let alone to regret him, is impossible.

The war in France provides Henry with "friends" of a rhetorical and special kind. It also allows him an ambiguous use of the pronoun "we" which momentarily clothes the abstract doctrine of the king's two bodies with flesh. Before Harfleur, Henry rallies "dear friends" to the breach, or urges them "to close the wall up with our English dead" (III.i.1–2). The good yeomen whose limbs were made in England are asked to "show us here the mettle of your pasture" (III.i.26–27). Later, before Agincourt, he will tell his cousin Westmoreland that "if we are mark'd to die, we are enow / To do our country loss" and speak of "we few, we happy few, we band of brothers" (IV.iii.20–21, 60). His encounter with Williams, Court, and Bates in act IV is prefaced by a speech addressed to Bedford and Gloucester in which the pronouns "we" and "our" are by implication both royal and collective:

> Gloucester, 'tis true that we are in great danger;
> The greater therefore should our courage be.
> Good morrow, brother Bedford. God Almighty!
> There is some soul of goodness in things evil,
> Would men observingly distil it out;
> For our bad neighbour makes us early stirrers,
> Which is both healthful and good husbandry:
> Besides, they are our outward consciences,
> And preachers to us all; admonishing
> That we should dress us fairly for our end.
> Thus may we gather honey from the weed,
> And make a moral of the devil himself.
>
> (IV.i.1–12)

In passages like these, where Henry's "we" and "our" seem to refer both to himself as king and to the nobles and soldiers around him as a group, a community in which he participates, the idea of the king's two bodies acquires a meaning that is concrete and emotionally resonant. Rightly considered, Henry's soldiers are part of his body politic and thus extensions of his own identity. But it is only in moments of stress and mutual dependence that the doctrine articulates itself naturally, allowing the king an easy jocularity which is familiar without being intimate, essentially distant at the same time that it creates an illusion of warmth and spontaneity. As the peril of the situation in France grows, so does Henry's sense of fellowship. It is almost as though he extracts from danger a kind of substitute for the genuinely personal relationships abandoned with Falstaff and Scroop.

Ironically, Henry's dazzling victory at Agincourt necessarily spells the end of this special accord. The king who speaks in the council chamber at Troyes in act V is once again firmly entrenched behind a royal "we" that is a diagram rather than a three-dimensional fact. Somewhat disconcertingly, he insists upon using the first person plural even in his request that the girl he intends to marry should remain in the room with him when the peers of France and England depart to discuss terms of peace:

> Yet leave our cousin Katharine here with us:
> She is our capital demand, compris'd
> Within the fore-rank of our articles.
>
> (V.ii.95–97)

For all its political realism, this seems a desperately awkward beginning to a declaration of love. In the wooing scene that follows, Henry falls back upon his soldier's persona. He resurrects this "I" to deal with a situation of peculiar difficulty. How should a king, encumbered by twin natures, embark upon what is necessarily the most personal of all relationships, that of love? Henry's particular compromise is witty, and yet the problems of communication in this scene do not spring entirely from the fact that the king's French is even more rudimentary than the lady's English. Most of Henry's blunders, his various solecisms, derive from his uncertainty as to whether at a given instant he is speaking as Harry or as England, and whether the girl he addresses is the delectable Kate or the kingdom of France. Certainly the princess, when informed that her suitor loves France so well that "I will not part with a village of it; I will have it all mine: and Kate, when France is mine and I am yours, then yours is France and you are mine," might well be excused for complaining that "I cannot tell wat is dat," even if her linguistic skills were considerably greater than they are (V.ii.178–83). The loving monarchs of *Fair Em* and *King Leir* recognized no such problems of expression. Whatever this wooing scene was like in the lost, original text of *The Famous Victories of Henry V*, it has been made in Shakespeare's play to serve the theme of the king's two bodies: the dilemma of the man placed at a disadvantage in the sphere of personal relations by the fact of a corporate self.

The first part of *Sir John Oldcastle*, a play belonging to the Lord Chamberlain's rivals, the Admiral's Men, was staged by 1600. Its four authors, Michael Drayton, Anthony Munday, Richard Hathway, and Robert Wilson, were certainly painfully conscious of Shakespeare's Henry IV plays and probably of *Henry V* as well. In the absence of any Elizabethan equivalent to Vasari, a writer who would have relished and also recorded the whole imbroglio, there seems no way of knowing precisely what steps the Brooke family took to try and dissociate their ancestor Sir John Oldcastle, the Lollard martyr, from Shakespeare's Falstaff. That Shakespeare had orginally christened his fat knight Oldcastle is clear from surviving allusions within *1 Henry IV*, from the public apology in the epilogue to the second part—"For Oldcastle died a martyr, and this is not the man"—and from the malicious references of contemporaries as anxious to press the connection as Sir Henry Brooke was to repudiate it.[13] Whether Shakespeare was forced to remove Falstaff from *Henry V* because of the protests of the Brookes and then permitted to display him at full length in *The Merry Wives of Windsor* at the direct request of Queen Elizabeth remains conjectural. It seems likely, however, that the Brooke family eventually realized that their repressive tactics were only serving to make them ridiculous and, in desperation, decided to fight fire with fire: to appeal to the stage itself to counteract the slanders of the stage.

There is no positive evidence that the mysterious sum of money received by Philip Henslowe "as a gefte"[14] to the four authors of *Sir John Oldcastle* came from Sir Henry Brooke. On the other hand, everything about the first and only surviving part of their history suggests a work especially commissioned as an answer to the Falstaff plays:

> The doubtfull Title (Gentlemen) prefixt
> Upon the Argument we have in hand,
> May breed suspence, and wrongfully disturbe
> The peacefull quiet of your setled thoughts.
> To stop which scruple, let this briefe suffise:
> It is no pamperd glutton we present,
> Nor aged Councellor to youthfull sinne,

But one, whose vertue shone above the rest,
A valiant Martyr and a vertuous peere;
In whose true faith and loyaltie exprest
Unto his soveraigne, and his countries weale,
We strive to pay that tribute of our Love,
Your favours merite. Let faire Truthe be grac'te,
Since forg'de invention former time defac'te.[15]

That the "pamperd glutton," the "aged Councellor to youthfull sinne" referred to in this prologue is Shakespeare's Falstaff admits of no doubt. Drayton, Munday, Wilson, and Hathway were out to soothe the Brooke family by presenting their ancestor as a hero, claiming in the process that they spoke truth where Shakespeare had lied. Furthermore, they had to construct an effective dramatic entertainment: a play which could support inevitable comparison with the popular *Henry IV* and *V* plays offered by the rival Lord Chamberlain's Men at The Globe. The result is curious. The first part of *Sir John Oldcastle* is, in effect, a detailed demonstration of how to turn a tragical into a comical history.

The four *Sir John Oldcastle* authors faced from the beginning a problem even more difficult than that of rivaling Shakespeare's invention. The historical Sir John Oldcastle, a follower of Wicliffe, had eventually given his life for the Protestant faith. As such, he was entirely eligible for the status of Elizabethan hero. Unfortunately, he happened to live in the reign of Henry V, a king who not only was not a Protestant himself, but one who firmly put down any outbreaks of this heresy that came to his attention. In writing his own Henry V play, Shakespeare had been able to ignore the inconvenient fact of the Henrician persecutions. The Oldcastle authors, on the other hand, could scarcely evade the religious issue, given a hero who was remembered solely because of it. Neither could they ask an Elizabethan audience to accept Henry V, the hero-king of the Agincourt ballad, the conqueror of France, as a villain. Because the second part of *Sir John Oldcastle* has been lost, it is impossible to know how they treated the awkward fact of the martyrdom itself. Part I, however, is remarkable for the consistency with which it romanticizes and obscures political and religious issues that were potentially dangerous. Carefully, and unhistorically, the four dramatists dissociated Oldcastle from a Lollard uprising aimed against the king as well as the pope. The rabble in the play is confused about its religious motives and activated chiefly by the hope of plunder. With this irresponsible and seditious mob the character Oldcastle is shown to have no connection. It is only the bishops, and certain nobles jealous of his popularity, who pretend that he leads the rebels. Henry himself is in no way distressed by Oldcastle's Protestantism, so long as it remains unconnected with the elements of political disorder in the state. It is almost suggested that Henry yearns to become a Protestant himself, except that the time is somehow not right. (There were, after all, limits to the liberties Elizabethan dramatists could take with history.)

That the Oldcastle authors were perfectly familiar with Shakespeare's histories is obvious. Indeed, they seem to have spent a good deal of their time wondering how to convert the fine things in the possession of the Lord Chamberlain's Men to their own uses. Like *Henry V, Sir John Oldcastle* opens just before the expedition to France. Here too, the clergy are scheming to divert attention from the wealth and rich livings of the church through the judicious dispensation of a portion of their gold: some is destined to help finance the war; some is offered to the Earl of Suffolk as a bribe to persuade him to speak against the troublesome Oldcastle—the most articulate opponent of ecclesiastical wealth and ceremonies—to the king. At the beginning of act II, a summoner engaged by the wicked Bishop of Rochester arrives before Oldcastle's house in Kent to serve a summons upon its master. Unluckily for him, he meets Harpoole, Oldcastle's brusque but loyal steward, first. Harpoole examines the legal document carefully:

Harp. Is this process parchment?
Sum. Yes, mary.
Harp. And this seale waxe?
Sum. It is so.
Harp. If this be parchment, & this waxe, eate you this parchment
and this waxe, or I will make parchment of your skinne,
and beate your brains into waxe: Sirra Sumner, dispatch;
devoure, sirra, devoure.

(II.i.56–65)

After a comic struggle, in the course of which the wretched summoner is threatened with a beating and administered a cup of sack with which to wash down the last scraps, he duly eats the summons including the seal. "Wax," as Harpoole opines, is wholesome: "the purest of the hony."

This episode has its obvious parallel in *Henry V*. In act V, Fluellen invokes the aid of a cudgel to force a reluctant and histrionic Ancient Pistol to eat the leek he had previously mocked. The New Arden

editor regards the similarity here as part of the evidence that the Oldcastle authors were familiar with *Henry V* as well as the two parts of
Henry IV when they wrote their own play.[16] He is probably right.
Yet it is surely important to note that there is a third scene of
this kind, earlier than either *Henry V* or *Sir John Oldcastle*, which
should be taken into account. In *George a Greene*, Sir Nicholas Mannering arrives at the town of Wakefield bearing a commission from
the rebellious Earl of Kendall for the requisition of victuals for his
soldiers. George a Greene himself, outraged both by the request and
by Mannering's insolence in urging it, first tears the parchment and
then compels this traitor to King Edward's throne to eat the seals
that were attached to it:

> Man. Well, and there be no remedie, so, George:
> [*swallows one of the seals.*]
> One is gone: I pray thee, no more nowe.
> George.   O sir,
> If one be good, the others cannot hurt.
> So, sir;
> [*Mannering swallows the other two seals.*]
> Nowe you may goe tell the Earle of Kendall,
> Although I haue rent his large Commission,
> Yet of curtesie I haue sent all his seales
> Back againe by you.
>
> (144–53)

The episode involving Harpoole and the Summoner in *Sir John
Oldcastle* may well have been inspired by Pistol's encounter with
Fluellen; it is nevertheless with this older scene from *George a Greene*
that its real affinities lie. Like the pinner of Wakefield, Harpoole is a
man of the people, someone who clings to a vanishing world of immediate feudal loyalties. His aggression stems not, like Fluellen's,
from the need to avenge a personal affront but from the desire to
defend his master from traitors who obscure simple right and wrong
with the aid of a new and suspect legalism. The spice of the incident
lies in the audacity of the underdog: the simple, honest man converting rotten parchment bonds into matter-of-fact fodder. It reflects
one of the wish-dreams of a lower class victimized by legislation
forced upon it from above, by a sea of paper which it could not understand. In both *George a Greene* and *Sir John Oldcastle*, the plain
old loyalties of master and servant, subject and king, achieve a triumph in the moment that the parchment (or the seals) slides down

Anne Barton

the officer's unwilling throat. When Shakespeare converted the original legal document into a vegetable, the dapper courtier worsted by the pinner into an entirely personal matter involving Fluellen's Welsh pride and Pistol's unconsidered boasting, he was moving away from traditional forms in response both to the spirit of the time and to the shape of his own history play. By 1599, the comical history was a consciously reactionary, an outdated dramatic mode. That cycle of Shakespearean plays which begins with *Richard II* and ends with *Henry V* had helped to make it so. Yet Elizabethans could still be made to respond emotionally to the ballad and folk material upon which the genre depended, while withholding actual belief in such distant and half-legendary types of social protest.

Harpoole himself has nothing but praise for the constable who enters immediately after the discomfited summoner has crept away. This functionary has been sent to make hue and cry after a thief who has robbed two clothiers. He means to search the ale-house for the culprit, but because that building stands in Oldcastle's "libertie" he refuses to exercise his function "except I had some of his servants, which are for my warrant" (II.i.140–41). In effect, the constable of his own free will recognizes and honors an older order of jurisdiction and responsibility based on the autonomy of the great house and its demesne. That the inviolability of Oldcastle's "libertie" from outside interference is no longer something taken for granted is apparent in Harpoole's cry of relief: "An honest Constable! an honest Constable!" The steward is old-fashioned, a believer in relationships and prerogatives which, in his time, were beginning to be questioned and superseded. Later in the play, he will engineer his master's escape from the Tower and loyally, without hope of reward, accompany Oldcastle and his Lady in their flight. His taste in literature reflects his attitudes toward society and the proper relationship of vassal and overlord. When the Bishop of Rochester orders the "heretical" books in Cobham's house to be burned, Harpoole makes a heated defense of his own personal library: "for I have there English bookes, my lord, that ile not part with for your Bishoppricke: Bevis of Hampton, Owleglasse, the Frier and the Boy, Ellenor Rumming, Robin Hood, and other such godly stories" (IV.iii.166–69).

Harpoole and his library are by no means the play's only links with the ballad and romance tradition. The cast of characters includes another Sir John besides the hero: Sir John the parson of Wrotham. This cleric is a hanger-on of precisely those covetous bishops who cause Oldcastle so much trouble. He follows them, however, purely to serve his own ends:

Me thinkes the purse of gold the Bishop gave
Made a good shew; it had a tempting looke.
Beshrew me, but my fingers ends do itch
To be upon those rudduks. Well, 'tis thus:
I am not as the worlde does take me for;
If ever woolfe were cloathed in sheepes coate,
Then I am he,—olde huddle and twang, yfaith,
A priest in shew, but in plain termes a theefe.
Yet, let me tell you too, an honest theefe,
One that will take it where it may be sparde,
And spend it freely in good fellowship.
I have as many shapes as *Proteus* had,
That still, when any villainy is done,
There may be none suspect it was sir John.
Besides, to comfort me,—for whats this life,
Except the crabbed bitternes therof
Be sweetened now and then with lechery?—
I have my Doll, my concubine, as t'were,
To frollicke with, a lusty bounsing gerle.

(I.ii.155–73)

As an example of Shakespearean influence, this speech would be hard to surpass. It is perfectly evident that Sir John of Wrotham represents an attempt on the part of the *Oldcastle* authors to make use of precisely the character their play was designed to discredit and obliterate from the memory of Elizabethan audiences: Sir John Falstaff. Somehow, Drayton, Munday, Hathway, and Wilson were going to contrive to introduce the Gad's Hill robbery into their work too. Doll, the parson's paramour, is sister to Falstaff's Doll Tearsheet and, in the course of the play, will display the same mixture of tenderness and fury as her prototype. The line about Proteus has been stolen from one of the speeches of the future Richard III, in *3 Henry VI* (III.iii.192). Otherwise, the speech appears on the surface to be all fake Falstaff. Yet something about the tone is alien. Falstaff, after all, was scarcely "an honest theefe," concerned to "take it where it may be sparde." A purse was a purse for him, whether it belonged to a wealthy traveler or was to be extracted from poor Mistress Quickly at the cost of all her plate. It is in the outlaw ballads of the late Middle Ages, particularly those centered upon Robin Hood, that the source of this Sir John's attitude may be found. What the *Oldcastle* authors have done is to reach back through Falstaff to resurrect the far older figure of Friar Tuck.

When Shakespeare's Henry V adopted disguise, the night before Agincourt, he found himself confronting men who inquired into the nature of the king's responsibility with uncomfortable particularity. The *Oldcastle* Henry V also resorts to disguise, perhaps in imitation of Shakespeare's play. At the end of act III, the king sets off to Westminster alone and incognito to gather news about the rebellion. On Blackheath he encounters Sir John disguised in green, the color traditionally worn by the followers of Robin Hood. Courteously and wittily the thief relieves his unknown sovereign of a purse containing one hundred pounds in gold. This Henry V, unlike his Shakespearean counterpart, evinces no hesitation in speaking about his disreputable past and old associates:

> Wel, if thou wilt needs have it, there 'tis: just
> the proverb, one thief robs another. Where the
> divil are all my old theeves, that were wont to
> keepe this walke? Falstaffe, the villaine, is
> so fat, he cannot get on's horse, but me thinkes
> Poines and Peto should be stirring here aboute.
>
> (III.iv.59–65)

Sir John, informed that his victim is a gentleman of the King's chamber, professes himself doubly pleased: this traveler can spare his money without hardship and may also be useful in future to "get a poor thiefe his pardon" (III.iv.82). With this latter contingency in mind, the concealed parson breaks a golden angel between them so that they may know each other again. Sir John swears that this token, when produced, will forestall any second robbery. Henry, in return, is to remember his promise of a pardon. In high good spirits, and without the least animosity on either side, the two men shake hands and separate.

Henry, now quite penniless, but delighted by this irregular encounter, proceeds on his way and joins his army in a field near London after dark. His lords greet their king ceremoniously, but find him strangely reluctant to abandon his disguise. "Peace, no more of that," he tells Suffolk, who has addressed him formally as "your Highnesse":

> The King's asleepe; wake not his majestie
> With termes nor titles; hee's at rest in bed.
> Kings do not use to watch themselves; they sleepe,
> And let rebellion and conspiracie
> Revel and havocke in the common wealth. . . .
> . . . this long cold winter's night

How can we spend? King Harry is a sleepe
And al his Lords, these garments tel us so;
Al friends at footebal, fellowes al in field,
Harry, and Dicke, and George. Bring us a drumme;
Give us square dice, weele keepe this court of guard
For al good fellowes companies that come.
(IV.i.6–10, 29–35)

Predictably, Sir John is the first good fellow to wander in. In the gaming that ensues, the disguised king wins back his hundred pounds. When the parson produces his half of the broken coin as a final stake, Henry matches it, and challenges the thief to a combat. The two take up their positions and are about to engage when a horrified noble intervenes and reveals the identity of the king. Without this interruption, the episode would fairly clearly have terminated in the manner sanctioned by the Robin Hood ballads and actually demonstrated in Peele's *Edward I*: with a victory for the king that vindicated his strength and manly prowess.

In *Sir John Oldcastle*, Henry amuses himself for a few moments by adopting a pose of mock severity toward this Friar Tuck. Reminded, however, by the culprit that "the best may goe astray, and if the world say true, your selfe (my liege) have bin a thiefe" (IV.i.182–84), the king freely admits the fact and contents himself with urging upon the parson a repentance and reclamation like his own. He makes him a free present of the stolen gold, a gift which Sir John receives with an unfeigned gratitude and delight that is worlds away from Williams's taciturn acceptance of the glove filled with crowns in Shakespeare's play: "*Vivat Rex & currat lex!* My liege, if ye have cause of battell, ye shal see sir John of Wrootham bestirre himself in your quarrel" (IV.i.197–99). One may well suspect the parson's ability to forswear cards and wine and become an honest man—indeed, on his next appearance, in act V, he is confessing to Doll that drink, dice, and the devil have consumed the hundred pounds and preparing to recoup his fortunes by way of another robbery—but not the sincerity of his admiration for King Henry as a man.

Consistently, in borrowing from Shakespeare, the *Oldcastle* authors turned their material back in the direction of balladry and romance. That doctrine of the king's two bodies which underlies all of Shakespeare's histories from *Richard II* to *Henry V* is nowhere visible in their play, any more than it is in *George a Greene, James IV,* or the old *Famous Victories of Henry V*. The *Oldcastle* Henry shifts from the first person singular to the plural form much as he might put on a furred cloak for a state occasion: to mark the momentary appropriateness of formality. This king is first and foremost a man, an understanding good companion, happy to try conclusions with a thief, prevented only by lack of time and the necessary affairs of state from engaging more often in the kind of light-hearted, picaresque adventure he so clearly loves. Not even his confrontation with the traitors Cambridge, Scroop, and Grey in act V can shake his confidence in the possibility of personal relations. The whole idea of kingship in this play is uncomplicated, stripped of sacramental overtones, and essentially gay. It is also deliberately unreal, a fiction deriving from a distant and half-legendary past. *Henry V* may seem, by comparison with Shakespeare's other histories, to be optimistic and celebratory, a simplified and epic account of certain events in the Hundred Years' War. To set it for an instant beside *Sir John Oldcastle* is to realize, not only that Shakespeare was an incomparably finer dramatist than his four rivals put together, but that his conception of history, even when he was chronicling one of England's moments of glory, was fundamentally tragic.

In the absence of any formal dramatic theory which could be said to connect with the productions of the public stage, Elizabethan drama seems to have developed to a large extent through a curious kind of dialogue among specific plays. The world of the London playhouses was small and intimate: everyone, as it seemed, knew everyone else. Kyd once shared a room with Marlowe, and lived to regret it; Ben Jonson loved Shakespeare but prided himself on being able to beat Marston and take his pistol from him; Shakespeare suffered from the animosity of Greene and was defended by Chettle; the so-called War of the Theatres sent a number of poets into battle with each other for reasons that must have been aesthetic and personal in about equal measure. The true history of the hostilities and allegiances, the jealousies and discipleships among the dramatists writing between 1587 and 1600 can never be recovered now. Yet the plays that have survived from this period are in a sense projections and records of these long vanished relationships and artistic controversies. Because the history play was a relatively new genre, without the classical sanction possessed by comedy and tragedy, and also because its brief flowering was effectively bounded by the reign of Elizabeth, it can provide a particularly rewarding study of the way writers tended to articulate their own dramatic ideas by reference to pre-existing plays. No Puttenham or Abraham Fraunce, no Sidney or Ben Jonson ever troubled to distinguish between the comical and the tragical history as dramatic forms. It is only from the plays themselves that these categories emerge as something more real and consequential than the private lunacy of a Polonius, or the rodomontade of Elizabethan printers concerned to imp out a title-page with words.

The roots of the tragical history lie, fairly obviously, in those Tudor entertainments which A.P. Rossiter called "the interludes of church and state."[17] The consequential dialogue between plays begins, however, in 1587 when Marlowe used the memory of Preston's *Cambises* (1561) and plays like it to launch his own counterstatement in the form of *Tamburlaine the Great*. Plays like the anonymous *Locrine* (1591) or *Selimus* (1592) reveal much about the impact of Marlowe upon his contemporaries: the need to assimilate and learn from *Tamburlaine* but also to domesticate and render it harmless. In *Edward II* (1592), on the other hand, Marlowe himself seems to have felt impelled to imitate Shakespeare's new style of history play, much in the way that Raphael, painting in the Vatican Stanza della Segnatura, suddenly was led to create figures patently Michaelangelesque after he had been shown the unfinished Sistine ceiling. Because Vasari thought such things important, the details of how and when Raphael managed to see the tormented grandeurs of the Sistine Chapel are known, even as the long hours Michaelangelo himself had spent absorbing the figure style of Masaccio in the Brancacci Chapel are known, even as the long hours Michaelangelo himself out the testimony of Vasari, there would only be certain stylistic features from which to construct a hypothesis that Raphael's experience of the Sistine ceiling was so unexpectedly intense that for a time it altered the character of his own work, or that Michaelangelo learned from Masaccio. The problem of identifying reaction and specific indebtedness would, in fact, strongly resemble the one which confronts the Elizabethan scholar trying to make sense of the development of dramatic forms during the crucial years 1587–1600.

As it was defined by Shakespeare, the tragical history became a serious, and politically a somewhat incendiary, examination into the nature of kingship. At the heart of the form lay the Tudor doctrine of the king's two bodies, which, in the fullness of time, was to provide the Puritans with justification for the execution of Charles I. Shakespeare himself, absorbed by the difficulties of royal incarnation, never wrote a comical history, unlike Peele, Greene, Heywood, Dekker, and a host of other contemporary dramatists. Yet he must have been aware of it as an alternative form, stemming originally from ballads and romances, made dramatic at least as early as 1560, and still wistfully alive in his own time. Certainly he introduced its most characteristic motif, that of the king disguised, into *Henry V* because he expected to gain, by his atypical handling of it, a calculated and powerful emotional effect. For Shakespeare, *Henry V* seems to have marked the end of his personal interest in the tragical history. He had virtually exhausted the form, at least in its English version, and not only (as it turned out) for himself. When the four *Oldcastle* authors accepted the doubtful task of competing with Shakespeare's Henry IV and V plays, it cannot have been only the religious difficulties posed by their subject matter which led them to turn tragical history so completely into comical. *Sir John Oldcastle* is a tribute to Shakespeare not only because it is haunted everywhere by characters, episodes, and turns of phrase taken from his own cycle, but also because its entire style and anachronistic ethos as a play stand as silent witness to the fact that in the English tragical history, the more consequential form Shakespeare had made peculiarly his own, little or nothing now remained for anyone else to do.

Shakespeare's Use of Oaths

Frances Shirley

Hotspur, through several scenes in *Henry IV, Part One*, shifts from a rather bantering comment on swearing to what seems an overly serious regard for an oath. In the process he not only reveals things about himself and the other rebels, but he also demonstrates an additional facet of Shakespeare's skill in the details of character-building and play construction. If this were an isolated instance, it would be worth only a footnote. But there are hundreds of examples of the careful use of oaths or the reactions to them, in situations ranging from the satiric to the deadly serious. The history plays provide a rich sampling of this variety when, for example, a comment on oaths and a single exclamation tell much about a hired murderer, a contrast in the use of certain phrases emphasizes the contrast between groups of characters, and a play-long series of broken vows punctuates the self-aggrandizing shifts of the politically ambitious at the expense of a suffering England. The histories also show Shakespeare increasingly relying on his audience's knowledge of the weight of certain oaths, the current fashions in swearing, and even the historical traditions attached to some phrases. That he was often far more subtle and detailed than his sources becomes obvious as one glances back at *The Famous Victories*, with Prince Hal's reformation, or Holinshed's *Chronicles*, which lacks the Temple Garden scene and Richard Plantagenet's appropriate vow by the symbolic white rose.[1]

One of the difficulties in working with the oaths, of course, is grasping the Elizabethan attitude toward particular words. Even though there would be changes over a decade, and certainly a variety of reactions within a given audience, there was still some consensus. Today, for instance, "zounds" seems quaint, and both the *Random House* and *Webster Collegiate* dictionaries call it "mild." A minced version of the word, "sounes," used exclusively by Jack Cade in *The Contention*, is almost meaningless to us. But there was no doubt in Elizabethan minds that a person was swearing "by God's wounds," and the word, along with similar elisions and even an occasional "in

118

faith," disappeared from many passages in the First Folio that were otherwise identical with the quarto versions. Obviously either Heminge and Condell, or others along the way, had deferred to the Act of May 1606, "for preventing and avoiding of the great abuse of the Holy Name of God in Stage Playes . . . and such like."[2] They may have been sporadically sensitive to the climate of opinion that produced a wider-ranging anti-obscenity statute in 1623.[3]

Guidelines to the acceptability of certain words are provided by this sort of change, not only in Shakespeare's work, where it is often carelessly made, but also in plays by his contemporaries, especially Jonson, who carefully chose substitute phrases. So, too, sermons, court records, numerous tracts on conduct, and even the rare recorded difference of opinion between author and censor reveal some Tudor and Stuart connotations.[4]

The moralists who inveigh against swearing in pamphlet, poem, and pulpit not only list dangerous words but also give us glimpses of the philosophy that would lead a Master of the Revels such as Sir George Buc to expunge an innocent-sounding "By this hand" from *The Second Maiden's Tragedy*.[5] There seems to have been an increasing tendency to explain, as the puritanical forces, emphasizing the aspects of spiritual sin, strove to convince people that "customary swearing" must be made a statutory offense.

Stephen Hawes, early in the sixteenth century, had Christ complain of physical pain if parts of His body were sworn by, and asks kings to punish those who use "cruell othes without repentaunce."[6] The tradition was carefully passed on that Henry VI "did not swear in common conversation; but reproved his ministers and officers of state when he heard them swearing."[7] Later, Stubbes, Gosson, and Joannes Ferrarius carried on the attacks against those who offend when

> in euery light talke upon eurie smal occasion, [they] do sweare continually not only by heauen, but also by God him selfe, and the verie blessed woūdes of our sauiour Christ, beside those that they use, by the elementes, by euery creature, by the most holy Sainctes: hereunto do they ioyne filthie talke, and gyue them selues to the deuill. . . . Which detestable blasphemie, although moste men do impute to those Ruffians and vnshamefast Villaines, which folowe the campes, as a speciall fruite of warre, yet it is certaine that childrē which can scarcelie speake do heare such othes of their mothers, nurses, and parentes, and so learne that while they be yonge.[8]

Had he lived a bit later, Ferrarius could have cited Falstaff's young page, seriously blurting out a mild "marry," but hearing rougher talk all around him (*2 Henry IV*, II.ii.96).

The third commandment was the starting point for many of the disquisitions, and Robert Boyle's mid-seventeenth-century logic was widely shared: because this law preceded injunctions against adultery, theft, and killing, and carried with it a promise of punishment, it was more important than the others.[9] Gervaise Babington pointed out two objections to even seemingly innocent oaths such as Plantagenet's "by this maiden blossom," which certainly looks weaker than the more commonplace phrases used by his companions. First, in the very act of swearing, people make "the thing [they] sweare by . . . greatest of all other."[10] The rose, like the ale Doll Tearsheet will call to witness, is made an object of idolatry. And (perhaps conversely, since the first implied at least unconscious religiosity) by using "Mary" or "mass, faith, and truth" or "any thing that is not God, [they] doo flatlie forsake the true God himselfe."[11]

This was surely an overly strict interpretation in the minds of many, but a generation or so later, under the 1623 law, it would have explained the conviction of William Harding of Chittlehampton and Thomas Buttand for "upon my life" and "on my troth."[12] With equal seriousness, officials called Ben Jonson from a sickbed to answer for some words that the players then admitted they had slipped into *The Magnetic Lady*.[13] At the end of Queen Elizabeth's reign, various unsuccessful attempts to pass laws against swearing would have kept the problem very much in people's minds and made them as sensitive to oaths as today's audience is to sexual aberration.

Hotspur himself casts aspersions on the "swearing" of moralistic tradesmen. He has been arguing rather explosively with the other rebels, but his confidence in their strength is as yet unshaken. There is still time for singing, and after Lady Mortimer performs in Welsh, Hotspur turns to his wife: "Come, Kate, I'll have your song too." Her response, "Not mine, in good sooth," precipitates one of his characteristic expostulations, more tangential than some of his earlier outbursts, as he talks not of her refusal, but of the way she has underlined it:

> Not yours, in good sooth? Heart! you swear like a comfit-maker's wife. "Not you, in good sooth!" and "as true as I live!" and "as God shall mend me!" and "as sure as day!"
> And givest such sarcenet surety for thy oaths
> As if thou ne'er walk'st further than Finsbury.

Swear me, Kate, like a lady as thou art,
A good mouth-filling oath; and leave "in sooth"
And such protest of pepper gingerbread
To velvet guards and Sunday citizens.
            (*1 Henry IV*, III.i.248–59)[14]

Obviously he would approve if Kate followed the well-known example of Queen Elizabeth, who might remind her sister Mary that "a king's word [is] more than another man's oath," but who laced her own informal speech with the strongest language.[15]

One is not surprised at Hotspur's stand. With the exception of Falstaff, he uses more oaths than any other person in the play, and in the first three acts, rips them off as part of his deeply felt impatience. Of course, this lecture to Kate loses some of its credibility in the Folio. There, "Yes, I will speak of him" has replaced a splenetic "Zounds," and "I protest" is in lieu of "By the lord," and where there is no problem of meter, words have often simply been cut.[16] The eruption issues pointlessly from a nonswearer. But in the quarto, Hotspur is the proper counterpart of a lady with a "mouth-filling oath," and he fits Elyot's dismayed "they . . . say he that sweareth deep, sweareth like a lord."[17] One feels more of Hotspur's youthful inability to contain himself when " 'Sblood" punctuates his attempts to recall the name of Berkeley Castle (I.iii.247), or "Heart!" stands in contrast to the "pepper-gingerbread" of a sweetsmaker. The oaths are an essential part of Shakespeare's transformation of Hotspur into a younger man, artistically balanced against the light-hearted Prince of Gadshill and the tavern.

There is a change, however, when more of the weight of rebellion falls on young Percy as word of their progressive weakness and the King's growing strength reaches him. "Zounds" he exclaims for the last time at the news of his father's illness (IV.i.17), then he uses Kate's favorite asseveration as he more calmly declares "in faith, it is not" too great a loss for their side (IV.i.44).

While this change in language and bearing is taking place, Hotspur and the rebels are becoming increasingly preoccupied with the other sort of oath, the solemnly taken vow. Shakespeare had passed a bit less quickly than Holinshed over the original episode in *Richard II*, where Henry Bolingbroke returned from banishment and the nobles pledged allegiance. A hand was shaken, some vows were mentioned, and Northumberland summed up their respective positions:

The noble Duke hath sworn his coming is
But for his own; and for the right of that

We all have strongly sworn to give him aid;
And let him never see joy that breaks that oath!
(II.iii.148–51)

Before the battle of Shrewsbury, that vow or series of vows becomes
of prime importance to the rebels defending their reprehensible revolt against a crowned and effective king. They are men raised in a
knightly tradition, who retain respect for an oath, as opposed to a
Richard of Gloucester, with his lack of conscience, or an Edward who
can glibly say "for a kingdom any oath may be broken. / I would
break a thousand oaths to reign one year" (*3 Henry VI*, I.ii.16–17).
Shakespeare early made use of this sort of scruple in that scene where
Richard and Edward convince their hesitating father that his oath to
King Henry VI is void. And over the years he examined the various
arguments men put forth in their psychological need to rationalize
or to determine when an oath may be forgotten.[18] The detailing of
Henry IV's seeming bad faith is a dramatic culmination of this sort
of self-justification.[19]

Hotspur begins by recalling Henry's rise: "My father and my uncle
and myself / Did give him that same royalty he wears" (*1 Henry IV*,
IV.iii.54–55). There had been a chain reaction, for when the Elder
Percy

> heard him swear and vow to God
> He came but to be Duke of Lancaster . . .
> Swore him assistance, and perform'd it too.
> Now when the lords and barons of the realm
> Perceiv'd Northumberland did lean to him,
> The more and less . . .
> proffer'd him their oaths.
> (*1 Henry IV*, IV.iii.60–61, 65–68, 71)

Henry, seeking the crown, "Broke oath on oath" (IV.iii.101). The
episode at Doncaster becomes a leitmotif repeated in three scenes,
with Worcester reminding Henry of the limits of the rebels' fealty,
saying that the King has occasioned the revolt

> By unkind usage, dangerous countenance,
> And violation of all faith and troth
> Sworn to us in your younger enterprise.
> (*1 Henry IV*, V.i.69–71)

Shakespeare neatly balances our sympathy with Hal's party against
our acceptance of the rebels' belief that they are men of honor who

would be justifiably angered by Worcester's emphasis that Henry is "now forswearing that he is forsworn" (*1 Henry IV*, V.ii.39).

This episode merits recounting at length because it illustrates the more serious aspect of the oath that pervaded *Henry VI, Part One*, was a major concern of both *Henry VI* and *Richard II*, and reached a peak in thematic use in *King John*. The emphasis is to be expected in the history plays, concerned as they are with loyalty and revolt in high places. Furthermore, Shakespeare's careful shift from exclamatory oaths parallels much Elizabethan thinking. The Queen's own practice notwithstanding, there was a real fear on the civil level that casual swearing, as done by Falstaff and the early Hotspur, led to a disregard of serious oaths, which could in turn lead to a judicial crisis.

Ferrarius and Alexander Nowell refer repeatedly to men whose word cannot be trusted, yet who take oaths blandly and expect to be believed.[20] Falstaff certainly would be an example as he talks of "a lie with a slight oath" (*2 Henry IV*, V.i.91) or as he plans the perversion of oaths after the Gadshill robbery. Pistol and Bardolph reveal that he had hacked his sword with his dagger, "and said he would swear truth out of England but he would make you believe it was done in fight." Bardolph adds that they were persuaded "to tickle our noses with speargrass to make them bleed, and then to beslubber our garments with it and swear it was the blood of true men" (*1 Henry IV*, II.iv.336–43). This perjury is part of Falstaff's character. A habitual liar who wants people to accept his statements, he automatically reinforces even the simplest utterance with an oath. He thinks nothing of breaking his word and imputes the same standards to others, defensively asserting that they dissemble. With the more honorable characters, however, it should be a different matter; and Shakespeare seems consciously to have turned from expletives later in the play, when they would have suggested rash swearing and undercut the references to serious vows.

Structurally, this shift enhances the parallel between Prince Hal and Hotspur as Shakespeare moves them toward the climactic battle. In many often-cited ways, such as King Henry's first comparison of the two, the change in Hotspur's age, and Hal's offer of single combat, Shakespeare has primed his audience for the final meeting. Hal's oaths also complement the shift in tone. Earlier he had sworn a bit, though never as strongly as Hotspur—a difference which adds to the feeling that he has more self-control than is expected. In act III, scene ii, however, he promises his father, "in the name of God," that he will be a better son, adding, "I will die a hundred thousand deaths

/ Ere break the smallest parcel of this vow" (*1 Henry IV*, III.ii.153, 158–59). There is an increasing sense of nobility, real or ostensible, with Hal fulfilling a princely vow and Hotspur battening on the insult of Henry's perjury.

Falstaff and his companions are, of course, unaffected by this change except that their standards are thrown into sharper relief, crystallized in Falstaff's rejection of honor. Again one feels a sense of artistic culmination in the Henry IV plays. A decade before, Shakespeare had noted the distinction in profanity that should separate rulers of state from the coarser elements of society, and he usually had only serious oaths uttered in the presence of kings. The Earl of Salisbury complained,

> Oft have I seen the haughty Cardinal
> More like a soldier than a man o' th' church,
> As stout and proud as he were lord of all,
> Swear like a ruffian and demean himself
> Unlike the ruler of a commonweal.
> (*2 Henry VI*, I.i.185–89)

Although there was no originality of thought here, since the soldier and ruffian were standards of vulgarity for almost every writer on conduct, the play does show Shakespeare beginning to broaden the cast of characters in his histories as he includes the fraudulent Simpcoxes, the perjuring armorer, and Jack Cade with his followers. *The First Part of the Contention*, for all its unreliability, gives a hint that the distinction in oaths may originally have been stronger than it is in the censored Folio. And the authoritative quartos for the mature histories preserve the subtle distinctions Shakespeare intended as he balanced tavern and court elements and placed Hal in the middle, understanding the low-life attitude toward oaths but not really partaking of it.

The Prince's early promise to reform has been regarded by some as a mechanical insertion to reassure the audience when Hal is genuinely enjoying the company of the rogues. More perceptive critics, however, have pointed out that he robs only the robbers and is in certain other ways distanced from them. If one glances back at *The Famous Victories*, one immediately sees Shakespeare making one area of careful distinction. In the older play, Hal's swearing is worse than Falstaff's—a steady stream of "Zounds," "Gogs wounds," and "blood" —before he becomes king. Then there is a complete reform that lasts until he utters a few mild asseverations while courting Kate. In Shakespeare, however, the shift is more believable. In *Part One*, Hal's strongest phrases, seldom used, are "By'r lady" (II.iv.329), said ironically and of diminishing importance in Protestant England, and "by the Lord" (II.iv.14), which was sometimes censored but seems not to have been as bad as those oaths reminiscent of Christ's physical agony.

Falstaff, however, does not grasp this distinction. In the tavern play scene, as he stands for the Prince while Hal plays the King, Hal's "The complaints I hear of thee are grievous" elicits an automatic " 'Sblood, my lord, they are false!" Hal replies in a moralistic vein that not only fits Henry IV, but may also point ahead: "Swearest thou, ungracious boy? Henceforth ne'er look on me" (*1 Henry IV*, II.iv. 486–91). Wright was partially correct when he commented that the Folio change to "y'faith" makes the rebuke pointless,[21] yet one must also compare each man's frequency of swearing, overall attitude, and actual words left by the censors.

Number and manner of use are even more telling factors in *Part Two*, where Hal makes another of his mid-play shifts to serious vows, and Falstaff, who may have dropped "Zounds" and " 'Sblood" in favor of "marry" and "by the Lord," still swears enough to impress an audience of 1600. Although Boyle and countless others argued that even one lapse endangered the soul,[22] Falstaff and Shallow's repeated utterances give an impression of casualness lacking in the Prince. Falstaff says Hal likes Poins partly because he "swears with a good grace" (*2 Henry IV*, II.iv.269–70), but in fact both young men only use their infrequent "gallant's oaths" early in the play.[23]

The distinctions in vocabulary come with Justice Shallow and the tavern frequenters. In a sweeping generalization that takes in even *The Merry Wives of Windsor*, Sharman has suggested differences that would not be apparent to spectators at a single play but do point a broader trend: "The asseverations employed by the Shallows and Slenders are as limpid and as timorous as those of Falstaff and Bardolph are downright and headstrong."[24] The contrast is not quite so neat in *2 Henry IV* alone, for Falstaff has become somewhat milder. But he never shares Shallow's use of "minced oaths." Like others who attempt to disguise their profanity, Shallow walks the tightrope between propriety and the desire to impress people with his daring and his wild youth. His selection of "by God's liggens" or "by cock and pie" certainly would place him in Crowley's classification of those who

> woulde seme all sweryng to refrayne,
> And ... inuent idle othes, such is theyr idle brayne:—
> By cocke and by pye and by the goose wyng;

By the crosse of the mouse fote, and by Saynte Chyckyn . . .
Not knowing that they call these thynges to wytnes
Of their consciences, in that they affirme or denye,
So boeth sortes commit Moste abhominable blasphemie.[25]

On balance, however, it is usually "in faith" and "marry" that punctuate his attempts to be vigorous and assertive, whether he is greeting the morning, insisting that Falstaff stay, or recalling Jane Nightwork. Falstaff accepts his attempts with some qualification and fortunately is not around to comment on his "by yea and no" (III.ii.10), a Puritan-approved phrase that Falstaff himself relegates to a rather elaborate letter.

In act II there is ample opportunity to see impressions of characters reinforced by profanity as one compares Doll Tearsheet and Mistress Quickly. Despite roughness and excitability, the Hostess has a genuine tenderness and simplicity that are shown in her enjoyment of the tavern play in *Part One*, or her narration of Falstaff's death in *Henry V*, and she possesses a certain restraint. At times, however, Falstaff tries her patience, and she finally calls in the officers and underlines her grievances with "in good faith." As she recounts her financial straits, she swears mildly "By this heav'nly ground I tread on, I must be fain to pawn both my plate and the tapestry of my dining chambers" (*2 Henry IV*, II.i.16, 152–54). Even in *Part One*, Falstaff had to accuse her before she was moved to a single "God's light!" (III.iii.71).

Doll Tearsheet, younger, fiercer, and a consummate sinner, matches the men in casualness of outburst. Her "i'faith" and "by my troth" are used in more tender moments with Falstaff. When Pistol makes advances, she unleashes a stream of comments, threatens "By this wine, I'll thrust my knife in your mouldy chaps," and exclaims "God's light," he will ruin the name of captain. The oaths are interwoven with other unlovely language. And all this after she has called him "the foul-mouth'dst rogue in England"! (II.iv.77 ff.) It would come as no surprise to the early audience that she seems more guilty than Mistress Quickly when arrests are made.

Henry IV complains repeatedly of the anticipated ascendancy of these ruffians who "swear, drink, dance, / . . . and commit / The oldest sins in the newest kind of ways" (IV.v.125–27). Numerous contemporary writers had described a similar sort, the "filthie talker of ribaldrie, a common swearer and blasphemer of God's name."[26] Even before 1623, court records refer increasingly to men like John Lyming, with their "swearing, swaggering, and blasphemy of the name of God."[27] Ferrarius regards it as a habit, more unconsciously done than digging roots in a garden.[28] Gadshill and the Carriers would immediately be recognized as no Puritans, although Gadshill's "zounds" seems merely exclamatory, while the Carriers are also emphasizing their dismay at conditions in the inn.

Despite the numbers of potential swearers, however, Shakespeare is careful to let Falstaff stand above the others. One wonders whether William Richardson was using the Folio, or whether, like the Reverend Bowdler, he was missing the import of some words when he wrote, "We have little or no swearing, and less obscenity than we might have expected."[29] For Falstaff is not only profane in himself but the cause of profanity in others. He exasperates the Hostess. He draws out Bardolph's strongest oath in three plays—" 'Sblood, I would my face were in your belly!"—by joshing "If thou wert any way given to virtue, I would swear by thy face; my oath should be 'By this fire, that's God's angel' " (*1 Henry IV*, III.iii.56, 37–40).

Sir John would be quick to remind us, even in *The Merry Wives*, that he is no mere tavern ruffian, despite his habits. As one glances at other characters, and at plays by Shakespeare's contemporaries, one realizes how completely he combines the profane aspects of rogue, gentleman, and soldier. Young gentlemen, as we saw, were notorious. Viola, in Dekker's *Honest Whore*, tells Fustigo to "Swear as if you come but new from knighting," and he counters, "Nay, I'll swear after four hundred a year."[30] Stephen, in Jonson's *Every Man in His Humour*, Sir Andrew Aguecheek in *Twelfth Night*, and even Slender in *Merry Wives* are satiric examples of the ineffectual gentleman trying to be stylish by spicing his vocabulary. Falstaff obviously has more native ability and, as his comments about Bardolph's face suggest, more imagination. He describes his own youth in exaggerated terms, commenting ironically that he "was as virtuously given as a gentleman need to be ... swore little, dic'd not above seven times a week" (*1 Henry IV*, III.iii.16–19).

Stubbes spoke of the "fashion for gallants, not only to swear generally, all round, but for each to have oaths special to himself."[31] A glance at the lines of Falstaff or Shallow, who think of themselves as erstwhile gallants, or at the young men in the comedies, reveals that Shakespeare does not generally follow fashion and attach a particular oath to one person. There are exceptions based on historical precedent, as with Richard III's "by Saint Paul," or for some national peculiarity of pronunciation, as with Dr. Caius' repeated "by gar" or MacMorris's various uses of "Crish." Frequently, however, Shakespeare points ahead to the appropriate oaths that Jonson would turn to so often after 1606. In a serious scene, Duke Humphrey of Gloucester had declared "Now, by God's Mother" to a priest, who might be more impressed by the phrase than a Protestant, and whose presence might logically have suggested the choice of oath (2 *Henry VI*, II.i.51). Here, as in the Temple Garden, the words grow organically out of the situation.

In a less serious scene, Falstaff, perhaps referring to Doll, greets Hal, "by this light flesh and corrupt blood, thou art welcome" (2 *Henry IV*, II.iv.320-21). Earlier he declared he killed "Seven, by these hilts" at Gadshill (1 *Henry IV*, II.iv.229). A man who emphasizes his title, he will even use "As I am a true knight," a phrase both he and his hearers must regard as ironically akin to the perjury-proof oaths mentioned by Touchstone (*As You Like It*, I.ii). Others make occasional use of "by this hand," but not so often as one might expect from soldiers taking up their weapons; and Douglas, in his frustration, exclaims "Now, by my sword, I will kill all his coats" (1 *Henry IV*, V.iii.26).

Falstaff utters neither phrase, although the third part of his profane heritage is that of the swearing soldier, especially the *miles gloriosus* who often relied on words to cover a lack of prowess. He says little when actually fighting at Shrewsbury; however, "before God" and "zounds" underline his boasts to Hal. But Sir Toby Belch explains the coward's strategy as he coaches the inept Sir Andrew in duelling techniques:

> as thou draw'st, swear horrible; for it comes to pass oft that a terrible oath, with a swaggering accent sharply twang'd off, gives manhood more approbation than ever proof itself would have earn'd him. (*Twelfth Night*, III.iv.195-200)

Here again, Shakespeare is selective. In the history plays, filled with soldiers, he is careful not to have too many of the blusterers and not to let those that do appear spout off too often He sometimes prefers to let a perceptive Gower describe talkative men who "con perfectly in the phrase of war, which they trick up with new-tuned oaths" (*Henry V*, III.vi.78-80).

Gower is correcting Fluellen's estimate of Bardolph, who also deceives us in a different way, especially on stage. At times we are sure that we have heard more oaths than he and Pistol have actually sworn. Their appearances and the comments of others help create a picture corresponding to Ascham's description of "Smithfield Ruffians," who look fierce, with "an ouer-staring frounced hed, as though out of euerie heeres toppe, should suddenlie start out a good big othe, when nede requireth."[32] In *Henry V*, they pale before Fluellen, a better soldier who shares some of Hotspur's explosiveness. But all elements of characterization work together, and we do find them swearing "when nede requireth."

Their use of oaths bolsters the contrasts Shakespeare again develops between the honorable world, now represented by Henry V, and the raffish elements who get swept into the French wars, but who lack the honest patriotism of Bates or Williams. Henry is leading his forces into Church-sanctioned battle. There is admittedly a certain lightness when he characterizes himself to Kate as one who has "no cunning in protestation; only downright oaths, which I never use till urg'd, nor never break for urging" (*Henry V*, V.ii.150–53). Yet he certainly expects people to believe him when he simply swears he will not be ransomed. The night before Agincourt, Williams's quarrel with the disguised King springs from his doubting the King's word. (After the battle, Henry must make sure no honorable men are hurt because of the vows and gloves.) Henry's determination had been underlined earlier by the simple "as I am a soldier" when, after some inconclusive skirmishing, he promised to show Harfleur no mercy (III.iii.5).

Gone is that measure of internal tension that was evident when Henry was keeping up a pose of profligacy, occasionally swearing casually lest he be called a hypocrite, yet grieving over his father's sickness (*2 Henry IV*, II.ii). But obvious contrast is sharpened, in part, by separating Henry and Bardolph, yet having them utter the same oaths. The early scene where Bardolph quiets the quarreling Nym and Pistol becomes a foil for the later English heroism and singleness of purpose. Pistol, who deals in appearances and will swear that cudgel marks are battle scars, welcomes a way out. He siezes on Bardolph's "as I am a soldier" as "an oath of mickle might," and backs away. To make sure we grasp the sardonic fun, Shakespeare repeats the episode thirty lines later, when Bardolph vows "By this sword, he that makes the first thrust, I'll kill him! By this sword I will." Again Pistol retreats, for "Sword is an oath, and oaths must have their course" (*Henry V*, II.i.69–107).

Bardolph fits Brathwait's description of the stock braggart: "They're blustering boys . . . / They have a mint of oaths, yet when they swear / Of death and murder, there's small danger there."[33] Surely Pistol knows he is relatively safe, though he is probably more impressed than a Gower would be. His eager belief, when it suits his purpose, contrasts with his later "oaths are straws, men's faiths are wafer-cakes" (II.iii.53). Eventually he will run into more problems when Fluellen, to whom the leek is a symbol, forces him to eat but rejects his appropriate "By this leek, I will most horribly revenge!" not because Pistol is no match for Fluellen, but because "There is not enough leek to swear by" (*Henry V*, V.i.49–53).

Shakespeare not only counts on his audience's reactions, but also makes frequent and varied use of the way swearers react to the oaths of others. The kings concentrate their attention naturally on the formal vows; Hotspur looks both ways; Pistol, Fluellen, and Falstaff comment on the oaths others use by habit. Sir John naturally disapproves of any person with puritanical values and the caution to refuse him credit. Dommelton, the tailor, was probably one of those "Sunday Citizens," and he is characterized as "a rascally yea-forsooth knave" (*2 Henry IV*, I.ii.41). Richard III would be equally scornful of Dommelton, but he knows how to cater to the citizens of London. He had already revealed part of his nature when he posed as a rational and virtuous man finding loopholes that would free his father from the oath to Henry VI. His posing reaches its height in *Richard III*, and there his reaction to the exclamatory oath is an integral part of his ability to convince people.

Buckingham, himself an actor, helps stage a persuasion scene for the doubting Londoners. He feigns disgust after Richard, holding a Bible and flanked by two bishops, has demurred at the throne. "Come, citizens. Zounds, I'll entreat no more!" Richard, the most profane character in the play, caps his performance with a mild "O, do not swear, my lord of Buckingham." Rather than being an example of extreme hypocrisy that the Folio did well to cut,[34] it is the sort of unexpected and seemingly automatic reaction that might convince a doubting populace, and it shows a depth of acting ability that is missing from the Folio (III.vii.219–20).

The hunchback is using an oath for political ends in a most unusual way here. More often, Shakespeare shows Richard and others in the convenient perjury born of ambition, and he usually includes a commentary on the lack of faith that makes their demise more appropriate. Not, of course, that all perjurers match Richard in villainy. We may have some doubts about the opportunism of Henry IV and his compromised allegiance to Richard II, or the vacillation of an Aumerle, but we are carefully kept aware of their good points and sometimes their own pangs of conscience.

Man's propensity to exchange spiritual safety for temporal gain is more explicitly shown in the earlier histories, although the sheer expanse of the Henry the Sixth plays, and the weakness of the King, lessen the impact there. In *Part One* the honorable Talbot contrasts with the wavering Burgundy, while nobles split into sworn factions that can only hurt their country. In *Part Two* Margaret is accused of having "suborned some to swear / False allegations to o'erthrow" Gloucester (III.i.180–81), and the political maneuvering gains momentum. Henry is moved to ask in helpless anger, "Hast thou not sworn allegiance unto me? / . . . Canst thou dispense with heaven for such an oath?" (V.i.179, 181). In *Part Three*, as power devolves to Edward and Richard of Gloucester, one becomes increasingly aware of opportunism and the chance for reward replacing steadfastness. Henry, honorable if inept, discovers more about the fleeting oaths of men when he encounters Sinklo and Humfrey. Now loyal to Edward, they answer his "And you were sworn true subjects unto me; / And tell me then, have you not broke your oaths?" with a simple "No; / For we were subjects but while you were king" (III.i.78–81). If pressed to explain, they might say the office was more important than the man, and leave the question of who had the right to depose a king to subtler minds.

The disastrous results of the interrelationship of ambition and perjury are presented far more clearly in *King John*, where oaths and broken faiths stand out in sharp relief. The Bastard Faulconbridge, a bit like Queen Elizabeth in his coupling of exclamatory oaths with a native sense of honor, discovers to his disgust that "commodity" is a "daily break-vow." He watches amazed as England and France "break faith upon commodity" and negotiate their short-lived treaty (II.i). Thus begins the pattern which dominates the play, of political maneuver followed by oath followed by shift of allegiance, as formal vows are discovered to be no safeguard against treachery.

Constance begins the accusations of perjury as she accepts Salisbury's report of the treaty and unleashes her fury against France and Austria for ceasing to champion her Arthur against King John. The Roman Church, exercising political and spiritual pressure together, works steadfastly for its own ends by convincing King Philip that his allegiance to the Church must take precedence, and "What since thou swor'st is sworn against thyself" (III.i.268). Philip's genuine concern at playing "fast and loose with faith" soon wilts before Pandulph's involved reasoning stiffened with the threat of a curse.[35]

The dramatic culmination of this wavering pattern, with its moral lesson driven home to the English audience, begins as John reassures himself at a second coronation. Pembroke tells him "the faiths of men were never stained with revolt," only moments before they ask for Arthur's release. The juxtaposition of scenes and allegiances here is complicated, for the audience must be kept aware of Hubert's mercy,

John's duplicity, and the mounting suspicion and anger of the nobles. Salisbury may be justified in his vow of revenge, despite sworn assurances that nobody killed Arthur, but that vow will lead him to the French side, always a bad thing in the history plays. The depth to which England has sunk, when the populace is "Swearing allegiance . . . to foreign royalty," leads John to reaffirm his "oath of service to the Pope."

The Dauphin meanwhile has drawn new courage from Salisbury and Pembroke, basically men of conscience who worry that they must turn against England to cure her. *The Troublesome Reign* had shown the even worse French treachery more explicitly by having the nobles "swear upon the altar, and by the holy Army of Saints" to support Lewis; moments later Lewis is revealed at the same altar vowing "by heaven's power" to destroy the English traitors.[36] Shakespeare prefers to let the dying Melun, pricked by conscience, summarize all and send the nobles back "to these bounds we have o'erlooked."

Faulconbridge, horrified at the outcome of such "inglorious league[s]," avers that Heaven is frowning upon the land. His "Zounds! I was never so bethump'd with words" (II.i.466) expresses his dismay at political palaver, and other oaths help emphasize his blunt steadfastness. His expletives are habitual and often come at moments of deep feeling. But in this play the affirming exclamations of Faulconbridge, Hubert, and King John pale in contrast to the dramatic importance of the more solemn vows. As the tides in the Washes destroy armies, so the ebb and flow of sworn allegiances destroy men and countries.

The same principle holds true in *Richard II*. With its all-pervading formality affecting even gardeners trimming apricots, the play not surprisingly has few exclamatory oaths. Angry knights facing each other manage "By all my hopes" and "by the glorious worth of my descent" (I.i.68, 107). When they meet again, it is in the formal setting of the lists. Mowbray and Bolingbroke answer in a formulaic way the formulaic questions put by the Marshall with his "Speak truly on thy knighthood and thine oath." Occasionally "by heaven" or "by my soul" graces the serious words of one of the nobles. But the Folio text, where "heaven" is carefully substituted for "God," need change few oaths to conform to the letter of the 1606 law. The poetic quality that suffuses the rest of the play affects the oaths, too, and they become longer. Richard will use "by my sceptre's awe" (I.i.118) or "by my seat's right royal majesty" (II.i.120) and will command others to "Swear by the duty that you owe to God" (I.iii.180).

In comedies written at about the same time, fun is made of long strings of oaths. There is irony, not laughter, however, when Northumberland lists the things Bolingbroke has called to witness:

> by the honourable tomb . . .
> That stands upon your royal grandsire's bones,
> And by the royalties of both your bloods . . .
> And by the buried hand of warlike Gaunt,
> And by the worth and honour of himself,
> Comprising all that may be sworn or said.
> (III.iii.105–7, 109–11)

In light of what happens in the next hundred lines, we cannot but think that Bolingbroke has protested too much. For the moment, though, the string of phrases seems to impress Richard, who in his self-pity will soon indulge in some lists himself.

This same conformity between a portion of the oaths and the other speeches or artistic principles in a play is obvious in *Richard III*. Perjury and past deeds haunt people. Curses and self-damning oaths seem to be fulfilled. The hypocritical Richard swears to emphasize true statements which he, in fact, does not believe.

In an exceptionally violent play, Clarence, far more than the nobles in the other histories, is violently reminded of his breach of faith. He had rationalized ending his allegiance to Warwick because "To keep that oath were more impiety" than to break it and avoid fighting his brothers (*3 Henry VI*, V.i.90). Captured Prince Edward accused him and received one of his three death wounds "for twitting me with perjury" (V.v.40).

The memory of the scene follows him into *Richard III* where, imprisoned and frightened, he dreams of a hellish afterlife with Warwick demanding " 'What scourge for perjury / Can this dark monarchy afford false Clarence?' " and the wraith of Edward repeating its charge (*Richard III*, I.iv.50 ff.). Even the murderers remind him of God's anger for his killing of the sovereign's son, "Whom thou wast sworn to cherish and defend." Far milder than he had seemed in *3 Henry VI*, he emphasizes his terror with "as I am a Christian faithful man" (I.iv.4). By contrast, Richard spends a haunted night, remembers that he is perjured, and a few lines later exclaims "Zounds" —the worst of oaths from the worst of men (V.iii.197, 209).

Out of the pattern of Margaret's cursing seems to grow a predilection for a kind of self-curse ironically carried out as people break faith and the larger curse is fulfilled. Richard's "so thrive I in my enterprise / . . . As I intend more good to you and yours" (IV.iv.236–37) and Hastings's "So prosper I as I swear perfect love!" (II.i.16) are preludes to eventual destruction. Boyle and others comment on the practice,[37] and Falstaff occasionally uses the same formula, but it seems less meaningful separated from Margaret's imprecations.

Richard himself seems unbothered by conscience or curse until that moment in act V when his control slips, although we have heard that he is a troubled sleeper. Part of our fascinated horror stems from his ability to dissemble. It has been suggested that men swear because they are at a loss for words, but this is certainly not the case with a man who can persuade the mourning Lady Anne of his love. In that scene, his oaths are reserved for threatening the corpse-bearers.

Nor can one say that Richard's oaths always give credence to lies, for he may use them with true statements. As old Margaret lashes out, he seems the soul of compassion: "I cannot blame her. By God's holy Mother, / She hath had too much wrong." This obvious truth is probably calculated to remove doubt from his hypocritical statement of repentance (I.iii.306–7).

Richard meets a temporary match in Queen Elizabeth, however, as he woos her daughter. In a combat of wits, he swears by everything from his anachronistic George to God Himself. Her premise, "If something thou wouldst swear to be believ'd, / Swear then by something thou hast not wrong'd" leads her to reject each oath, cataloguing his evil deeds in the process. Finally, he slips into another of the self-curses, soon to be fulfilled:

> Myself myself confound!
> Heaven and fortune bar me happy hours!
> Day, yield me not thy light, nor, night, thy rest!

There is more, and this turn from the usual pattern of swearing seems to soften Elizabeth's resolution (IV.iv.166–401 *passim*).

Shakespeare matches Richard's oaths to the man. Sometimes they are as unthinking as his rashest actions, more often as considered as his carefully planned moves to the throne. Sir Thomas More seems to have started the tradition that he swore by Saint Paul, and Shakespeare, like Holinshed, followed it.[38] But the careful reservation of "zounds" for Richard, Buckingham, and the Murderers is Shakespeare's own.

It is with the Murderers that we have a last example of the way oaths and conscience can be used to form a distinguishing vignette when a lesser dramatist might have created two mere functionaries. The Second Murderer, more sensitive to good and evil, must be reminded of the reward. For an instant he gathers himself together: "Zounds, he dies! I had forgot the reward." "Where's thy conscience now?" he is asked, and he replies cavalierly, "O, in the Duke of Gloucester's purse." He adds, scoffingly, "I'll not meddle with it; it makes a man a coward . . . a man cannot swear, but it checks him" (I.iv.128–31, 137–39). The Folio's replacement of "Zounds" with "Come" is certainly less effective in showing this man's temporary surface callousness, for when he denigrates conscience he touches on the swearing that has probably just given him a twinge.

The most important use Shakespeare made of the oaths in the history plays is the way he associated them with other aspects of characterization or with thematic patterns. Henry VI is obviously sincere in his humble "by his majesty I swear / Whose far unworthy deputy I am" (*2 Henry VI*, III.ii.285–86). Were Richard III to use the qualifying phrases during his brief reign, we would regard it as hypocritical.

If ignorant of their existence, we would not miss casual oaths omitted from a censored text any more than we would a description of "the morn, in russet mantle clad." Nor would we be aware that the formal oaths had lost some of their strength. But when we compare quartos and Folio, we see immediately the added richness and think how controlled Falstaff or Hotspur must have seemed in theatres where censored texts were used. Had Shakespeare written after 1606, of course, he would have been careful to use only oaths that complied with the law. The collaborative *Henry VIII* is an example of the amazing amount that could get by so long as "Zounds!" or other words incorporating God's name did not attract the censor's attention. But unless the actors slipped in "safe oaths," of which we have no record, the early histories must have seemed rather mild in post-1606 revivals. The audience might have assumed oaths of allegiance and would have had frequent reference to them. But they would have missed the extra spice of vulgarity necessary to Doll Tearsheet. Sins never went singly, and courtesans were supposed to swear.[39]

One is most struck by economy, however, when one compares Shakespeare's plays with those of his contemporaries. Though few Elizabethan dramas match the plethora of oaths uttered in *Gammer Gurton's Needle*, many of them load the speeches of gallants or soldiers with so many expletives that they lose all force. Shakespeare tends to push one of a group of characters to the fore, then give him a few oaths and some commentary in a cluster, or in reaction to the swearing of another, so that dramatic effect is served. Or he heightens the impact of a single example by its placement. Prince Arthur's "By my Christendom" rings out at a moment when the Christianity of others is based purely on commodity.

These things are obvious to us today. We must remember, too, that many of the phrases or attitudes we merely note had much greater force for the Elizabethans. After all, Shakespeare was writing when people were weekly told that perjury was a sin, not merely a civil crime, and a man could end up with a court record for uttering some casual oath over a tankard of ale.

In the Margin

J. C. Trewin

Once, years ago, towards the end of an unimportant production of *Twelfth Night*—if any revival is unimportant: still, this needs no further identification—the Sir Toby, who until then had been a solid fellow, not noticeably consanguineous, entered with a "bloody coxcomb," according to text. Turning off the Duke's question with a blunt, "That's all one; has hurt me, and there's an end," he called to Feste: "Sot, didst see Dick surgeon, sot?" He emphasized the name, so that for almost the first time in many revivals, I was conscious that there was a doctor in the house. Feste responded with mischievous pleasure: "O, he's drunk, Sir Toby, a hour agone; his eyes were set at eight i' th' morning." "Then," insisted Toby, "he's a rogue and a passy-measures-pavin; I hate a drunken rogue." He insisted with so much fervor that I have never met *Twelfth Night* since without imagining this unseen Dick surgeon, occasionally—and in spite of Toby's note on his dignity—a ready drinking companion, never about when needed professionally, but one of the true Illyrians, somebody in the margin of the spacious picture—somebody, too, that Malvolio would have scorned.

We are unlikely to see him on the stage, though nobody has yet charted all the ingenuities of a contemporary director; nowadays anything may happen, and often does. Still, "Dick surgeon" remains one of the Shakespearean outer circle, the strange, rarely considered company that the dramatist created with a cheerful ease when he needed to fill out a passage or to cover a join in the plot. It is dangerous to be told too often of people we do not see (certain late-Victorian-Edwardian dramatists, particularly Henry Arthur Jones, could overdo the trick). But Shakespeare, as any drama critic will witness, can always manage it without worrying us in the theatre.

I am not speaking, of course, of the regiment of innominate Gentlemen who can be found about the place; these, as in *Hamlet, Othello, Cymbeline, All's Well that Ends Well, The Winter's Tale,* usually have lines that it is left to a director to distribute according to the resources of his cast. As speakers the Gentlemen are just in sight, on the edge of the picture. Dick surgeon and his friends are out in the margin. There must have been a real Sir Topas, the curate, whom Feste impersonates above Malvolio's prison. I often wonder, too, about the Duke's young nephew, Titus, who lost a leg in the sea-fight. And did Feste really entertain a "leman" at his house by the church—somewhere near Dick surgeon's, no doubt—or was Sir Andrew merely spluttering drunkenly when he said, "I sent thee six-pence for thy leman: hadst it?"

All of these are marginal matters, but now and again someone from outside is given an entry and remains speechless. Such a man as this is Antenor, the Trojan for whom Cressida is exchanged. There are, indeed, two entries for him, but he does not get in a word, though he finds himself in excellent company. First, at the beginning of what would become the fourth act of *Troilus and Cressida*, we have a Folio direction (and spelling):

Enter at one doore Aeneas with a Torch, at another Paris, Diephoe-bus, Anthenor, Diomed the Grecian, with Torches.

And again, later on, at what we gather is before the house of Pandarus (this is the scene with the grand first phrase for Paris, "It is great morning"):

Enter Paris, Troylus, Aeneas, Diephoebus, Anthenor and Dio-medes.

Antenor has been talked about, his name has been bandied round; for a moment he is brought from the margin, but he remains a property. Shakespeare has forgotten him. I do not know whether an unlucky actor ever complained. In any event, was *Troilus* "acted . . . at the Globe," or was it a new play, "never staled with the stage"?

Jane Shore, in *Richard III*, is a property as well, but a more important figure. She is mentioned repeatedly at the beginning of the play where, as Professor Sprague, who has considered her in detail,[1] said, "These references would have carried more meaning [to the Elizabethans] than they do to us, since the story of the adultery of Shore's wife, her pride of place, fall from greatness, and pitiful end, was once a very popular one." It is extremely tempting to bring her, without warrant, from the margin to the picture; and in late years she has been increasingly popular. At Stratford-upon-Avon in 1970 we heard her voice (a naughty interpolation) in the parting from Hastings; but as a rule she remains—as I said once in *Punch*—decorative but dumb. Pauline Wynn played her, as "mistress to the King," in the Olivier *Richard* (John Burrell's production) as the New Theatre in September 1944—she is in the cherished first night programme that described the Earl of Richmond as "afterwards King *Edward VII*"—and Pamela Brown was Jane in the Olivier film in 1955. Peter Bull, in his first brisk volume of autobiography,[2] said of Pamela Brown: "Among her favourite roles, she confesses, are long parts in films which require the minimum of speaking, but which lurk in the background . . . and [let her] look enigmatic for weeks on end." Olivier telephoned her anxiously about Jane Shore: "You see, Pam, the trouble is that there aren't any lines." "No lines?" said Miss Brown. "No, I'm afraid not," said Sir Laurence, abashed. "Snap!" said Miss Brown quietly. And how well she played the silent Jane.

We have entries, Antenor-fashion, but no lines, for Violenta (*All's Well that Ends Well*, III.v), who stands with Mariana (22 lines) as one of the Florentine widow's neighbors and friends and—a familiar exhibit—for Innogen, Leonato's wife, that ghost-character of the Folio's *Much Ado About Nothing*. If she had been allowed to speak, she would surely, as Hero's mother, have had a good deal to say to Claudio and Don Pedro.

Professor Sprague has also discussed the wholly marginal Kate Keepdown, Lucio's mistress in *Measure for Measure*, and the Indian Boy in *A Midsummer Night's Dream*, both of whom in performance are becoming visible.[3] Indeed, they might even preen themselves on having parts, whereas the real people of the margin do not even lurk enigmatically. Who are they? I have not long come from a *Hamlet* in which, I am sorry to report, one of my favorite imaginary personages was not mentioned. I notice a gradual tendency to cut the beginning of the Graveyard scene; even when a Second Gravedigger is present, he may not be sent to Yaughan to fetch a stoup of liquor. Yaughan has always been an off-stage favorite; I dread to guess at the riddles and the small talk he must endure when the First Gravedigger, merry soul, is off-duty. John Dover Wilson, in the New Cambridge edition, has a happy time considering Yaughan's identity; we can suppose that he was "deaf John," the keeper of a tavern near the Globe: both a friendly advertisement and a local topicality. In any event he is much more alive to me than is Lamond, the visiting "gentleman of Normandy," "the brooch, indeed, and gem of all the nation," who, two months earlier—according to the King—had brought to Elsinore so glowing an account of Laertes's prowess with sword and rapier, "for art and exercise in your defence." Lamond is just a useful reference, a property, and so is the "mountebank" of whom

Laertes bought the mortal poison to anoint his sword. But Yaughan, as the late Baliol ("Bay") Holloway said once, and unblushingly, can conquer with stoups.

In *Romeo and Juliet* the most obvious marginal figure is Rosaline ("O, she is rich in beauty; only poor / That, when she dies, with beauty dies her store"). The pale, hard-hearted wench has appeared very seldom indeed, though Irving had her prominently at the Capulet feast and in the program. We have never yet seen Susan Grindstone and Nell (I.v.10) who, presumably, are to come to a servants' party when the feasting is over; the First Serving Man asks a porter to be sure to let them in. Others present on this occasion will be Peter, Anthony, and Potpan; the last two are serving men whose names can slip by us, just as we might not know, without catching the single reference, that the infinitely more important Nurse is called Angelica.

I do not remember seeing on any program the name of Hesperia, "the princess's gentlewoman" (*As You Like It*), though I have seen her brought in at act II, scene ii (for example, in a Bridges Adams production at the Greenhill Street Cinema in Stratford, 1930) while the Second Lord tells Frederick that she

> Confesses that she secretly o'erheard
> Your daughter and her cousin much commend
> The parts and graces of the wrestler
> That did but lately foil the sinewy Charles.
> (II.ii.11–14)

Of all the plays one would expect marginal bounties in such a comedy as this, with the palm tree and the green and gilded snake and the lioness. There are two people (among others) that we do not see: the Old Religious Man and the old "carlot" (peasant) of churlish disposition, who is Corin's master and who shears the "fleeces" the shepherd has to graze. It is his "cote, flock, and bounds of feed" that Celia and Rosalind will buy, thus removing what seems to have been a bargain from young Silvius, too much in love to care for buying anything. It is the cottage, in Celia's direction to Oliver, that some Stratford historians (notably Edgar Fripp) suggest must surely be a direct reference to Anne Hathaway's, or what was originally the double message of Hewlands Farm:

> West of this place, down in the neighbour bottom,
> The rank of osiers, by the murmuring stream,
> Left on your right hand, brings you to the place.
> (IV.iii.79–81)

Nobody at Stratford would give such a direction now; but it is a pleasant thought.

But the chief off-stage figure in *As You Like It* is not the "carlot"; it is the Old Religious Man. Because this must be, in the end, the happiest of comedies, Shakespeare had to do something to dispose of the usurping Duke Frederick, left many scenes earlier in a foul temper. Otherwise, how does the Banished Duke recover lands and title? It is perfectly simple. Frederick and his "might power" have reached only the fringe of Arden when they meet the Old Religious Man, clearly so much of a spellbinder that I regret we never see him in mid-picture. Three lines of a messenger speech by the other Jaques, the second de Boys brother—an example of Shakespeare's carelessness with names—tell us that Frederick,

> meeting with an old religious man,
> After some question with him, was converted
> Both from his enterprise and from the world.
>   (V.iv.166–68)

It is then late in the day, and there is little time for anyone to show special enthusiasm. Few Banished Dukes, in my experience, have ever done more than acknowledge the news with rapid, expansive geniality and then get on with the business. The other Jaques does go off—a reasonable idea—to join the "convertite" from whom much matter may be heard and learned; and Shakespeare leaves us with the tantalizing sense that somewhere in Arden there is another play waiting to be discovered.

No other people from the margin are so wrapped into the plot of a play as Antenor, the Old Religious Man, and the Indian Boy; but we can mark some unexpected accessories. The Clown in *Titus Andronicus*, whom Saturninus dismisses so ruthlessly, is going to "take up a matter of brawl between my uncle and one of the emperial's men." The preceding stage direction is:

Enter a Clown, with a basket and two pigeons in it.

Titus calls: "News, news from heaven!" Peter Brook, in the famous Stratford-upon-Avon production of 1955, let Edward Atienza appear, lowered in a basket, with the line, "My uncle the gibbet-maker and I have been up on the walls." That was collaborating with Shakespeare, for the dramatist has indeed mentioned a gibbet-maker. Consider more straightforward figures. Thus, in *The Two Gentlemen of Verona*, Silvia and Eglamour meet at Friar Patrick's cell, apparently in a Milanese abbey. The Friar himself is absent—a pity. Nor do we discover Friar Laurence (no relation of another reverend father) who, while wandering "in penance . . . through the forest," met Silvia and Eglamour: "Him he knew well; and guess'd that it was she, / But, being mask'd, he was not sure of it."

In *The Taming of the Shrew* Shakespeare indulges himself with a catalogue of Petruchio's country house servants (besides one named Curtis whose part has sometimes been adjusted to a woman). They are Nathaniel, Joseph, Nicholas, Philip, Walter, Sugarsop, Gregory, Peter, Adam, and Rafe. I have known a selection of them on various programs, though none of them has lines except a concerted "Here, here, sir; here, sir." They are then both in the margin and on the fringe; a director can summon as many of them as he likes, though he seldom bothers about "my spaniel Troilus"—I seem to remember Grumio filling the gap with a not very successful bark in the New Theatre *Shrew* of 1937—and "my cousin Ferdinand," whom Petruchio also calls for, never turns up for Kate to kiss and be acquainted with. Another catalogue, which in the text is simply part of a general soliloquy by Pompey, Peter Brook ingeniously chose to illustrate in the Stratford-upon-Avon *Measure for Measure* of 1950. There he brought in from the margin a line of prisoners, Master Rash, Master Caper, young Dizzy, Master Deepvow, Master Copper-spur, Master Starvelackey, young Drop-heir, Master Forthright, Master Shoe-tie, and— at the end of a string of remarkable grotesques—a kind of glazed and shuffling dummy, "wild Half-can that stabb'd Pots." I have not encountered them since; and certainly I have never been introduced to Flavius, Valentinus, Rowland, and Crassus, whom the Duke asks for in act IV, scene v. And what, too, of the mysterious Varrius, who has a couple of entries, here and in act V? He speaks no word, though the Duke addresses him:

> I thank thee, Varrius; thou hast made good haste.
> Come, we will walk. There's other of our friends
> Will greet us here anon, my gentle Varrius.
>
> (IV.v.11–13)

Varrius, presumably an attendant Lord, is not mentioned in "The names of all the Actors" at the end of the First Folio text; but he gets his place, often without explanatory suffix—except now and then "a friend to the Duke"—in the *dramatis personae* of various editions. I try to conjecture what Shakespeare might have intended for him; probably he was the victim of a last-minute cut.

Some others I wonder about: the off-stage player, not very skilled, of the music that Richard II hears in imprisonment at Pomfret

("Ha, ha! keep time: how sour sweet music is, / When time is broke and no proportion kept"); Margery Gobbo, Launcelot's mother, who had, we surmise, some trouble with old Gobbo ("My father did something smack, something grow to, he had a kind of taste"); Isbel, woman to the Countess Rousillon, whom Lavache talks of in *All's Well*; the unfortunate fever-stricken Ragozine (*Measure for Measure* again), "a most notorious pirate" of the same age and coloring—beard and head—as Claudio; old Nedar of Athens, Helena's father (*A Midsummer Night's Dream*); Jane Nightwork ("she lives, Master Shallow"), the bona-roba who had Robin Nightwork by old Night-work before Shallow came to Clement's Inn; and the "host" of Caius Marcius in Corioli. The last of these rises from a little scene that snatches at the imagination and is sometimes passed over too quickly. Though the victor of Corioli refuses princely gifts he craves the freedom of a poor Volscian, now a Roman prisoner, who had befriended him. "O, well begged," Cominius replies:

> Were he the butcher of my son, he should
> Be free as is the wind. Deliver him, Titus.
> *Lartius*: Marcius, his name.

> (I.ix.88–90)

There is a pause. Slowly, Coriolanus answers, "By Jupiter, forgot! I am weary; yea, my memory is tired. Have we no wine here?" The good Volscian's fate we cannot know. The surge of the play hides the brief scene and swells again toward a distant shore. John Clements was most affecting in this moment during the 1948 Old Vic revival at the New Theatre.

What happened, I ask sometimes, to Marcus Luccicos of the pre-posterous name, whom the Doge asks for in that rapidly convened midnight Senate of *Othello*? "He's now in Florence," the Duke is told; and I confess that whenever I am in Florence I think of him, the absent Marcus opening the Doge's letter (sent post-haste) and deciding that, after all, Othello would deal with that matter comfortably and well. Various people have tried to rationalize the name ("Lucchese," for example); but I rather like Professor Sisson's suggestion that Shakespeare simply turned Mark and Luke into some sort of Greek form as Marcus Luccicos, "not without amusement." A last figure I want to bring in from the margin is old Doctor Bellario, of Padua, Portia's cousin, who presumably provides her with the quibble that saves Antonio's life. But I recall a Portia—it was in Henry Baynton's company, touring in the West of England during 1922—who looked up suddenly from the bond in the Trial scene, with a sadly overacted indication that she herself, and just at that moment, had realized the flaw. It was eccentric; but *The Merchant of Venice* has often lent itself to eccentricity.

True marginal figures aside, we have many others we can call peripheral, an army of near-supernumeraries who get into the picture simply because they have stray lines often re-allocated by directors (without anybody worrying) to suit a moment's need. Here are the Lords, Gentlemen (*"Enter a Gentleman"* at the end of *Lear*, with a bloody knife), Senators, Messengers, Soldiers, Citizens, Servants, Watchmen, and Guards who have their work to do round the edges. Some minor named figures can often defy immediate recognition. Who are Gallus, Phrynia, Margarelon, Sir Michael, Urswick, and Friar Thomas? I have seen them all, I am certain—programs beside me say so—but how they were acted at this moment escapes me. Few people bothered, I remember, when in two revivals of *Antony and Cleopatra*, one at the St. James's in 1951 (by Michael Benthall), another at the Old Vic in 1956 (by Robert Helpmann), the directors ran together some of the characters to make composite parts: Philo Canidius, Scarus Dercetas, Alexas Diomedes, Euphronius Lamprius. There I did object because Euphronius, Antony's schoolmaster, is not a figure to be merged with anybody else. He is the man who goes as ambassador to Octavius Caesar after the defeat at Actium, and who is given a first speech rarely treated as it deserves, an example of Shakespeare's generosity to the lesser people:

> Such as I am, I come from Antony:
> I was of late as petty to his ends
> As is the morn-dew on the myrtle-leaf
> To his grand sea.
>
> (III.xii.7–10)

Superb; but why merge Euphronius with the Soothsayer, quite another type?

In the matter of names, Shakespeare was always agreeably maddening. He would grab at them, whether or not he had used them before, and whether or not they were plausible. We revert naturally to the repetition of "Jacques" in a single play; but the Folio can become a vast echo chamber: Escalus, Prince of Verona; Escalus, an ancient lord of Vienna; Escalus, snatched from the air for an officer of the Florentine army in *All's Well*. The relevant phrase here is: "That is Antonio, the Duke's eldest son; That, Escalus." Antonio? Yes; but he is also father to Proteus, a merchant of Venice, the brother of Leonato, a Sea Captain, and the usurping Duke of Milan.

J.C. Trewin

We must make it clear whether we speak of Helena (*A Midsummer Night's Dream*) or Helena (*All's Well*); moreover, there are Helen of Troy and a casual "my woman Helen" who has two lines in Imogen's bedchamber scene. We have Rosalind and Rosaline. We have three Emilias, two Juliets and a Julia, a brace of Sebastians, two Marias, a variety of assorted Katharines (or Katharinas); Ventidius, Cornelius, Angelo, Portia, Mariana, Valentine, Francisco, Balthazar, Demetrius, Gregory, all appear twice, as does Vincentio, though we usually know the Duke of Vienna simply as the Duke.

Apart from the cheerful confusion of Gremio and Grumio in *The Taming of the Shrew*, I am most conscious in *Hamlet* of Shakespeare's waywardness. The King is Claudius, a name used before only as a three-line soldier in *Julius Caesar*, though there had been a Claudio in *Much Ado* (and another would come in *Measure for Measure*). But in *Hamlet*, an attendant, not specified in the *dramatis personae*, runs in suddenly from the margin; letters have come from Hamlet to the King, and the attendant tells Claudius: "They were given me by Claudio—he received them / Of him that brought them." It is possible to make the useful attendant into a composite man-about-Elsinore, and that is what Tyrone Guthrie did in the famous Olivier production of 1937 that later went to Elsinore, though he labeled the part simply "Messenger." The young player, Crichton Stuart, was given the Gentleman's "Save yourself, my lord" before the entry of Laertes, and he spoke it with so much fire that Charles Morgan awarded him a special note in the next morning's *Times* review.

It must always be exciting in the theatre when something can rise from these minor characters. Barely visible in the text, on the stage they can enter for a moment and leave themselves firmly in our minds and our debt. Some more talkative personages can be hard to separate—Solanio and Salarino, Rosencrantz and Guildenstern—or, of lesser partners, Valentine and Curio, Adrian and Francisco. But I do not forget, say, Balthazar (*Merchant of Venice*) and that stately fellow's "Madam, I go with all convenient speed," which I fear has become a rubbed joke—we can see in Balthazar the tiny embryo of Malvolio when Olivia adjures him to "Run!" Balthazar, textually, has only a single line, but usually (and with some cause) he is amalgamated with the Servant who brings to Portia news of Bassanio's approach, and to whom she says: "I am half afeard / Thou wilt say anon he is some kin to thee, / Thou spendst such high-day wit in praising him." Then, none can forget the marvelous little part of Mercade (three lines), the messenger who enters with the news of death ("Even so; my tale is told") upon the revel at the end of *Love's*

145

Labour's Lost. Peter Brook had a heart-stopping pause in the Stratford production of 1946. Any Second Gentleman, too, should be proud to find himself crying in *Othello*:

> For do but stand upon the foaming shore,
> The chiding billow seems to fret the clouds;
> The wind-shak'd surge, with high and monstrous mane,
> Seems to cast water on the burning Bear
> And quench the guards of th'ever-fixed Pole.
>
> (II.i.11–15)

When I sit back to recall a really transforming creation of a character that seems, from the text, to be nobody in particular, my mind returns inevitably to the nights (well over a dozen of them) in the spring of 1937 when I met the Olivier *Hamlet* at the Old Vic. In this a young actor named Alec Guinness was cast as Reynaldo, a character to which few of us had given earnest thought. Certainly no actor had been heard to brag of his success in it. Reynaldo, who belongs to the household of Polonius, has some nine or ten lines in a brief scene, and not all of the lines are inflammable: "I will, my lord"; "My lord, I did intent it"; "But, my good lord"; "Well, my lord."

The man is being sent to Paris to keep an eye on Laertes and to find out what he can in the peculiarly roundabout way that Polonius prescribes. Polonius is here at his most dithering and inconsecutive; and Reynaldo listens with amused deference. It is a passage that for many years was utterly forgotten except in "entirety" performances. Now, on this spring night when Tyrone Guthrie—just the director to pick on Reynaldo—revived *Hamlet* at the Vic, Polonius's envoy was very much of a personage as he stood with a discreet, hooded smile and observed his master's haverings. I can hear now the gentle emphasis in his reply to Polonius's "You have me, have you not?"— "My lord, I *have*." That night, and at other times during the run, I felt that I knew Reynaldo so well it would have been possible to make a Stanislavsky record of his early life.

I might think similarly were Guinness to appear as Dick surgeon, the learned Bellario, or—gloriously—as the Old Religious Man; but there hope must fade. These are eternally figures of the margin, just out of the picture though forever in Shakespeare's imagination and our own. "You have me, have you not?" says the dramatist. And in the theatre we answer, briefly but gratefully, "My lord, we *have!*"

III
The
Playwright
and
Performance

The Duke and Isabella on the Modern Stage

Jane Williamson

Anyone investigating twentieth-century literary criticism of *Measure for Measure* quickly discovers that this play, for which earlier criticism is relatively scanty, has aroused an extraordinary amount of interest and an extraordinary amount of disagreement among modern critics. Critical interest in *Measure for Measure* has been reflected in an extensive bibliography of articles and, in the last two decades, three books devoted exclusively to the play. Probably the outstanding feature of this criticism is its diversity. There are differences of opinion on virtually every aspect of *Measure for Measure*; Professor Ernest Schanzer has suggested that perhaps no other Shakespearean play has called forth "such violent, eccentric, and mutually opposed responses."[1]

But contemporary interest in and diversity of opinion about *Measure for Measure* has by no means been confined to the critic's study. After having been seldom performed in the theatre for nearly a hundred years, *Measure for Measure* has found increasing prominence on the twentieth-century stage. Among the professional presentations of the play in this century have been nine productions at Stratford-upon-Avon, six productions at the Old Vic, two productions at the Bristol Old Vic, two productions at Stratford, Ontario, and two at Stratford, Connecticut. The play has also found increasing popularity in provincial theatres, in summer drama festivals, and in college and university theatres. Like the literary critics, the actors and directors have shown notable differences in their approaches to the play. Unfortunately, as J.M. Nosworthy indicated in prefatory remarks to his recent edition of the play, "Those who wish to know something of the impact of *Measure for Measure* as a stage piece will find little to enlighten them in the literature about the play."[2] *Measure for Measure* stands in need of a thorough study of its stage history. Within the scope of this essay I can focus on only a limited

149

aspect of that history: the fortunes of the Duke and Isabella (the two characters who have been the subject of most controversy among the literary critics) in recent major professional productions of the English and American stage. Here Peter Brook's production at Stratford-upon-Avon in 1950 seems the appropriate starting point. The most widely discussed and applauded revival of the play since Tyrone Guthrie's presentation with Charles Laughton and Flora Robson at the Old Vic in 1933, it sparked an increased theatrical interest in *Measure for Measure* which has continued for two decades. And, like the Guthrie production of the early 1930s, it resulted, on the one hand, in numerous comments from theatrical reviewers suggesting that the problems raised by the scholars in the study seemed to disappear on the stage and, on the other hand, in renewed interest and scrutiny by those in the study, the scholars and literary critics.

Although the Duke and Isabella have had their difficulties in gaining a sympathetic reading from the critics, Harry Andrews and Barbara Jefford managed to win a sympathetic response for these characters from the audience at the 1950 Brook presentation at Stratford. Both managed, too, to avoid being overshadowed in a production in which there was an extraordinary interest in the treatment of the Viennese low-life and in the masterful portrayal of Angelo by John Gielgud.

Barbara Jefford's Isabella was presented against a rowdy background in which the sense of corruption and sordidness, vitality and humanity, and inherent humor were all simultaneously heightened; and she was placed opposite an Angelo who was a proud, self-righteous deputy, a figure of "suppressed and twisted nobility"[3] whose inner struggle was such that his fall seemed a minor tragedy. The nineteen-year-old Jefford possessed one important requisite for her role which unfortunately many Isabellas have lacked—youth. The character she presented was no "ice-maiden," but a warm, young, innocent, ardent novice endowed with youth's single-mindedness. She had "no mature *savior-faire* with which to meet her predicament, but only the burning conviction that two blacks cannot make a white."[4] And as the dreadful situation unfolded before her, she never became strident; she condemned "proud man, dressed in a little brief authority" with "an air of bitter discovery rather than cynical denunciation."[5] Reviewers who were critical of Barbara Jefford's performance generally complained on one of two counts. Either they criticized her for being too emotionally restrained and for lacking sufficient power and force of passion,[6] or they disagreed in general with her conception of the role, with the soft, sympathetic interpretation she gave to the part.[7] But most critics applauded the young actress's achievement, and while perhaps noting some imperfections arising from inexperience, concurred with the reviewer for *Time and Tide* (17 March 1950): "It was an Isabella we could well accept and even feel with."

If a sense of "flaming protestation" was not conveyed in her scenes with Angelo, this Isabella never seemed cold or especially withdrawn in her pleadings with the deputy; and the two encounters of the pair possessed a "grand tenseness."[8] In the first interview with Angelo the ardent Isabella several times stopped the deputy from leaving, as she knelt and clutched his arms.[9] (At one point as "she grasped his hand in fervor, Gielgud showed, subtly, the response of the awakened Angelo. His voice was somewhat less sure, his motions not flagrantly but just perceptibly less steady. The audience was aware of the change. Isabella was not."[10]) At the second meeting, she knelt and kissed Angelo's hand to intensify her assurance that for him to revoke the sentence would be "no sin at all, but charity."

In her soliloquy at the end of the second scene with Angelo, Isabella revealed an agonized excitement, and when she came to the harsh and perilous couplet, "Then, Isabel, live chaste, and, brother, die; / More than our brother is our chastity," she "turned from speaking full to the audience, to hide her face passionately against the wall behind her, as if herself ashamed that her intellect could find no more adequate expression of her heart's certainty."[11] Richard David applauded Jefford's technique here: "It was indeed skillful, and a good illustration of one kind of 'translation,' to substitute the pathos of the inarticulate for an affronting insensitivity, and to convert what is often an offence to modern playgoers into the very engine to enforce their sympathy." He noted that a similar technique was used in the interview with Claudio to retain sympathy for the anguished novice despite her bitter rebuke of her brother. Her tirade against her brother "was made to appear as much anger with her own failure as a witness to truth, her own inability to communicate it to others."[12] Another reviewer observed that after the denunciation of Claudio, one had the feeling that Isabella might apologize to him later. He continued: "It is in conformity with this presentation that when the Duke tells her of Claudio's death, there is a pause for grief before she cries out, 'O, I will to him and pluck out his eyes!' "[13] The moment of Jefford's presentation which drew the most comment, however, was a different pause which provided a climax for the play that was "breath-taking":

Mariana has passionately implored Isabella to kneel to the Duke for Angelo's pardon; the Duke has warned her to do so would be "against all sense"—"He dies for Claudio." The pause that followed must have been among the longest in theatre history. Then hesitantly, still silent, Isabella moved across the stage and knelt before the Duke. Her words came quiet and level, and as their full import of mercy reached Angelo, a sob broke from him. It was perfectly calculated and perfectly timed; and the whole perilous manoeuvre had been triumphantly brought off.[14]

As her natural youthfulness proved to be a particular asset to Barbara Jefford as Isabella, a naturally rugged and towering physical appearance proved a special advantage to Harry Andrews as the Duke. Harold Hobson wrote that Andrews "is so fine and frank in appearance as the Duke, he speaks in so manly a fashion, that one forgets he is a masquerader and an eavesdropper, a practical joker, and a liar."[15] Andrews played Vincentio as such a good ruler endowed with so much authority and benevolence that antipathies to the character or questions about his strange and circuitous procedures did not develop. Richard David observed that Brook found in Harry Andrews "a Duke whose commanding presence could dominate the play, as the half-seen arches the stage, and whose charm of manner could convince us of his integrity and wisdom."[16]

Andrews, although clearly reflecting a royal presence and nobility of mind, did not bring out any extrahuman or supernatural overtones in the character. He was strictly an earthly prince. The ritualistic couplet soliloquy that concludes act III ("He who the sword of heaven will bear"), which in productions a decade later was often delivered as the pronouncement of a Godlike figure, was spoken quite naturally by Andrews as "a rumination, moving, as well as in character."[17] One of the few complaints against Andrews's very human Vincentio came from a critic who thought that he seemed "too amiable to conduct such a rigorous and dangerous experiment." This critic objected especially to the actor's manner with Lucio in the final scene. "Mr. Andrews is too roguishly pally; the threat is never real."[18] The reviewer for the *Birmingham Post* (10 March 1950), however, judged that Andrews kept "an exact measure of aloofness, which is always that of the authentic *deus ex machina*," and the critic for *The Stage* (16 March 1950) thought him "quite capable of dealing with the rich authority of the final scene." This final scene, it should be noted, involved a good deal of compression. Andrews's Duke omitted the repeated deception of Isabella about

Claudio's death (which, given the emphasis on Isabella's test suggested by the long pause, might have seemed more appropriate than usual in this production); he omitted the direct expression of his proposal to Isabella ("Give me your hand and say you will be mine"); and he omitted the pardon of Barnardine (played here as "a gentleman who has gone downhill"[19]), which seals the mercy theme.

The conception of Vincentio as the model prince—wise, omniscient, beneficent—was the predominant one in subsequent professional productions of *Measure for Measure* in the 1950s. In 1954 when the play was chosen as the opening production for the second season of the Stratford, Ontario, Shakespeare Festival, Cecil Clarke presented it "as a sober probing into the complexities and inconsistencies of human nature—with a generous injection of low and often bawdy comedy";[20] but this probing was directed toward the citizens of Vienna not the Duke. Lloyd Bochner's portrayal of Vincentio was a clear, sharp performance which glossed over inconsistencies and made the Duke "a heroic figure even in those moments when it appears his little masquerade is going to lead to all disaster."[21] Herbert Whittaker suggested that potential problems of implausibility and inconsistency in the character were minimized as Bochner managed "to lead us through the mazes of the Duke's justice with conviction and give us a feeling that his purpose was at all times high, though his ways were certainly devious."[22] Walter Kerr reported that Bochner's Duke "was not only a regal but a passionate figure, driving the play forward with do-or-die urgency."[23] His was a Vincentio who could maintain his dignity despite a tweaking of his nose by a decadent Lucio, played here to suggest a sharp "satire on the faithlessness of fops."[24] As was the case in Harry Andrews's performance, the actor's physical appearance was "an enormous contribution to the dignity and style of the production."[25] Unlike the English Vincentio, however, the Canadian Duke extended his mercy in the last act to a hairy and disheveled Barnardine.

As Isabella in the Canadian production, Frances Hyland, a twenty-five-year-old Regina-born actress, brought to the role a fragile, delicate "flower-like beauty marked by great purity."[26] Hyland, like Jefford, managed to win sympathy for the novice. This Isabella conveyed a strong sense of vocation; and, in the opinion of the reviewer for the *Toronto Star* (29 June 1954), the actress was able "to turn what amounts to an unfeeling wench of fluctuating principles into a woman of some tenderness and even considerable provocation." Isabella contended here with James Mason's grim, deeply brooding Angelo, a "cold, cruel martinet,"[27] who won considerably less sympathy than Gielgud's deputy. Although tiny, Frances Hyland could dominate the stage, and in exchanges with Angelo and with Claudio "reached considerable heights of emotional power."[28] Walter Kerr judged her virtuous Isabella "anything but a plaster saint; she is a spit-fire in her scenes with Angelo."[29] In the last scene as staged by Cecil Clarke not only was the dramatic effect of Isabella's charges carefully intensified by the usual crowd reaction, but the great moment of her decision to kneel before the Duke and ask mercy for Angelo was heightened by the responses of a group of her fellow novices who were prominent among the onlookers.[30]

When in 1956 the American Shakespeare Festival directed its attention to *Measure for Measure*, the result was a production which can scarcely be compared with other presentations of the decade.[31] John Houseman and Jack Landau apparently determined to prove that with a little help from the directors this reputedly dark and difficult piece could be turned into very light comedy. By decking it out in late nineteenth-century costumes and playing it like a Strauss operetta, they managed to avoid the central acting and interpretive problems and to present an entertainment which was greeted kindly by some reviewers, if not by Shakespeare enthusiasts. "Director John Houseman—with the assistance of Jack Landau—has whisked that corrupt Vienna of Shakespeare's forward into the nineteenth century, splashed it over with Japanese lanterns and Lautrec-type posters of dancing girls, planted derbies on the town rakes and feather boas on the bawds, and called it a nose-thumbing carnival," Walter Kerr reported with some sense of enthusiasm for the project.[32]

The appearance of Arnold Moss's Duke in the first scene set the tone of the production. Vincentio's departure, with footmen, parading dogs, hatboxes, and fur-lined coats, started the play on a preposterous note. Moments later this Lehar prince, with feather in his hat and twirling moustache, reappeared as the friar, "a bespectacled, bearded dodderer, rather like a Mack Sennett comedian, eavesdropping as a perpetual busybody, quivering with indignation when he hears himself traduced."[33] Moss's portrayal of the Duke as a "playful prince who enjoys a spot of incognito for its own sake—rather than for any deeper purposes of investigation of the state of his principality,"[34] met with some applause. Kerr had kind words for this "engagingly antic figure":

> The Duke is, nine times out of ten, a tedious go-between, windily tangling and untangling the threads of Shakespeare's cynical plot. By lowering his voice, planting eyeglasses on the end of his nose,

and bustling into the role with the air of an incurably prying old goat, Mr. Moss has not only made the man tolerable, he has made us take a chess-game delight in the machinations of a complicated and garish narrative. (*New York Herald Tribune*, 29 June 1956)

This Duke, who "takes apparent delight in donning a false beard and mingling with the populace," who "enjoys the situations his deception brings about and positively twinkles as he plots in the death-house," appealed also to the reviewer for the *Toronto Globe and Mail* (29 June 1956): "He has the seedy air of a traveling actor, and proves himself a good, lively, even low, comic. With the Duke relieved of his darker responsibilities, his actions now seem capricious rather than wounding, and the sour aspects of his double dealings less puzzling." If Duke Vincentio could be turned into a purely comic figure and survive in this presentation, Angelo, Claudio, and Isabella could not. As an otherwise enthusiastic Kerr had to admit, "At the center of the play stand three figures that cannot be peeled from a deft cartoonist's drawing board." There was no complexity and no interest in Nina Foch's Isabella, who emerged as "no more than a tricksy heroine, a pawn in a game of masquerade."[35]

English productions of *Measure for Measure* in the mid-1950s placed increasing emphasis on the Duke. When the Shakespeare Memorial Theatre offered *Measure for Measure* in 1956 under the direction of Anthony Quayle, Duke Vincentio became the most important figure in the play.[36] The following year when the Old Vic presented it (for the first time in twenty years) under the direction of Margaret Webster, the Viennese ruler once more clearly stood at the center of the action. The Vincentio in each case was Anthony Nicholls. At Stratford, Nicholls's commanding, forceful, manly Duke was also an especially compassionate and comforting Vincento who, in his friar's robes, kneeled beside the distraught Isabella as he explained his unusual remedy. And in the end he was a most happy and triumphant Duke whose face was "illuminated with joy when the miracle happens and Isabella kneels for mercy for her enemy."[37] A critic for the *Stratford-upon-Avon Herald* (17 August 1956) suggested that this look of joy and triumph was "one of the great moments of emotion." Typically, reviews of this production tended to note the drama of the Duke's response to Isabella's action, rather than Isabella's action itself, which, emphasized by the long pause, had been such a memorable moment in the Brook production. To enhance the nobility of Vincentio, lines that might possibly cast an unfavorable, puzzling, or doubtful light on him were cut, including the

Duke's repeated probing of Juliet's penitence, his assurance to the Provost that he might safely be left alone with Isabella, his deceptive praise of Angelo to the Provost, and his reference to giving Barnardine shrift. (As in the Brook production, the pardon of Barnardine was omitted.[38])

If Nicholls clearly created an honorable Duke endowed with great dignity and grace, he nonetheless portrayed him, as had his predecessors, as a man, not a figure of Providence, not a God. Interestingly, for the first time a number of theatrical critics, perhaps stimulated by Nevill Coghill's essay of the previous year,[39] began to comment upon the matter of a supernatural dimension in the character. The reporter for the *Daily Telegraph* (15 August 1956) wrote that Nicholls's Vincentio "only momentarily becomes the symbol of the loving God which Shakespeare clearly intended, so that his Prosper-like act at the end came as too much of a surprise." The reviewer for the *Leamington Spa Courier* (17 August 1956) remarked on a trend in modern criticism to emphasize a twofold aspect to the role, "a temporal Duke and more as the play proceeds a personification of God himself," and he declared that "at Stratford there is not the smallest suggestion of this duality." This reviewer observed that Nicholls's Vincentio was only a temporal Duke, but he noted: "You feel that after all it is reasonable to suppose that a man of such ardent certainty of purpose should stage this whole complex of stratagems as the only way to lay open the virtues and weaknesses of his court and having done so dispense justice tempered with compassion." He thought the Duke's outburst of very human irritation (he "thumps his stick in anger" when the Provost reads the order for Claudio's execution[40]) at the setbacks to his plans seemed "to fall more naturally than usual into place"; however, he noted a loss when the Duke had to play down and hurry through the passage, "Look, th'unfolding star calls up the shepherd." "What was Shakespeare's purpose in putting Christ's words into the Duke's mouth if it was not to indicate that he had become in some way more than a man?"[41]

Reviews of Margaret Webster's Old Vic production of 1957 stressed its success in fusing what had often appeared as two incongruent halves of the play and in preventing a sense of anticlimax in the second part. Much of the credit for this fusion and for the coherence of the production rested with Nicholls's Duke. "Miss Webster sees that it is not Angelo's conscience but the Duke's Wolfenden survey which is the crux of the play, and if you can make the Duke seem a true sociologist and not a mere Arabian Nights *farceur* the usually intractable and tedious second half will come fully alive," reported the reviewer for *Time and Tide* (30 November 1957). "This she achieves with a strong, important seeming Duke." Philip Hope-Wallace suggested that Anthony Nicholls managed to bind the audience "in the belief of a man pursuing a mission with a positively biblical zeal."[42] Miss Webster believed that the Duke could be humanized and strengthened by an actor's personality; he could be given "a variety of thought and feeling which is not immediately apparent from his actual words"; he could "become much more than 'a tall dark dummy' ":

> Shakespeare knew, and no doubt counted upon, the interpretive possibilities of silence. The Duke does quite a lot of listening and quite a lot of learning as he listens; there is, further, much ironic humor implicit in his lines. He is dispassionate; he has the power to end all the threatened evils of the play, or, rather to resolve its immediate problems in terms of a pattern roughly just. Over the dark emotions which have caused these problems he has no power. When Shakespeare is writing full tragedy, there will be no Duke to say "Thus far, and no further"; but this play is to be insulated from a consummation of pity and terror, and the Duke will do it for us, interpreting between the audience's normal pulse of thought and the underground currents of emotion which the play so nearly lets loose. He is, supremely, a part for an actor of imagination who has the ability to project unspoken thought.[43]

Among the critics who thought that Miss Webster had found such an actor were the reviewers for *Punch* (27 November 1957) and the *Evening News* (20 November 1957). The former reported: "As the Duke Anthony Nicholls assumes a commanding dignity which is unpompous, and survives even the more inexplicable tricks; there is a flicker of humour in him which suggests he knows better than we do what he is about." The latter judged: "Anthony Nicholls did the impossible. He actually prevented one of Shakespeare's moralising Dukes from being a bore. With its lightness of touch, intelligence, and easy dignity, his was the performance of the evening." That "flicker of humour" and "lightness of touch" were qualities which had not been seen in many earlier portrayals of Duke Vincentio.[44] The critic for *The Times* of London (20 November 1957) detected, too, a slightly ironic light to fall on this Vincentio. He left the production believing that while Shakespeare ultimately "condemns no one high or low . . . hardly anyone escapes his ironic criticism." And he included in this "anyone" the good Duke. He wrote: "Mr. Anthony Nicholls is . . . set to expose what is equivocal in the Duke's behaviour. He speaks many of his lines in such a way as to convey a touch of absurdity in the absentee ruler playing providence with a gusto that is essentially childish. Mr. Nicholls discharges this delicate task effectively."

Opposite responses to the Duke's proposal to Isabella were evoked in the 1956 Stratford and 1957 Old Vic presentations. At Stratford Mr. Nicholls's sudden offer of marriage and its acceptance by Margaret Johnston's Isabella drew more harsh criticism than usual; at the Old Vic his offer and its acceptance by Barbara Jefford's novice were viewed as seeming especially appropriate. The cause of the different responses lay in the portrayal of Isabella.

In the latter presentation the reviewer for *Punch* responded with pleasure to Miss Jefford's appearance in the play's final moments and spoke of her conveying humanity "in the acceptance, without false modesty, of the Duke." In this production, as she had in the Brook presentation, Jefford offered a basically sympathetic interpretation of Isabella, a beautiful, warm-blooded young woman, "no cold neurotic but a maid passionate in her own sense of right and wrong."[45] Again a few critics wanted a novice who was more austere, but most applauded the portrayal, which J.C. Trewin judged "enriched and deepened" since 1950.[46] The remarks of reviewers suggest that Barbara Jefford's performance on this occasion engendered a greater variety and complexity of response than had her earlier study. The reporter for *The Times* of London thought that the actress brought out "many ironical references to the vanity of self-regarding virtue," and that at the end she showed that Isabella, "like Angelo, has need to concede something of her idealism to the world"; Kenneth Tynan, writing for *The Observer* (24 November 1957), interpreted Jefford's Isabella as "almost, for an instant ('we are all frail')" succumbing to Angelo, played here by John Neville as "a man in whom the flesh and spirit are truly at war."[47] The critic for the *Daily Telegraph* (27 November 1957) noted that this time she "came out fullthroated with that dreadful line, 'More than our brother is our chastity,' giving it a sort of defiant integrity." To Tynan, however, she uttered it "as if it were the most anguishing thought that had ever crossed her mind."

In comparison with Miss Jefford's Isabella, Margaret Johnston's was quite austere; and the actress's acceptance of Duke Vincentio at the end of the play brought forth the complaint that "this Isabel is nothing if not a nun."[48] Cast opposite Emelyn Williams's rather villainous Angelo who, black garbed and pale faced, looked "like an ambitious and callous churchman in charge of an inquisition,"[49]

Johnston offered "a performance of spirited, almost militant saintliness."[50] She was "no maiden hiding her bashfulness in a nun's habit, but a woman of character and integrity virtually crucified by the intolerable strain to which her dedicated loyalty is subjected."[51] She was judged especially successful in the scene with Claudio in "making her passionate abuse of his cowardice the expression only of her own moral agony."[52] (This was an Isabella who nearly fainted when Angelo said, "Your brother is to die," and who in the last scene, finding her brother restored, crossed herself and rushed impulsively into his arms.) For most reviewers, a matter of principle and religious faith clearly governed her response to Angelo's base proposal, and most of these critics responded with understanding if not with sympathetic affection for this "correct nun." One reporter, however, disagreed that religious principle was the sole basis for her action: "Miss Johnston . . . offers us a modern glass—the repressed spinster to whom the idea of sacrificing herself is intolerable on intense, personal grounds."[53] All agreed that this Isabella's acceptance of Duke Vincentio at the end of the play seemed fundamentally inconsistent with her character.

In the early 1960s professional productions of *Measure for Measure* began, increasingly, to present the Duke as the semiallegorical, Godlike figure that some theatrical reviewers had been looking for in the mid-1950s and that literary critics had been discussing since the 1930s. And, even more emphatically than Quayle's production of 1956 or Webster's production of 1957, these presentations made Duke Vincentio the leading character in the play. At the center of John Blatchley's 1962 production at Stratford-upon-Avon, with its stark, bare, almost claustrophobic set, stood Tom Fleming's Vincentio. To Harold Hobson the most striking feature of this *Measure for Measure* was "its exaltation of the Duke."[54] As portrayed by Fleming, he was certainly no sober, retiring prince who "loved the life removed." He was a lively, purposeful, imposing, assured, energetic, and above all ubiquitous ruler. The bare stage set, with its massive stone wall at the rear and a floor of similar rough stone, across which ran diagonally a slightly raised platform which filled more than half the stage, facilitated the swift movement of the Duke. It allowed him "to pass rapidly from point to point, to dart hither and thither, to be (almost) omnipresent."[55] Hobson recalled:

This man, played by Tom Fleming with eager authority, zestfully disguising himself as a monk, teaching Isabella how to trap Angelo into bed with another woman, popping up in prison to decide whose head is to be chopped off today, ranking as blasphemy any joke made at his expense, punishing sin, rewarding virtue, playing cruelly with his creatures till his moment comes to dispense final judgement, grew larger and larger as the play progressed. At the end he was everywhere, on the magistrates' bench, in gaol, in robes of state, under the monk's cowl, all-interfering and omnipotent.[56]

Fleming's prominent Duke consistently impressed the critics as being a providential, Godlike character. But to some, at least, he seemed to be a God with repellent as well as attractive qualities, to be an enigmatic, mysterious deity who controlled a universe in which happiness seemed to be achieved only through pain. To the critic for *The Times* of London (11 April 1962) his attitude toward Angelo appeared puzzling and a little cruel: "It resembles that of a schoolmaster towards an intelligent pupil for whom he has conceived a dislike. Disliking him, while outwardly praising him, he persecutes him by setting an elaborate trap, putting Angelo in a position of authority in the expectation that he will find temptation there and succumb to it." He added that "given the way Mr. Marius Goring plays Angelo [a pathetically neurotic deputy], the Duke's trick seems extremely cruel." This Duke "can bring out his aims by a wave of the arm. Why, then, does he not give the immediate signal that would end all ills? Why does he choose to accomplish his desires by means so unnecessarily tortuous, unnecessarily torturing?" Such questions were raised in the mind of Harold Hobson, who suggested that Blatchley's production set out to explore the philosophical "question of government and of evil still continuing despite the existence of incontrovertible moral power."[57]

When *Measure for Measure* was undertaken by the Old Vic for the last time in its final season, director Michael Elliott acknowledged in a program note advice given him by Nevill Coghill. And in this 1963 production, which began with a clap of thunder and ended with the sound of bells and fireworks, reflections of Professor Coghill's view of the play as a comedy cast in the medieval form, a play that starts in trouble and ends in joy and that carries an allegorical meaning which, however, "should neither supplant nor overbear the literal, human meaning" was evident,[58] particularly in the treatment of the Duke. James Maxwell's severe and just Duke, at whose first entry the nobles prostrated themselves "with a sudden arresting thunder of their knees upon the stage,"[59] was "the focal point of the production, no mere lurking shadow or *deus ex machina*."[60] A figure of "aloof dignity," and "indisputably ducal," Maxwell's Vincentio impressed the critic for *The Times* (4 April 1963) as "a mysterious semi-divine personage who has better license than an ordinary mortal to treat other characters like flies" and who, "cowled like a Bergman spectre, arbitrates over the action with lofty authority." The reporter for the *Sunday Telegraph* (14 April 1963) wrote that Maxwell invested the Duke "with awesome saintliness." The reviewer for *The Spectator* (12 April 1963) noted the production's strong suggestion that the final scene stands for the Day of Judgment itself with the previously cowled and barefoot Duke now robed in Cardinal's red entering triumphantly to ecclesiastical music in front of a great sun, with onlookers falling prostrate before him. Responses of the critics to the religious overtones in the presentation were somewhat mixed. Among those offering complaints were the critics for the *New Statesman* (12 April 1963), who thought this ending, with the Duke stepping forth "with the sun for his halo, like Christ . . . coming into his Kingdom" seemed "a staggering impertinence," and the critic for the *Catholic Herald* (11 April 1963), who judged this Vincentio "over-deified."

In 1966 Tyrone Guthrie, with his memorable 1933 and 1937 Old Vic productions of *Measure for Measure* now more than a quarter of a century behind him, turned to the play once more, this time directing a Bristol Old Vic production which, the following year, toured major cities in America.[61] This Guthrie *Measure for Measure* presented a notable contrast to his Old Vic presentations of the 1930s. In those earlier efforts the intense and emotionally charged scenes between Charles Laughton's frightening Angelo and Flora Robson's passionate Isabella and between Emelyn Williams's proud, pale, disturbed deputy and Marie Ney's impulsive, high-strung novice had provided the center of interest for audience and reviewers. In the Bristol Old Vic presentation, however, the play, as in the 1962 and 1963 productions of Blatchley and Elliott, revolved around the Duke, a figure of God Almighty, as it expressed thematically the idea that "Justice must be tempered by Mercy, Authority by Love."[62] A program note by Guthrie suggested that the play was to be given a theological interpretation not unlike that of the Old Vic production of 1963, that it was to be interpreted as a divine allegory with the disguised Duke representing the absent deity. With respect to the Duke and the various aspects of his role Guthrie wrote explicitly:

I suspect he is meant to be something more than a glorified portrait of royalty. Rather he is a figure of Almighty God; a stern and crafty father to Angelo, a stern but kind father to Claudio, an elder brother to the Provost . . . and to Isabella, first a loving father and, eventually, the Heavenly Bridegroom to whom at the beginning of the play she was betrothed.

In appearance John Franklyn Robbins's Duke seemed a Christlike figure. "In his white habit and cowl, with his temporal face and disciplined beard, Robbins looks like every traditional conception of Jesus Christ—except that he must be a little more arrogant," remarked the reviewer for the *South Wales Argus* (4 March 1966). The Duke's divinity seemed effectively emphasized to critic Sheila Huftel in his "initial appearance coming into the darkness" and in the opening to the second half, in the prison where "the friar stands in white and there is a fleeting impression of a white cross against the dark."[63]

There were, however, aspects of Robbins's Vincentio which seemed difficult to associate with the idea of divinity, at least in the Christian sense. Unlike the awe-inspiring, aloof, dignified, mysterious figure of the Old Vic production, Robbins's omnipresent ruler was an extremely lively, jovial, puckish prince who engaged in various pieces of comic business, including getting lost in the folds of his hood when he dons the unfamiliar habit of a friar. Faced with this lively side of the Duke the reviewer for *The Times* of London (4 March 1966) remarked that he was grateful for Guthrie's program note: "Without it one might not have guessed that this jovially eccentric figure, whirling his crucifix like a propeller, was intended to possess metaphysical significance." He concluded that this Duke seemed "related not to Christian drama but to the sprightly classical immortals of modern French comedy." And the reviewer for *The Scotsman*, who had noted the moments in which the religious overtones in the character seemed effectively pronounced, was surprised by this other side of the "whirlwind" Duke: "The part can surely never have been played so fast, so breezily, or with such boisterous humour. A friar can never have been more secular." She observed that "the Duke unfolds the Mariana plot as happily as a successful conjurer" and speculated that "Guthrie might have been a trifle bored" with the character "and decided to brighten him up."[64] Walter Kerr, viewing the Bristol Old Vic performance in New York, noted that the tone of Vincentio's character was established in the first scene with the "raffish Duke spitting out farewells to his city and quite jovially anticipating the trouble he's going to cause when he sneaks back into it disguised as a friar."[65] Another New York critic wrote that Robbins "appeared to take a Mephistophelean pleasure in drawing out the suspense of Angelo's assorted victims."[66] That Guthrie had intended at least some of the complexity of interpretation and perplexity of response to his Duke seems indicated by his final remark on the character in his program note: "And may we not suppose that in showing the Duke's considerable and calculated ruthlessness, as well as his wisdom and humour, Shakespeare is permitting himself a theological comment upon an all-wise, all-merciful Father-God, who permits the frightful and apparently meaningless disasters which unceasingly befall his children?"

The Isabellas which these Godlike Dukes of the 1960s assisted were presented with varying degrees of youthful innocence, passion, humanity, and fallibility. At Stratford-upon-Avon in 1962 Judi Dench offered a very young, robust, outgoing Isabel, a girl who was not yet of the cloister and who never wore the habit of a religious order.[67] ("This is the first time I have seen Isabella in so low-cut a gown," observed Philip Hope-Wallace.[68]) She had to contend with an Angelo presented as a man frozen by fear who—with unseeing, psychotic, staring eyes, blanched face, stiff neck, and sleepwalker gait—went about the attempted seduction like someone "in the grip of a nightmare."[69] Faced with an Angelo of this sort, Isabella's struggle became "a struggle to keep her own balance, to remain sane and independent."[70] Although very young, inexperienced, lacking in guidance, and unpredictable, this Isabella seemed "already formidable as a member of secular society."[71] The production suggested that Isabella's experiences were an "initiation into life," and, as one critic noted, she proved "to be a very tough and courageous fighter."[72] A few reviewers, such as the critic for the *Glasgow Herald* (11 April 1962), indicated that they wanted Isabella to be a little more of a prig and suggested that Judi Dench was "too soft and kittenish," but most commended her simple, direct portrayal of "an urgent desperate girl with the ring of truth in every phrase."[73]

In the 1963 Old Vic production Dilys Hamlett (who like Judi Dench discarded the religious habit in favor of secular dress) presented a very "taut and distraught"[74] Isabella. She was a fiery tempered, extremely passionate young petitioner, too passionate and strident to suit the tastes of some who criticized the actress for excessive shouting, ranting, or screaming.[75] With respect to the first interview with Angelo, Philip Hope-Wallace remarked that "while it is fine to let fly and pull out all the stops as Marie Ney or Flora Robson did at 'man, proud man,' . . . the scene is more not less effective for being played with gradations of volume and not all *fortissimo*."[76] So strong-tempered was this Isabel that W.A. Darlington wondered how she and the dictatorial Duke could possibly live happily ever after.[77] In contrast to the situation which Judi Dench's Isabel faced, this young girl encountered a nonascetic, virile looking Angelo (Lee Montague), who received her at the second meeting "unbuttoned to the chest hair." As was the case at Stratford, there was a sense of Isabella's being initiated into life's realities. Alan Brien noted that Dilys Hamlett interpreted Isabel as a "clever innocent young woman who knows all the words for good and evil but has never felt them incarnated in flesh and blood. A blue-stocking debater, she can out-orate a politician and out-quibble a theologian," but she "takes refuge in a burst of screaming hysteria" when faced at last with the gulf between appearance and the reality of the Puritan Angelo's lust and her brother Claudio's fear of death. He found her ultimately "one of the few Isabellas who can awaken our sympathy without demanding our approval."[78] A moment of Hamlett's performance which was remembered especially by the critic for *The Times* (4 April 1963) was her reaction to the news of Claudio's death, which, he remarked, was "a terrifying demonstration in which one seems to be witnessing the destruction of an identity."

Tyrone Guthrie suggested in the program note to his 1966 production that Shakespeare was not concerned with creating "good" people or "bad" people but "real people in whom good and bad are inextricably commingled"; Isabella is not a simple "heroine" but a complex young woman. He explained: "She does behave outrageously to Claudio. But reasons for her irrational cruelty are strongly suggested: she has been taught that a woman's "purity" is her greatest treasure, and she feels an overwhelming and irrational regard for her father." Reviewer Sheila Huftel judged that Guthrie's Isabella, Barbara Leigh-Hunt, "unflinchingly" exposed "the contradictions in Isabel."[79] She presented the novice as a young woman who is tested, who grows through suffering, and who is shaped by experience.[80] Initially she suggested an Isabel "by no means alien to Angelo." As the critic for the *Western Daily Press* (3 March 1966) observed, "She strives for ideals as abstract as his. . . . This is a pairing of fanatics, not an oversimple confrontation of good and evil." The actress seemed a devout, passionate novice in the early scenes, a figure that "could well persuade Angelo that a saint had baited the hook." Later she made Isabella's weaknesses clearer. Isabella's "hysterical fury at Claudio turns all sympathy from her, and the 'saint' becomes a virago on hearing of Angelo's treachery."[81] Reviewing her performance in Bristol, the critic for *The Times* (4 March 1966) thought that Miss Leigh-Hunt realized "the physical nausea and sheer wrath of the part were considerable power"; and, commenting upon her presentation in New

York, the critic for the *World Journal Tribune* (15 February 1967) spoke of being "emotionally swayed by this Isabel." Interestingly, however, Walter Kerr suggested that ambivalent responses to Isabel and the ambiguities of the action were such that emotional involvement was at a minimum by the scene of the meeting with Claudio when the novice tells her brother of Angelo's proposal. "We don't groan with her, we grin. Values are being stood on their heads too rapidly for us to take this particularly grisly sport in earnest."[82] Richard Watts, Jr., writing for the *New York Post* (15 February 1967), remarked, too, that "under Guthrie's direction, the playing is interestingly cool and detached."

In two recent offerings of *Measure for Measure* at the Festival Theatre, Stratford, Ontario (1969), and the Memorial Theatre, Stratford-upon-Avon (1970), Duke Vincentio has returned to human dimensions, and the productions, in contrast to many earlier presentations, have sought—as did Guthrie's—to emphasize rather than minimize the complexities and ambiguities of character and action. David Giles, the director of the 1969 Festival Theatre presentation, who remarked that the tone of the play "makes it difficult to fit into any slot but black comedy,"[83] explained his approach in a program note: "In approaching the play we have tried to avoid all of the simplistic extremes in the hopes of finding and capturing the humanity with which Shakespeare illuminates every situation. In doing so we have found that the apparent discrepancies and violent swings of mood, so objectionable to most critical opinion, are in fact organic to a drama very much of the mood of our own times." Giles "turned away from heavy-handed symbolism"[84] to present *Measure for Measure* as a play dealing with "a difficult journey of self-discovery for many of its characters."[85] Indeed so strong was the sense of reality, "so 'real' was the immediate action on this occasion," Professor Clifford Leech observed "that one wondered whether, after the events were well in the past, there might be dinner-parties for Vincentio and his Duchess, Angelo and his wife, and what their table-talk would have been like."[86]

The Duke received a special introduction in Giles's presentation in an opening sequence which gave an initial sense of reality to the situation, established an atmosphere of lawlessness, and provided additional background and motivation for Vincentio's actions at the beginning of the play. The play opened to a gloomy setting, to somber music, and to the tapping of the cane of a blind man who made his way across a semidarkened stage, strewn with derelicts and muffled figures, as various robberies and stabbings were taking place.

Finally, with screams in the night, the stage emptied except for the blind man, who casually removed his visor and beggar's cloak and revealed himself to be Vincentio in disguise, already spying on conditions in his city. For Arnold Edinborough these opening minutes effectively established the sense of violence and license in Vienna and brought a recognition that such corruption had to be curbed. However, he noted that they also suggested too that the solution to the problem would have to come from "someone other than this spectator Duke who had watched the scene . . . so passively," and who, after removing his disguise, "had washed his hands—a Pilate-like gesture."[87]

This Vincentio as subsequently developed by actor William Hutt was characterized by the critic for the *Winnipeg Tribune* (12 June 1969) as "an aristocrat with a sardonic turn of mind and a sophisticated outlook. He is no mealy moralist. He is rather a man who likes to see the wheels go around and likes to be the one who helps them turn." Walter Kerr remarked that Hutt endowed the part with "surprising humor." The Duke developed his complicated plan "with the benevolent humor of an insane guardian angel."[88] Generally Hutt projected to reviewers a character who was mischievous, whimsical, but basically well intentioned. "A prankish man, yet a good one, learning much about human nature in each adventure," was the description given him by the critic for the *Record American* (12 June 1969); "a benign pixie, dabbling in lives without a moment's hesitation," was the interpretation recorded by the reporter for the *Globe and Mail* (13 June 1969). Professor Leech noted especially the sense of delight in his various schemes that Hutt's Duke conveyed. He is "the first actor to show that Vincentio takes an almost feline pleasure in his small Machiavellian tricks, and smiles as he thinks up device after device."[89] To the reviewer for the *Vancouver Sun* (18 July 1969) Hutt's Duke seemed "a benevolent humanist, an amused . . . observer of human weakness. Nothing shocks him; he can be angry but it is not the sort of anger that produces lightning bolts. He does not insist on perfection."

Director Giles decided on an extremely young Isabella and cast "the childlike, lovely, and automatically winsome"[90] Karin Fernald in the part. Her youthful novice was "a child at sea,"[91] overwhelmed by the circumstances she encountered. Her rage at Claudio was finally dissolved in tears, and later she collapsed as she delivered the harsh threat to Angelo ("O, I will to him and pluck out his eyes") upon hearing of her brother's death. This was a young woman who desperately needed outside support, and who, finding no such support from her brother, was particularly thankful for the Duke's assistance. Professor Leech recalled that "Isabella's demonstration of relief when the Duke brought out his apparent ace in the hole was one of the most poignant moments in the play."[92] Some critics suggested that the young actress's performance suffered from lack of experience,[93] but Professor Leech found her "a most moving Isabella."

John Barton's 1970 production at Stratford-upon-Avon was "as far removed from the direct Christian allegory of the 1963 Old Vic version as from Peter Brook's riotous low-life spectacular" of 1950.[94] The focus here was on "man, proud man," and each of the characters was presented from ever-varying perspectives, "like the turning of a many faced stone."[95] Ultimately none of the characters, including the good Duke and Isabella, emerged unflawed. "Isabella's purity conceals an hysterical fear of sex which scarcely allows her to speak of her brother's fault, and leads directly to her unlovely attack upon him in prison," Anne Barton remarked in a program note. Estelle Kohler's beautiful Isabella, who could forgive but not give herself, impressed Irving Wardle as "an ambiguous figure held on course only by sustained sexual nausea. Beyond this," he noted, "she has a range of direct emotional impulse and sheer coyness that make the big scenes with Angelo and Claudio exceptionally rich in moment to moment development."[96] Basically this was a cold, young Isabel, a commanding self-assured novice who responded to Angelo's dreadful offer not with fear but indignation and disgust.

In the first interview with Angelo there was a touch of anger and bitterness in her voice as she delivered the famous plea for mercy. Although initially reluctant to plead her brother's cause, this novice was a skilled debater used to winning arguments, and she showed "an increase of passion in each rebuff."[97] She knew how to enforce her points with gesture, and she managed to capture Angelo's position behind the desk, leaving him on the defensive before her. In their second encounter she again got the upper hand. "Seeming, seeming!" she exclaimed, bending over the seated deputy. When, later, she came to the sympathy-destroying declaration, "More than our brother is our chastity," Kohler's Isabella not only declined to omit it, hasten through it, or camouflage it with tears as some of her predecessors had done, she spoke the last word with considerable emphasis. "Here," Robert Speaight observed, "in a flash of defiant self-revelation, Miss Kohler let us see that her chastity—like the chastity of Angelo himself—is corrupted by pride. The pride that betrayed *him* to lust has betrayed *her* to cruelty. Each will have to be punished by humiliation—he by public exposure, and she by pleading forgiveness for the man she had accused."[98]

In the prison scene with Claudio when the latter declares that he will embrace death willingly, Estelle Kohler's Isabella registered a tremendous relief and for the first time seemed to soften and release her pent-up feelings. Interestingly, when he then vacillates and Isabella speaks the sharp words of reproach, this novice was in tears and spoke with muted tones. Moments later she and Claudio were reconciled, and they embraced as the Duke and Provost exchanged words. In the final scene she fainted upon seeing Claudio, and subsequently the pair shared a touching reunion. "We do not know how Isabella reacts to her sovereign's extraordinarily abrupt offer of marriage in the final moments of the play, because she says nothing to him in reply. It is at least possible that this silence is one of dismay," Anne Barton conjectured. In the Stratford production dismay and bewilderment, at the very least, seemed registered in her silence. The reviewer for *The Listener* (9 April 1970) interpreted an even stronger response from this "feminist" Isabella. He thought that Isabella, "glaring at the audience," had "silent rage written all over her high forehead and stubborn chin."

If Duke Vincentio "is, as some critics maintain, an image of Providence, there would seem to be chaos in Heaven. His attempt to stage-manage a human reality far too complex for such arbitrary ordering is inefficient. It also reveals his inability to understand the thoughts and feelings of other people." As suggested by these remarks of Mrs. Barton, Sebastian Shaw's Vincentio, who met with Isabella's negative silence, was clearly one of the flawed figures in the play, a character who, like everyone else, stands in need of redemption and who, like everyone else, gets his come-uppance. Certainly no God figure, he was an aging, spectacled Duke, a genial but rather smug and slightly eccentric fellow who was constantly surprised and foiled in his efforts to manipulate the complicated individuals and circumstances he encountered. This Vincentio is "a middle-aged academic who likes to think he understands human nature," noted the critic for the *Oxford Mail* (2 April 1970) in describing Shaw's "fascinating conception" of the part. "In appearance, with his Holbein cap and spectacles, he suggests a university vice-chancellor: a paternal administrator whose encouraging smiles are always contracting into icy severity," declared the reviewer for *The Times* (2 April 1970). "The performance captures all the possible aspects of the character, except its awful authority; by turns he is sly, petulant, crafty, philosophic, resourceful. But no view is pushed to the limit and in the end he is as much an enigma as ever."

Handing Angelo a heavy law book and leaving behind a desk cluttered with dusty volumes, Shaw's Duke went forth to investigate his city, and he immediately began to encounter problems with its citizens. Juliet became indignant at his probing of her penitence and cut him off in mid-sentence; Claudio rather inattentively continued to eat while he counseled him to "be absolute for death" and seemed not to find any lasting persuasion in his message; Barnardine rejected his blessing and comfort, desecrated his cross, and flatly refused to die; Lucio slandered him and haughtily tossed him a coin for his prayers; and Angelo of course upset his scheme for rescuing Claudio by sending to the Provost a message ordering Claudio's execution, an action which proved especially startling to this Duke. His most notable setback, however, came at the end of the play when he offered his hand in marriage to Isabella and she, shocked at his proposal, rejected it. This spectacled Duke's concern with growing old and his futile love for the young Isabella struck a note of pathos. In the philosophic speech of consolation to Claudio, Shaw's friar seemed quite detached, almost speaking the words as a mere exercise until he came upon those dealing with the emptiness of life for the "old and rich," when he suddenly registered sincere emotion in his voice. In the last scene it seemed clear that the Duke's one true feeling was his love for Isabel—there was a special tone as he repeated her name. And although he somehow sensed it was a hopeless case, he could not help but try to win her for his bride. "Give me your hand and say you will be mine—He is my brother too," said the Duke. But this young Isabella simply leaped to Claudio's arms, ignoring Vincentio. After a long pause he sighed, "But fitter time for that." Later, trembling, he made his last bid. "What's mine is yours, and what is yours is mine." After a long pause of silence, he uttered a resigned, "So," put on his glasses, and departed with all the others, leaving a bewildered Isabella alone on stage looking out at the audience. The royal prince of the 1950s and the Godlike Duke of the 1960s had given way to a genial bumbler.

Realism Versus Nightmare: Problems of Staging The Duchess of Malfi

Lois Potter

The most lucid account of Webster's dramatic technique is found in Inga-Stina Ewbank's article on the masque of madmen in *The Duchess of Malfi*:

> The scene as a whole neither fits into a realistic scheme of cause and effect or psychological motivation, nor does it consistently embody convention. It balances between those two alternatives. It is a precarious balance, and at other points we see Webster losing it. But in this scene he holds the tension between the two and draws strength from both sides.[1]

"The 'Impure Art' of John Webster" has been called "the most convincing answer yet written to Eliot's charge that convention is ruined by realism."[2] But it is not an answer for the would-be producer of the play. This is not simply because the particular convention discussed by Mrs. Ewbank—the marriage masque—is one which no modern audience can be expected to understand;[3] it is also because, as Mrs. Ewbank herself says, Webster's balance between convention and realism is achieved "'by poetic means"—and by a kind of poetry (embodied in action as well as statement) which a modern production could hope to bring out only through a high degree of stylization. Thus, far from being able to reconcile convention and realism, the director is likely to find himself forced to choose between them. This, at least, is the view expressed in a review of the most recent Stratford production of the play:

> Either you believe *The Duchess* a profound and truthful statement about the human condition, that evil reigns inexorably and inexplicably at the heart of things. Or else you consider that it can be given a human explanation, traceable through the tangle of ordinary men's mixed motives. In the first case, you can't try to act

Webster's tragedy, you can only perform it, turning it into an abstract ballet or poem about cruelty, blood and darkeness.

A realistic approach like that taken by Clifford Williams at Stratford, the reviewer went on, works for such characters as the Duchess and Antonio, but not for those who embody evil: "The harder [the director and actors] work to present them as people, the less plausible their efforts become." Reluctantly he concluded that "the performance-groups who treat the play simply as a circus of evil are right."[4]

It is true that the Duchess and her brothers belong to separate worlds, not only poetically but also dramatically. The court of Malfi is seen in practical, domestic terms: Antonio may not literally smell of ink and counters, as Ferdinand says, but we are never allowed to forget that his main job is to keep the Duchy solvent; his and the Duchess's many references to children may symbolize innocence and fruitfulness but are also strikingly vivid in their images of riding "a cock-horse / Upon a painted stick,"[5] eating sweetmeats "As fearful to devour them too soon" (I.i.466–67), spinning tops, (III.v.79–81), and taking syrup for a cold (IV.ii.203–4). On the other hand, Ferdinand and the Cardinal inhabit an atmosphere whose horror and grotesqueness, appearing first in the imagery and then in the action of the play, have made nearly every critic since G.H. Lewes want to use the word "nightmare."[6] Webster presumably intended us to see his play both through the Duchess's eyes and through her brothers', as in one of those perspective pictures of which Mrs. Ewbank gives such a fascinating account;[7] it is obviously necessary, then, to find a style of production which does not tip the balance too far in either direction.

W. Bridges-Adams has maintained that this can best be done through a realistic rather than a poetic approach: "Surprisingly, this dream of horror will prove a frigid thing if there is anything dream-like in the playing. . . . Precisely because the events are almost beyond belief, they must be presented as if they were everyday happenings; the magic brew must be concocted of the most ordinary ingredients."[8] However much they have differed in their external features, most recent productions of the play have in fact followed this advice in their treatment of the characters. The first *Duchess* in my experience—and perhaps for that reason the most fondly remembered—was Colin George's 1966 version at the Sheffield Playhouse. It combined realism and fantasy in its set, an ornate Baroque structure of twisted pillars, colonnades, and balconies which, deliberately out of proportion, seemed about to collapse. But its characters did not seem fantastic; in particular, Bridges-Adams's insistence that "no Bosola should take the stage who cannot bring his galley servitude before our eyes" was admirably fulfilled by an actor who looked capable of pulling the whole galley single-handed and whose bewildered, futile gropings toward virtue after the death of the Duchess seemed doubly moving by contrast with his massive physique.

The same realistic approach to character could be found in Brian Shelton's *Duchess* at Pitlochry in 1967. Playing on an Elizabethan-type stage and with full awareness of Elizabethan conventions (I remember that Antonio and Delio directed their "methinks 'twas yesterday" dialogue straight at the audience), the actors drew their parts in broad strokes but avoided symbolism or caricature.[9] By all accounts, the same was true of two major productions which I did not see, the 1960 one at Stratford and the Aldwych and the 1971 *Duchess* at Stratford, Ontario.[10] At the Aldwych, sets appear to have been both symbolic and realistic: the focal point for the opening scene, a fountain, both suggested the gracious atmosphere of the Duchess's court and picked up an important image from Antonio's first speech; to set the beginning of act II in a market, however—so that the audience actually saw Bosola buy his apricots—seems more like an attempt to cover up the static nature of the scene by a gratuitous injection of local color. Reviewers often made fun of the plot but found the performances believable, though their disagreement as to whether Eric Porter did or did not intend to give Ferdinand an incestuous motivation suggests some uncertainty of effect,[11] as does the apparent belief of many of them that it was a sign of failure for the play to get any laughs at all. There was no doubt about either of these points in the Canadian production: Ferdinand seems hardly to have kept his hands off the Duchess in their scenes together, and the deliberately modern readings of such lines as "Be yourself" and "Awake, awake, man," ensured that the play, especially in the first half, was not uniformly dark in mood.

A further example of how Webster can be played on a realistic level was "a straightforward, lusty Italianate version" of *The Duchess* in translation, at the Amfiteatro Michelangelo in Rome, which left one reviewer astonished at "how acute was Webster's understanding and familiarity with the Italian scene."[12] Paradoxically, to emphasize the Italianate aspect of the work in an English production, as happened in Frank Dunlop's highly successful *White Devil* at the National Theatre, can only have the effect of distancing it from us; the

Jacobeans' Italy comes across as a never-never-land of sex and violence. For *The White Devil* this may be appropriate, but it seems too easy a way out for *The Duchess.*

Perhaps for this reason, some recent productions have eliminated almost everything which makes the play Italian, or even Jacobean, in feeling. At the Royal Court in early 1971 the actors played against a background of building-site doors, inspired by the lines about death having ten thousand several doors for men to take their exits. Their quiet, unemphatic speaking irritated many critics, but others found the effect hypnotic and dreamlike. Yet this delivery was really intended to be naturalistic rather than surrealistic; in an interview, director Peter Gill described his approach in terms which, for the unsympathetic readers, inevitably recall *The Girlhood of Shakespeare's Heroines*: "I tried to create the feeling that apart from being a royal family the audience were watching two brothers and a sister who might have shared beds as children. During rehearsals we improvised Stanislavski-like ways of showing the brothers' neurotic love for their sister—deciding on her hair styles, ordering her around, that sort of thing."[13] As in the Stratford production, this approach worked better for the Duchess and Antonio (Judy Parfitt and Desmond Gill) than for the "Arragonian brethren." I have seen only one interpretation of the play in which the horrors came across as successfully as the quieter passages, and this was probably the one which Bryden meant when he referred to the "circus of evil" approach: the extraordinary one-hour version which the Freehold Company presented at the Young Vic in the autumn of 1970. Like the Royal Court production, it was badly received on the whole, yet I felt there were some aspects of the play which it caught superbly.

Balletic and acrobatic movement replaced much of the dialogue: for instance, the family pride of the House of Aragon was indicated by a raising of the arms (like someone being held up by a gunman), which the Duchess nervously copied from Ferdinand and the Cardinal in the scene where they warned her not to remarry, and she adopted again—now with her fingers twisting desperately in her hair—when she was trying to retain her sense of identity in prison. The play, in this version, ended almost immediately after the murder of the Duchess. Her body, roped to a scaffolding tower, dominated the otherwise bare arena where the rest of the cast huddled together, looking very like Rupert Brooke's "writhing grubs in an immense night." The only phrase audible through the hissing and swaying of the crowd was Bosola's

when thou kill'd'st thy sister,
Thou took'st from Justice her most equal balance,
And left her naught but her sword.

(V.v.39–41)

A rather good equivalent, I felt, for what many critics feel happens to the play after the death of its heroine.

What the Freehold and Royal Court had in common was that they were both aspiring to the condition of music. This became clear to me when I saw the most recent of English *Duchess*es, an operatic version by a young composer, Stephen Oliver, which had its premiere at the Oxford Playhouse in November 1971. Though its clean, uncluttered staging (by Julian Hope) was more realistic than that of the two productions I have just been describing, it carried still further their emphasis on the choric, commonplace-book elements in the play. The Freehold actors had all been dressed alike in hideous drab Hessian rags; at the Royal Court, both major and minor characters wore yellow. In both cases, there was a deliberate depersonalization of most of the actors, who faded in and out of the ensemble —not very courtly looking, perhaps, but nevertheless conveying something of what Webster meant by the court: a sense of group pressure being exerted on the main characters. In Stephen Oliver's libretto for *The Duchess of Malfi*, many speeches—for instance, Bosola's dirge —were transferred from the central characters to an offstage chorus. They sang a setting of "Go and catch a falling star" after the "mandrake" scene between Ferdinand and the Cardinal, thus picking up not only that image but also the cynicism expressed by the Cardinal in his earlier scene with Julia. It was they at first who answered Antonio's voice in the echo scene; only later did we become aware of the Duchess's voice rising above the others, as the messages became increasingly urgent and personal.

Apart from his very moving setting of this scene, Mr. Oliver made little attempt to deal with the last act of *The Duchess*. Bosola's character was the main casualty; despite the fact that the composer sang the part himself, he cut out the whole series of vacillations between high moral purposes and grubby actions which constitutes his behavior after the death of the Duchess. Antonio met his death at the hands of anonymous assassins, and Bosola, Ferdinand, and the Cardinal died in even more of a mist than usual. The chorus held the opera together at this point, picking up Bosola's dying speech, after he trailed off on "In what a shadow . . . ," and following it with the more hopeful words which Webster gave to Delio: "Integrity of life is fame's best friend." Here, as elsewhere, they bridged the gap between Webster's *sententiae* and the action of the play.

Though he cut, altered, and in some cases added to *The Duchess* so extensively that, as he said in the programme, "It is hardly fair to saddle [Webster] with the responsibility of our imaginations," Oliver's opera nevertheless seemed to get closer to the workings of Webster's own imagination than many versions which have been superficially more faithful to the text. However, this is not much help for the producer without benefit of music. It is only in music, for instance, that the different imaginative worlds of the play's characters can be sharply contrasted without becoming ludicrous. In opera, the Duchess and Antonio can sing highly melodic love duets while the chorus expresses itself in what sounds like medieval plainchant and Ferdinand swoops eerily up and down in his high tenor. What would the equivalent be in a nonmusical production?

The sketchy history of recent *Duchesses*, running the gamut from realism to nightmare, represents a variety of solutions to the problems posed by the play. In turning now to the play itself, I may at first seem to be offering some solutions of my own, but in fact what I want to do is to show that the problems are even more complex than I have already indicated. To look at *The Duchess* simply in the hope of understanding what Webster intended to be happening on the stage at any given moment—an approach which I think is too seldom taken by students of the play—leads to an awareness of a reality of detail to which few performances have done justice. On the other hand, the more familiar type of analysis in terms of imagery and structural patterns seems to me to point to a conscious use of techniques which only the most surrealistic production could hope to put across on anything but an unconscious level.

Before looking at these complex effects, I should like to examine some simple problems of literal meaning and tone—problems that I think *can* be solved in the theatre. The first and last scenes of the play are good examples. The difficulties of the last scene are obvious —hence the cutting of it in two recent productions. But the opening of the play also poses difficulties because it has no recognizable context for a modern audience. The first encounter of Antonio and Delio is described by F.L. Lucas as a "desultory discussion,"[14] a phrase that would describe equally well much of what happens before the dialogue between Ferdinand and Bosola which starts the plot moving. Critics since Lucas have pointed to the dramatic significance of

175

Antonio's first speech, with its reference to the corrupt court as a poisoned fountain; J.R. Brown, still more helpfully, has found an explanation for the fact that all the characters come drifting onto the stage: they are all supposed to be gathering in the Duchess's presence-chamber, which he sees as one of the major images of the play.[15] The difficulty, of course, is that neither of these points is easy to put across in performance. The first is apparent only in hindsight and the second only in a particular social context. It is not surprising, therefore, that most directors use Antonio and Delio throughout the first scene simply as chorus characters who deliver highly stylized comments on the rest of the cast. At the Royal Court, they went round tilting back the heads of the characters under discussion; at Stratford, Ontario, the brothers and sister were spotlighted in turn as Antonio described them. This approach would seem in keeping with the frankly artificial, literary nature of the "Character" speeches.

But there is a good deal more than this going on in the scene. As Ferdinand's opening line—"Who took the ring oftenest?" (I.i.88)— makes clear, it is set against a background of revels and tournaments. It was a virtue of the two productions by the Royal Shakespeare Company and of the operatic *Duchess* that they both picked up this hint: in the 1960 production, Antonio made his first entrance still dressed for the tournament, then gave back his helmet, gloves, and pike, and, going to the fountain, wet his handkerchief and mopped his brow. A good deal is said later in the play to suggest that the Duchess's court has been a gay and extravagant place. Ferdinand warns her to "give o'er these chargeable revels" (I.i.333); she herself tells Antonio that they need to review their financial position "after these triumphs, and this large expense" (I.i.365), and the thought of this past gaiety seems to come back to her in the last moments of her life, when she tells Cariola:

> In my last will I have not much to give;
> A many hungry guests have fed upon me.
> (IV.ii.200–201)

By taking part in, and winning, the riding at the ring, Antonio associates himself with the mood of the Duchess's court, but Delio's comment that he is "a very formal Frenchman in your habit" (I.i.3) implies that his dress ought somehow to set him apart from the other courtiers.

Ferdinand, on his entrance, immediately contrasts the "sportive action" in which Antonio has just taken part with "action indeed"— that is, with the wars:

Ferd. I shall shortly visit you at Milan, Lord Silvio.
Sil. Your grace shall arrive most welcome.

(I.i.137–39)

Ferdinand is not talking about a state visit but about his intention to take part, under Silvio's generalship, in the siege of the castle of Milan, then occupied by the French. Though he does not make a great deal of this historical background of warfare, which he got from his sources, Webster obviously takes it for granted as part of his action. In particular, he is aware that Milan, on which all the characters converge in act V, has the atmosphere of an armed camp; even the ruined cloister where Antonio hears the echo has been made into a fortification. The movement from Malfi to Milan is part of the disintegration of civilization under the pressure of violence, most memorably symbolized in the scene where the Cardinal ceremonially exchanges his religious robes for a soldier's dress. The historical Cardinal of Aragon was a famous soldier, but Webster also gave some of his warlike qualities to Ferdinand. The Duke's obsession with the falsehood and pretense of women, especially his sister, makes him cling to the idea of war as the only situation in which there is no falsehood,[16] and hence it is not surprising that when he arrives onstage, insane, in the final scene, he should imagine himself on a battlefield.

Thus the formal character speeches of this first scene are presented against a complex background. We are shown two contrasting groups: the Duchess and her court enjoying a time of revels which is about to be succeeded by a period of austerity; Ferdinand and the Cardinal, merry only on the "outside" as Antonio warns us, either bound for the wars or talking of them, and anticipating, in their concern for military honor, their later obsession with that of their sister. In the court but not of it, and hence set aside from either group, are Bosola and Antonio; both comment on the other characters from their differing points of view and both, significantly, are held together for a moment in our minds when Ferdinand wonders whether Antonio would have been "far fitter" than Bosola for the office of spy on the Duchess (I.i.228–29). Other parallels between these two characters will soon be established, as both are offered, in exchange for their secrecy, the long-awaited reward for their past services. Their roles, as we shall see, continue to be intertwined throughout the play.

But let us jump ahead to the final scene. Performances of *The Duchess* are generally thought to fail if the deaths of Ferdinand and the Cardinal are greeted with even the faintest titters, and yet it seems odd that an expert in stage deaths like Webster should have miscalculated his effect here. The difficulty seems to be that the scene fits neither into the black comedy framework familiar to us from recent productions of *The Revenger's Tragedy*, *The Jew of Malta*, and *The White Devil* nor into that of high tragedy like the death of the Duchess herself, where Webster might well have felt that he had observed "all the critical laws, as height of style, and gravity of person."[17] The very number of deaths following in quick succession seems to prove the Bergsonian proposition that repetition is comic, yet there is none of the obvious fantasy that we find in the incredible bravado of Vittoria, Flamineo, and Zanche.[18]

Nevertheless, there are indications all through the last act of *The Duchess* that Webster wants to undercut violence with laughter. Bosola's question to the dying Julia,

> O foolish woman,
> Couldst not thou have poison'd him?
> (V.ii.286–87)

is one example. Another is his anticipation of an effect which Harold Hobson noted in a scathing review of the Royal Court *Duchess*: the mounting laughter with which audiences greeted the business of getting rid of the bodies.[19] Webster obviously realized that whereas Bosola's carrying the Duchess's body offstage could be a moving conclusion to act IV, there was bound to be a sense of parody when he came to do the same for Julia. Hence his self-mocking reply when the Cardinal orders him to "Take up that body":

> I think I shall
> Shortly grow the common bier for churchyards.
> (V.ii.311–12)

Similarly, Ferdinand's madness, particularly his encounter with the doctor, is funny in a way that the madmen in act IV are not. And the Cardinal's careful precautions which ensure that no one will come to his rescue when Bosola attacks him lead to a scene of pure comic cross-talk between him and the actors on the upper level:[20]

> *Card.* The sword's at my throat:—
> *Rod.* You would not bawl so loud then.
> (V.v.26)

When Ferdinand comes charging in on top of this confusion, shouting for a fresh horse in the manner of Richard III, the director may as well give up any hope of a high tragic effect. The Cardinal later says that Ferdinand "gave us these large wounds, as we were struggling / Here i' th' rushes" (V.v.88–89). Though no performance that I have seen has picked up this point, it seems obvious that Webster imagined Bosola and the Cardinal rolling about on the floor at the point where Ferdinand enters. Since both Antonio's body and that of the servant are already lying there as well,[21] it is not surprising that Ferdinand immediately starts behaving as if he were on a battlefield. The whole of the Bosola-Cardinal-Ferdinand *scuffle* (this is the word used in Webster's stage direction) is clearly meant to be undignified and confused.

Besides providing a contrast with the slow and dignified death scene of the Duchess, this pile-up of bodies on the floor has an obvious symbolic appropriateness in a play so much concerned with the rise and fall of men in "places at court." The cliché "*All things do help th' unhappy man to fall*" (III.iv.44) is applied to Antonio after the Loretto scene, and Ferdinand's attempt to catch his shadow by falling on it has been shown to have its source in an allegory about the vanity of worldly honor: "the onely waye to cache it, is to fall downe to the grounde vpon it."[22] So, when Bosola says to the Cardinal,

> thou fall'st faster of thyself, than calamity
> Can drive thee,
>
> (V.v.43–44)

he may not only be speaking figuratively. If the Cardinal has actually knelt to beg for mercy it would be easy, after his recovery of courage—

> Shall I die like a leveret
> Without any resistance?—
>
> (V.v.45–46)

for him to pull Bosola down to the floor, where Ferdinand, a moment later, finds them both.

After all the confusion and scuffling, Webster then uses Bosola's lines, and particularly his hint that Ferdinand is no longer to be taken as a raving lunatic—

> He seems to come to himself,
> Now he's so near the bottom—
>
> (V.v.69–70)

179

to re-establish the somber note which he wants for his ending. Pescara's "How fatally, it seems he did withstand / His own rescue" (V.v.91–92) has a similar effect; the Cardinal's overclever behavior suddenly ceases to be comic. One might compare the technique which Middleton used later in *Women Beware Women*: a series of ludicrously appropriate deaths in a masque is given comic perspective by being set against the naive attempts of the spectators to follow events in a synopsis, until the long speech of Hippolito, the last of the masquers to die, puts an end to the laughter and reminds us that retribution has been not only comically but also terrifyingly apt.

It must be apparent now that there is no simple choice to be made between a realistic and a stylized approach to the play. Sometimes, indeed, as I have suggested with the "scuffle," a symbolic point may be more effectively made by realistic staging than by, say, a series of slow-motion deaths under a red spotlight. It is not always true, however, that the director can have it both ways. I have already noted a number of patterns in the first and last scenes. Now, theoretically, patterns ought to be easy for the director to bring out, by similarities of costume, grouping, and so on. The trouble is that *The Duchess* has far too many of them. Although normally one would be wary of imposing too much sense of pattern on a Jacobean play, I suspect that in Webster's case the cross-references and parallels are as intentional as the coincidences in a novel by Dickens. His obsessive interest in a relatively small number of topics, his apparent determination to make *The Duchess of Malfi* "the most sententious tragedy that ever was written,"[23] and his fascination with the idea of repetition, whether for ritual, irony, or parody, have resulted in an element in the play which no conceivable performance can fully exploit.

A simple example is the scene in which Delio tentatively suggests that Julia should become his mistress, which has puzzled most readers, who generally assume that it is meant either to provide still more evidence of court corruption or to make us (quite unnecessarily) suspicious of Delio. From the point of view of the plot, it is useless, yet it has many reverberations in the rest of the play. Delio's offer of the gold parallels Ferdinand's offer to Bosola in act I, which was the first of many versions of the "service and reward" motif also found in the Duchess's wooing of Antonio and Julia's later wooing of Bosola. None of these cross-references, however, does anything to help the scene itself, which must inevitably be confusing in performance. J.R. Brown has suggested that this is precisely its purpose—not to lead anywhere, but to add to "the audience's sense of a growing web of intrigue and an increasing complexity of character."[24]

There is another parallel to which Webster makes Antonio himself draw our attention:

> I have got
> Private access to his [the Cardinal's] chamber, and intend
> To visit him, about the mid of night,
> As once his brother did our noble duchess.
>
> (V.i.64–67)

Presumably Antonio has a false key such as Ferdinand had, and such as Bosola is about to be given by the Cardinal. It is a curious fact that whereas most of his contemporaries allow characters to come and go on the stage as they please, Webster seems anxious to make us visualize where they come from, how they leave, and how difficult it is to gain "access to private lodgings" (I.i.281). His characters are sometimes locked in as well as out. It is not only the Duchess who eventually finds herself a prisoner in her own palace. In a particularly complicated bit of plotting, all the Duchess's officers are locked into their rooms so that the birth of her first child can be kept secret; Julia apparently locks Bosola in ("Nay, the doors are fast enough") before beginning to woo him (V.ii.152), and Bosola locks the Cardinal in, leaving him no escape except to the room that holds Julia's body.[25] Though Webster often uses an unlocalized stage in the same manner as other Jacobean dramatists, at moments like these he seems to be insisting on the same kind of concentration as the old-fashioned type of detective story which comes complete with a plan of Sir Jasper's country house and timetables of all the suspects.

On a similar level of confusion is the use of disguise in the play. Like many other features of the plot, it starts as metaphor and then becomes literal. Ferdinand's warning his sister against "a visor and a mask" (I.i.334) is probably meant to be taken on both levels. The disguise imagery spreads into the Duchess's language as she is forced from the beginning to

> leave the path
> Of simple virtue, which was never made
> To seem the thing it is not.
>
> (I.i.446–48)

Though she tries to "put off all vain ceremony" (I.i.456), act II shows her, now disguised in a loose-bodied gown, trying vainly to make

Antonio dispense with the ceremony of keeping his hat off before her in public. Her recognition of the need to save his life by a *magnanima menzogna* draws from her the cry:

> O misery! methinks unjust actions
> Should wear these masks and curtains, and not we.
>
> (III.ii.158–59)

As if in response to this wish, the Duchess, in her feigned pilgrim's dress, is met at Loretto by the Cardinal in military dress and later by Bosola with his "counterfeit face"; it is in his disguise as an old man, moreover, that he supervises her death, where, with courageous wit, she again uses the image of undressing:

> I would fain put off my last woman's fault,
> I'd not be tedious to you.
>
> (IV.ii.226–27)

Has Antonio perhaps been wearing a disguise also, while he "lurks about Milan" (IV.i.139)? Though there is no such indication in the stage directions, there are a few hints of it in the text: his intention to "go in mine own shape" to the Cardinal's lodgings (V.i.69), his reference to the "infamous calling" which he has to practice (V.i.73), and his reply to Bosola's "What art thou?"—

> A most wretched thing,
> That only have thy benefit in death,
> To appear myself.
>
> (V.iv.48–50)

The "disguise" might not be more than a tattered cloak, but it would help explain Bosola's mistaking him for a hired assassin like himself.[26] In any case, it does not matter whether it is real or metaphorical; Webster's audience would have been familiar enough with the Stoic view that man takes off the mask and shows his true self only at the moment of death. But the acting out of this adage, which obviously lies at the heart of Websterian tragedy, involves all the characters in a series of pretenses, complicated lies, and half-explained changes of "shape," which, like the other mysterious intrigues and keys passing from hand to hand, are likely simply to bewilder and irritate a modern audience. Somehow it is necessary to make clear that uncertainty and confusion are not flaws in the construction of the play, but its very essence.

This can be seen still more strikingly in Webster's treatment of the physical likeness between the three members of the royal house of

*Neglected plays, traditionally
regarded as critically inferior or
theatrically unmanageable, have been brought
to life in exciting productions on the modern stage.
All photographs are by Angus McBean,
courtesy of
The Harvard Theatre Collection.*

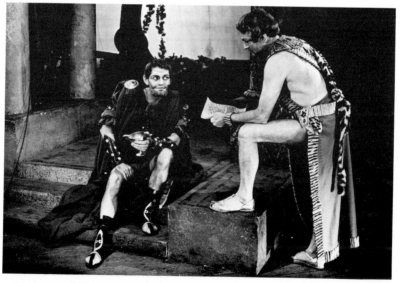

1. *Antony and Cleopatra,* with its problem of alternating scenes between Egypt and Rome on older proscenium stages, has been given full scope on the bare stages of the modern theatre. This setting, with Laurence Olivier as Antony and Norman Wooland as Enobarbus, was designed by Roger Furse for the Michael Benthall production, St. James's Theatre, London, 1951.

2. Peter Hall realized both the elegance and farce of *Love's Labour's Lost* in his 1956 Stratford-on-Avon production designed by James Bailey.

3. Difficult scenes of speechless communication after the mutilation of Lavinia astonished audiences in Peter Brook's production of *Titus Andronicus,* a play once considered hack-work. Michael Denison as Lucius, Vivien Leigh as Lavinia, Laurence Olivier as Titus, and Alan Webb as Marcus Andronicus are shown in the 1955 Stratford-on-Avon production.

4. Modern productions of *Henry VIII* have reinforced arguments for Shakespeare's authorship. In the Old Vic production of 1958 directed by Michael Benthall, John Gielgud as Cardinal Wolsey and Edith Evans as Catharine of Aragon capture the drama of their confrontation.

5. and 6. The 1960 Stratford-on-Avon production of *The Duchess of Malfi*, directed by Donald McWhinnie, attempted to resolve the clash between convention and realism in the play. For the entrance of Peggy Ashcroft as the Duchess, Leslie Hurry designed a symbolic set with the fountain as focus. Characterization, however, was realistic as shown by Patrick Wymark as Bosola and Eric Porter as Ferdinand at the death of the Duchess.

7. *Measure for Measure* was seldom performed in the Victorian theatre because of such scenes as this, represented in the 1950 Stratford-on-Avon production directed and designed by Peter Brook. Here the imprisoned Claudio (Alan Badel) pleads with Isabella (Barbara Jefford) to save his life by yielding her virginity; the disguised Duke (Harry Andrews) overhears.

8. Not acted since Shakespeare's time, *Troilus and Cressida* has become a popular play in the twentieth century. In 1938, Michael Mac Owan stressed its relevance with a modern dress production. Max Adrian as Pandarus sings to Helen (Oriel Ross) and Paris (Michael Denison) at the Trojan court.

Aragon. Ferdinand and the Cardinal look sufficiently alike to make Delio ask whether they are twins (I.i.172); Bosola calls Ferdinand the Duchess's elder brother (IV.i.21); and Ferdinand later calls himself her twin (IV.ii.266). The vagueness may be deliberate. However, a family resemblance is easy enough to create, and at the cost of some far from ideal casting, the 1971 Stratford production succeeded in making its Duchess, Cardinal, and Ferdinand look remarkably alike, a fact that was emphasized in the opening tableau when they were seen side by side as if in a family portrait. It is an idea I had always hoped to see carried out, yet as the play progressed it became increasingly difficult to understand why Webster had insisted on this resemblance. Nothing in the plot depends on anyone mistaking one member of the family for another, as in Shakespearean comedy, and the theory of Ferdinand's incestuous attraction to his sister is neither confirmed nor refuted by our awareness of the likeness between them. One wonders, in fact, whether Webster's original cast—Burbage, Condell, and the boy actor, Sharpe or Robinson—could have borne much actual physical resemblance to one another. Perhaps this is a case for symbolic rather than realistic interpretation.

In stressing both the family resemblance and the spiritual difference between the brothers and their sister, Webster was taking to its furthest extreme the fairytale pattern—three children, of whom two are bad and one is good—which he had already used in *The White Devil* for the Vittoria-Marcello-Flamineo and the Isabella-Francisco-Montecelso group. In *King Lear*, of course, a similar contrast in the King's three daughters had already given rise to metaphysical questions about the origin of good and evil, and at first it seems as if Antonio is going to pursue the same theme:

> You never fix'd your eye on three fair medals,
> Cast in one figure, of so different temper.
>
> (I.i.188–89)

But Antonio takes for granted, rather than questioning, the existence of the Duchess's goodness and her brothers' evil. What really fascinates Webster can be seen in the imagery of the speech. The three characters are compared to works of art ("fair medals") and the speech itself is seen as a portrait of the Duchess ("I'll case the picture up"). *The Duchess* is full of references to likenesses of human beings in inanimate objects: medals, pictures, figures cut in alabaster, waxworks, princes' images on their tombs, and so on. But Antonio goes one step further when he claims that his picture of the Duchess— or the Duchess herself—could serve as a mirror for other women:

Let all sweet ladies break their flatt'ring glasses,
And dress themselves in her.

(I.i.204–5)

He is, of course, using a favorite Elizabethan conceit.[27] To say that one person is a mirror for another may mean, as here, that he is a model of perfection; it may also be a way of describing a likeness between the two. But Webster's habit of revitalizing a familiar metaphor or proverb by taking it literally is nowhere more clearly seen than in the surrealistic effects which he creates on the basis of Antonio's graceful compliment.

Objects in dreams tend to lose their own identities and merge into others. Webster found one such example in the French historian Matthieu, and put it into the mouth of the Duchess:

Methought I wore my coronet of state,
And on a sudden all the diamonds
Were chang'd to pearls.

(III.v.13–15)

Much more frightening than this kind of transformation, however, is the one that attacks the dreamer's own identity; he may be transformed into something else, or he may be threatened by the self in the mirror, which suddenly takes on a separate existence. It is at such moments as these that *The Duchess of Malfi* most truly deserves to be called a nightmare.

The first such instance occurs immediately after a light-hearted scene in which Antonio has talked jokingly of comic and romantic metamorphoses into "flow'rs, precious stones, or eminent stars" (III.ii.32). The Duchess thinks she is talking to Antonio and Cariola, they think they have left her talking to herself, but the figure standing behind her, who appears over her shoulder in the mirror, is Ferdinand holding a poniard.[28] Other "reflections" are equally sinister in character: the echo in the cloister, which picks up only those words that foretell death, speaks not in Antonio's voice but that of the Duchess, and the "thing, arm'd with a rake," appears in the fishponds in the Cardinal's garden where one would expect him to see his own reflection.

Ferdinand's shadow, on the other hand, really *is* a reflection, but he takes it for another person. That he should try to throttle it may be part of the "fatal judgement" which Bosola recognizes as having fallen on him, for he is now obsessed with the nature of the death which he devised for his sister, and his words when he saw her dead face—

She and I were twins:
And should I die this instant, I had liv'd
Her time to a minute—

(IV.ii.267–69)

suggest that he feels her murder to have been a kind of suicide for him. In a hideous version of the lovers' metamorphoses Antonio had joked about, he now imagines himself transformed into a wolf, then into other animals, and in his eyes all the other characters become "beasts for sacrifice" (V.ii.80–81).

We have seen that Ferdinand can "come to himself" in the last moments of his life, just as the Duchess asserts her own identity and Antonio is able to "appear myself" only in death. Their deaths reveal not only what they are but also where their natural affinities lie. Thus Ferdinand, though he had imagined himself dying at the same moment as his twin sister, actually lies alongside the brother who is, as Antonio says, his twin "in quality."[29] This is a theme which Middleton developed with biting clarity in *The Changeling*: Beatrice's death beside De Flores makes apparent to everyone the spiritual kinship which has all along existed between them.[30]

Similarly, the Duchess and Antonio, who die thinking of their children and of one another, are further linked through the symbolism of the echo scene. The idea that husband and wife are one is common enough, but Webster draws our attention to its strangeness by the curious imagery in which he expresses it throughout the play: their parting is compared to the taking apart of a clock (III.v.61–65), and the Duchess says that the sight of the "dead" Antonio (though she does not know that he is a wax image) affects her as if her own image had been made in wax and used to torture her (IV.i.62–65). In the wooing scene, Antonio had realized that she was, as it were, acting his part for him—"These words should be mine" (I.i.472)— and she had reassured him: "You speak in me this, for we now are one" (I.i.497). This means that the echo scene, unlike the other reflections discussed, is not merely ominous but also tender: in the union of perfect love, one partner can be a true mirror of the other.

As one would expect from the fact that he is both the murderer and the revenger of the Duchess, Bosola finds himself, like Richard III after his nightmare, in a position where his only logical course is to "revenge myself upon myself." The saying that "Revenge proves its own executioner," to be specifically stated and acted out in Ford's *The Broken Heart*, finds many variations in the earlier drama: the straightforward suicide of Hieronymo; the deaths, at each others' hands, of Hamlet and Laertes, alter egos ("For by the image of my cause, I see / The portraiture of his"); the ludicrous situation where Vendice in one disguise is hired to kill himself in another disguise. The killing of Antonio by Bosola is likewise something of a symbolic suicide, since it puts an end to his "long suit" and his "hope of pardon" no less than to Antonio's. I have already noted how Webster establishes a parallel between the two characters in the opening scene of the play.[31] In a sense, Bosola's behavior after the Duchess's murder can be seen as an attempt to take on Antonio's role; he declares that he will "execute" her "last will" (a task which, in the wooing scene, she intended for her steward), but his accidental killing of the man he hoped to rescue shows that to the last he, however unwittingly, is acting on the orders of Ferdinand and the Cardinal.

The darkness in which he kills Antonio is later extended, in Bosola's mind, to the symbolic darkness in which he sees all mankind as living. *The Duchess of Malfi* contains a great many nocturnal scenes, and J.R. Brown thinks that Webster was probably relying on the special lighting effects available at the new indoor theatre: "What would be difficult, clumsy, and grotesque at the Globe, could be thrilling and sensitive in the darkened auditorium of the Blackfriars."[32] There is no doubt that Webster, like his contemporaries, was influenced by the lighting and staging effects which reached their height in the court masques of the period. Some of the play's imagery may have been inspired by the two most striking features of the masque: its chiaroscuro vision of life and its use of metamorphoses and transformation scenes at the climax of a performance. At the Globe, both actors and audience shared the daylight, and darkness could only be indicated symbolically by the carrying of torches or lanterns; at Blackfriars, where candles illuminated the auditorium as well as the stage, a complete blackout would have been impossible but the overall effect must have been one of twilight even when Ferdinand supposedly sees his shadow in the sunshine (V.ii.35–37).

A modern producer, with sophisticated lighting effects at his disposal and a darkened auditorium to set them off, might seem better equipped than Webster's original performers to bring out the play's image of life as "a shadow, or deep pit of darkness" (V.v.101). But complete realism in lighting can be a disadvantage. Many crucial scenes in *The Duchess* take place at night and depend on characters not being able to see one another clearly: Antonio's meeting with Bosola in act II, the scene in which he is killed by him, and the sinister visit of Ferdinand to the Duchess in act IV. If the director is committed to realistic lighting he will have to play these scenes in an almost total blackness, which may not only confuse the audience but also lose its attention; if he decides to sacrifice realism to intelligibility he risks making the characters' mistakes and misunderstandings look merely silly instead of tragic. The "dead man's hand" scene is a particular problem. In my experience, Ferdinand's "Where are you?" generally gets a laugh when this scene is played in total darkness. Webster probably inserted the line to help his audience imagine a completely darkened stage, since both characters would in fact have been visible at Blackfriars as at the Globe. When the stage really *is* dark Ferdinand tends to sound embarrassed rather than sinister. It also seems to me vastly preferable that we should be able to see the Duchess's face as the truth of what she is holding dawns on her.

The fact that darkness was metaphorical at the Globe and literal at Blackfriars has implications for *The Duchess* which go beyond such local effects as these. One can best understand the significance of the new staging by looking back at *Othello*, another play which makes great use of nocturnal scenes but which was written for the outdoor playhouse. Like *The Duchess*, it depends a great deal on confusions and misunderstandings between characters, and it contains a scene of stabbing in the dark which may be compared with Bosola's killing of Antonio. The constant emphasis on uncertainty—where the Turkish fleet is going, who is approaching in the dark streets of Venice, whose ship is coming into port in Cyprus, who started the street fight, and so on—creates a background for Othello's being "perplex'd in the extreme" and leads, in the scene of Iago's attempted murder of Cassio, to the question (ironically, it is Iago himself who asks it, and he does not need an answer), "What may you be? Are you of good or evil?"

The difference is that at the Globe the audience could see what was really happening on the stage, just as they could see what was happening to Othello and know, as he did not, whether Iago was "of good or evil." The characters might be in physical and moral darkness, but the spectators were never in doubt as to how they themselves were to respond to events. The peculiar horror of Othello, often blunted in productions with overatmospheric lighting effects, is that we are forced to watch in helpless clarity as the hero walks blindly, in his private darkness, over a precipice. The darkness in which Bosola stabs Antonio, however, is a darkness which the Blackfriars audience would have shared with him. It is not at all clear from the scene exactly whom Bosola thinks he is killing—Ferdinand, the Cardinal, or an anonymous assassin. The voices come from different parts of the stage and then disappear; he is perhaps meant to think that they are all the same voice. When he gives up all attempt to explain what has happened—"Such a mistake as I have often seen / In a play" (V.v.95–96)—we can almost join with him in feeling that his actions are preordained by a script written somewhere else, and that no one can be expected to make much sense out of "this gloomy world" where "we cannot be suffered to do good when we have a mind to it" (IV.ii.359–60).

Yet the moral generalizations which fill the play seem to belong to a different climate, that of the outdoor playhouses, where good and evil could be clearly recognized for what they were. Perhaps this explains what Ian Jack among others has pointed out in Webster's work: "this background of moral doctrine has nothing to do with the action of the plays."[33] Bosola's last speech (V.v.94–105) alternates between cries of despair—

> In a mist . . .
> We are only like dead walls, or vaulted graves,
> That ruin'd, yields no echo. . . .
>   O, this gloomy world!
> In what a shadow, or deep pit of darkness,
> Doth womanish and fearful mankind live! . . .
> Mine is another voyage—

and straightforward moralizing—

> It may be pain, but no harm to me to die
> In so good a quarrel. . . .
> Let worthy minds ne'er stagger in distrust
> To suffer death, or shame for what is just.

The more optimistic *sententiae* sound like fragments which he has shored against his ruins, and it is not just the coincidence of the image that makes me wonder whether, like Eliot in *The Wasteland*, Webster was aware of the ironic contrast between these moralistic literary echoes and the moral chaos of the background against which they are spoken.

It is generally true of poetic drama that more things are going on in the language than can possibly be conveyed to an audience on any one occasion, but *The Duchess of Malfi* outdoes all its contemporaries in the sheer complexity of its patterns and cross-references. Webster, like his Cardinal in act V, was suicidally clever; from the beginning his play has had to be cut heavily in performance. Una Ellis-Fermor suggested long ago, with particular reference to the final scene, that although *The Duchess* was susceptible of a "more or less naturalistic presentation," its musical and poetic values were "utterly alien to any plausible stage representation."[34] One need not agree with her suggestions about either a naturalistic or a poetic delivery of the lines to understand her uneasiness. I think it explains why the much cut and altered operatic version was in many ways the most successful fusion of the realistic and dreamlike qualities of the play: the one conveyed in the production, the other in the music itself. The effect of a Jacobean masque, if we could recreate it, might be rather similar. No doubt one reason why Webster and his contemporaries were so fascinated by the form was that they realized how much of what they really wanted to do could be better expressed by nonverbal means.

The Darkened Stage:
J. P. Kemble and
Troilus and Cressida

Jeanne T. Newlin

What are we to make of dramatic judgment which darkened the stage for one Shakespearean play for almost three hundred years? No professional productions of *Troilus and Cressida* in its original form are recorded since the disputed entry in the *Stationers' Register* of 7 February 1602/3, "as yt is acted by my Lord Chamberlens Men vjd," until 1907. We might not be surprised at such blank pages in the stage history of *1 Henry VI* or *Titus Andronicus*, plays whose structural weaknesses, melodramatic or episodic plots, dated conventions, and thematic irrelevances fail to interest producers. These plays have been performed with somewhat greater frequency in the twentieth century only in the several attempts to produce the Shakespearean canon. This is not the case for *Troilus and Cressida*, whose twentieth-century stage history is an amazing reversal of earlier opinion. Its dramatic effectiveness has been so vindicated in the theatre that today the spectator might have less trouble finding a performance of *Troilus* than one of *Henry V*. From Shaw onward, critics and audience have come to term *Troilus* the most "modern" of Shakespeare's plays.[1] No doubt part of its appeal has been its deflation of military honor and romantic sensualism in a cynical, war-weary world. Beyond that, however, the play has been shown to be a complex and sophisticated work of Shakespeare's maturity.

At its very best, modern criticism has been able to make only sweeping allegations to explain the failure of earlier tastes to appreciate the play and to defend its own enthusiasm. We see the Restoration trapped in its critical theory, dismayed by the seemingly disjointed double plot, and outraged by the indecorous handling of characters from classical myth. Only Dryden's remolding of the play into heroic drama could satisfy the late seventeenth and early eighteenth centuries. Even his version was dropped from repertory after 1733. In the following age of Shakespearean revivals, dominated by Garrick, we blame the star system for the indifference to *Troilus*. No

190

modification of the original play would provide a *tour de force* as
thrilling as the usual Garrick role. The late eighteenth century's indifference coincides with the emergence of sentimental drama, making the ungallant Troilus and the unfaithful Cressida of doubtful
appeal. With sentimentality hardened into an ethical cast through
the Victorian period, Shakespeare's lovers could only offend morals
and his warriors only ridicule imperialism.

Historical generalizations such as these may foreshadow as easy
a dismissal of the modern delight in the play by future critics. However, there is a piece of theatrical evidence, positive evidence at a
fortuitous moment in Shakespearean stage history, which explains
the darkened stage, reinforces the generalizations, supports recent
judgment, and, in fact, sheds light upon the nature of the play. Even if
the play was not performed, at least one producer gave much thought
and work to an intended production. His thinking is a barometer of
the age. His failure to present even his whitewashed version indicates
the distance between popular theatre of his day and Shakespeare's
play.

At the turn of the nineteenth century, John Philip Kemble decided
to revive the play. Using an inexpensive 1791 edition of *Troilus*, he
prepared a promptbook by rearranging scenes, transposing and ex-
cising lines, and casting some of the roles.[2] Surely aware of the bleak
stage history, his decision was a risk. Covent Garden, then in financial
difficulty, could not afford the luxury of producing an uninviting
classic.[3] The risk was underscored by a carefully argued warning,
which, it seems likely, Kemble had before him as he prepared his
promptbook. In the 1774 Bell Acting Edition of the play, Francis
Gentleman had expressed the popular consensus:

> The great end of every drama is, or should be, *instruction relished
> by amusement*; so far as any production fails of this, it fails in
> value. Judging similarly of *Troilus and Cressida*, it is a very cen-
> surable effusion of dramatic fancy; for except some very fine senti-
> ments scattered up and down, it is void of the essential requisites;
> besides, characters are so oddly blended, the scenes are so multi-
> plied, and the plot so strangely wound up, that we think it stands
> but a poor chance of giving either public or private satisfaction.[4]

It is a curious advertisement for an "acting edition," but Bell's
Troilus and Cressida was an acting edition in name only. Bell's editions of Shakespeare, published in the 1770s, printed acting versions
of the plays as they were then performed in the London theatres.
Francis Gentleman wrote the introductions and notes. In those cases

where the plays were not performed, the original Shakespearean texts were published with suggested alterations and omissions by Gentleman; they were advertised nonetheless as straight from the London stage.

Kemble recognized that the play in its original form had "but a poor chance" of satisfying the public. Apparently guided by Gentleman's suggestions as he had been in so many of his other Shakespearean alterations, however, Kemble set to work on a promptbook that would overcome popular objections. He hoped to attract an audience by portraying on stage the epic struggle between Greeks and Trojans. Whatever proportion (and critics argue this) Shakespeare assigns to the themes of love and war, Kemble made the siege of Troy his heroic main plot and relegated the unhappy love affair to a tragic subplot. To ensure this focus and an appropriately serious tone, he stripped the play of any comedy. His adaptation was intended to satisfy the decorum which he associated with classical legend and simultaneously to cater to the sensibilities of an audience prone to take offense at the bawdy and sexual coarseness of the original.

Correlating Gentleman's commentary with the alterations adopted by Kemble provides fascinating documentation of what the late eighteenth century believed necessary for a successful production of *Troilus and Cressida*. Moreover, Shakespeare's intention and design are placed in relief by Kemble's omissions and transpositions.

In his alteration, Kemble begins the play with the Greek council scene. Gentleman had suggested this but worried that we would "be less acquainted with the disposition of Troilus." Because he diminishes that role, Kemble is less concerned. (Furthermore, the promptbook establishes Kemble himself in the role of Ulysses!) Shakespeare's three scenes of act I are redistributed among four scenes; by dividing the council scene at the news of Hector's challenge into his act I, scene i and act I, scene iv, Kemble begins and ends his act I with the war. The middle scenes are given over to Troilus and Cressida, so that their love becomes a personal, tragic countertheme played out against the epic victory of Greeks over Trojans. Instead of the Shakespearean emphasis on Troilus and his lovesickness expressed in terms contemptuous of the war, Kemble introduces the action with Agamemnon's state-of-the-war- speech, an exposition which plots out the major action.

Gentleman frequently is alarmed about the length of Shakespeare's speeches for stage presentation. Kemble cuts even more ruthlessly than the Bell edition recommended. Agamemnon's opening speech is cut from its original thirty lines to twelve. In fact, this entire first scene is a characteristic example of Kemble's technique in compression. The scene is cut by more than a third. Where Shakespeare elaborates, Kemble ferrets out the simplest expression of the idea. Gentleman thought the degree speech "too long, and too redundant"; Kemble reduced it by forty-five percent. Ulysses's extended discussion of the chaos which results when the planets are in disorder becomes baldly

> Oh, when degree is shaked,
> Which is the ladder to all high designs,
> The enterprise is sick!

Where Shakespeare offers a second or third simile, Kemble allows but a single image. He permits Agamemnon to describe the Greek setbacks as "the protractive trials of Great Jove," but cuts nine lines of metaphor in which their constancy is compared to fine metal tested "in the wind and tempest" of Fortune's frown. For both Gentleman and Kemble, simple and direct communication obviously is more manly for Homeric warriors than the pompous rhetoric which some critics have argued is Shakespeare's intent. The speech of Nestor is an illustration. Whether or not Shakespeare intended Nestor as an old garrulous figure of fun, his lines have been so pared in Kemble's council scenes that he can be played only as a venerable sage. In the same way, wherever Shakespearean lines may be read as ironic, Kemble cuts, as with Ulysses's affected tributes to Agamemnon and Nestor and Agamemnon's bewildering if not ironic, reply:

> Speak, Prince of Ithaca, and be't of less expect
> That matter needless, of importless burden,
> Divide thy lips than we are confident
> When rank Thersites opes his mastic jaws
> We shall hear music, wit, and oracle.
>
> (I.iii.70–74)

Inevitably, characterization lost flavor when Kemble catered to an increasing refinement. His audience would not tolerate such vulgarities as

> to cough and spit
> And, with a palsy-fumbling on his gorget,
> Shake in and out the rivet.
>
> (I.iii.173–75)

Kemble begins his story of Troilus in the second scene. Here, his most pressing problem was a modification in character; Gentleman's note warned, "Troilus, here finely, describes himself, in a far gone state of amorous imbecility." Kemble wanted a Trojan hero, tragic in his love, not a lovesick adolescent "less valiant than the virgin in the night" who refuses to "war without the walls of Troy." Critics who readily interpret Shakespeare's Troilus as the tragic hero may be surprised at the extensive cuts which Kemble believed necessary to rescue his Trojan from "amorous imbecility." One soliloquy may be considered:

> Peace, you ungracious clamours! peace, rude sounds!
> Fools on both sides! Helen must needs be fair,
> When with your blood you daily paint her thus.
> I cannot fight upon this argument;
> It is too starved a subject for my sword.
> But Pandarus,—O gods, how do you plague me!
> I cannot come to Cressid but by Pandar;
> And he's as tetchy to be woo'd to woo,
> As she is stubborn-chaste against all suit.
> Tell me, Apollo, for thy Daphne's love,
> What Cressid is, what Pandar, and what we?
>
> (I.i.92–102)

Kemble felt obliged for his purpose to delete both excessive emotion and insistent sexuality. Instead of fifteen lines, Kemble reduced the speech to four:

> But Pandarus,—O gods, how do you plague me!
> I cannot come to Cressid but by Pandar;
> And he's as tetchy to be woo'd to woo,
> And she is stubborn-chaste against all suit.

Troilus is much less vulnerable when his dismay with the war and his sexual desires are limited to a mere expression of annoyance that he must win Cressida through the unsavory Pandarus. Even where Gentleman would allow Troilus "strange flights . . . however fanciful and extravagant" since he is a lover, Kemble deletes these so that the character conveys only an appropriately heroic stature.

Cressida is introduced in the third scene of the adaptation. Unlike Dryden's heroine, she does betray Troilus but Kemble traces her downfall in much fainter lines than Shakespeare. Reflecting theatrical taste in the late eighteenth century, she is sketched as the fallen woman of sentimental drama—not quite more sinned against than sinning, but certainly led by circumstance rather than character. The first clue to this Cressida is visual. Instead of entering alone with her servant Alexander, she is accompanied more modestly by "two virgins." To sustain that modesty and refinement, Kemble cut her suggestive repartee with Alexander and Pandarus sharply. Blending with her ladies-in-waiting, she loses her Shakespearean personality, her wit and coquetry. Gone are her methods, "Upon my back, to defend my belly, upon my wit, to defend my wiles . . ." and gone is her premise:

> Therefore this maxim out of love I teach:
> Achievement is command; ungained, beseech.
>
> (I.ii.318–19)

Her purpose is little more than the revelation of her feelings for Troilus. The entire scene is converted from Shakespeare's flippant gaiety to the more serious game of courtship set against the cadence of marching Trojan soldiers. Although Gentleman here had marked more lines for omission than Kemble actually deleted, an example of their agreement in interpretation is their mutual cutting of Pandarus's long joke about the single white hair in Troilus's youthful beard. When Pandarus baits Cressida with this jest of Helen's supposed love for Troilus, Shakespeare incorporates the extreme youth of Troilus, the flirtations of Helen, the merriment of the court, including the hearty laughter of Hecuba, Cassandra, Hector, and Paris, and the cuckolding of Menelaus, interrupted frequently by clever retorts from Cressida. Kemble's rejection strips away the comedy, refines Cressida's character, bowdlerizes the mocking allusions to cuckoldry, forbids the humanizing of the legendary Trojan court, and suppresses indication of Troilus's age. Throughout, Kemble's tone requires maturity in lover and warrior.

To emphasize the war, Kemble closed act I with a fourth scene, the last 180 lines of Shakespeare's act I, scene iii reduced by about half. Here too Kemble coincides with Gentleman, for, although he deleted more than is noted in the Bell edition, they both agree that the banter between Aeneas and the Greeks should be omitted and that the challenge itself should be kept. Gentleman had written, "This challenge, though a whimsical one in its nature, has something very manly and spirited in it." Nestor's amusing reply is dropped since there is no need in this adaptation to fear that the challenge will go unanswered. Surprisingly, Kemble kept Nestor's concluding lines:

Now I begin to relish thy advice;
And I will give a taste of it forthwith
To Agamemnon: go we to him straight.
Two curs shall tame each other: pride alone
Must tarre the mastiffs on, as 'twere their bone.
(I.iii.388–92)

Gentleman had protested, "A most low idea concludes this Act; which is through the whole uninteresting, and by no means advantageously calculated for representation."

Kemble might have been expected to follow as well Gentleman's advice to cut the first scene of act II entirely, "surely too immaterial to be retained." Kemble, however, had already listed the popular comedian John Bannister for the role of Thersites and it cannot be imagined that either Bannister or the audience would tolerate Thersites's first scene omitted. Kemble must have realized that for his audience the trouble would not be the pertinence of the scene but its scurrility. Consequently, he deleted the most offensive terms, "bitch wolf's son," "Mistress Thersites," "whoreson cur," and "bowels." He rewrote others: "How if he had boils" became "How if he did itch." Such concessions to taste run through the text.

Kemble made only minor changes in the Trojan council scene (II.ii) but the interpretation of the scene is clear. All the changes support a comment which occurred to Gentleman as he was writing his notes for the scene, "All the chiefs, both Trojan and Grecian, require dignified externals, and graceful oratory, for stage representation." Both adapters omitted the angriest exchange, that between Helenus and Troilus. And even though he compressed Hector's speech against the war, Kemble kept the sense, surely in approval of Gentleman's judgment, "The soft moral sensations, which appear in this speech, deserve great approbation and strict attention, as sensibly appealing to one of the tenderest feelings of life, though seldom properly attended to; we mean, matrimonial chastity."

Act II, scene iii holds up well in both alterations. Gentleman wrote, "The principle of flattery is well maintained through this scene; and the act in general has much more merit and importance than the former." Working some twenty-five years later, Kemble was keenly aware of theatrical strictures without Gentleman's protest, "*Thersites* aims much at the ludicrous, but is a little too licentious in some of his ideas, and therefore should be occasionally retrenched." The major changes are in Thersites's lines with such peculiar substitutions (for the modern reader) as "wenching" for "lechery."

The textual changes prompted by the sensitivities of editors and audiences result in expurgations, the rule in the theatrical history of the period. Moral taste and dramatic decorum being closely linked, it is not surprising that both Kemble and Gentleman worked toward heroic drama in the major plot and sentimentalism in their subplot. What may be more germane to an understanding of Shakespeare's *Troilus and Cressida* are the tonal changes which the adapters thought necessary. Critics of the play have wrangled for centuries about its genre. It has been labeled tragedy, comedy, satire—with every variation and combination imaginable. When a director decides upon a single genre and a consistent tone, he inevitably diminishes the complexity of Shakespeare's play. To sustain the dignity associated with heroic drama and with tragedy, Gentleman and Kemble excised a great deal which they surmised to be comic and ironic.

Gentleman would begin act III with the entrance of Paris and Helen instead of the opening "buffoonery" between Pandarus and the servant. Kemble, however, went even further and cut the entire scene. The original scene is essentially comic, with its jests and repartee either sexually explicit or implicit through double entendre. The mere presence of Helen so undermines tone that Kemble dropped her role. He began his third act with Shakespeare's scene ii, the rendezvous of Troilus and Cressida. Despite the difficulty of his task, Kemble alters the scene to evoke a romantic image of the lovers. Troilus is the hero-lover; Cressida appears almost innocent and shy. The lines and appearances of Pandarus are reduced. Gentleman had defined the sentimental tone and its discordant element, "This scene is rich with very fanciful feeling ideas, worthy of our author, but *Pandarus* is a very great disgrace to them, and the conclusion is rather fulsome; some lines are therefore marked for omission." Kemble denotes Troilus's entrance as manly without the extravagances in his anticipation of Cressida that Shakespeare had written. In a significant instance of omission changing tone, the hero is denied his fantasy, "where I may wallow in the lily beds." Cressida is brought in as a blushing maiden. Any suggestions to the contrary, as in Pandarus's lines, are dropped. Pandarus neither urges the lovers to kiss nor hints that, were it night, no urging would be necessary. Unlike Shakespeare's leering bawd whose intrusive presence qualifies every protestation of love, Pandarus departs. As they confess their feelings, Cressida acts with restraint. There is no evidence of her impatience for Kemble cut her thrice-repeated invitation to enter the house and her coquettish plea for a kiss. After Pandarus re-enters, Kemble transposed lines so that the scene ends not with the bawd leading the lovers to bed but with the uncle protesting his family's fidelity:

> Nay, I'll give my word for her too.
> Our kindred, though they be long ere they are wooed,
> They are constant being won. They are burrs,
> I can tell you, they'll stick where they are thrown.
>
> (III.ii.117–20)

Kemble structured his third act around two crucial situations, the union of the lovers and the baiting of Achilles. The latter scene (III.iii) followed Shakespeare's treatment closely. Gentleman had considered the third act much more important than the first two though he still objected to the lengthy speech, "too prolix to bear speaking to the general ear; argumentative harangues, on the stage, should be concise." What alterations Kemble made aimed at the prolixity; as usual he compressed for the sake of pacing and directness. He deleted morally offensive lines. The particular lines which he chose, however, had the deliberate effect of improving Achilles's image. Achilles is less proud and, of course, not tinged by suggestion of homosexuality.

The five scenes in act IV follow Shakespeare's arrangement. The first scene has only minor omissions, Diomedes's mockery of lust in Paris and Menelaus as a significant example. Curiously, Kemble kept some of the dialogue whereas Gentleman thought the entire segment "should unquestionably be expunged. . . . Diomed's expressions trespass strongly on decorum." The awakening of the lovers in scene ii was toned down "to abridge indecency, trifling, and superfluity." The frankest lines of the lovers and the jests of Pandarus were cut. One example will illustrate the difference in portrayal. Kemble's Cressida sighs romantically, "Night hath been too brief," but Shakespeare's continues petulantly:

> You men will never tarry.
> Oh foolish Cressid! I might have still held off,
> And then you would have tarried.
>
> (IV.ii.16–18)

There is a sense of the tone in the modification of stage business as well. When Cressida hears knocking and calls Troilus back to her chamber in alarm, Kemble omits her line and the implicit stage business, "You smile and mock me, as if I meant naughtily." The lines which Kemble retained for Cressida would in no way threaten Gentleman's picture of the sentimental heroine, "*Cressida* should have elegant delicacy, and considerable powers of expression." After the brief scene in which Paris and Troilus meet, the lovers are shown at their parting. Again, the role of Pandarus is reduced. The farewell embrace for the Shakespearean audience is conditioned by Pandarus's recollection of an appropriate rhyme. Kemble restricts Pandarus to but few expressions of grief throughout the scene so that nothing detracts from the couple. Again the more emotional cries of Troilus are omitted. Cressida's infidelity is not foreshadowed but merely hinted at. Troilus does warn Cressida about the Greeks' charm but without the Shakespearean emphasis. The "delicacy" of the heroine does not permit her to retort, "My lord, will you be true?" nor is Troilus allowed to subvert morality by declaiming that faithfulness is his vice. Cressida's sincerity extends into the fifth scene where she is delivered to the Greeks. Agamemnon greets her with a kiss, but Kemble, agreeing with Gentleman, cut the kissing exchange and the familiar repartee. Gentleman had omitted Ulysses's lines including the famous "daughters of the game." Amusingly, Kemble, cast as Ulysses, restored these even though they violate decorum as much as the ones he deleted. Throughout the rest of the scene, alterations are made to reinforce previous points: comments about Troilus's youth are cut, Nestor's verbosity is cropped, and mocking allusions to Menelaus are excised. On Kemble's stage, then, the scene would move very quickly from a ten-line introduction of Cressida at the Greek camp to the greater interest, the combat between Hector and Ajax.

The last act of Shakespeare's play disturbed Gentleman. In note after note, he suggests omissions and rearrangements. He would begin seventy-four lines into the first scene because "every preceding syllable seems to us much fitter for rejection than acceptance" (Thersites-Achilles-Patroclus banter). Later lines he terms "unpleasing," "superfluous," "very gross." One section has "an intolerable quantity of trivial matter . . . without anything tragically affecting, or comically amusing." Another is "too free"; a third "has no business here." In despair, he writes, "All these excursionary scenes are much too full of action for representation." The action itself is despicable. Concerning the death of Hector, he deplored, "This is a most cowardly mean conquest." Concerning the humiliation of Hector's body, he grudgingly admitted, "This shows a most brutal conqueror, or rather warlike assassin, but is consistent with history."

Kemble no doubt felt the same dismay. Furthermore, since his project was not simply a criticism of Shakespeare as the Bell edition was but an acting version for performance, Kemble's interpretation had to draw together the two threads of plot and subplot. The link was Troilus, but the dramatic burden which Kemble imposed on the part could not be borne. The last act is the least satisfying in the adaptation. In the subplot, Troilus is to witness the loss of his love and respond tragically. In the major plot, when he hears of Hector's death, he is to convert his personal tragedy into a heroic cry for revenge. The play is to end with his assumption of Trojan leadership. Yet, whether Kemble intended it or not, our attention has been engaged throughout by the Greeks. There has been no preparation for identification with Trojan tragedy. So restricted has Kemble been by his concept of heroic decorum that he changed Hector's cowardly murder to a death effected by Achilles in single combat. Consequently, the audience must see this act as the logical and dramatic conclusion to the major plot, something with which it had sympathized all along, a Greek victory.

Kemble handled Troilus's personal tragedy adequately within a romantic interpretation. Cressida must fall, but she does not fall tauntingly. Troilus must watch, but he does not do so contemptuously. Kemble deleted the familiarity between Cressida and Diomedes which Shakespeare shows immediately. Her first words and the stage business of her whispers are cut. So too are Ulysses's condemnation, "She will sing any man at first sight" and Thersites's agreement. Kemble intended his audience to hear only Cressida's protest, "In faith, I cannot. What would you have me do?" It is Diomedes who woos; Cressida neither baits nor begs. She yields under his pressure, but the pressure extenuates her betrayal considerably. In addition, Thersites is deprived of his sharpest barbs. The effect of the scene upon Troilus, of course, is grievous. Still, the exclamations of grief are so much more disciplined than in Shakespeare that Kemble may delete as unnecessary Ulysses's impatient, "Oh, contain yourself." The difference between sentimental tragedy and Shakespeare's intention may be illustrated in Kemble's change of a single word. When Troilus confronts Diomedes, Kemble's line reads, "And pay thy life thou owest me for my love." Shakespeare had written the bitter challenge, "And pay thy life thou owest me for my horse" with the unmistakably damning echo of the word whore.

Kemble made his major structural changes by scrambling the final scenes. With his consistent respect for his classical heroes, he could not accept the brutal murder of Hector by the Myrmidons. Regardless of the dramatic consequences of his interpretation, Kemble seems compelled to maintain dignity for all the warriors just as he keeps decorum for his lovers. He postponed the entrance of Achilles by dropping him from Shakespeare's scenes v and vi and eliminated scene vii in which Achilles plots the murder with the Myrmidons. Achilles enters the battle for the first time when he confronts Hector. In Shakespeare, the two giants back off in this encounter and exit without a struggle. Kemble patched together Achilles's entrance with lines transposed from earlier scenes. The adaptation was to be staged with Achilles shouting for Hector. Hector enters and is challenged. Kemble gives him a Shakespearean line but in a context which excuses his impending defeat:

> I would have been much more a fresher man
> Had I expected thee.

The two warriors then do glorious battle until the one is slain. The fight is honorable, and Kemble punctuates it with Achilles's victory cry shifted from Shakespeare's scene viii:

> So, Ilion, fall thou next! now, Troy, sink down!
> Here lies thy heart, thy sinews, and thy bone.
> On, Myrmidons, and cry you all amain,
> "Achilles hath the mighty Hector slain."

Gone from the last act are the ironic commentaries which Shakespeare provided in a Thersites groveling for his life and a Pandarus rejected by an enraged Troilus.

Kemble did assign the last word to Pandarus but not the mocking epilogue of his final Shakespearean speech. In a condensed form, his lines have the ring of a moral satisfying the ethical demands of the audience:

> A goodly medicine for my aching bones! Thus is the poor
> agent despised! O traitors and bawds, how earnestly are
> you set a-work, and how ill requited! What instance for
> it? Let me see:
> "Full merrily the humblebee doth sing
> Till he hath lost his honey and his sting,
> And being once subdued in armèd tail,
> Sweet honey and sweet notes together fail."

Francis Gentleman had begun his commentary on Shakespeare's play with the pose of the disinterested critic, "From so grand an assemblage of eminent characters, as we perceive in the drama of this play, some transactions, situations, and sentiments, particularly interesting, may reasonably be expected; investigation will gratify, or defeat our hopes." When he finished his explication, he concluded that Shakespeare had failed, our hopes defeated. Despite the reworking of the material into epical and ethical form, apparently Kemble too felt defeated. The risks remained too high. His prompt-book was left unacted. It would take the investigations of the twentieth-century theatre to gratify an audience more in tune with Shakespeare's irony.

The Taming of the Shrew
—with
"Additional Dialogue"?

Robert Hamilton Ball

Probably everyone who reads about film is aware of the story that the Pickford-Fairbanks *Taming of the Shrew* (1929) carried after acknowledgment to William Shakespeare as author an attached credit: "Additional Dialogue by Sam Taylor." Historians and reviewers, reporters and columnists, distinguished professors and undistinguished popularizers, lecturers, directors, and actors have enjoyed and repeated the absurdity. At a luncheon of British film critics which I attended some years ago, many admitted to having perpetuated the tale. Mary Pickford in an interview professed annoyance that the credit line had ever been permitted. There is no need to list those responsible for the proliferation, especially since I hope to embarrass them, and, by way of extenuation, I have to admit that in an unguarded moment I once contributed myself, and therefore have to take my share of the responsibility. It was, I suppose, too good a laugh at Hollywood fatuity to miss. Nevertheless, I have come to believe that the credit is a fable, especially since Sam Taylor denied that the ridiculously supererogatory line ever existed except in someone's imagination. Moreover, though people have told me that they remember seeing the "additional dialogue" on the screen, none of them could defend the allegation with any evidence except recollection after a long interval. I have not been able to find any responsible documentation to support it. The purpose of this essay is to examine the evidence by presenting an account of the production and presentation of the film, to account for the origin of the story, and to show why I think it is a canard.

By 1929 sound pictures were established and spoken dialogue was here to stay. To be sure, silent versions of sound films were sometimes made to accommodate those theatres which had not yet been wired to carry words, music, audible effects, and frequently cacophony to audiences who had been essentially spectators, but the revolution in the industry was rapid. Directors had to deal with a new dimension;

actors had to learn to speak effectively or be replaced by those who had been stage trained. Among the busiest and most sought after people in the movie industry were those who could teach and train the management of voice. If sound were to be not merely an obtrusive addition to silent film but an amalgamation with motion, the reigning stars had to look in new directions.

The most famous couple in Hollywood were no exception. Douglas Fairbanks began using sound in *The Iron Mask*. Mary Pickford was in production in her first "all-talking" film, *Coquette*, an adaptation of a successful Broadway play, under the direction of Sam Taylor. They had been thinking of breaking the pattern further by co-starring in a picture as soon as a suitable vehicle could be found.[1] At this point the Stratford-upon-Avon Festival Company from the Shakespeare Memorial Theatre, on tour in the United States, arrived in Los Angeles for the presentation of its repertoire. On 31 December 1928 and on 5 and 10 January 1929, the play presented was *The Taming of the Shrew*, the story of another famous couple. Miss Pickford, Mr. Fairbanks, and Sam Taylor, invited by Fairbanks, attended one or more of the performances at the Mason Theatre. This was the germ of the first full-length sound film of a comedy "by William Shakespeare," as it was to be listed on the film credits. As such it was to achieve a modest success, not to be discussed here.

The reaction of Fairbanks and Taylor to the stage performance was an enthusiastic welcome of *The Taming of the Shrew* as a film vehicle. Pickford has indicated that she was reluctant but was finally persuaded to give her approval. *The Iron Mask*, a "part-talkie," and *Coquette*, still in the studios, were released in March, and the stars flew off for a brief vacation in Mexico. Taylor, who had come to Hollywood as a scenarist and worked as such for six years before becoming a director as well, began preparing the script. Constance Collier and John Craig were engaged as dramatic coaches. Fairbanks's and Pickford's companies were for the one and only time to be joined, and the stars were to co-produce for release by United Artists. The cast would include Edwin Maxwell as Baptista, Joseph Cawthorn as Gremio, Geoffrey Wardwell as Hortensio, Clyde Cook as Grumio, and Dorothy Jordan as Bianca, playing in sets and costumes designed respectively by William Cameron Menzies and Laurence Irving, and photographed by Karl Struss. Sam Taylor would of course direct. By 20 April *The Taming of the Shrew* was publicly announced, in June it was in rehearsal, and filming began early in July. By 17 August a trade paper could announce that production had been brought to a close "with a celebration participated in by all members of the Pickford-Fairbanks producing unit. . . . Both stars and Director Sam Taylor will spend many weeks putting the finishing touches on the picture." The stars sailed for Europe on 4 September, to be followed shortly by Mr. Taylor. A preview of *The Taming of the Shrew* at the Belmont Theatre, Hollywood, was reported in the *Exhibitors Herald-World* of 14 September. It was officially released on 26 October in 6116 feet and was given a quiet East Coast tryout in continuous performance at Loew's State Theatre, Boston, beginning on 11 November. Neither Douglas Hodges in the trade journal nor E.F.M. in the *Boston Transcript* of 12 November mentions "additional dialogue." Hodges minimizes the amount of dialogue to twenty percent compared with eighty percent pantomime; E.F.M. wrote: "They have held to the Shakespearean language. Some of course has been cut. Some of the speeches have been transferred to other characters than those who had them originally. But still it is recognizable blank verse."

Pressbooks were of course prepared for exhibitors of the film; two are in the Theatre Collection of the New York Public Library and from them I quote or summarize: "It will take an expert to detect any variation from the original text of Shakespeare's play. The tradition of 'not changing Shakespeare' has been faithfully observed, with the exception that the marriage service is read; but even in this service Petruchio and Kate affirm their vows by nodding their heads instead of speaking. This is information for you to give to people who might try to kick about someone's attempting to write new dialogue for a Shakespeare play." Elsewhere it is indicated that Garrick's version provided the clue to bringing the picture to appropriate running time, and that assisting Taylor in the preparation of the script were Thomas Patton (described as "the noted Shakespeare authority"), the veterans of the Shakespearean stage, John Craig and Constance Collier, and the principals. It is worth noting that Fairbanks had written the stories of his last three pictures under the pseudonym of Elton Thomas. In an interview in one of the pressbooks he said, "We shall not presume to write Shakespearean dialogue. . . . We will delete lines and even characters, since . . . the length of the film is standard."

The gala premiere of *The Taming of the Shrew*, a presentation by C.B. Cochran, was at the London Pavilion on 14 November 1929. The programme bore a note by James Agate: "Hollywood has carried what is already extraordinary reverence to the length of only using those words which are common both to Shakespeare's and to Garrick's version." M.E., writing in the *Daily Herald* the next day, said,

"The curtailed text is pure, the only alterations being that we see the wedding and the bedroom scene, to which the 'sun and moon' scene has been transferred." None of a dozen other London reviews examined mentions "additional dialogue," yet London, one would think, would be the very place where such an excrescence would have been derided.

In New York the film opened at the Rialto Theatre on 29 November. Richard Watts, Jr., reviewed it in the *Herald Tribune* on the thirtieth: "The director of the film has announced proudly that no line of dialogue is used in the work that is not in the original play. Strictly speaking, his claim is not entirely justified, for there is a scene in which the wedding ceremony is recited. With that minor exception he is entirely correct, however. The screen 'Taming of the Shrew' is, so far as the speeches go, entirely Shakespeare's, but the cinema has retained its right to retain its own interpretation." Mordaunt Hall in *The New York Times*, same date, remarked that "it sticks closely to the Bard's immortal lines." In the *World* of 2 December, Quinn Martin emphasized that "the speech [is] culled carefully from the original Text." The astute Sime Silverman in *Variety* on the fourth said nothing about "'additional dialogue," nor did Peter Vischer in two accounts in the *Exhibitors Herald-World* on the seventh, nor "Eddy" in *Film Daily* on the eighth, yet surely commentators with their ears so close to the reverberations of the industry might have been expected to mention it. Finally John C. Mosher in the *New Yorker* of 7 December is explicit: "A good deal of common sense, I feel, has been used in the adaptation from the play. Adequate lines have been culled from the original version, and incidentally, no others have been added by contemporary geniuses to indicate that there are in Hollywood those who aspire to Elizabethan rhythms. Where the screen demanded departure from the continuity of the play, pantomime only has been substituted." I have looked elsewhere too, but I can find not a single review which mentions the absurd credit line, and the number I have quoted should raise serious doubts about its basis in fact.

A close examination of the shooting script shows that Taylor visualized descriptive passages, transposed and cut language, telescoped characters, but contributed almost no words except for substitutions for speech that might not be understood and casual interpretive bits for characters in otherwise pantomimed scenes, the sort of thing that might be expected even in a shortened stage version of the play.

Since clearly Garrick's *Catharine and Petruchio* suggested the means of reducing Shakespeare to appropriate length, a comparison of it with Shakespeare's text will simplify a later treatment of the script in relation to Shakespeare's play by removing Garrick from further consideration except as he contributed dialogue.[2] The British actor-manager condensed *The Taming of the Shrew* into three acts. The Christopher Sly Induction and his brief reappearance are entirely eliminated. Bianca is not wooed and won by Lucentio, who is not in this version at all, but is already the wife of Hortensio. Catharine breaks the lute on the head of a real music-master, not on Hortensio's. The account of the wedding of Catharine and Petruchio is assigned to Biondello, not to Gremio, whose part disappears. The old man whom Catharine is compelled to recognize as a blushing virgin becomes her own father, met by the couple together with Bianca and Hortensio on the way to Baptista's house, and it is apparently on the journey—there is no place designation—that Bianca is rebuked by Catharine after her submission. There is no banquet or Widow. By and large, Garrick's method of adaptation was to cut subplots and many lines, to transfer speeches from characters dropped to characters retained, and to revise or add lines to suit these prunings and transpositions. Except for such changes, he stayed close to Shakespeare's text.

Garrick's act I is Shakespeare's act II, scene i, from "Signior Baptista, my business asketh haste" with some interpolation of lines from act I, scene ii. The scene in Baptista's house includes the conversation between Baptista and Petruchio, who receives permission to woo Catharine, with side comments by his servant, Grumio; the breaking of the lute; the stormy interchange between Catharine and Petruchio; the delighted interposition of Baptista with the arrangement for the next day's wedding; the exit of Petruchio; and the furious opposition of Catharine. Act II is the return of Petruchio in ridiculous garb, the off-stage wedding and after it the departure of bride and groom for Petruchio's house, which becomes the second scene. Here are the servant's preparations for the reception of the pair, the account by Grumio of Catharine's misadventure with the horse, the arrival of the newlyweds, the supper episode after which Petruchio leads Catharine to the bridal chamber, and the return of Petruchio to proclaim that Catharine will not only not eat but will be kept awake all night with his dismantling of the bed and the clamor of his raging. We have here then portions of Shakespeare's act III, scene ii and act IV, scene i. The final act includes the rejection of apparel prepared by the tailor and the haberdasher, the departure for Baptista's house, the meeting with Bianca, Hortensio, and Baptista, and Catharine tamed, as already described; in other words, material adapted from act IV, scenes iii and v and act V, scene ii.

Taylor's script used less than a dozen lines original to Garrick, and it cut characters still further. Only Katherine, Petruchio, Baptista, Gremio, Grumio, Hortensio, and Bianca are listed for cast credit. Christopher Sly and the accompanying characters disappear with the Induction. Gremio is not a wooer of Bianca, and Hortensio has no rivals for her hand, but he is not married to her at the beginning of the action, as in Garrick, and his success depends upon Petruchio's. Bianca has almost nothing to say. Gremio and Grumio are built up by being assigned lines which Shakespeare gave to others. Basically Taylor used some of Shakespeare's act I, scene ii for atmosphere, exposition, and the initiation of the action; then parts of act I, scene i and act II, scene i to introduce Katherine, Baptista, and Bianca, brought into combination with Petruchio and Hortensio by further material from act II, scene i. Act III, scene i is entirely omitted. The third section, revolving around the wedding, which is shown, depends on act III, scene ii. Shakespeare's act IV, scene i provides the bridal couple's travel, made visual, and their arrival at Petruchio's house. All of scenes ii, iii, and iv are cut. Scene v is transferred from the journey to the bridal chamber and much built up. Act V, scene i is dropped. The last section is the wedding feast but changed to Baptista's house; it is from the latter part of act V, scene ii with a suggestion of the cap business from act IV, scene iii. Taylor then used the same scenes of *The Taming of the Shrew* as Garrick had, with the addition of portions of act I, scene i. His settings are of course something else, either more Shakespearean as in the opening street scene and the final banquet, or less so in the depiction of the wedding, the bridal journey, and chamber. There is more transferral of dialogue in the script and suitably a great deal more variety of visual action. Shakespeare's text runs to about 2650 lines; Garrick has cut to about 1000. Admitting the difficulty of dealing with broken lines and speeches, I count in Taylor's script about 500 Shakespearean lines, occasionally modified. The diminution should not be surprising with the emphasis in a film on what is seen rather than heard. What little dialogue Taylor has added will be evident from a full analysis.

Taylor's script for *The Taming of the Shrew* can be most conveniently examined through division into the several sequences called for in the film. The first sequence shows a street opening off a public square in Padua. It was constructed on the back lot of the studio to make use of tracked perambulator shots, numbered 1 to 4. Hortensio's house with colonnade and balcony is on a corner. The camera, at first stationary, fades in on a Punch and Judy show covering the whole frame. The operator of the show in progress speaks shrill Italian during a roughhouse and skeletonized performance of *The Taming of the Shrew*. Judy, made up to represent Katherine, drives a fat Baptista to flight; Punch enters dressed as Petruchio, tries to drag her away; when she resists fiercely, he knocks her down repeatedly with a stick until she pleads for mercy and is tugged off. The camera pulls back disclosing the booth and a laughing and applauding peasant audience, then pans for a wider view of the public square, and moves toward a narrow street to take in its entire length, revealing as it perambulates a series of activities which will create the atmosphere of an Italian street scene. Twenty-four such bits of action, accompanied by appropriate noises, are enumerated in a partial list in the script. Near the end of the street, Petruchio and Grumio appear out of a crowd for a full-figure shot before the camera tracks back keeping them in view for various business designed to show Petruchio as an irresistible force sweeping into the picture. As the camera passes through a series of arches and then moves laterally, Gremio and Hortensio at the balcony railing both call Petruchio by name. The second shot shows them in medium close up as Gremio exclaims, "My good friend, Petruchio!" The third shoots down from the balcony, as Petruchio recognizes him and speaks his name. To his servant he explains, "Here, Grumio, is the friend I seek!" After the salutations, a fourth shot through the arches shows Petruchio and Grumio crossing the square and clambering up the colonnade to the balcony. Not counting the reiteration of proper names from Shakespeare, used in identifying greetings, all the dialogue in this essentially visual sequence consists of seven words rearranged from act II, scene i by Taylor to indicate and explain relationships and two which are implied by Petruchio's purpose in coming to Padua.

The second sequence comprising shots 5 to 18 is entirely based on act I, scene ii, the involvement of Petruchio in the wooing of Katherine and of Hortensio in winning Bianca. Since this sequence, unlike the first, puts more stress on what is heard than on what is seen, it is impossible to present the dialogue in detail without reprinting the script, a method which would expand this analysis out of all reasonable compass. The setting is the colonnade and balcony, but this is a new sequence on an indoor sound stage with the camera shooting down a side street toward Hortensio's house. A long shot including the roofs of other houses is followed by a variety of medium shots and closeups focusing on the characters. The last shot is a lap dissolve to the next sequence. Many of Hortensio's lines are assigned to Gremio, who is not on stage in the first part of Shakespeare's scene; a few lines of Gremio's are later transferred to Hortensio. The purpose is to break up lengthy speeches, to achieve more equal assignment, and to simplify the intrigue. Shakespeare's other characters do not appear at all.

The lines are almost entirely Shakespeare's, in his order, but with much omission. Proper names and certain words or phrases are repeated for further identification of the characters or for clarification by emphasis. A more colloquial, less metrical effect is achieved by the repetitions and the insertions of exclamations ("Ha!," "Oh!"), affirmations ("Ay!"), hesitations ("Er . . ."), query ("Wherefore?"), explanations and simplifications ("If perchance she be . . . ill tempered," "good Hortensio cannot wed the younger daughter / Till Katherine, the elder have a husband," "You would woo this Katherine . . . And *marry* her?"). There are a few modernizations ("wed" instead of "wive"; "have her" instead of "board her"). Except for this sort of minor and reasonable tinkering, necessary because of the change of form from drama to film, Shakespeare wrote the dialogue, and there is, in sum, hardly anything which could seriously be called addition by Taylor.

Shots 19 to 75 technically contain several sequences since the photography is both interior and exterior and special sets are necessary for certain frames, but because they all center at the home of Baptista and his daughters and depend, after introductory business from act I, scene i, almost entirely on Shakespeare's act II, scene i, it is best to treat them as a group. Shakespeare's lines, now that exposition and the inciting incidents have been completed, relinquish much of their inherent importance to visual involvement, though sound itself plays a substantial part. Shot 18 overlapped Petruchio's confident laughter with Katherine's furious vehemence as well as transferring the setting from balcony to loggia, a large room with a broad stairway at the top of which is Katherine's room. The camera is on a platform suspended from an overhead track; it focuses on the closed door. We hear Katherine's voice coming from the room, at first indistinctly and unintelligibly because of Petruchio's laughter; only the latter part of her speech of protest from act I, scene i, is understandable as the laughter dies away. (The scene was photographed silently with the sound dubbed in afterward.) The speech is not addressed to Baptista as in Shakespeare but to Bianca in Katherine's room; accordingly the pronouns are changed. Lines are cut but there are about eight of Shakespeare's followed by four more of his which mark the transition to act II, scene i, berating Bianca for being her father's treasure and swearing revenge. A stool comes crashing through the glass in the door; there is a hint of rough action behind it; but we do not see Katherine's face. As the camera tracks back to take a long shot of the loggia, a fat woman servant stumbles out of the door and collides with a man servant going up the stairs. Both tumble to the bottom. Baptista and two other servants enter from a ground-level door. In a medium shot (with sound) at this side door, the fat woman servant identifies Baptista and Katherine with five words added by Taylor. There is no further dialogue until shot 30. The interval is filled with rapid flashes (to which sound was added later) taken up with identifiable flying objects, cowering servants, a terrified cat, a shaking chandelier, and the like, interspersed with two closeups in Katherine's room of Bianca's feet being lashed with a whip. The servant (not Hortensio, as in Shakespeare) prays to heaven: "From all such devils, good Lord, deliver us" from act I, scene i. Two exterior shots on special sets show a servant climbing out of Katherine's window and dropping to the ground. Bianca rushes from Katherine's room into her father's arms; five words are added by Taylor, again for identification. What might be called this series ends at 35 with the camera peering into Katherine's room, presenting the wreckage and panning to Katherine sitting on a broken chair with the whip in her hand. In this series there has been then only one line of Shakespeare and ten explanatory words by the script writer; all else has been the sound and fury.

Shots 36 to 58 introduce Petruchio, Gremio, and Hortensio; only six carry dialogue; only three carry a significant number of lines. The dialogue is Shakespeare's except for minor additions and adaptations, such as we have met before. Bianca leaves; Baptista sighs on the stairs: "Was ever gentleman thus grieved as I?" Petruchio, followed by Gremio, strides in: "Ah. good sir! Pray have you not a daughter / call'd Katherine, fair and virtuous?" Baptista is at first too bewildered to answer, so the question is repeated before he replies in the affirmative. Gremio expostulates at Petruchio's unceremoniousness, and Petruchio identifies himself and is welcomed. Hortensio, disguised with a beard, and Bianca at an open door delightedly but warily recognize each other. They remain in the background until Petruchio introduces "Signior Licio" and recommends him as a musician and tutor. Here Taylor has to add a few lines before Bianca, at Baptista's bidding, leads him to Katherine's room. A combination of slightly adapted and Shakespearean lines concludes the bargain between Petruchio and Baptista. A crash is followed by Hortensio's falling the full length of the stairs with the lute broken over his head. Gremio leads Hortensio off, as Petruchio exclaims in admiration at Katherine's intransigence. The lines are Shakespeare's except that now for the first time Taylor substitutes a line of Garrick's: "Oh how I long to have a gr-r-r-raple with her!"

There is further slight adaptation of Shakespeare as Baptista climbs the stairs to bring Katherine to the waiting Petruchio. There is no dialogue in shots 48 to 58. The meeting of Katherine at the top of the stairs and Petruchio at the bottom is photographed from three angles, a profile long shot, one over Katherine's back shooting down the stairs, a third shooting over Petruchio's back up the stairs. There are also medium closeups. The purpose is to contrast Katherine's haughty antagonism and Petruchio's carefree swagger, Katherine's small flicking whip and Petruchio's great cracking one. Until 65, all shots have dialogue, preponderantly in 63. It begins at "Good morrow, Kate," and extends with breaks and rearrangement to the re-entrance of Baptista and Gremio at 64. Petruchio and Katherine, two menacing animals, meet on the stairs in shots from closeup to long to the accompaniment of Shakespeare with minor variations. Petruchio grabs Katherine and tries to kiss her. As she resists, they stagger down the stairs, and Petruchio succeeds. There is much roughhouse byplay to illustrate the speech. Katherine refuses to sit down but, lassoed by Petruchio's whip, lands on his lap. During this action two lines of Garrick's replace Shakespeare's bawdy about the wasp with a sting in his tail: "The fool knows where the honey is, sweet Kate." / " 'Tis not for [the] drones to taste." Baptista and Gremio, entering behind, are amazed to see the "lovers" in apparently intimate embrace; a reverse shot shows that Petruchio is holding Katherine forcibly on his lap by throwing a leg over both her knees and gripping her throat with his hand (shots 64 through 68 with no dialogue).

Shots 69 to 71 use Shakespeare's words to carry the business through the arrangement for the wedding to Petruchio's departure except that, as in Garrick, Katherine is constrained to give her hand first to Petruchio before both give their hands to Baptista, and Taylor adapts parting lines from Garrick rather than Shakespeare. Petruchio, laughing as he leaves, tosses Katherine's whip to her; she uses it to drive her father and Gremio from the room. The rest of the series (72–75) involves a special set, apparently built on location. From a window, at which Katherine stands, she looks out on Petruchio riding away through a courtyard arch waving and calling "Adieu!" She angrily slams the shutter and concludes with three lines slightly modified from Garrick:

Look to your seat, Petruchio, or I throw you.
Cath'rine shall tame this haggard; or if she fails,
Shall tie up her tongue, and pare down her nails.

Fade out.

Shakespeare's act III, scene ii provides the basis for shots 76 to
140, the awaited arrival of Petruchio, the actual arrival, the wedding,
and the departure of the bride and groom, but in the film the center
of activity is the church, outside and in, and the wedding is actually
shown. The extent of the visualization is suggested by the fact that
from some ninety lines, there are sixty-five shots covering action,
much of which Shakespeare has described and kept off-stage. There
is no dialogue at all until 84 (two lines), none again until 94. Shots
76 through 78 are exterior shots connected by lap dissolves of the
bell tower and the dome (done in miniature) and then a long shot
of the church. The bells are heard ringing. The long shot shows steps
leading down to a public square thronged with restless bystanders.
As the camera moves toward the church, we see the groups more in-
timately and hear church music. A distracted Hortensio hurries out
of the church looking for Petruchio. Shots 79 to 95 show the interior
with various focuses: the altar, a door to the sacristy, the rear of the
church, the vestibule in shots long, medium, and close. The church
is crowded, the people impatient, the priest nervous. Katherine in
bridal costume sits in the vestibule, forlorn and furious, tapping her
feet. Bianca and Baptista are chagrined and impatient. At 84 Taylor
adapted Shakespeare's opening lines to assign them to the Priest:
" 'Tis past the appointed hour that they be married, / And yet we
hear not of the bridegroom." Shots 85 to 94 pick up the action of
various participants. Baptista shushes the Priest and watches the
dynamite about to explode in Katherine; the guests fidget; a fat man
snores and is rudely awakened by his wife; one couple get up to
leave. Shot 94 contains the first extended dialogue from "What
mockery. . . ," transferred from Baptista to Bianca through Katherine's tirade to the Priest's cold comfort, transferred from Tranio. The
lines are somewhat cut and modified to adapt them to Taylor's
dramatis personae. Gremio, not Biandello, hurries into the vestibule
with the news that Petruchio is coming, and Baptista, Bianca, and
Katherine react. At 96 there is a shift to a courtyard outside the
sacristy into which Petruchio, grotesquely attired on a swayback
horse, rides with Grumio. At 98 dialogue resumes with their greetings and the expostulations of Baptista and Gremio. It is Shakespeare,
much cut, with Tranio's lines given to Gremio and consequently

suitably adapted. Shot 102 moves indoors to the sacristy with further expostulation and reply and similar minor changes. There is no further dialogue at all except a few words at 119, until 131; church music drowns out the words of the wedding ceremony. We see in various shots Katherine and her attendants getting ready, the priest at the altar rail, guests craning their necks looking for the bride, the bridal procession. Petruchio, approaching the altar rail, is jauntily eating an apple. At the sight of him and his apparel, Katherine stops dead in her tracks and then advances slowly and resentfully. Petruchio passes his apple to Gremio, who puts it in his pocket. The ritual is heard only in muffled tones, but Petruchio's "I do" becomes loud and clear with "Ay, by gogs-wouns!" taken from Gremio's report in Shakespeare. Katherine is so angry she refuses to give her pledge until Petruchio stamps on her foot and she lets out a howl which is accepted as agreement. The fat man laughs uproariously, and other guests are shown as the camera perambulates back the center aisle during the giving of the ring and the pronouncement that the two are now man and wife. A lap dissolve at 126 takes the participants outdoors for a final sequence. There is no dialogue until 131. A decorated carriage drawn by two beautiful horses awaits the bride and groom to take them to the wedding feast. Other carriages are ready for the wedding guests. Baptista, Gremio, Hortensio, and Grumio are at the foot of the steps. The camera is on a perambulator with first a medium shot; then it pulls back to a full long shot, in which Katherine appears on Petruchio's arm. In a medium closeup, she has somewhat softened as a result of the occasion and as she greets friends forgets her anger. Taylor adds an explanatory line for Baptista: "Come, my son! The wedding feast awaits!" Shakespeare's dialogue resumes with Petruchio's thanks to his friends but his determination to leave despite the shock to Katherine, Baptista, and Gremio. There is minor adaptation and cutting. Katherine swings her whip, which has been inconspicuously attached to her cloak, but Petruchio only grins at her. Half a line assigned to Hortensio in the Garrick version goes to Gremio. Petruchio takes command with his whip and sword, cows the assembled individuals and throng, throws Katherine over his shoulder and carries her to his horse, oblivious to her blows. They ride away, Katherine grimly hanging on for dear life. The final shot has Gremio picking up an adaptation of Lucentio's line to Bianca: "Baptista, what think you of your daughter?" with Baptista replying: "That, being mad herself, she's madly mated," and Gremio commenting "I warrant him, Petruchio is Kated." Fade out.

Shots 141 to 219 derive from description and action in act IV, scene i, but whereas Shakespeare's scene is entirely within Petruchio's house, the film also used adjacent exteriors though with little dialogue. The camera first shoots through an arch into the front yard, a kind of farmhouse court, toward the house itself with a porch and lighted windows. Pigs wallow in the mud formed by the pouring rain. The courtyard was set up on an ordinary stage and filmed silently with the sound of the wind and rain added later. In a fade in, Grumio on horseback gallops in from the arch, hurriedly dismounts and ties his horse, and splashes through the mud, shooing a pig out of the way, to the front door, shown in a medium closeup and duplicated on a soundproof stage, since there is to be brief speech. Shivering and sneezing he calls for Curtis and is answered at the door by him, as in Shakespeare. Curtis is the only servant who has any lines to speak, save for five words spoken in concert, but the actor of Curtis was not given cast credit. As Grumio hurries in the door, the setting changes to the main downstairs room of the house, where a table is partly set for supper, and logs are laid in a huge fireplace. Rear center is a stairway to a balcony, off which is the bridal chamber to be used later. Grumio and Curtis continue their dialogue; the fire is lit, and preparations are made by servants for the imminent arrival of bride and groom. Portions of some dozen of Shakespeare's lines, much broken to indicate the mounting tempo, are used so far, with one line of additional explanation by Taylor. From 145 there is no dialogue until 157. The interval is filled with the direct depiction of the arrival of Katherine and Petruchio at the exterior of the house, enlarged from the description given by Shakespeare to Grumio. The camera is on a perambulator and the shots run from long to close up. On the ungainly horse sit the two principals, Petruchio wrapped in a great cloak and singing lightheartedly; Katherine, drenched and bedraggled, holding on to Petruchio for self-protection. Petruchio dismounts unconcernedly and jerks the reins toward the hitching post. As the horse lurches forward, Katherine tumbles off into the mud to the amazement of curious pigs. She is too furious to move, as Petruchio at first does not notice her and then pretends to ignore her. As he knocks at the door, she arises, almost stumbles over a pig, but walks determinedly away from the house toward the arch. At 157 Grumio opens the door; there are a few words between him and Petruchio, supplied by Taylor, partly adapted from Shakespeare. The lure of warmth and food is too much for Katherine; she reverses her course and hurries to the door just as Grumio is about to close it.

All the rest of the action is interior; through 188 it is based on about forty lines of Shakespeare with a few assisting words by Taylor. Kate, huddled in a corner, is perfunctorily welcomed to her new home by Petruchio, who goes off to change his clothes, leaving his bride to remove her soaking cloak and water-filled shoes. Servants bring in appetizing food at which she sniffs eagerly. When Petruchio reappears on the balcony, he has softened somewhat, but as Katherine removes her whip from her cloak and attaches it to her dress, he becomes grim and lashes the stairs with his own whip. There is no dialogue from 161 until 170 where he calls his servants and berates them, as in Shakespeare, for their supposed neglect, a section which continues with violent slapstick through 179, where Katherine tries to intervene by remonstrating. The dinner and its rejection follow through 188 at the end of which Petruchio bounds up the stairs to wait for a hesitant Katherine at the foot and to bring her to the bridal chamber. Gazing wistfully at the food she hesitates, then timidly follows him. Shots 192 through 201 are in the bridal chamber, except for 200 in an adjacent dressing room, and carry no dialogue; they have no basis in Shakespeare. The chamber contains a large fireplace, an easy chair, a table, and a stool and of course a prominently featured bed. Katherine, embarrassed, shies from the bed, as Petruchio warms his hands in front of the fire, then sits in the chair and begins a game of solitaire as if she did not exist. As she goes into the dressing room and slams the door, he leaves the bridal chamber toward the balcony.

There is no dialogue from 202 to 211 except for one Taylor line, but the shots alternate between the living room, the dressing room, the bridal chamber, and the balcony. We see Petruchio return to the dining table where he eats ravenously, Katherine removing her shoes and stockings in the dressing room, Petruchio consuming delicacies brought in by the servants, Katherine slipping into a negligee over her nightgown, Petruchio finishing his meal and calling his dog, "Ah, Troilus, good dog! T'was a hearty meal!" The dog's name is Shakespeare's, but he is appropriately large, not a spaniel. Katherine finds the bridal chamber empty, hears the dog bark and Petruchio's laugh, goes to the balcony, and sees the dog sitting in her chair and being fed by Petruchio. In 211 Petruchio's speech beginning, "Thus have I politicly begun my reign," is addressed to the dog, and therefore has to have minor modification. During the speech, which continues, though cut, through several shots, Katherine realizes that Petruchio's temper tantrums have been put on for her benefit and learns about his plan to dismantle the bed and keep her awake with singing. It is clear that she is planning a counterattack as she returns to the chamber. Petruchio climbs the stairs and calls back to Curtis for wine. Shots 220 through 233 have no dialogue. Petruchio hesitates at the door when he sees Katherine in bed, apparently asleep. He slams the door, deliberately stumbles over a stool which he hurls against the door of the dressing room, and sings raucously. Katherine pretends to awaken gradually, sits up in bed and joins in the song. Petruchio throws open a window letting in the wind and cold; Katherine opens the other window; Petruchio, having failed to discomfit her, slams both windows shut. The moon-sun dialogue from act IV, scene v, transferred from the road to the chamber, follows in shot 234. Curtis brings the wine, and substitutes for Vincentio in the original as "a fair lovely maid" succeeded by "a man, old, wrinkled, faded, withered" until he retires in relief (235–241). The rest of the sequence through 250 is in action entirely original except insofar as it is based on "I'll fling the pillow" from act IV, scene i. Its purpose is to show Katherine triumphant. There are perhaps the equivalent of five lines of dialogue in nine sequences, about half of which are Shakespeare's. Here Taylor has had to provide enough words to carry the reinterpreted action. Petruchio, irritated at Katherine's demure composure, jerks the pillow away from her head, which hits the head of the bed with a loud bang. Katherine, all pretense gone, engages in a furious struggle for the pillow. A pushing contest ends with Katherine sprawling and then throwing a stool, which hits and momentarily stuns her husband. Horrified, she cradles his head in her arms, soothes his bravado as he comes to and declaims Shakespeare's "I who have heard the lions roar / And the rage of an angry sea," from act I, scene ii, and gets him to bed, "only a child after all," says Taylor's explanatory direction. Her whip, no longer necessary, she tosses into the fireplace. He recovers long enough to repeat with her two lines from the sun-moon dialogue, then relaxes contentedly at her affectionate agreement. Fade out. It is worth noting that most of the servants' dialogue, the argument about the clothes tailored for Katherine, and all of act IV, scenes ii, iii, and iv have been omitted.

The banquet scene from Shakespeare's act V, scene ii provides the material for the final sequence of the film, but it is of course at Baptista's house, not at Lucentio's. It contains forty-six lines of dialogue, about forty-one of Shakespeare's, about five, though suggested by Shakespeare, altered by Taylor. Shots 251 to 259 vary from medium to close with the emphasis upon the latter; the camera is on a perambulator. The banquet hall is a loggia with one side of the room open to provide a background of moonlight. The feasting guests at the table listen to music, toast the bride and groom, chatter merrily ad lib, but the words are not recognizable over the music. Petruchio is at the head of the table, his braggadocio rendered ludicrous by a huge bandage about his head. Katherine sits demurely beside him. As the banquet concludes, the guests except Petruchio rise and form groups with Katherine, for a reason to be apparent, in a position where she faces women rather than men. She takes a pillow from her own chair to make Petruchio more comfortable and stands beside him. Confident now that he has tamed the shrew, he decides on a public demonstration: "Katherine, that cap of thine becomes thee not. / Off with the bauble! Throw it under foot!" These are Shakespeare's lines slightly altered by Taylor. She smiles, throws the cap on the floor, and to the astonishment of the guests stamps on it. Bianca is indignant: "Lord, let *me* ne'er be brought to such a silly pass!," a modification of the Widow's words in act V, scene ii which Garrick had already assigned to Bianca. Gremio's wife speaks Bianca's, "Fie, what foolish duty call you this?" Petruchio leaps to his feet with Shakespeare's words (except for clippings): "Kate, I charge thee, tell these headstrong women / What duty 'tis they owe their lords and husbands." The subsequent objection is assigned to Bianca but otherwise follows Shakespeare. It is to Bianca that Katherine reprovingly addresses her final speech of thirty-seven lines, Shakespeare again except for the omission of three words and a change of order from Garrick, so that the speech will end with the suggestion of the marriage service, ". . . to serve, love and obey." During the speech there are closeups of the reactions of Baptista, Hortensio, Gremio, Bianca, Grumio, and Petruchio. At its conclusion, Katherine solemnly winks at the other women, but the wink is not visible to the men. Petruchio, self-satisfied, bursts into a triumphant guffaw and ends the dialogue with Shakespeare's, "Why, there's a wench! Come on and kiss me, Kate!" As she sits on his lap, the guests resume their indistinguishable conversation, the music grows louder, the camera pulls back into a long shot with everyone singing, and the picture fades out.[3]

This detailed analysis of the script should lay the ghost of "additional dialogue by Sam Taylor." He changed much in his adaptation of play to film, but supplementary dialogue is clearly minimal and nothing for which a sensible man could or would claim credit, and Mr. Taylor I found in discussion to be not only a sensible man but a highly intelligent one. It could just possibly have happened of course that, despite the evidence of the script, the credit was inserted at some point or on some prints and later deleted. During this era many plays and novels which were to be made into pictures needed new or adjusted dialogue. Dramatists and novelists such as Sidney Howard and S. S. Van Dine were brought to the Coast to augment or rewrite. Credits in the *Film Daily Year Book* list such "dialogue directors" who assisted in production, as Frank Reicher, Dudley Digges, Richard Boleslavsky, and Frank Craven. Sometimes they added dialogue themselves. The *Year Book* carries three pages listing "dialogue writers," with the comment, "The dialogue writer . . . has earned a definite niche in the new scheme of talking-picture production." Sam Taylor was named as a dialogue writer for *Coquette*. This wholly new practice easily led to the juxtaposition on initial frames of original authors and writers of additional dialogue, sometimes with results ludicrous enough to cause mild hilarity among viewers.

Yet the evidence again denies this possibility. Sam Taylor was not listed in the *Year Book* as a dialogue writer for *The Taming of the Shrew*. There is no ground for thinking that someone else mistakenly assigned him unwanted credit. He was the director and supervisor of the film and any policy would have been dictated by him or by the co-producers, Pickford and Fairbanks. No underling would have dared to make such an insertion, and Joseph M. Schenck, the president of United Artists, was a businessman who did not oversee, once a director had been assigned, the productions of the constituent companies. As a matter of fact, in this case, Taylor's contract with Schenck had been modified before the picture was released so that he would continue to direct Pickford films and would thereafter receive twenty-five percent of the profits. He was indeed, subject to the wishes of the stars, in complete control. Mr. Taylor told me that he did not hear the rumor of the credit line until he was in London, where he saw the film without such credit. He cabled Bob Fairbanks, Douglas's brother, to kill the canard, but apparently nothing was done about it. As for Miss Pickford's belief that the credit existed, she and her husband had embarked for England even before the picture was previewed in Hollywood. The only screening they could have seen beforehand was a rough cut run-through without credits or titles. Miss Pickford's will to believe may perhaps have been affected by the domestic tensions she describes in her book, by her dissatisfaction with the role of Katherine, and by the more favorable notices which the press gave Fairbanks. Taylor certainly reduced lines and reassigned speeches, but increments, excepting a few by Garrick, were expository for the purpose of identifying characters, eliminating minor bawdiness, emphasizing by exclamation, hesitation, or query, or providing brief bridges made necessary by pantomimic adaptation and simplification. The story of "additional dialogue" has to be, as I see it, a fantasy and trick of fame. The evidence of the reviews, the pressbooks, the script, the time schedules, and the director himself all contradict its reality.[4]

If all this be so, how did the legend arise? On the same date as the *Exhibitors Herald-World* announced the "celebration" for the completion of production, 17 August, "The Talk of the Town" in *The New Yorker* carried a paragraph containing a report from "a courier who made a forced ride from Hollywood."[5] He brought news of *The Taming of the Shrew* "which Douglas Fairbanks and Mary Pickford have filmed out there. The picture is titled thus: '"The Taming of the Shrew," by William Shakespeare. Additional Dialogue by Sam Taylor.' He doesn't know whether it will be shown generally that way, however, as there was considerable comment about it up and down the Pacific Coast." But by 17 August the picture had not yet been titled. One can speculate that the "courier" had heard the comment, that at some time, unknown to Taylor, there may have been an unthinking *intention* on the part of a title-writer to use such a credit in conformity with current practice, although this is doubtful, or the reporter may have been inaccurate. It seems to me much more probable, however, that he had happened on an "in" joke and passed it along as humorous humbug, covering himself with the warning that it was uncertain that the subsidiary credit would ever appear on the film. Moreover, the canard, if it is fair to call it that, in *The New Yorker* of 17 August is corrected by the evidence of its own review in the issue of 7 December. It is hardly reasonable to assume that John C. Mosher, its author, did not read the magazine for which he wrote. It seems much more likely that he deliberately stressed that no lines other than those in the original "have been added by contemporary geniuses."

The conclusion of the matter, I think, has to be that "additional dialogue by Sam Taylor" is a myth, that what has been proliferated as fact was actually a satirical jape which was funny enough to bear oral and then written repetition. Alas, poor ghost, I hope you are not "as the air invulnerable." If you be an honest ghost, you have the power to haunt me.

IV
The
Playwright
and
Theatre

Macbeth *at The Globe,*
1606-1616 (?)
Three Questions[1]

Nevill Coghill

I have three brief questions to ask about the staging of *Macbeth* at The Globe in the early seventeenth century when Shakespeare was in charge of it, and a little later, when absence and lastly death left his plays in the hands of the theatre. With these questions I shall offer some not absolutely hesitant answers, though I must start by admitting that there is scarcely enough evidence to burn a witch. At first they formed themselves with a cautious *Num*, but now they press forward with a more confident *Nonne*; I shall, however, put them bluntly and directly, without either of these question-begging adverbs.

IN THE ORIGINAL PRODUCTION OF C. 1606, WERE THE WITCHES, AT THEIR SEVERAL EXITS, FLOWN OUT ON WIRES?

At that time, of course, all Europe, not to mention America, knew that witches were able to ride the air. It might almost be said to be expected of them. Reginald Scot in many passages asserts the prevalence of this superstition,[2] and King James, in his *Daemonologie*, expounds more than one method by which such aerial journeys might, perhaps, be powered; he says, for instance, that they might be "carried by the force of the Spirite which is their conductor, either above the Earth or above the Sea, swiftlie."[3] This is the climate of belief in which to consider the evidence given in *Macbeth* about their movements. The 1623 Folio seems at first to be prodigal of question but niggard of reply; all we are told in the opening scene is:

Thunder and Lightning. Enter three Witches.

At the end of the scene they get a simple *Exeunt*, as if they were purely pedestrian; but, as so often happens in Folio, we can find far fuller stage directions in the dialogue, for Shakespeare loves to pile up language which contains instructions to the actors who are to speak it; and so we discover from their own mouths how the Witches were to make their exit:

> faire is foule, and foule is faire,
> Houer through the fogge and filthie ayre.

Fog and filthy air are easily provided on the stage; there had been techniques for it ever since the first Hell-mouths had belched their terrors forth two hundred years before, and further back still. Let us not pause, then, on that, but on the word *hover*. It has been noticed before, I need hardly say by whom, in *Shakespeare and the Actors*.[4] "Perhaps," says Professor Sprague, "there is a hint of action in that 'hover.'" There is, I think, more than a hint. I take it for a concealed stage direction.

Why should Shakespeare use this very explicit and visual verb to describe the exit of the Witches, if the whole audience could see that they were *not* hovering, but going out on their own flat feet? Such a thing would be the opposite of Shakespeare's habitual practice; he liked to boast "your eares vnto your eyes Ile reconcile"[5] and he advised actors to "suit the action to the word, the word to the action."[6] Yet, it might be countered, why place so much weight on one brief poetical image that may have escaped him, for the nonce, in the speed of his fancy? Perhaps he used the word "hover" to raise the imaginations of the audience, rather than to raise the Witches? But if we look a little further we find he by no means uses this air imagery "for the nonce"; he uses it continuously and consistently through the play to describe their disappearances, and, what is more, he never uses any other. They are associated with the winds which they claim to control:

> 2. Ile giue thee a Winde.
> 1. Th'art kinde.
> 3. And I another.
> 1. I my selfe haue all the other.

and at the end of their second scene (in which they all-hail Macbeth and Banquo) when they make their exit, the text has a new verb to describe it and directs: "*Witches vanish.*" Banquo, in commenting, uses the same word:

> The Earth hath bubbles, as the Water ha's,
> And these are of them: whither are they vanish'd?

Macbeth replies:

Into the Ayre: and what seem'd corporall,
Melted, as breath into the Winde.

This is a strong endorsement of the air imagery of "hover."

At Macbeth's second and final meeting with the Witches, in act IV, scene i, the dialogue again insists on a magically airborne disappearance for them in a little interchange with Lenox, which has no other dramatic or poetic purpose but just that. This interchange comes at the end of the apparition scene: The situation is as follows: Macbeth has just been shown the blood-boltered Banquo, pointing to his royal progeny, as it stretches to the crack of doom, and is appalled at the sight; he falls into one of his habitual brown studies (cf. "Looke how our Partner's rapt," I.iii.143) and "stands amazedly," as the First Witch tells us. She calls on her sisters to entertain him with a dance. It is clear Macbeth takes no notice of this entertainment; he remains under the effect of the apparitions he has just seen. It is reasonable to suppose him a little downstage, because the apparitions must have been upstage of the "Heavens," where the machinery for them was, and it is not hard to imagine him looking out over the heads of the audience, into the futurity of Banquo's seed, and showing the audience his full face, with its varying emotions, as actors are wont, and indeed wanted to do, while the dance went on behind him. And then we should hear the galloping of horses, since this seems to be what awakens him from his brown study; for, a few lines later, he tells us

I did heare
The gallopping of Horse.

The galloping may well have been the cue to interrupt and end the Witches' dance, for when Macbeth swings round on the sound of hooves, they are no longer there. The text reads:

[*The Witches Dance, and vanish.*]

Macb.   Where are they? Gone?
Let this pernitious houre,
Stand aye accursed in the Kalender.
Come in, without there.
[*Enter Lenox.*]
Lenox.   What's your Graces will.
Macb.   Saw you the Weyard Sisters?
Lenox.   No my Lord.
Macb.   Came they not by you?
Lenox.   No indeed my Lord.
Macb.   Infected be the Ayre whereon they ride.

The whole point of this tiny incident is to underline that the Witches have flown out as Lenox walked in, and he has therefore not met or see them; the dialogue confirms what the audience has seen happen; ears and eyes are thereby once again reconciled. What else can the lines mean? And so, three times out of three, in these authentic scenes, their airborne exits are strongly stressed, for all these examples come from Shakespeare's hand—from the uncontaminated parts of the play—and belong, so far as we can ever know, to the 1606 text; it is preposterous to imagine that at some later date he revised the play in order to intersperse these tiny, scattered indications of flight which, taken together, are so powerful, so insistent—*Hover* through the fog; *the Earth hath bubbles* as the water has; *into the air;* as breath *into the wind;* infected be *the air on which they ride.* This is the way a man writes out of a steady and consistent vision, as if it had not so much as occurred to him that they should not fly.

Let me now take into account the contaminations of which I spoke. They are, of course, those taken from Thomas Middleton's *The Witch*, conjecturally dated 1609–10. They are the easily detachable act III, scene v (of *Macbeth*), in which Hecate appears to rate the Witches for their traffic with Macbeth, and the five-line speech she is allowed in act IV, scene i (the apparition scene) together with the two songs that grace, or rather disgrace, these two occasions, "Come Away, Come Away" and "Black Spirits and White," which the actors have obviously interpolated at some date after Shakespeare's retirement but before the compilation of the Folio. These interpolations greatly reinforce the flight imagery; at her first exit, Hecate says:

> I am for the Ayre: this night Ile spend
> Vnto a dismall, and a Fatall end.

and again

> Hearke I am call'd: my little Spirit see
> Sits in a Foggy cloud and stayes for me.

and that is followed by the song which begins "Come away, Come away":

> Come away: Come away:
> in ye aire
> Heccat: Heccat, Come away
> *Hec.* I come, I come, I come I come,
> with all the speed I may,
> with all the speed I may.

wher's Stadlin?
                    Heere in ye aire
wher's Puckle
         heere
And Hoppo too, and Hellwayne too
we lack but you; we lack but you in ye aire
Come away, make up the count
Hecc.   I will but noynt, and then I mount

and finally we get the explicit stage direction

> [*Hec. going up*]
> Now I goe, now I flie,
> Malkin my sweete Spirit, and I.
> oh what a daintie pleasure 'tis
> to ride in the Aire
> when the Moone shines faire

and so on.[7]

Anyone who writes for the stage, to this very day, knows that he has only to turn his back to find that some actor or director has cut some necessary passage, or added some senseless gag, to draw attention to himself. That is evidently what has happened in the scenes we are discussing; it looks as if *Macbeth* had started a fashion in Witch entertainments which used flying techniques, and some bright interpolator had thought it would improve the effect (for one cannot have too much of a good thing) if a little more were made of the Witches, and a couple of jolly songs were thrown in from Middleton, all into a play which already had flying Witches but was pining for more use to be made of them.

As I have said, Shakespeare seems to have created a brief fashion in witches, and it is strange that Jonson's *Masque of Queens*, with its anti-masque of Witches, which was performed on 2 February 1609, perhaps the year of Middleton's *The Witch*, and was obviously a part of the witch trend, has virtually no flight imagery at all. It is a nobly comic poem, replete with great quantities of other witch lore, poured in from the enormous wealth of Jonson's classical and anthropological learning, but except for one oblique reference in the command to anoint, and

Sadle yor Goate, or yor greene Cock,

which seems to prelude flight, as Jonson's textual footnote learnedly explains,[8] there is absolutely no reference to, or imagery taken from flying; he is not thinking in such terms, and indeed seems deliberately to avoid them, in contrast to Shakespeare, who, as we have seen, always envisages them as disappearing into the air.

We know also that Shakespeare could translate his dialogue into action on stage in this matter; if we look at *Cymbeline*, act V, scene iv, we find these directions in Folio:

> *Iupiter descends in Thunder and Lightning, sitting vppon an Eagle.*

I can recall how thrilling this descent was in a production at the Royal Shakespeare Theatre a few years ago; never was Iupiter more august, never was eagle more golden. However, there is no reason to suppose that the Elizabethans were any less skilful or ingenious than we are, with respect, at least, to carpentry, carving, paint, and winch; they could do all that we can do, except what can be done by gas or electricity.

But I can hear an objection forming itself to these arguments: could there have been the machinery to fly *three* witches? One witch, perhaps, but surely not three! Yet Professor Glynne Wickham, in his indispensable and authoritative work, *Early English Stages*,[9] quotes an account of work done on the *Mystère des Trois Doms*, given at Romans in 1508:

> Pay Amien Gregoire for six long, strong bars for the great winch, and three belts for the three angels, with lynch-pins for their descent from Heaven . . . 3 florins and 3 sous.

If three angels in 1508, why not three witches in 1606? It is the mere difference between the Middle Ages and the Renaissance.

In this brief opening to a question of some interest and complexity I ought, perhaps, to say a word about that strange astrologer, Simon Forman, who has left us what purports and even seems to be a partly eyewitness account of *Macbeth* and of *The Winter's Tale* at The Globe in 1611. The document is very oddly worded; he uses phrases like "ther was to be obserued," never directly stating that he was the observer, and much of what he tells us of *Macbeth* is manifestly taken out of Holinshed and not from Shakespeare at all. For instance, he describes the Witches as "women feiries or Nimphes," which are Holinshed's words for them and which would show an astounding insensitiveness to language if used by anyone who had actually seen Shakespeare's hags; indeed they might be the forgery of such a man as John Payne Collier was, having a joke with himself, as he attempted to puzzle posterity. But if these entries are truly the work of Simple

Simon, and if he actually *saw* the 1611 production, could he possibly have seen them fly and have forgotten it? Could he have omitted to tell us of so spectacular an effect if it had really happened? I am afraid the answer is "Yes, he could," for he tells us nothing about the resurrection of Hermione in the statue scene of *The Winter's Tale*, the most spectacular *coup de théâtre* in all Shakespeare. We can argue nothing from the silences of so shaky a witness; so I mention him only to leave him out of the argument.

Thus in determining the means by which the witches exit, six points should be considered: (1) All the unquestionably Shakespearean witch-exits particularly specify an exit into the air; this is a simple certainty of the true text. (2) Shakespeare knew, and later used, the flying techniques needed for supernatural effect in *Cymbeline* and *The Tempest*. Three goddesses (like the three angels or the three witches) are certainly flown in the latter play, and are described as having "melted into air, into thin air," almost exactly Macbeth's phrase for the disappearance of the Witches that "melted as breath into the wind." (3) Shakespeare saw and thought of them as sorceresses, but Jonson saw *his* Witches as personifications, allegories, like something out of Prudentius, to represent various moral turpitudes, which he names, such as *Ignorance, Credulity, Suspicion*; he then loaded them with learning and left them firmly earthbound from first to last. (4) Jonson kept his texts to himself, hoarded them with care. He knew they were poetry. Even if his twelve Witches had been originally suggested to him by Shakespeare's three, he scrupulously— one might say ostentatiously—avoided the charge of plagiary, or of trading on a reminiscence of Macbeth, and particularly on anything connected with flying, while he quietly showed that he knew a thousand times more about witch lore than an amateur like Shakespeare. (5) Jonson's *Masque* was performed in February 1609; we have no exact date for Middleton's *Witch*, but the Malone Society editors assign it to 1609–10. Perhaps while Jonson was planning his royal entertainment, he saw or heard about Middleton's plans for his more vulgar adventure, *The Witch*, with Hecatean song and dance in the air, and was disgusted, determining to banish even the hint of flying from his moral *Masque*, lest it should be thought unserious, infected by the ignobility of Middleton's piece. But this is mere conjecture; all we know is that he refused all such aerobatics. (6) But the actors had none of these qualms, and when Shakespeare's back was at last turned on London, they took advantage of this to gild his lily by the interpolation of Hecate and her saucy songs; so she flew into Folio unobserved.

HAVE WE LOST
SOME PART OF THE SCENE AT THE COURT OF
KING EDWARD THE CONFESSOR?

In his planned buildup for this famous, popular, and sainted King, Shakespeare uses the same technique he had used to build up Fortinbras, of whom we hear in act I, scene i, although we do not meet him until act IV, scene iv. As far as I can recall, St. Edward is the only saint in all Shakespeare's sources; his sanctity is a necessary element in the play and is held out to us as a kind of consolation or replacement, in the second half of the play, for the sanctity of Duncan, murdered in the first; the mere thought of him helps to keep the balance against the Instruments of Darkness.

We are forewarned of his distant presence as early as act III, scene vi, in a passage worked up out of Holinshed and given to an unnamed Lord, talking to Lenox:

> The Sonnes of *Duncane*
> (From whom this Tyrant holds the due of Birth)
> Liues in the English Court, and is receyu'd
> Of the most Pious *Edward*, with such grace,
> That the maleuolence of Fortune, nothing
> Takes from his high respect. Thither *Macduffe*
> Is gone, to pray the Holy King, vpon his ayd
> To wake Northumberland, and warlike *Seyward*,
> That by the helpe of these (with him aboue
> To ratifie the Worke) we may againe
> Giue to our Tables meate, sleepe to our Nights:
> Free from our Feasts, and Banquets bloody kniues;
> Do faithfull Homage, and receiue free Honors,
> All which we pine for now. And this report
> Hath so exasperate their King, that hee
> Prepares for some attempt of Warre.

Lenox presently rejoins:

> Some holy Angell
> Flye to the Court of England, and vnfold
> His Message ere he come, that a swift blessing
> May soon returne to this our suffering Country.

We are thus told to expect an interview between Macduff and Saint Edward, that will result in an alliance with Northumberland, and a blessing from the Priest-King. So, when act IV, scene iii is reached, attentive members of the audience will think "Ah! Now we shall have the promised scene between Macduff and the Confessor!" And I think they would be entirely right, if something absolutely unique and almost inexplicable had not happened to the text. It runs like this: Malcolm has just inculpated himself and confessed to all the crimes he can think of, and then unsaid them all, to Macduff, who rejoins:

> Macd. Such welcome, and vnwelcom things at once
> 'Tis hard to reconcile.
>   [*Enter a Doctor*]
> Mal. Well, more anon. Comes the King forth I pray you?
> Doct. I Sir: there are a crew of wretched Soules
> That stay his Cure: their malady conuinces
> The great assay of Art. But at his touch,
> Such sanctity hath Heauen giuen his hand,
> They presently amend.   [*Exit*]
> Mal. I thanke you Doctor.

Consider this extraordinary thing: the entry of a character never seen before and never seen again, who has no other function than to announce the immediate arrival of a great and long-expected personage, with a positive "Aye, Sir!," and who then departs, having appeared only to give his message, which is immediately proved false; the King does not appear. Is it not unheard of that an authoritative, purposeful messenger-speech of this kind should be belied in the event? If Shakespeare had not intended the Confessor to enter at this point, what can he have been thinking about to introduce this pointless Doctor with his lying announcement?

As if the buildup he had already given to St. Edward were not enough, Malcolm adds a long cadenza on his sanctified power in healing scrofula:

> Tis call'd the Euill.
> A most myraculous worke in this good King,
> Which often since my heere remaine in England,
> I haue seene him do: How he solicites heauen
> Himselfe best knows: but strangely visited people
> All swolne and Vlcerous, pittifull to the eye,
> The meere dispaire of Surgery, he cures,
> Hanging a golden stampe about their neckes,
> Put on with holy Prayers, and 'tis spoken
> To the succeeding Royalty he leaues

The healing Benediction. With this strange vertue,
He hath a heauenly guift of Prophesie,
And sundry Blessings hang about his Throne,
That speake him full of Grace.

Even Fortinbras is not so richly prepared for as this; for Shakespeare had ransacked Holinshed to build up this fabulous national figure, someone on the side of the angels, who would at last appear, to link England and Scotland in amity and order at this very moment, which is the watershed of the play. Imagine how the scene implied in this speech would lift up all hearts, out of all the blood and darkness, when most they need to be lifted, just before the news of a last holocaust—the slaughter of Macduff's family—is to assail them. In the scene that seems to have been lost I would suppose there to have been the solemn procession of the holy King, under a canopy, borne perhaps by monks, with a ceremonial bell before it, and, behind, a troupe of scrofulous wretches; then a solicitation of Heaven, during which all would kneel; and the bestowal of a golden stamp on each would follow, with the ensuing miracle of a cure, so easily effected on the stage by the concealed removal of an ulcerous mask; and after that some notes of a *Gloria* or a *Te Deum*, and finally a prophecy of victory to Malcolm and a blessing on Scotland pronounced by the Saint. This would indeed justify the last lines of the scene, as they now stand in the text for Malcolm to speak:

Macbeth
Is ripe for shaking, and the Powres aboue
Put on their Instruments: Receiue what cheere you may,
The Night is long, that neuer findes the Day.

All this the otherwise inexplicable entry of the Doctor allows us to imagine; but we have been deprived of it. It has been suggested to me by Professor E.A.J. Honigmann that we need not go so far as to suggest the loss of so large a slice of the scene; all we need suppose is the loss of some such stage direction as:

Enter a Dumb-Show of St. Edward the Confessor with monks and a troupe of scrofulous wretches. All kneel. The King touches the sufferers and hangs a golden chain about their necks and they arise healed. A Gloria is sung. The King blesses Malcolm at a distance, and exit.

This is clearly a possible view, though I do not hold it myself because it does nothing to fulfill the notion of a prophecy of victory to

Malcolm, which we have been led to expect by the text; but I think it would be justifiable in a modern production on the grounds that it seems in consonance with Shakespeare's intention, in which case the purely antiquarian speculation here offered would turn out to have a practical utility.

Another critic, R.J.C. Wait, suggested that it might be pertinent to inquire what King James I himself would have thought of such a scene; as it happens this detail among his many opinions is particularly well documented from contemporary sources; there is the following testimony of Arthur Wilson (1593–1652) in his *Life and Reign of James I*:

> He was a King in Understanding, and was content to have his Subjects ignorant in many things: As in Curing the *King's-Evil*, which he knew a Device, to aggrandize the Virtue of Kings, when Miracles were in fashion; but he let the World believe it, tho' he smil'd at it in his own Reason, finding the Strength of the Imagination a more powerful Agent in the Cure, than the Plaisters of his Chirurgions prescrib'd for the Sore.[10]

An even subtler estimate is to be found in the Vatican Archives in the letter of an anonymous papal spy which records the ambivalent attitude forced upon King James at the outset of his reign in this matter of curing the "Evil." The letter is quoted fully in Professor Marc Bloch's fascinating *Les Rois Thaumaturges*,[11] and it greatly helps us to sympathize with the King's dilemma. Here was a Protestant King, educated by Calvinists, who abhorred the invocation of saints but expected to perform a miracle, though the Age of Miracles had passed, at the outset of his reign. To accede to this demand was publicly to surrender to a superstition just such as was forbidden by the twenty-second of the *Thirty-nine Articles*, annexed to the *Book of Common Prayer* by his illustrious Protestant predecessor; to refuse the demand was to break with an ancient custom of the realm, performed for the benefit of his subjects.

James gave way; to do so may have tickled his royal vanity by a sense of "aggrandizement" not out of keeping with his many-times trumpeted doctrine of the Divine Right of Kings, but he was careful to disclaim any special powers; the papal spy tells us that the rite of touching was preceded by a sermon by a Calvinist minister, after which the King explained his personal difficulties in a second sermon, the substance of which was how could he effect a cure without miracle? But miracles no longer happened; he was afraid of committing some superstitious act yet unwilling to discontinue a benevolent tradition. However, he had resolved to perform the ceremony, though only in the manner of a prayer, in which he begged all present to join with him. The spy amusingly adds that the King, as he spoke, turned his eyes toward the Scottish clergy that stood by, as if seeking their approbation.

There are, alas, no documents to tell us what King James thought of Shakespeare, if he thought of him at all. The King's opinions about miracles and the baleful effect of promulgating superstitions, however, may have been noted by the Revels Office; in this case it may have been deemed wise to cut out the visual presentation of so glamorous a scene, recalling the good old days, when miracles and superstition were still happily allowed; for even if King James thought there was no offence in them (as in certain moods he may have) there were still those puritan, Calvinist clergy from Scotland to reckon with.

WHERE DID MALCOLM'S ARMY ENTER FROM IN THE BIRNAM WOOD SCENE (V.iv)?

Let me first recall an important but little noticed article by Professor Allardyce Nicoll called "Passing over the Stage." It gives good reason, with many examples, for believing that the phrase "passing over the stage" was used as a technical term, meaning "an entry of actors in the yard, and their walking onto and over the platform." His conclusion "that there was provision in the Elizabethan theatre for some way of stepping up onto the acting area from the yard, although there is no positive evidence to support it, finds justification in the longstanding tradition in boothstages of ladder-like steps from the ground to the raised acting-level."[12] Professor Nicoll draws hardly any of his examples from Shakespeare, though his plays teem with occasions when such entries seem mandatory. I shall offer at least one that I think can be demonstrated as absolutely certain, for there is no thinkable alternative. If it be asked why so striking a way of mounting the stage is nowhere mentioned in contemporary records, the answer must be that what is taken for granted is seldom noted for a wonder, and that although tens of thousands of London theatre-goers knew what The Swan Theatre was like, only one has left us a drawing of it, and he was a Dutchman.

Let us, then, take his drawing as our basis of inquiry and follow in Folio the last act of *The Merchant of Venice*, with regard to the entries necessitated by the text.

Nevill Coghill

Actus Quintus. Enter Lorenzo and Iessica.

Lorenzo opens the dialogue by telling us that the moon shines bright, and that

> In such a night
> Did Jessica steale from the wealthy Iewe,
> And with an Vnthrift Loue did runne from Venice,
> As farre as Belmont.

This establishes De Witt's *mimorum aedes* as Belmont, an identification reconfirmed many times during the scene. Lorenzo and Jessica have just come out of the building into the (imagined) moonlight of the garden. Presently a Messenger enters at speed, running, as messengers should; for Lorenzo calls out into the "darkness":

Who comes so fast in silence of the night? [my italics]

It is Stephano, coming from Portia.

> *Stephano* is my name, and I bring word
> My Mistresse will before the breake of day
> Be heere at Belmont. . . .
> I pray you it [is] my Master yet return'd?

From these lines we can safely infer (1) *that Stephano must have room to run* on stage; (2) that, since he comes from Portia, he comes from the direction she will come from and not from the Bassanio direction.

But Shakespeare immediately establishes Bassanio's direction by the words of Launcelot Gobbo. Gobbo (as we know from act III, scene v) has been taken on as part of the Belmont household. He now appears, shouting into the (imagined) darkness:

Sola, sola: wo ha ho, sola, sola.

Where does he make this appearance? *Certainly from Belmont,* either by the other great door (imagined as the servants' entry) or, more likely, on the balcony, where he can achieve a jack-in-the-box effect with his sudden irruption of comedy. He tells us that a post full of good news has just come, announcing Bassanio's return before morning. This creates an expectation that Bassanio will enter *from the house,* since he is said to be following his "post," as Portia and Nerissa are following Stephano. They will therefore meet from opposite directions, from the (imagined) front and back of Belmont, in the garden before us, their journey's end.

Lorenzo sends Stephano into the house to join Gobbo in the work of preparing for the joyful return of their master and mistress, and

235

it is perhaps Stephano who places a welcoming candle in the gallery (the only place in the De Witt drawing that it could be seen from), which will in a few moments be seen and commented on by Portia from a distance.

The stage is now empty except for Jessica and Lorenzo, and, as it happens, we can tell almost exactly where they are standing and where they sit. They are sitting on a bank under the "heavens," that is, a little upstage of the pillars in the Swan drawing; we know this from Lorenzo's lines:

> How sweet the moone-light sleepes vpon this banke,
> Heere will we sit . . .
> Sit Jessica, looke how the floore of heauen
> Is thick inlayed with pattens of bright gold.

They are looking up at the painted "heavens" above them; the bank on which they recline must be of such a kind as to make a group that will justify Portia's description of them when she presently comes upon them:

> Peace, how the Moone sleepes with Endimion,
> And would not be awak'd.

Music streams forth from the house.

> [*Enter Portia and Nerissa*]
> *Por.* That light we see is burning in my hall:
> How farre that little candell throws his beames.

Now it would be absurd for her to say that if she entered through either of the doors in the *mimorum aedes*, whereas if she entered downstage by steps onto the apron it would be most natural; the candle would seem to shine its welcome *from afar*, as she says it does; she sees her hall with a sense of homecoming and is approaching Belmont not by the front door (which Bassanio will use) but by the privacy of her garden. But even if we swallowed such an absurdity, as repugnant to common sense as it is to the imagination, and allowed her to enter from the house toward which we have been told she is wandering, there would still be a further absurdity to accept, for she would be coming down past Lorenzo and Jessica without noticing them. It is thus inescapable that Portia and Nerissa can make this entry only from the apron, at least in a theatre such as we see in the Swan drawing. And this is corroborated by what we have noted of Stephano's entry, which needs the room given by the apron to allow him to approach *fast*.

All we need imagine, then, is a removable flight of wooden steps affixed (for this scene at least) to the apron, at the point which De Witt has labeled *proscaenium* and protected by light wooden railings under the guard of a stage servant or two. Once we have imagined this simple set of steps, everything in the action and dialogue coheres. It is a paradigm.

Let us, however, take another example, almost as convincing, before we come to Birnam Wood. It comes from an equally if not more famous scene in *Henry V*, at the opening of act II. Chorus is on stage telling us of Harfleur, encircled and about to be stormed by King Harry and his "choyse-drawne Caualiers"

> and the nimble Gunner
> With Lynstock now the diuellish Cannon touches,
> [*Alarum, and Chambers goe off.*]
> And downe goes all before them.

As he speaks, we hear the deafening bang and see the (property) doors of the Swan drawing collapse in smoke. The Chorus makes his exit, then,

> *Enter the King, Exeter, Bedford, and Gloucester.*
> *Alarum: Scaling Ladders at Harflew.*

Undependable as Folio often appears to be in the matter of stage directions, it may be worth noting in passing that at this point there is no mention of soldiers entering on *stage*, only the King and his nobility enter this way; but scaling ladders are specified. What better way of clambering out of the yard—the *planities siue arena* of De Witt's sketch—than by scaling-ladders, after the King's oration? What better platform from which to deliver it than the apron stage, from which it seems that all England could be addressed? With the King and his nobility in full view, with the smoking town before them, and their English troops below them, with their scaling-ladders at the ready, all would be set for the charge to which King Harry exhorts them in his peroration:

> Follow your Spirit; and vpon this Charge,
> Cry, God for *Harry*, England and S. George.
> [*Alarum, and Chambers goe off.*]

The King and his Lords race forward, the soldiers clamber up their ladders and rush the length of the stage, shouting "God for Harry!" in the din of battle, and assault the ruined doors.

How could such a charge be made if they had all come in upstage, through one or the other of the doors? How could they enter from the breached city they were about to take by storm? Consider, too, the immediate sequel of the entry of Nim, Bardolph, Pistol, and Boy. They must surely be detached from the general *mêlée* to make their ironic comments; should not they come up from among the groundlings, their natural companions? Bardolph, on the apron, encouraging the troops from well behind, with his "On, on, on, on, on, to the breach, to the breach" must surely have clambered up onto the *proscaenium*, safely to the rear of the heroics, if he was to be seen and heard, and not up among the soldiers so bravely assaulting and scaling the *mimorum aedes*; and Pistol must surely stand where Harry had just stood, parodying his noble rhetoric with

> Knocks goe and come: Gods Vassals drop and dye:
> and Sword and Shield, in bloody Field, doth winne
> immortal fame.

Let me take a leaf from Mr. Emrys Jones's recent book, *Scenic Form in Shakespeare*; there he suggests that, in his later life, Shakespeare frequently and deliberately imitated the solutions he had found for certain problems in scene construction in his earlier plays, and repeated them (with the appropriate variations) in his later ones.[13] I think this scene of the assault on Harfleur may have served him as his model for the Birnam wood scene in act V, scene iv of *Macbeth*. Folio reads:

> *Drums and Colours. Enter Malcolme, Seyward, Macduffe, Seywards Sonne, Menteth, Cathnes, Angus, and Soldiers Marching.*
>
> . . . .
>
> *Seyw.* What wood is thus before vs?
> *Ment.* The wood of Birnane.
> *Malc.* Let euery Souldier hew him downe a Bough,
>   And bear't before him.

Now Birnam wood must be a practicable wood of green trees, with boughs easily detachable by the soldiery; such a wood could not be set out on the apron; it could only be prepared upstage, under the "heavens," during the previous scene, played on the apron, before a traverse. This is evidently the intention, for the previous scene ends thus:

> *Macb.* I will not be affraid of Death and Bane
>   Till Birnane Forrest come to Dunsinane.
> *Doct.* Were I from Dunsinane away and cleere,
>   Profit againe should hardly draw me heere. [*Exeunt*]

After their *Exeunt* the curtains of the traverse would be parted to reveal the long-expected wood thus introduced; it has come pat upon its cue and is masking the great doors of the *mimorum aedes*, awaiting the miracle of its removal that the audience has been kindled to expect.

Malcolm and his army are marching *toward* it, for Siward says "What wood is that *before* us?" If he had come in upstage (from the wood itself), he would have had to say "What wood is that *behind* us?" or, simply, "What wood is this?" But it is *before* him as he steps onto the apron with Malcolm and the others, as King Harry did with his nobles before Harfleur. And so they lead their soldiers up onto the stage, and forward to the wood, and when every soldier has hewn him down his carefully prepared bough and passed on through the doors, the back wall has instantly become the Castle of Dunsinane, and Macbeth is ordering his banners to be hung out where, a moment before, had been Birnam wood. The three scenes make a smooth sequence in stagecraft.

Some scholars will, I know, feel reluctance to admit the solutions I have proposed to my three questions, especially the last; so I will ask them further to consider the domination of our mentality by the picture-frame stage and what goes with it—the impassable gulf of the orchestra pit and beyond that the impregnable protection of many rows of comfortable stalls, *fauteuils*, as they are called in France, armchairs, whose privacy may be purchased. It is as if actors and audience were like the goods for sale in a supermarket, separately packaged in cellophane, untouched by human hand. And indeed, though we may not have walked with Kings, we have a little lost the common touch in our modern Shakespearean theatres, that so perfectly encapsulate us. So, in judging of the answer offered to my third question, I hope it will be remembered that there was a long tradition in this matter of entry from the yard in Jacobean times. A year or so after *Macbeth* was first performed, The Citizen and his Wife, followed by their inimitable Ralph, leaped up from among the audience in *The Knight of the Burning Pestle* and took possession of the stage. That was in 1607 or so. In like manner, A and B emerged from the audience in 1497 and joined in with the actors in Henry Medwall's delightful *Fulgens and Lucres*; so too, in contrary motion, a hundred years before, Herod had descended from his pageant to rage in the street. Perhaps this would not have seemed so strange to the audiences of those days as it does to us; perhaps it would not have seemed strange at all.

Heavenly Mingle:
Antony and Cleopatra
as a Dramatic Experience

Alan S. Downer

A half-century of industrious effort on the part of stage historians has finally made it imperative for critics of Shakespeare to acknowledge the importance of the theatre, its conventions, and its actors in evaluating his works. Yet, however knowingly they write of the open stage, their minds' eyes will be seeing the proscenium arch and illusionistic scenery. However glowingly they write of actor and playwright without crib, cabin, or confine, they still think of another part of the forest, and act I, scene vi. And the play is once again cast into an alien mode.

For the first thing to understand about *Antony and Cleopatra* is that, despite the kind assistance of latter-day editors, there is no possible interruption in the play from the first line to the last. Ariel-like it leaps and glides, dips and flirts, expands, contracts, winks, starts, and rushes on. Its intense, unbroken, relentless drive is as much a part of its meaning, of the experience the audience will carry away, as any of its most quotable lines. And unfortunately for those whose experience must be confined to the theatre of the mind, this effect of the play's structure can be realized only in the theatre. It was lack of a theatrical experience of *Antony and Cleopatra*, or failure of theatrical imagination, that led Dr. Johnson to declare the play's structure haphazard: "the events, of which the principal are described according to history, are produced without any art of connection or care of disposition." Quite the contrary; the design of *Antony and Cleopatra* is as meticulous as *The Cherry Orchard*; the connecting (or juxtaposition) of events is all art, and is disposed with as much care as a young bride dressing for her first wedding.

Coleridge's enthusiasm for the play is perhaps closer to its effect as a dramatic experience. For him, *Antony and Cleopatra* exhibited "a giant power in its strength and vigor of maturity" with "*Feliciter Audax* (happy valiancy)" the motto for its style. In few other plays, Coleridge goes on, does Shakespeare express "the notion of a giant strength so much, perhaps none in which he impresses it more strongly . . . [the playwright] *lives* in and through the play." To move from such heady evaluation to the arena of practical theatre is to descend indeed; yet a play *is* a play and perhaps neither Coleridge nor his subject will be diminished by a visit to the wooden O.

ENOBARBUS

The contemporary American playgoer is being introduced, somewhat hesitantly, to the pleasures and limitations of repertory theatre. He is learning that, if each actor in his season must play many parts, there will inevitably emerge among the parts certain similarities not readily apparent to the reader's eye; this is a fact of repertory which makeup and costume and a voice "suiting with forms" to changes in age and status cannot deny. If this is true for present-day companies with their four or six programs a year, it could hardly have been less valid for Shakespeare's own company offering dozens of plays, old and new, each year. Rehearsals must have been generally perfunctory, and performances must have had some of the improvised quality of a *commedia dell' arte*, each actor taking his cue from the *platt* at the stage entrance, his words from the prompter, his gestures and actions from his own resources. Conversely, in a theatre where it was not customary, indeed not possible, to seek out just the right actor for a role, playwrights customarily designed roles for actors; theatre, like politics, is the art of possibility. Shakespeare, good workman that he was, never quarreled with his tools, though he sometimes found unexpected uses for them.

There must have been in his company an actor (John Lowin?) "of a stout blunt humour," solid of body, gruff of voice, with a firm gaze and a weathered face well suited to a grizzled wig or a variety of martial beards. He was seldom, in the actor's phrase, "at liberty," for play after play involves one whose business it is to be plain, "to serve him truly that will put me in trust, to love him that is honest, to converse with him that is wise and says little, to fear judgment, to fight when I cannot choose, and to eat no fish." In archetypal form, of course, he is named Kent, the faithful servant of his master even in direst circumstances; more interestingly he is Enobarbus, faithful servant of a less than honest master and deserter of a lost cause, who, almost at once, dies of remorse.

He has some of the qualities of the fool-stereotype as commentator on the action, though his comments are more often cynical than didactic. When the queen's women beg the soothsayer to read their fortunes, Enobarbus observes accurately that the fortunes of most of the court shall be "drunk to bed." When Antony orders him to speak no more during the meeting with Caesar, he apologizes for forgetting that truth should be silent and fires an oxymoron over his shoulder: "Go to, then! your considerate stone."

The cynicism which provides the distinctive coloration of his stereotype is important in demonstrating to the audience the fullness of Cleopatra's witchery. Antony is too far gone, even at his first appearance, to serve as a measure, but Enobarbus has kept his distance. Even to her lover's face he can "affect a saucy roughness," as he prophesies that "Cleopatra, catching but the least noise of this [Antony's departure], dies instantly; I have seen her die twenty times upon far poorer moment. I do think there is mettle in death, which commits some loving act upon her, she hath such celerity in dying." And when his master resolves to return to his Roman duty and repair the business his late wife had broached in the state, Enobarbus does not fail to remind him that "the business you have broach'd here cannot be without you; especially that of Cleopatra's which wholly depends on your abode."

So, when Maecenas and Agrippa in Rome ask him about the Egyptian dish, he launches into a set piece embroidering his own conceits on Sir Thomas North's velvet brocade:

> She disdained to set forward otherwise but to take her barge [like a burnish'd throne / Burn'd on the water] in the river of Cydnus, the poop whereof was gold, the sails of purple [and so perfumed that / The winds were love-sick with them] and the oars of silver which kept stroke in rowing after the sound of the music of flutes. [and made / The water which they beat to follow faster. As amorous of their strokes]. . . . And now for the person of herself [it beggar'd all description], she was laid under a pavilion of cloth-of-gold of tissue [O'er picturing that Venus where we see / The fancy out-work nature]; and hard by her, on either hand of her, pretty fair boys, appareled as painters do set forth god Cupid, with little fans in their hands . . . [whose wind did seem / To glow the delicate cheeks which they did cool, / And what they undid did]. (II.ii.191–205)

The embroidery, of course, is what makes the speech memorable; it also makes it characteristic. Such phrases from the bluff and cynical warrior ring with mockery long before his cartoon of Antony, "en-

thron'd i' th' market-place . . . / Whistling to the air." Yet a moment
later Enobarbus is overcome by the picture he is painting:

> I saw her once
> Hop forty paces through the public street;
> And having lost her breath, she spoke, and panted,
> That she did make defect perfection
> And, breathless, pow'r breathe forth.
>
> (II.ii.228–32)

As in his hearers, the mockery is gone and only wonder remains:

> Age cannot wither her, nor custom stale
> Her infinite variety. Other women cloy
> The appetites they feed, but she makes hungry
> Where most she satisfies.　　(II.ii.235–38)

O, rare for Antony! Rare Egyptian! Royal wench!

Enobarbus's portrait of Cleopatra overwhelms the senses most
with color, odor, sound, as her presence had, despite duty and profession, overwhelmed Antony and the holy priests. And it is Shakespeare's embroidery on the conventional interpretation of his subject
matter that overwhelms the audience and must have left the playgoers of 1607 (as it seems to have left later critics) somewhat bewildered.

THE DOTARD AND THE WITCH

Shakespeare, of course, did not hesitate to surprise his audience.
Within a few years he had presented them with a Hamlet who did
not follow the rules for revengers and a King Lear who in defiance
of history and a familiar old play did not regain his throne. Now he
offered not only a tragedy (if the First Folio's title be Shakespearean)
with a highly ambiguous action, but a hero and heroine who burst
the moral bonds they had been forced to wear at least since the
judgment of Plutarch.

That the audience accepted, at least in principle, "'the Elizabethan
world picture" there can be little doubt; Shakespeare himself had
refreshed their memories with Ulysses's famous discourse on degree
in *Troilus and Cressida*, and *Lear* is relentlessly enclosed in it. The
Elizabethan world picture was a tidy assignment of place and function of all elements in man, the family, the state, nature, and the

cosmos, fixing the relationship of man and superman, man and man, man and subman, all painstakingly reassembled by propagandists for the Tudor monarchy from defrocked rule books of the medieval church. Medieval philosophers may have quibbled over details, but they knew the absolute values of everything in a divinely ordained world order, and Tudor historians had little difficulty transferring the same principles to a society ordained by Henry VIII.

The key word was, of course, order; the evil word was chaos. Order came from obedience to divine decree, chaos came from listening to the devil. Translation: order came from obedience to one's political, social, familial superior, to the voice of reason; chaos came from listening to one's own will, one's own ambition. There was plenty of evidence to defend such evaluations: by hearkening to ambition, Satan fell, Adam fell, Faustus fell, Richard III fell (a particularly choice example for the Tudor mouthpieces). By hearkening to God, to reason, by serving the necessities of order, Isaac was saved, and Noah, and England through the grace of the Duke of Richmond (chosen by the Tudor agents to put down Richard III).

And there were Antony and Cleopatra. The pre-Shakespearean view of this paradigmatic pair of sinners may best be set forth by referring to Thomas Beard, whose moralizing treatise *The Theatre of Gods Iudgements* was published in London in 1597.

According to Beard (who is in no way original) Mark Antony was "the most dissolute and impudent in this case of diuorce"; he forsook his first wife to marry Octavius's sister, then forsook her to be with Cleopatra, "from whence sprung out many great euils." Shakespeare worsens the situation by putting the liaison with Cleopatra between Antony's two marriages. But the great evils spring out of Cleopatra; Adam, after all, would still be weeding his garden if Eve had not presented herself.

Beard declares that Cleopatra "by her flattering allurements rauished the hart of this miserable man" and was the cause of the second divorce. Thus, "as she partaked of the sin so she did of the punishment," killing herself, which indeed would have been a sin if she had been a Christian. He continues, "'this was the miserable end of those two, who for enjoying of a few foolish and cursed pleasures together, receiued in exchange infinite torments and vexations, and at length vnhappy deaths togither in one & the same place, verifieng the old prouerbe: For one pleasure a thousand dolours."[1]

Octavius, during the Renaissance, was the chosen agent of God in the defeat of Antony and Cleopatra. Historians customarily pointed out that Jesus was born during his reign and that he was the Caesar whom Christ accepted as temporal ruler. Plutarch, who was a moralizer long before the Roman Church or the Tudor apologists got to work, declares that Cleopatra was set up by the goddess Fortune so that Antony would destroy himself through her, leaving Octavius to "survive and reign alone" for a golden age.

From these bits and pieces it would not be hard to assemble a true Renaissance tragedy of Antony and Cleopatra. The great warrior and political leader, flawed by lust, neglecting his responsibilities to the state (resigning his god-ordained duty) to indulge himself in base pleasure with a woman who had her own designs on the order of things, defeated in simple combat by the strength and honesty of Octavius, armored in Christian symbolism like the Earl of Richmond.

If that scenario might have furnished the plot for an acceptable Renaissance tragedy of Antony, perhaps for Shakespeare as a very green apprentice, it is clearly worlds away from the play he wrote in 1607. The place names are the same but Plutarch would not recognize the territory. The character names are the same but they are attached to utterly different embodiments. The *tragedy* of a dotard and a witch? The *tragedy* of a warrior who botches his own attempt at suicide, and whose half-dead but still articulate body gets stuck in the air as his mistress and her maids haul it up the side of the monument? The *tragedy* of an aging vamp who unmans a warrior, runs from battle, cheats on a truce agreement, and has played footsie with the top echelon of the SPQR? Tragedy should be made of sterner stuff.

Sir Philip Sidney might have reacted as to a black comedy. In *The Apology for Poetry* he had remarked that the relationship of Hercules and Omphale "breeds delight and laughter," and Shakespeare develops this mythological analogue to his Queen and General at some length. There are other comic elements—Cleopatra's whims, Pompey's banquet, the clown—but the ending is faulty. Jack doth not have his Jill, and the fatal Cleopatra with the baby at her breast, crowned and enthroned among the women of her court as if she would catch another Antony in her strong toil of grace, is somewhat lacking in the high spirits that used to be associated with comedy.

Vital drama, even when dressed in the clothing of past ages, is inescapably a response to its own world, and only a world that is absolutely sure of itself and its values can produce a dramatic reflection which is rigorously tragic or indulgently comic. The Elizabethan world picture was beginning to dissolve.

The basis of the fabric for Shakespeare and his fellows had been Elizabeth herself. When that great presence departed, the departure, as history had repeated over the ages and as many of her subjects feared, left a gap in nature. The succeeding age (the Jacobean) was not comprehensively aware that it was revolutionary. But the Renaissance was growing old, and society was growing restive. The middle of the century was to be a time of chaos, of civil war, society against itself, but also of war on the moral and intellectual as well as political and social levels. Preliminary battles were going on, even now in 1607. Alchemists begin turning into scientists, looking at what happens rather than for what they wanted to happen; Puritans draw further and further from the politically directed state church; merchants begin to dispossess knights as figures of power; country squires begin recognizing their own strength; and "new Philosophy calls all in doubt." Shakespeare was no middle-aged liberal; he was, apparently, by instinct a conservative businessman who had his eye on social respectability and comfortable means. But one of the things that characterize the major artist is a sensitiveness to influences from all sources; some he is doubtless unaware of, some he might reject if he were aware of them. That Shakespeare responded to the established influences of his time is readily apparent in the earlier plays where English history is reshaped to follow the lines of established moral principles, where his tragedies are built upon the nature of the true governor, and of right reason. But if he is responsive to the conventional influences of his time, he is also sensitive to the influences that are going to disturb those conventions, and these are the influences which have a bearing on the dramatic experience of *Antony and Cleopatra*.

The dramatic experience will also depend, in a special way, on Shakespeare's method as a playmaker. In spite of centuries of research this "method" still remains hypothetical, but by 1607 he had written some thirty plays in two decades, a rate of production possible only to a disciplined talent. Other playwrights in his own time and after exceeded his productivity—Thomas Heywood, Lope de Vega, Eugène Scribe, Dion Boucicault—but their discipline was the creation of a formula within a genre; Shakespeare never employs exactly the same dramatic structure twice and genre is, more often than not, only a point of departure.

In one thing he is consistent. He may have begun his London career as a play-doctor, fixing other men's work or assisting them in their operations. And the habit stuck, for he was always an adapter. But he was never a parrot; whatever he takes up becomes transformed: stories, conventions of form, conventional characters, all are transformed by his fusing genius. And the transformation need not always have been deliberate. The changes were made in response to some inner demand, not an intellectual demand, but a shaping idea. Hamlet's story, for example, whether he read it in Belleforest or Kyd, became in his poet's mind a metaphor and the central character was transmuted from fashionable revenger to tragic hero imprisoned by a way of life. Is it too risky to suggest that Shakespeare might also adapt conventional ideals, ways of looking at things, values, to the demands of this shaping idea?

The shaping idea of *Antony and Cleopatra* is not a conventional tragic one. To be sure the action deals with the falls of princes and the mutability of worldly things, but at least Cleopatra appears to be ennobled by her fall, while the exemplary figure (the well-governed man, the Edgar) looks rather foolish standing beside her shrine. Somehow the spectator feels that the nobleness of life *is* to do thus, when such a mutual pair and such a twain can do it. Does the play glamorize lust and dereliction of duty? Or does it expose the appetite-governed man, the chaotic state? Or does it, somehow, do both? The shaping idea is not the tragedy of man but the ambiguity of human experience, an ambiguity which wears a precious jewel in its head.

SYMBOLIC STAGECRAFT

If Shakespeare was no great respecter of genres, if he relied little on dramaturgical formulas as an aid to composition, to one restriction he rigidly adhered: what he wrote might challenge but must never exceed the resources of the stage and its actors. From the modern point of view Elizabethan stage conditions were primitive: a bare platform, backed by two doors, with an upper level, standing in full sunlight and more or less surrounded by spectators. Plays written for this theatre were performed without scenery, and locale, when significant, was made explicit through the dialogue. The actors themselves must set forth the scene, but they waste few words on architecture or topography; they present the idea of the world of action.

Consider the opening of *Antony and Cleopatra*. Onto the bare stage come two Roman soldiers to begin the exposition. If Shakespeare wants his audience to have a clear picture of Alexandria he is certainly uninformative, for the two soldiers speak only of the dotage of their general, his rejection of his proper sphere of action, his devotion to a lustful gypsy. They are interrupted by the arrival of Antony and Cleopatra and their attendants, a sort of street parade or public pageant illustrating the dotage, the passion, the rejection of Rome: a Wagnerian prelude, establishing the leitmotifs to be developed in subsequent action. The lovers and their train depart through one door, the baffled messenger from Rome through the other, and the two Roman soldiers remain briefly to reassert the original point of view. As prior audience they have made the spectator see Antony and Cleopatra through Roman eyes; therefore the spectator has seen only the surface, the public front.

As the Romans leave, the stage is immediately occupied by Cleopatra's chattering maids, Charmian and Iras, Alexas, her chief steward, a Soothsayer, and Enobarbus, Antony's closest friend. The girls rattle about the Soothsayer begging forecasts of happy lives of unlimited sexual experience, while Enobarbus orders the night's banquet to be brought in. The focus is narrowing and the idea of the world is becoming more textured. From the street, where the externals of the world can be spied on, the spectator is moved to an inner room where the idea lives. Once again the Roman messenger appears, and this time Antony, struck by "a Roman thought," receives him. Antony even speaks as a Roman. Where, earlier, he had cried in his Egyptian voice:

> Let Rome in Tiber melt and the wide arch
> Of the rang'd empire fall! Here is my space.
> Kingdoms are clay; our dungy earth alike
> Feeds beast as man. The nobleness of life
> Is to do thus [embracing]; when such a mutual pair
> And such a twain can do't, in which I bind,
> On pain of punishment, the world to weet
> We stand up peerless   (I.i.33–40)

he can now say

> Things that are past are done with me. 'Tis thus:
> Who tells me true, though in his tale lie death,
> I hear him as he flatter'd.   (I.ii.94–96)

In the third scene, the focus of the action narrows once more: from the introductory pageant, to the way of life, to the crystallization or embodiment of that way of life in Cleopatra. The spectator has heard a good deal about her from Antony and especially from Enobarbus, but she now assumes in action the dramatic values she has been given by her associates. In one brief scene she fully reveals herself: superstitious, loving, crafty, ironic, violent, self-pitying, and generous. She represents a world of appetite, self-indulgence, excess, all to be condemned and yet:

> Eternity was in our lips and eyes
> Bliss in our brows' bent, none our parts so poor
> But was a race of heaven.   (I.iii.35–37)

As the embodiment of the idea of Egypt leaves the stage, enter Octavius and Lepidus to establish through speech, situation, and manner the contrasting idea of the Roman world. Since Egypt has been developed so carefully, it takes only a few selected strokes to present Rome. Duty, the business of the state, the maintenance of order; no rattling females here, no soothsayer, no banquets, only reports, messengers and guns, and drums and wounds. And at its center, its embodiment: Octavius Caesar, the Augustus that is to be, who may be best summed up as a man who is complete master of his syntax at all times. The idea of Rome, duty-cum-order, is to be praised, but there is news of pirates and malcontents in the city, and there is a touch of superiority and personal ambition in this Octavius. Cleopatra returns briefly to fix the symbolism, and the audience has been prepared for the developing action of the play.

The opening sequence (to borrow a term from the movies) is carefully calculated not just to provide necessary information but to establish a point of view from which to evaluate the apparently sprawling events of the play. Thus the design of the action is anything but casual, "produced without any art of connection or care of disposition"; the structure is rather a part of the dramatic experience for the spectator. It will not do to tamper with Shakespeare's scenic arrangements. To combine the first two scenes (street and banquet hall) into one as some editors and all producers do is to weaken the important effect of progressive revelation of the nature of the Egyptian world. To postpone the first Roman scene until all the Egyptian scenes have been run through is to weaken the principle of juxtaposition or contrast which governs the experience of the play. For example, in the (editorial) second act, Shakespeare develops at greater length the idea of the Roman world. First comes the conference between Octavius and Antony, the two great pillars on which the world must rely for stability (with Lepidus as a feeble little strut between them). Their agreement goes forward shot full of pettiness, opportunism, and a clear hint of future quarrels. Antony emerges as the superior man, for all his flaws, and Octavius's cold-blooded opportunism (nicely sugared with hypocrisy) in offering his sister to the man whose sex-life he so thoroughly condemns suggests that something is rotten in the state of Responsibility and Order.

Before the Roman marriage can be performed, enter Egypt, not in person but in Enobarbus's famous description of the first meeting of Antony and Cleopatra. The speech could come at no other place in the play, for its function is to maintain the structure of juxtapositions, and to show Enobarbus bewitched by his own recollections.

Then, having tasted Egypt, the spectator is introduced to the Roman Woman and married love: she exits with her brother and leaves Antony whistling at vacancy. Immediately Egypt rushes into the vacuum as Cleopatra's Soothsayer works to make Antony jealous of Octavius. Antony's mind is made up; married or no, in the East his pleasure lies. The dramatic structure—which takes the spectator from Rome to Egypt and Egypt to Rome either physically or through embodiments of the ideas of the places—allows him to participate vicariously in Antony's dilemma. As the spectator moves back and forth across the waters, so Antony's mind or heart or conscience swings like a pendulum. His mind, heart, or conscience is never permitted to be at rest, and the quick succession of scenes and the uninterrupted movement of the action make the spectator "see feelingly" his experience.

One other instance of juxtaposition will sufficiently confirm its function as part of the dramatic experience. At the end of the second act, the triumvirate conclude a truce with Pompey and thus restabilize the world. To celebrate, a feast is held on Pompey's galley. During this celebration of honorable concord one of Pompey's men takes him aside and prompts him to become lord of the world by setting the galley adrift and cutting the throats of the Triumvirs when they are helplessly at sea. Pompey, Man of the Roman Idea, is shocked:

> Ah, this thou shouldst have done,
> And not have spoke on't! In me 'tis villainy;
> In thee't had been good service. Thou must know,
> 'Tis not my profit that does lead mine honour;
> Mine honour, it. Repent that e'er thy tongue
> Hath so betray'd thine act. Being done unknown,
> I should have found it afterwards well done,
> But must condemn it now. Desist, and drink.
>
> (II.vii.73–80)

To cite another of Shakespeare's ethical philosphers: "What is honor, a word; what is that word honor, air; a trim reckoning!"—and a revealing juxtaposition.

Pompey returns to the brawl, which increases in riotousness; Lepidus is carried off drunk, the others carouse and reel. Only Octavius retains his head, but this seems more from calculation than moral principle. The party begins to leave the boat, Enobarbus warning Antony not to fall overboard, then Enobarbus and the former pirate go off to the cabin for more wassail, hiccuping and flinging their caps at the main mast.

Enter Ventidius as it were in triumph [with other Roman officers and the corpse of his enemy] borne before him.

The editors, who always will be editing, have inserted an act break between the carousal on the galley and the entrance of Ventidius, thus destroying one of Shakespeare's most artful devices. The triumphs and dangers of Roman armies in the field are freely reported by messengers in the play as they might this incident, except for the dramatic comment that is gained by the immediate juxtaposition of the workaday dutiful Roman officer and the drunken, hypocritical superior officers of army and state to whom he owes allegiance. The dialogue supports the intention of this structural device as the officer is urged to pursue the enemy forces to total victory: Ah no, says the officer,

> Better to leave undone than by our deed
> Acquire too high a fame when him we serve's away.
> (III.i.14–15)

Once again the play emphasizes that if Egypt is to be condemned, the high and palmy state of Rome is not unblamable. Wondrous blind are the editors who can worry that such a scene "cannot be fitted with any historical time scheme," and industrious blind is their insistence on finding a place where acts begin and end. The time scheme of the play is not historical but dramatic; if there are possible moments of pause, or rather moments for which large units of the total play seem to be preparing, they are not the Aristotelian five but the Shakespearean three.

The first major movement of the play concludes with the truce between Octavius and Antony and Cleopatra's violent despair at the news (II.v). The second movement includes the breaking of the

251

truce, the initial victory of Octavius, and the revival of Antony's determination (IV.ii). The third movement sees the final triumph of Octavius over Antony and at the end, Cleopatra.

The division into movements suggests the creation of chaos and restoration of order which is one of the elements of Renaissance tragedy. But in *Antony and Cleopatra* a kind of order is restored three times, once within each movement: first by a bargain (and a political one at that), second by victory in war, third by defeat (the death of Antony, the death of Cleopatra, the frustration of Octavius). That is, the dramatic structure, though it suggests and employs many of the conventional devices of panoramic, historical, moral tragedy, does not respond in conventional ways to the same impulses.

At the end of *Hamlet* enter Fortinbras, the conventional figure to restore order; at the end of *Macbeth*, Malcolm; at the end of *Lear* (with some modification), Edgar; at the end of *Antony and Cleopatra*, Octavius. If Octavius represents order-restored the action of the play insures that he does so in a purely conventional way, without conveying much conviction on Shakespeare's part that the order reflects a true *idea*.

There is a kind of ambivalence about nearly all the characters in this play. Cleopatra's infinite variety is extensively declared, but it goes deeper. To be sure lust does not become virtue, but Cleopatra does not die like other lustful women in the plays of Shakespeare and his contemporaries, like Goneril, for example, who also had lusted adulterously and brought chaos into the state. Instead, the Egyptian dish of the first movement becomes the Eastern Star of the last.

There is the same ambivalence about Antony. He turns his back on duty to wife and state, and this is not presented as virtue. His failure to kill himself is a kind of emblem of the failure of his career, yet can the spectator readily moralize upon him as on earlier characters, on Angelo, and Troilus, and Edmund? He is a senior citizen bewitched by passion, but also (and here is the ambiguity, even blasphemy) he is caught by Cleopatra's "strong toil of *grace*."

And as for the positive character, the restorer of order, Octavius: Caesar is the true governor, he governs himself (no drunkenness), he governs the army and state, and self-control does not become a vice. But the spectator's admiration for him is tempered by his opportunism, by his ambition and pride, by his *policy* (always a pejorative term in Shakespeare), and by the frustration of his designs for a personal triumph at the expense of Antony and Cleopatra. True, he makes the best he can of it:

Alan S. Downer

> Take up her bed,
> And bear her women from the monument.
> She shall be buried by Antony.
> No grave upon the earth shall clip in it
> A pair so famous. High events as these
> Strike those that make them; and their story is
> No less in pity than his glory which
> Brought them to be lamented. Our army shall
> In solemn show attend this funeral,
> And then to Rome.

(V.ii.354–63)

—a few well-chosen *expected* words, like the telegram of a defeated candidate to the winner. But there is a bitterness behind them and perhaps a momentary grinding of the teeth, before he says, "And then to Rome." "The ass unpolicied" beside the "lass unparalleled." He has got what he wanted, though not with the sweetness of personal triumph.

In a sense Enobarbus is a key to the ambivalence of the characterization in this panoramic action. He should be the faithful follower and confidant of the hero: the Horatio, the Kent. But he is also the reflector: the Laertes, the Gloster; Antony's fortune (fate, experience) has corrupted him. From noble warrior Antony has become an adulterer, bad governor; and Antony's fortunes (as Antony points out) have corrupted honest men, the honorable Enobarbus falls away to the enemy. Reason told him that only disaster lay with Antony. Still, he dies regretting his reasonable action. In the world of this play, personal loyalty, the personal feeling of man for man (and for woman?) was suddenly more important than the abstract, reasonable order of the conventional chain of command. Personal relationship, the feeling of this man for this man, is the only secure thing in this world, this world so carefully built up by Shakespeare in the structure of the action of his play: the world-idea of Antony and Cleopatra. It is not the world-idea of Plutarch, or of Christian doctrine.

As so often the tragic hero is presented with a choice of worlds (or ways of life), but the choice is not to be directed by law or reason, for the worlds are not clear-cut. The world of government is ambivalent, the world of love is ambivalent; and yet he must choose. And in either choice lies destruction. This is an idea which had been growing throughout Shakespeare's tragedies; it is first stated at

253

length in *Hamlet*, and here declared with finality. It is the central idea of *Antony and Cleopatra*, not the moral, but the idea developed through the dramatic experience. The structure is designed to reveal Cleopatra and Octavius not as lustful figures or dramatic stereotypes but as representations of world-ideas. Enobarbus, who perceives so much, does not quite perceive the truth of his comment on the elimination of Lepidus:

> Now world thou hast a pair of chops
> And throw between them whatsoe'er thou hast
> They'll grind the one the other.
>
> (III.v.13–15)

He speaks of Antony and Octavius as the jaws of the grinding world; the play structure shows us that the jaws are Octavius and Cleopatra and what is thrown between is Antony.

How marvelously it is all done, this nontragedy, this play, this "heavenly mingle." With what ease the playwright moves through the known world manipulating persons and places into a unique structure, unprecedented (except for *Troilus and Cressida*) and unduplicatable. It is dangerous to put words into the mouth of a dead critic but perhaps this is what Coleridge meant when he spoke of the happy valiancy of its style and the giant strength with which Shakespeare lives in and through the play.

> His legs bestrid the ocean; his rear'd arm
> Crested the world. His voice was propertied
> As all the tunéd spheres. . . .
> For his bounty,
> There was no winter in it; an autumn 'twas
> That grew the more by reaping. His delights
> Were dolphin-like; they show'd his back above
> The element he liv'd in. In his livery
> Walk'd crowns and crownets; realms and islands were
> As plates dropp'd from his pocket.
>
> (V.ii.82–92)

With those words Cleopatra remembered Antony; they are equally descriptive of Antony's only begetter, William Shakespeare.

The Alphabet of Speechless Complaint: A Study of the Mangled Daughter in Shakespeare's Titus Andronicus

Rudolf Stamm

In a recent article on Shakespeare's mirror technique in *Titus Andronicus*[1] I tried to show how the young playwright, conscious of his power of language and his sense of the theatre and stimulated by the competition of Kyd and Marlowe, experimented in this play with various methods of coordinating speech and gesture, elaborate poetical patterns, and effective stage situations to create a poetic tragedy capable of satisfying the demands of the learned lovers of classical poetry as well as those of the naive friends of sensational spectacle and of uniting the two groups in a common theatrical experience. The problem was pursued in connection with a small group of scenes, all of them dominated by the titular hero, and little attention was paid to the most extraordinary secondary figure in the play: Lavinia, who is deprived of the power of speech in the second act and can express herself through gestures only in all her later scenes, in which she becomes, of necessity, a purely visual theatrical element, in danger of being no more than a passive image of horror, a stimulus for the violent emotions and speeches of her relatives. This inquiry observes how Shakespeare uses her in this function, but is also at pains, often with the help of his mirror technique, to give her sparks of an active life and touches of individuality. In doing this it will throw light on the larger theme of the playwright's struggle to come to terms with the competing claims of his poetic and his theatrical ambition.

In the opening scenes of the play Lavinia appears to be very much her father's daughter. She shows the same fatally idealistic bent, the same respect for duty and righteousness, the same readiness to neglect the claims of instinct, natural emotion, and common sense. She is ready to marry Saturninus because her father wills it so, although she is betrothed to Bassianus, with whom she is clearly in love. When the new emperor suddenly shows his extraordinary interest in the captive Queen of the Goths and makes her rather ambiguous promises, Lavinia remains unperturbed. To his tactless question:

> Lavinia, you are not displeas'd with this?
> (I.i.270)[2]

she answers politely, patiently, and according to the highest ethical standards:

> Not I, my lord, sith true nobility
> Warrants these words in princely courtesy.
> (I.i.271–72)

This is a proud answer, too, since it rejects both Saturninus's suspicion that she could feel jealousy and the idea that he could be as weak and foolish as to desert her for the sake of Tamora. A moment later Lavinia is claimed by Bassianus, and, without comment, she allows him to carry her off. This foreshadows the mainly passive role that will be hers throughout the rest of the play with the exception of the forest scene (II.iii). When her husband is killed before her eyes and she finds herself at the mercy of the cruel empress and her lustful sons, desperation makes her eloquent for once. She refuses to believe possible the utter depravity of her three opponents, and frantically searches for a spark of humanity in their breasts. She does so without humiliating herself before the vile creatures. Realizing that they are obdurate she renounces her pleas for mercy and curses Tamora until she is silenced by brute force and carried off by Chiron and Demetrius.

The next entry of Lavinia and Tamora's sons is introduced by the stage direction: *Enter the Empress' sons,* DEMETRIUS *and* CHIRON, *with* LAVINIA, *her hands cut off, and her tongue cut out, and ravish'd.* It is a superfluous direction since Lavinia's condition becomes perfectly clear through the derisive mirror speeches of the two ravishers:

> Dem.   So, now go tell, an if thy tongue can speak,
>   Who 'twas that cut thy tongue and ravish'd thee.
> Chiron. Write down thy mind, bewray thy meaning so
>   An if thy stumps will let thee play the scribe.
> (II.iv.1–4)

The rape as well as the loss of her tongue and hands are mentioned in transitive mirror passages to clarify the physical means used by the actor (or actress) to illustrate Lavinia's plight. At the same time these passages are integrated in the characterization of the two ogres by their brutal tone. Demetrius's "See how with signs and tokens she can scrowl" (II.iv.5) stands apart from the rest as it depicts her present behavior; a wild kind of gait, posture, and gesticulation, expressive of mental and physical torture. This mirror passage is of the suggestive rather than the representative type as it leaves it to the reader's or actor's imagination to find the gestic equivalents of the "signs and tokens."

Thus when her ghastly figure is discovered by her uncle Marcus the audience is already aware of her condition. The effect of contrast sought by the playwright is between the cruel contempt of the two cowardly criminals and the horrified solicitude of Marcus. Marcus's famous—or perhaps notorious—soliloquy is the most ambitious experiment with the mirror technique in the play. It is a question whether it can properly be called a soliloquy as it is, in fact, the language part of an exchange between a speaking and a mute character. What it aims at first is to transform the grotesque figure of horror left by Chiron and Demetrius into an object of sympathy and pity. Lavinia's mutilations are not mirrored directly again; instead, they are subjected to a double process of comparison. The images appearing in it want to function as bridges between a spectacle so horrific as to deaden and pervert our responses and our normal human experience. If they do not quite succeed in doing this the excessive elaboration characteristic of the whole speech is responsible. It is clearly inspired by the ideals of Euphuistic rhetoric. The three themes—the lost hands, the lost tongue, the rape—are arranged in a balanced pattern. From the motif of the hands the speech moves to that of the tongue; the central position is taken—as it implies the loss of honor—by the rape; then the motif of the hands is resumed, and the parallel pattern is completed by a second handling of that of the tongue.

The peculiar complications of the passage are due to what we have called a double process of comparison, in the course of which Lavinia's present condition is on the one hand expressed by poetic imagery and on the other confronted with her former state of perfection. It appears clearly in Marcus's second address:

> Speak, gentle niece. What stern ungentle hands
> Hath lopp'd and hew'd, and made thy body bare
> Of her two branches—those sweet ornaments
> Whose circling shadows kings have thought to sleep in,

And might not gain so great a happiness
As half thy love?

(II.iv.16–21)

The initial metaphor, comparing Lavinia's body to a tree whose branches have been lopped, is a striking synchronic mirror passage. It passes into diachronic description when the speaker, in a daring development of his imagery, contrasts the present mutilated state of Lavinia's arms with their former beauty. The combination of the two images of sleep in the shade of the beautiful branches of a tree and sleep in Lavinia's beautiful arms is unexpected and original, but the passage peters out in the redundant:

And might not gain so great a happiness
As half thy love?

Even without this unfortunate coda it is open to criticism. Its second, diachronic part disturbs the dramatic rhythm by introducing an epical slow-motion effect; it makes Marcus dwell too long and insist too much on one single aspect of his niece's disaster; it oversteps the limits within which the relation of imagery to fact can be dramatically effective. Besides, it entirely disregards Lavinia's feelings: to remind her at the present moment of her former perfection and beauty is to increase her suffering instead of alleviating it.[3]

The four lines mirroring the flow of blood from Lavinia's mouth suffer less from the same blemishes:

Alas, a crimson river of warm blood,
Like to a bubbling fountain stirr'd with wind,
Doth rise and fall between thy rosed lips,
Coming and going with thy honey breath.

(II.iv.22–25)

The diachronic element is present again, but it is restricted to the two short and comparatively inconspicuous words "rosed" and "honey." The simile built into the main metaphor is artificial, but the description of Lavinia's intermittent hemorrhage itself is impressive: it is a striking illustration of our author's method of taming horror by poetic elaboration.

Now, invoking the fundamental myth of the play, Marcus jumps to the correct conclusion:

But sure some Tereus hath deflowered thee,
And, lest thou shouldst detect him, cut thy tongue.

(II.iv.26–27)

These and the following sixteen lines are given to the central theme of the rape of Lavinia. They are, as we shall see, rather successfully integrated in the dramatic score with the exception of two of the similes included in them. Whereas the line "As from a conduit with three issuing spouts" (II.iv.30) is strong and sufficiently rapid, what follows appears too elaborate and slow again:

> Yet do thy cheeks look red as Titan's face
> Blushing to be encount'red with a cloud.
>
> (II.iv.31–32)

The same objection is provoked by the sententious insertion:

> Sorrow concealed, like an oven stopp'd,
> Doth burn the heart to cinders where it is.
>
> (II.iv.36–37)

The following comparison of Philomel's and Lavinia's plights stresses the connection between the myth and the play once more, introducing at the same time the dramatically relevant problem of the identification of the authors of Lavinia's misery. Then the symmetrical rhetorical pattern is completed in a return to the retrospective description of Lavinia's former perfection. The lost hands, as well as the lost tongue, are praised as sources of delightful music. The idea that the sight of Lavinia's fingers moving on the lute and the sound of her voice could have influenced Tamora's ruffianly sons is not without a piquant touch of irony. Essentially, this passage is another epical element not completely assimilated to the dramatic style. Although it contains gestic images and a number of dramatically effective references to Lavinia as she is now standing before Marcus, it offers her no opportunity of action or reaction, thus forcing upon her the posture of a frozen statue of misery, which she must keep up too long.

But the young Shakespeare had too much of the playwright's instinct to have the whole scene spoilt by the demands of the rhetorical pattern in his mind. In fact, it was his ambition to integrate this pattern in a thoroughly dramatic event, and he was at least partially successful in realizing it. In what follows we shall observe his method of theatrical innervation in some detail.

The opening line:

> Who is this?—my niece, that flies away so fast?
>
> (II.iv.11)

is a question asked and immediately answered in Marcus's mind, but it is given the form of a spoken aside, which might draw passionate assent from an excited audience. It implies a situation: Marcus unexpectedly catching sight of his niece as she is running away from her torturers; and it introduces at once the motif to which the scene owes its dramatic life: Marcus seeking his way, step by step, from his happy ignorance to the knowledge of the full extent of Lavinia's violation. The dramatic and the mirror function of the line are combined with the help of a very unusual syntactical form. Hardly has the main question been asked when the recognition occurs, forcing Lavinia's name into its forward position, before the relative clause can complete the question. This sequence is so unusual that its punctuation has proved difficult from the start as is shown by the differences between the poor solution found in Q_{1-2} and the various improvements offered by Q_3, and F, and by the modern editions. The most adequate form would probably be as follows:

Who is this—my niece!—that flies away so fast?

In the first three words of the next line Marcus requests his niece to stand and speak:

Cousin, a word: where is your husband?
(II.iv.12)

In this four-stress line there is a rhythmical gap after the heavy caesura, which is not without a theatrical function. It permits Lavinia to stop and remain standing with her face averted from her uncle, and Marcus to approach her. Before he realizes her condition he utters the first thought that struck him when he recognized her: why should she be alone here in the woods? A moment later he has seen that she is without her hands. So far the movement of the scene has been very rapid; now the first retardation occurs, Marcus being given three lines to express his reaction to the enormity before his eyes:

If I do dream, would all my wealth would wake me!
If I do wake, some planet strike me down,
That I may slumber an eternal sleep!
(II.iv.13–15)

This carefully balanced rhetorical structure is also dramatically effective. The thought of dreaming and sleeping suggests a low use of the voice and the eleven monosyllabic words of the first line a staccato effect of even stresses, toned down by the alliteration of four w's to a kind of thick speech, expressive of the paralysis of emotion under the impact of horror. The same paralysis is in the anaphorical beginning of Marcus's second antithetical wish. Then a more energetic rhythm makes itself felt, indicating that paralysis is giving way to pity, sorrow, and anger. The gestic implications of all this remain unspecified, but the rhythm suggests that Marcus comes to a sudden standstill in his rapid approach to his niece, that he remains nailed to the ground for a few seconds, closing his eyes and stretching out his arms with raised hands to protect himself from the nauseating sight. The moment of immobility passes; with the words "Speak, gentle niece," he completes his advance to her in an impetuous movement of sympathy. Now instead of the simple direct question "Who had done this?," which the mature Shakespeare would have given him, we find the complicated metaphorical structure discussed above. Lavinia must continue in her posture of distress, her face turned away from her uncle. Since she fails to respond to his question, there is a pause at the end of his speech. It provokes his next urgent inquiry: "Why dost not speak to me?" Before he speaks again an implied gestic event intervenes: in a shy, hesitant movement Lavinia turns her face to him so that he can see the blood flowing from her mouth or—another response to the implication—can take her head between his hands in an affectionate way and turn it toward him. As he declaims on the flow of blood, she stands motionless again, with lowered eyelids rather than with wide-open, horror-stricken eyes, until he reaches his conclusion that she must have fallen victim to a new Tereus. Her reaction to this is the subject of the following mirror passage, which almost sinks under its burden of simile and metaphor. Lavinia turns her face away again, but not before Marcus has seen the blush of shame on it. Taking this for an affirmation he insists eagerly:

> Shall I speak for thee? Shall I say 'tis so?
>
> (II.iv.33)

His next lines presuppose an unmistakable reaction of hers: a grave and meaningful nod or one of the more passionate forms of gestic assent. Now Marcus becomes obsessed by the thought of the unknown author of Lavinia's disaster and indulges in his long declamation on his own suppressed emotions and on the influence her former charms should have exerted on the ravisher. The playwright tries to make the most of the contrast between the mute, immobile, disfigured Lavinia before our eyes and her former active and lovely self. The references to her presence are few: she is addressed twice, as "lovely niece" and "cousin." A very extraordinary effect is achieved by the demonstratives in "those pretty fingers," "those lily hands," and "that sweet tongue." The spectator tends to take them in their primary local sense and directs his attention to the places on Lavinia's person where her hands and tongue should be, only to realize more acutely than before that these limbs are lost things of the past, the demonstratives having acquired a temporal function.

The return to present action is introduced by the impulse words "Come, let us go," followed by a prospective mirror passage heavily charged with metaphor:

> Come, let us go, and make thy father blind,
> For such a sight will blind a father's eye;
> One hour's storm will drown the fragrant meads,
> What will whole months of tears thy father's eyes?
> (II.iv.52–55)

This is a perfect introduction to Titus's coming reaction and tear imagery, but it is hardly an encouragement for Lavinia to appear before her father. Her reluctance to become the cause of so much sorrow makes her move away from her uncle, a movement mirrored in the first words of his final couplet:

> Do not draw back, for we will mourn with thee;
> O, could our mourning ease thy misery!
> (II.iv.56–57)

To overcome her scruples he mentions the little her family can do to relieve her misery: their sympathy of woe. At this Lavinia acquiesces and follows her uncle.

Looking back upon the whole of this fascinating speech we conclude that its author tried hard to integrate a pattern derived from epical poetry in a dramatic event and that, although he did not fully succeed, he was able to create a scene with a greater theatrical potential than is usually conceded.

In the next scene in which Lavinia appears (III.i.) she plays a secondary role. She acts as a foil for the lamentations of the titular hero; her fate is one of the blows of fortune driving him from one paroxysm of grief through the next into half-madness and dreams of revenge. Yet the playwright tries to make more of Lavinia than a passive emblem of suffering by giving her opportunities of reaction and, on rare occasions, even of spontaneous action. When Lavinia is led in by Marcus she remains a passive object at first. Lucius uses the very word when he exclaims:

> Ay me! this object kills me.
> (III.i.64)

Her whole plight is not sized up by Titus and Lucius at a glance although they see at once that she is handless. For Lucius the shock is so severe that it not only wrings from him the above exclamation but literally knocks him off his feet. This is the implication of Titus's line:

> Faint-hearted boy, arise, and look upon her.
> (III.i.65)

The imagined action seems to be that of a few steps backward ending in a kneeling posture with hands clapped to face so as to wipe out the horrid vision. Titus's reaction is verbal. He wants Lavinia to name the perpetrator of the crime and develops, in his highest rhetorical style, the half-crazy punning associations striking his fevered imagination at her sight. As Lucius repeats his question Marcus finds himself obliged to tell his brother and nephew of the loss of her tongue. Shakespeare is using the device developed in the scene of her encounter with Marcus: the step-by-step discovery of Lavinia's condition, but, having taken the first two steps, he omits the third. The rape is not mentioned, nor is there any reference to it in the whole of the present scene. It is reserved for act IV, scene i, where it will become the dominating theme: a point to be remembered before we accuse our author of writing in terms of individual scenes only and of neglecting the overall structure of his play. Instead of pursuing his inquiry into Lavinia's plight, Titus is sidetracked by the punning possibilities in the word "deer." Then his mind wanders to the desperate situation of all his family, and he undertakes an emblematic representation of it, referring to himself in a powerful simile, to the way his wretched sons have gone to death, to Lucius, and, finally, to Marcus and Lavinia, who are shown weeping. This allusion to her tears is the first sign that she is more in this scene than a mere object of the scrutiny and sympathy of her family. The end of Titus's speech mirrors a more specific reaction:

> Look, Marcus! Ah, son Lucius, look on her!
> When I did name her brothers, then fresh tears
> Stood on her cheeks as doth the honey dew
> Upon a gath'red lily almost withered.
> (III.i.110–13)

It is when she hears Titus speak of the possibility that his two condemned sons might really have killed Bassianus that her response becomes more active; indeed, she is able to reject this possibility unequivocally. This is made clear by the following mirror speech coming from Titus:

> No, no, they would not do so foul a deed;
> Witness the sorrow that their sister makes.
>
> (III.i.118–19)

It is suggestive rather than representative, implying gestures of revulsion and sadness at the thought that even her father can entertain suspicions of this kind while she is unable to clear her brothers of them. The passage introduces a new and moving motif into the play: an ideal relationship of paternal and filial love endows Titus with a partly intuitive faculty of reading Lavinia's imperfect gesticulation correctly and of becoming her best interpreter. At the present moment he is so touched by her mute but energetic defense of her calumniated brothers that he wishes to show her his gratitude and love:

> Gentle Lavinia, let me kiss thy lips,
> Or make some sign how I may do thee ease.
>
> (III.i.120–21)

The unmistakable implication is that she avoids his kiss, probably because she considers her wounded mouth and her dishonored self unworthy of receiving it. He does not resent this repulse, sensing the honorable motives behind it, and therefore adds his second, rather helpless invitation, which remains without visible response. Thus Titus resorts to his verbal method of consolation again. He depicts an imaginary scene of shared sorrow, an emblem of the family's "sympathy of woe." As he is speaking, his mind becomes clouded, and his imaginings turn violent and bitter. This is not the way to assuage her grief. Lucius interrupts his father reproachfully:

> Sweet father, cease your tears; for at your grief
> See how my wretched sister sobs and weeps.
>
> (III.i.136–37)

The scene is then brought to a provisional conclusion by two parallel pieces of business. Marcus, in an attempt at supporting Lucius's intervention, offers Titus his handkerchief with the words: "Good Titus, dry thine eyes." The offer is rejected because the handkerchief is soaked with Marcus's own tears. In spite of this Lucius tries a similar experiment with Lavinia when he says:

> Ah, my Lavinia, I will wipe thy cheeks.
>
> (III.i.142)

She turns away from him, and Titus interprets her gesture:

> Mark, Marcus, mark! I understand her signs
> Had she a tongue to speak, now would she say
> That to her brother which I said to thee:
> His napkin, with his true tears all bewet,
> Can do no service on her sorrowful cheeks.
>
> (III.i.143–47)

In the subsequent parts of act III, scene i, Lavinia intervenes on two occasions with spontaneous actions of her own, and in either case they express her sympathy with her father. When Titus, after the Aaron episode and the sacrifice of one of his hands, resumes his complaints and tries to pray, he mirrors and appreciates her gesture of sympathy with the words:

> What, would'st thou kneel with me?
> Do, then, dear heart; for heaven shall hear our prayers.
>
> (III.i.210–11)

Quite soon the two kneeling figures rise again as Titus's exasperated mind converts his prayer into threats and hyperbolical lamentations, identifying Lavinia's sighs with the wind thrashing the sea and herself with "the weeping welkin" inundating the earth. When Titus sees himself as the tormented sea and as the drowned earth her sighs and tears become the expression of her dismay at the sight of her deranged father. Her behavior, not mirrored but implied in the text, could be a sudden frightened jumping up from her kneeling position, a few steps backward, away from the raving old man, the raising of her miserable stumps in an imploring gesture, and a solicitous stare at him, accompanied by the sighs and tears referred to in his speech.

Now the messenger with the cut-off hand and the heads of the executed sons arrives, and the horror of the scene reaches its climax. Lavinia's reaction is as unexpected as that of her father a moment later. She cannot go beyond her earlier demonstrations of woe, nor does she try to. Instead, she shows her fine mettle by simply walking up to her father and kissing him affectionately. The fact that this kindly action has no effect whatsoever on him becomes a measure of his suffering. Like the rest of the family Lavinia witnesses his paroxysm of laughter and is relieved when he saves himself by turning his thoughts toward revenge. She participates in the ceremony of revenge staged by him and accepts his vow and, as well, the gruesome and grotesque role he provides for her in the crazy procession in which she finally leaves the stage.

Thus Lavinia is an agent in this scene in spite of all her handicaps, and the touch of Shakespeare's humanizing hand makes itself felt in the way the father-daughter relationship is developed. Although this relationship is a secondary theme, it was considered promising enough to be resumed in the first part of the following banquet scene. At its beginning Titus shows himself troubled by the question how he and Lavinia, in their maimed condition, can express the only emotion that interests him: grief. His preoccupation has its origin in the sight of Marcus standing there with his arms folded before his breast, a gesture seen by Titus as the classical expression of grief:

> Marcus, unknit that sorrow-wreathen knot;
> Thy niece and I, poor creatures, want our hands,
> And cannot passionate our tenfold grief
> With folded arms.[4]
>
> (III.ii.4–7)

His mind then goes in search of the second-best gesture, within the reach of crippled complainers like Lavinia and himself. For himself he finds the thumping of his breast with his remaining right hand; and he not only describes this gesture but demonstrates it as well while he is speaking the defective line:

> Then thus I thump it down.
>
> (III.ii.11)

The beating of his breast coincides at first with the stressed words "thus," "thump," and "down," and after that it may supply the missing stresses. Turning to his daughter, Titus continues:

> Thou map of woe, that thus dost talk in signs!
> When thy poor heart beats with outrageous beating,
> Thou canst not strike it thus to make it still.
>
> (III.ii.12–14)

The irregular accentuation of the second line successfully represents the irregular heartbeat:

$$\smile \; \bar{} \; \bar{} \; \bar{} \; / \; \bar{} \; \smile \; \smile \bar{} \; \smile \; \bar{} \; \smile$$

The "thus" in the first line is best interpreted as a reference, accompanied by a glance, to an imploring gesture Lavinia is making in order to assuage the agitation of her father. The "thus" of the third line is a retrospective and therefore nongestic reference to Titus's preceding demonstration. As he pursues his line of thought his mind becomes increasingly deranged. His ravings about what Lavinia should do to her heart and about the loss of their hands come to an end when he remembers the purpose of the "banquet" and invites the company:

> Come, let's fall to; and, gentle girl, eat this:
> Here is no drink. Hark, Marcus, what she says—
> I can interpret all her martyr'd signs;
> She says she drinks no other drink but tears,
> Brew'd with her sorrow, mesh'd upon her cheeks.
> Speechless complainer, I will learn thy thought;
> In thy dumb action will I be as perfect
> As begging hermits in their holy prayers.
> Thou shalt not sigh, nor hold thy stumps to heaven,
> Nor wink, nor nod, nor kneel, nor make a sign,
> But I of these will wrest an alphabet,
> And by still practice learn to know thy meaning.
>
> (III.ii.34–45)

After his general invitation to the company he turns to Lavinia, who has sat down by his side. He starts feeding her, lifting a morsel to her mouth with his remaining hand. She accepts it but seems to find the chewing of it difficult. This is implied by what seems to be a question ("Here is no drink?") inspired by his solicitude for his daughter and accompanied by a searching glance across the table. Before any other response is possible Lavinia declines the offer by a gesture interpreted by Titus in terms of one of the tear conceits by which he is obsessed. This is one of the passages in the play where we are tempted to think that the conceit was first in the playwright's mind and that he was then at pains to invent a dramatic situation for it. The situation does not suit the conceit too well. There is a touch of homely realism and of spontaneous human feeling in Titus's attempt to feed his mangled daughter, qualities conspicuously absent from his rhetorical interpretation of her gesture as well as from most of his other poetic flights. They make themselves felt again in the following address to the "speechless complainer," in which Titus reasserts his wish to be his daughter's best interpreter, enumerating specifically five of the "signs" by which she tries to make herself understood. After Lavinia has shown her appreciation of her father's kind intentions by gestures that have left no sign in the text, she becomes a mute and unobserved witness of the fly episode, in which the correlation of speech and action is strikingly successful. At the end of the scene Titus's tender concern for her appears once more in his invitation:

Lavinia, go with me;
I'll to thy closet, and go read with thee
Sad stories chanced in the times of old.
(III.ii.81–83)

This passage provides an easy transition to the next scene (IV.i.), in which Lavinia is more active and shows more initiative than anywhere else in the play. This scene, especially its first part leading up to the disclosure of Lavinia's secret, aims at the same kind of interaction of speech and gesture as the fly episode, but it lacks its finish. The theatrical notation in it is so defective it suggests that it was printed without having gone through the author's final revision. Forming a clear idea of what happens in the scene is a difficult task. The following reconstruction is based on an evaluation of, it is hoped, all the available direct and indirect data.

If we want to make theatrical sense of what follows, a critical view of the initial stage direction is necessary: *Enter young* LUCIUS *and* LAVINIA *running after him, and the boy flies from her with his books under his arm. Enter* TITUS *and* MARCUS. It is a full direction, but leaves out of account the boy's remark:

Which made me down to throw my books, and fly—
(IV.i.25)

The solution of this puzzle seems to be that the boy drops his books immediately after his entry at the start of act IV, so that they remain scattered on the floor on one side of the stage. Then he runs up to Titus, crying "Help, grandsire, help!" Coming to a stop in front of him he adds breathlessly:

my aunt Lavinia
Follows me everywhere, I know not why.

Before he has finished Lavinia arrives in pursuit of him. As Titus, knowing too well the harmless good nature of his daughter, hesitates to respond to his appeal, the boy turns to Marcus:

Good uncle Marcus, see how swift she comes!

He tries to hide behind him and, from this shelter, addresses his aunt, who has come to a stop in front of Marcus:

Alas, sweet aunt, I know not what you mean.

Marcus, gently pulling the boy from behind him to his side, comforts him:

> Stand by me, Lucius; do not fear thine aunt.

Titus walks up to the group to second his brother's admonition:

> She loves thee, boy, too well to do thee harm.

The boy, being only half convinced, replies:

> Ay, when my father was in Rome she did.

Now Marcus turns his attention to Lavinia's gesticulation and asks his brother:

> What means my niece Lavinia by these signs?

In the light of what follows her "signs" would seem to be friendly gestures inviting Lucius to accompany her to the spot where his books are lying. Instead of answering Marcus's question, Titus decides to take over the care of the boy and to reassure him by an explanation of Lavinia's behavior. When he says

> Fear her not, Lucius; somewhat doth she mean,

the boy is still standing by Marcus. Turning from his general to a more specific interpretation of Lavinia's "signs," Titus takes young Lucius by the hand and talks to him in a very personal way adapted to his youthful psychology:

> See, Lucius, see how much she makes of thee.
> Somewhither would she have thee go with her.

This is the correct interpretation of her behavior. F and Qq are certainly right in giving these lines to Titus, who proves in this scene that he has realized his plan of becoming an expert in the reading of Lavinia's "signs," whereas Marcus, to whom the lines are transferred by Maxwell, shows himself puzzled by her gesticulation in line 8 and completely misunderstands it in lines 38ff., as I hope to show. Maxwell justifies his transfer by pointing to the use of the name Lucius in two successive lines; the apparent awkwardness of this disappears if the lines become part of the theatrical action described above.

For all that, I should agree with Maxwell that F and Qq are in error where they give all the lines from 9 to 15 to Titus, since line 18, in the boy's answer,

> For I have heard my grandsire say full oft

makes it clear that Marcus, and not Titus, is addressed. I have substantiated the view that lines 9, 10, and 11 should come from Titus. The following lines 12 to 15 can plausibly be given to Marcus:

Ah, boy, Cornelia never with more care
Read to her sons than she hath read to thee
Sweet poetry and Tully's Orator.
Canst thou not guess wherefore she plies thee thus?

The last line, with its uncertainty about the "signs," fits Marcus extremely well and cannot possibly come from Titus. The reason for giving him lines 12 to 14 as well is less cogent: Titus appears too much absorbed by his observation of Lavinia's present behavior to switch over suddenly to memories of her past actions.

At the end of his long answer to Marcus's question Lucius has regained enough confidence in his aunt to say:

And, madam, if my uncle Marcus go,
I will most willingly attend your ladyship.

(IV.i.27–28)

The next line is very short, a hint that, after Marcus's remark "Lucius, I will," the group begins to move in the direction indicated by Lavinia. According to such a reading their expedition comes to a standstill where the books are lying. Here Lavinia expresses a new intention by a new kind of gesture. Most probably she is searching for the book she desires with the help of one of her stumps, or feet, or both. Titus is at a loss for a moment, then he understands:

How now, Lavinia! Marcus, what means this?
Some book there is that she desires to see.
Which is it, girl, of these?—Open them, boy.

(IV.i.30–32)

Lucius, on his knees, helps her in her search, opening book after book to show her the title page. At the sight of this Titus is struck by the thought that these are merely schoolbooks and that he could put a much better supply at Lavinia's disposal. He tells her so in four lines (33–36) to which she pays no attention, absorbed as she is by her search, which ends during his speech when she has found the desired volume. Her gestures at this moment are mirrored in Titus's question:

Why lifts she up her arms in sequence thus?

(IV.i.37)

It sends Marcus off on a wild-goose chase, which deserves this name although he stumbles on a fact in the course of his mistaken diagnosis of Lavinia's gestures:

270

I think she means that there were more than one
Confederate in the fact; ay, more there was,
Or else to heaven she heaves them for revenge.
(IV.i.38–40)

In reality Lavinia's thoughts are less disconnected and her gestures more practical than he thinks. The signs she is making are an invitation to Lucius to take the chosen book up from the floor and place it before her on a table. Her wish is fulfilled during Marcus's speech, at the end of which Titus sees her already busy with the book. He asks:

Lucius, what book is that she tosseth so?

The boy replies that it is Ovid's *Metamorphoses* and throws in the extra information: "My mother gave it me," very much in the manner of a child. At this, Marcus comes in with a particularly obtuse interpretation of Lavinia's action:

For love of her that's gone,
Perhaps she cull'd it from among the rest.
(IV.i.44–45)

This, taken together with his earlier vague and confused guesswork, but with the fact also that it is he who, eventually, renders the discovery of Lavinia's secret possible, might suggest that the playwright was tempted to enhance the interest of the scene before us by making it an illustration of the proverb "A fool's bolt may sometimes hit the mark," and that he cast Marcus for the part of the fool, a part that is certainly not his in the rest of the play. Conversely, Titus is given the role of the wise man for the time being.

He keeps observing his daughter closely and giving correct and helpful interpretations of her behavior:

Soft! So busily she turns the leaves!
Help her.
What would she find? Lavinia, shall I read?
This is the tragic tale of Philomel
And treats of Tereus' treason and his rape;
And rape, I fear, was root of thy annoy.
(IV.i.46–50)

Titus's "Soft" is a friendly hint to Marcus not to distract attention from Lavinia by his irrelevant talk. Its gestic equivalent is a light silencing movement with the hand. While Titus observes his daughter and mirrors her activity in speech, he feels the need to help her. It seems a good idea to take the extra metrical "Help her," found at the beginning of line 47 in Qq and F, as an exclamation and to assign a line of its own to it,[5] one of the defective lines pointing to stage action. After his exclamation Titus moves up to where Lavinia is standing (or possibly sitting) at the table. As soon as he is in reading distance of the book, he asks himself rather than the rest of the company: "What would she find?" before he addresses Lavinia: "Lavinia, shall I read?" Upon an implied nod from her he adjusts the book to his own sight-line and finds that she is busy with "the tragic tale of Philomel." Marcus, now standing on the other side of his niece, puts in his:

> See, brother, see! Note how she quotes the leaves,
> (IV.i.51)

implying that she not only wishes to draw their attention to the tale as such, but to a particular passage in it. She finds the passage, points it out to Titus; he reads it and understands:

> Lavinia, wert thou thus surpris'd, sweet girl,
> Ravish'd and wrong'd as Philomela was,
> Forc'd in the ruthless, vast and gloomy woods?
> (IV.i.52–54)

With his isolated "See, see!" he triumphantly points out her eager nods and other signs of assent. He shows a rather disproportionate interest in the similarity of the wild places where Philomela and where Lavinia were wronged and expatiates on it in a way that reminds us again how often the playwright and the poet were at odds with each other in the author of *Titus Andronicus*. What is excessive dramatically becomes a bridge to a striking expression of one of the play's key themes in Marcus's question:

> O, why should nature build so foul a den,
> Unless the gods delight in tragedies?
> (IV.i.60–61)

With his next speech Titus shows that, at long last, he has discovered the way of common sense to the ravishers' names:

> Give signs, sweet girl, for here are none but friends,
> What Roman lord it was durst do the deed.
> Or slunk not Saturnine, as Tarquin erst,
> That left the camp to sin in Lucrece' bed?
> (IV.i.62–65)

Lavinia's answer to this must be a shaking of her head. Titus could now go on enumerating the other possible authors of the crime, and, with the help of Lavinia's signs of affirmation or negation, the detection of Demetrius and Chiron would be easy. But this would be a bad anticlimax, which could raise such awkward questions as why so obvious a method had not been used immediately or soon after Marcus's discovery of the maimed Lavinia, and it would deprive the play of one of its most spectacular scenes. Therefore Titus is not allowed to pursue his inquiry; Marcus silences him with his more sensational plan, and the writing in the sand is staged.

After it Lavinia kneels down in the new ceremony in which the family swear again to revenge their wrongs and then disappears from the stage until she is called upon to play her part in Titus's cruel rites of revenge and, finally, to become a willing sacrifice to her father's and her own sense of honor.

Practically, our author's experiments with his mute heroine come to an end at the beginning of act IV. I hope I have shown that they were important experiments because they permitted Shakespeare to train himself in one of the playwright's most essential skills, in the art of expressing emotion and meaning not through language alone, but through gesture and the other visual elements of the theatre as well.

Hubert Herkomer's
Theatrical Theories and Practice
and the New Stagecraft

Sybil Rosenfeld

Hubert Herkomer's contributions to the reform of staging have been unduly neglected and he hardly rates a mention in histories of the Victorian theatre. Yet his theories and practice were well in advance of his time and influenced the new stagecraft, particularly in the person of Gordon Craig. His experiments in his little theatre at Bushey, 1887–93, and his beliefs as promulgated to a knowledgeable audience in his lecture on scenic art in 1892, merit a niche in the history of the revolutionary shift from naturalistic painting to the abstract plasticity of the new movement.

Herkomer was a fashionable painter of easel portraits and landscapes when he first turned his attention to the stage. Like Adolph Appia he was inspired by Wagner, whom he met in England in 1878. As an amateur musician Herkomer was impressed by Wagner's ideal of a *Gesamtkunstwerk* and, more practically, by his reform in the shape of the Opera House which he had built at Bayreuth in 1876. The galleries there had been abolished in favor of a single-tier, fan-shaped auditorium. Herkomer agreed that it was not possible to fully convey movement to an audience, part of whom was seated 30 or 40 feet above the stage and another part in the front below it. A theatre, he said, should "provide seats from which the full intention of both actor and scenic artist can be perfectly seen by the audience."[1] This preoccupation with the relationship of audience to stage, so important in theatre planning today, had not till then been much considered in this country except for specialized cases such as E.W. Godwin's attempt to recreate a Greek theatre in Hengler's Circus for *Helena of Troas*, 1886, or Poel's determination to produce Shakespeare on a stage approximating Elizabethan conditions. Herkomer was one of the first to realize the importance of Wagner's experiment and to preach his reformed auditorium which has now become the usual form in new theatres.

It was Richard Wagner's son Siegfried, then at Harrow, who

persuaded the artist to give some private theatricals for Christmas in 1887. For this purpose Herkomer adapted a chapel near his house in Bushey. Though he believed that a theatre audience should be placed on one floor curving up from stage level, he seems to have been unable to carry this out in practice, probably because he was converting a building with a gallery already there supported by a huge wooden column.[2] The interior was remarkable for its craftsmanship. Pitch-pine walls were decorated with a frieze, the ceiling panels with a stenciled pattern, the gallery front with a carved design of oak leaves, the lamp-holders were of wrought iron and the screen which concealed the orchestra was ornamented with bronze scrolls, while the gold silk curtains were embroidered with a simple design. All this handwork was done by the artist and his student assistants and is evidence of the care which had been taken to create an artistic ambiance. Here Herkomer produced a slight, romantic medley called *The Sorceress* for which he was designer, composer, and stage manager and in which he also acted. His reforms consisted of abolishing the footlights and experimenting with a new kind of sky and moonlight effect. After this he enlarged his stage to 40 feet deep, 30 wide, and 60 high, and in 1889 he presented his "pictorial-music play," *An Idyl*. This curious piece was first conceived of as a picture with music attuned to it, and then as a story on which to hang it. Dumb-show played a large part in conveying the simple plot, augmented only when necessary by sung words.[3] Herkomer again composed and orchestrated the music, which was conducted by the famous Wagnerian, Richter. This was the most outstanding of Herkomer's productions. He and his students designed the two scenes: a fourteenth-century village street with a smithy and landscape background of meadows broken by huts and farmsteads for acts I and III, and a room in the smith's house for act II. The hamlet rose gradually to the back of the stage where an ancient cross marked the parting of two roads. The surface was built up unevenly and the cobbles of the street were actually modeled, which would seem the acme of realism. But Herkomer believed that a stage floor had to be as true to nature as the rest and pointed out that houses, rocks, and hills rarely rose from a perfectly level surface. This attention to the stage floor was a feature that had been neglected since the seventeenth-century baroque designers had used it for squared patterns to emphasize their perspectives. Tree's *A Midsummer Night's Dream* with its real grass was more than twenty years ahead, and in our own day John Bury has declared the floor to be the leading feature in a design. The middle scene of the room was simply let down from above over the

275

solidly built street scene. The flats had been folded against the upper part of the front stage wall and moved on hinges, being unfolded as they were lowered. This was a more practical version of a system which had been introduced into a production of Sardou's *Peril* in 1876, where the scenery was so solid that a boudoir scene could be played only inserted inside it. It also maintained some spatial relationship between the size of a street and the size of a room. Not only the cobbles but the houses and trees were modeled. The method was to build up a solid back scene in order to create a real perspective and true shadow effects. The difference from current practice was that the three-dimensional pieces were not only built up but modeled in plaster and papier-mâché with the help of glue and occasionally of tow, which produced a stereoscopic effect: "an admirable union of objects modelled in the round with painting which produce scenic effects of marvellous beauty."[4]

It was, however, his sky and his lighting that represented his major reforms. Since the usual painted sky meant unalterable color, Herkomer introduced a kind of canvas cyclorama: "The sky there is no flat surface but a blue vault painted in skilfully-graduated modulations of blue. Over this azure dome float misty gauzes superimposed in delicate varieties of line, illumined by an ever-shifting play of light."[5] This domed sky created an atmosphere in depth not hitherto achieved by canvas borders hanging from the flies "like washing on a line" with awkward joins at right angles in the corners.[6] The grey gauze on a frame was stretched at an angle in front of the graduated sky canvas and onto it were projected moving cloud effects. The gauze was illuminated by lights passing through colored glasses in Renaissance fashion. The moon was a round tin box closed at the back with three electric lamps inside; the front was closed with a lens covered with tissue paper on which were painted the moon mountains. It was secured to the painted sky behind the gauze by concealed wires and could be raised slowly by means of a lever worked by one man. The advantage was in its slow movement instead of the usual quick, perpendicular one which used to come to a sudden stop. Light, reduced to a glow for the moon's rising after the sunset, increased as it ascended. So complete was the illusion that Herkomer had to take members of his audience, including Irving, Ellen Terry, and young Gordon Craig, onto the stage afterward to convince them that what they had witnessed was not the actual sky seen through a removed back wall but pure artifice.

Herkomer just forestalled Appia in his insistence on the importance of light: "Light is the most potent factor in scenic art. . . . It is proper lighting rather than good painting upon which the success of a scene depends."[7] It was through light that mystery could be achieved and for him mystery was the backbone of scenic art: "It is through the management of light that we touch the real magic of art." Only a few years later Appia was to expound his theory of painting with light, though not on painted canvas or modeled scenery but on symbolic abstractions.

Herkomer wished to compose a scene on the stage, as he did on an easel picture, where some part of the landscape was seen in mysterious shadow, suggestive and indistinct, not flooded by an overall, even glare. He therefore abolished footlights which illuminated the foreground and cast upward shadows on the faces of the actors as they approached. Light, he insisted, does not come from the ground in nature. This idea was not altogether new. Giambattista Pasquali had suggested it, along with the abolition of footlights, long before the era of gas, in Venice in 1773: "If instead of illuminating the entire stage equally, the lights were concentrated on one part in such a way as to leave the other darker, one could then be able to admire in the theatre the same force and vivacity of light and shade which one sees in the paintings of Titian and Giorgione."[8] Both Pasquali and Herkomer took their cue from paintings, though the latter always emphasized that he was trying to get nearer to natural effects. This was something of a contradiction since works of art compose and do not imitate nature.

To secure a diffused effect and to soften the shadows on the actors' faces, Herkomer placed a group of lights at the side level with them, and boxed the lights so that they were hidden. The result was as near as he could come to diffused daylight. He was a pioneer in this method of diffusion which was not to be superseded until, in the twentieth century, Fortuny invented a system which could reflect light from the cyclorama. Herkomer's pictorial brilliance was obtained not by extravagant but by economical lighting.

His reforms provoked some disagreement. For instance, a writer in *The Builder* considered that footlights should be retained for the very reason that they were unnatural, removing scenery from the pretense of realism and giving it an idealized appearance.[9] William L. Telbin, scene painter for Irving and Tree, defended footlights on the ground that they formed a curtain of light between the stage and the auditorium softening over the front scenery.[10] But then Telbin was averse to reforms that might threaten traditional scene painting.

In staging his *An Idyl*, then, Herkomer realized the paradox that realism must be produced by means of deception. The eye of the spectator must not be allowed to see how the semblance of reality was obtained. Thus he said that "through the management of lights, the strangest deception could be practised upon the visual organs."[11] The aim was to recreate reality by means of illusion. By his mingling of painting and modeling, by his gauzes and his illumination, he succeeded in reproducing subtle atmospheric effects.

His two succeeding pieces, *Filippo* adapted from the French by Alfred Berlyn and given in 1889, and *Times Revenges* by W. L. Courtney in 1890, 1891, and 1893, continued to embody his ideas but seem to have added little to his previous experiments. More important was the lecture he gave on "Scenic Art" in 1892 in which he set out his theories and recorded his practices. He spoke to his audience of the desirability of the amphitheatre shape. He suggested that the proscenium arch should be capable of adjustment so that a palace chamber was not the same size as a cottage room. He did not hit on the idea of a false proscenium but proposed movable screens behind the arch which could diminish the framed space where necessary. Whether he ever used them is not clear but he did make a model worked by a left- and right-handed screw enabling one man to make the sides of the proscenium come closer while the upper section was lowered by means of a counterweight. In fact, a similar attempt had been made in 1842 at Drury Lane by the installation of sliding panels, though they only reduced the aperture by five feet.[12] Again Herkomer was challenged by Telbin, who disagreed because of sight-line difficulties from the side boxes, but these would not occur in an amphitheatre auditorium. Telbin preferred, as in his design for *Tristan and Isolde*, to use painted draperies placed about ten to twelve feet behind the proscenium to reduce the deck area of the ship.

Herkomer evidently employed some form of projection for his clouds; furthermore, he foresaw the possibilities of the magic lantern for a range of projected scenery hitherto undreamed of and even proposed an experiment of projecting an entire scene by this means.

He had come to know that positive realism on the stage was an impossibility and that the foundation of scenic art was artificiality. The scenery must be in harmony with the actor and should complete the dramatic situation for him. The artist and the actor together contributed to the whole work of art: "I hold the stage to be the medium through which the greatest truths in nature can be brought home most directly to the minds and hearts of the people, and all the arts can, to their fullest capacity, be united in this most complete form of human expression. But we should not be satisfied until all the arts

278

are placed on an equal footing *not necessarily of importance but of perfection.*[13] It was Wagner's ideal and it was to be one of the bases of the new stagecraft. Both Appia and Craig sought an aesthetic union to which all elements contributed. Craig, who attended both the performance of *An Idyl* and Herkomer's lecture, was greatly impressed. We are told that he bought the report of the lecture and pasted it in his scrapbook. Herkomer had criticized the contemporary theatre for its unnatural lighting, its wobbly canvases, its two-dimensional cutouts, its tatty sky borders, and its footlights which threw the shadows of the actors onto the scenery. He had paid tribute to Irving, in whose company Craig had enlisted in 1889, for the artistic wholeness of his productions, directed by one man, but he hinted that they were insufficiently experimental.

Craig adapted this conception of the planning and direction by one man. He was also impressed by more practical matters, such as the value of the adaptable proscenium and the atmospheric sky achieved by the lit gauze which he used in *Dido and Aeneas.*[14] Both Herkomer's theories and practice thus influenced the revolution in scenic design. He himself never made the leap away from the painted scene which had dominated the stage for nearly three centuries, and he never conceived of scenery as other than pictorial illustration. He still spoke in the name of nature and not in the name of symbol, architecture, or abstraction. Yet he believed that tradition must not block the way to future development and that experiment must be ceaseless. Some of his experiments pointed the way forward while his discontent with the theatre of his day was influential in producing a climate of change. He did not claim to be a reformer but the serious thought he gave to problems of staging deserves to be remembered.[15]

Arthur Colby Sprague
Bibliography: A Chronological List of Books and Essays

BOOKS

1926 *Beaumont and Fletcher on the Restoration Stage.* Cambridge, Mass.: Harvard University Press.

1930 *Samuel Daniel, Poems and A Defence of Ryme.* (Ed.) Cambridge, Mass.: Harvard University Press. Reprinted by Routledge and Kegan Paul, London, 1950, and the University of Chicago Press, Chicago, 1965.

1935 *Shakespeare and the Audience: A Study in the Technique of Exposition.* Cambridge, Mass.: Harvard University Press. Reprinted by University Microfilms, Ann Arbor, Mich., 1959, and Russell and Russell, New York, 1966.

1944 *Shakespeare and the Actors: The Stage Business in his Plays (1660–1905).* Cambridge, Mass.: Harvard University Press. Reprinted with corrections and additions by Harvard University Press, 1945 and 1948, and by Russell and Russell, New York, 1963.

1946 *Sixteen Plays of Shakespeare.* Edited by George Lyman Kittredge with introduction by A.C. Sprague; notes to *Hamlet* and *The Merchant of Venice* edited by A.C. Sprague from Kittredge's manuscripts. Boston: Ginn and Co.

1950 *The London Theatres in the Eighteen-thirties: Selections from Charles Rice.* Edited in collaboration with Bertram Shuttleworth. London: The Society for Theatre Research.

1953 *Shakespearian Players and Performances.* Cambridge, Mass.: Harvard University Press. Reprinted by A. and C. Black, London, 1954, and Greenwood Press, New York, 1969.

1954 *The Stage Business in Shakespeare's Plays: A Postscript.* London: Society for Theatre Research, Pamphlet Series, no. 3.

1964 *Shakespeare's Histories: Plays for the Stage.* London: Society for Theatre Research. Chapter I has been reprinted as "Shakespeare's Histories on the English Stage," in *Shakespeare's Histories: An Anthology of Modern Criticism,* ed. William A. Armstrong (Harmondsworth: Penguin Books, 1972), pp. 270–82.

1970 *Shakespeare's Plays Today: Some Customs and Conventions of the Stage.* In collaboration with John C. Trewin. London: Sidgwick and Jackson (Columbia: University of South Carolina Press, 1971).

Bibliography of Arthur Colby Sprague

ESSAYS

1927 "A New Scene in Colley Cibber's *Richard III.*" *Modern Language Notes*, 42: 29–32.

1944 "The First American Performance of *Richard II.*" *Shakespeare Association Bulletin*, 19: 110–16.

1945 "Off-stage Sounds." *University of Toronto Quarterly*, 15: 70–75.

1946 "Did Betterton Chant?" *Theatre Notebook*, 1: 54–55.

1947 "Edwin Booth's Iago: A Study of a Great Shakespearian Actor." *Theatre Annual*, pp. 7–17.

"Shakespeare and William Poel." *University of Toronto Quarterly*, 17: 29–37.

1953 "Gadshill Revisited: Falstaff and His Critics." *Shakespeare Quarterly*, 4: 125–37. Paper first read at the Shakespeare International Conference, Stratford-upon-Avon, 1951; reprinted in *Shakespeare, Henry IV, Part I*, ed. James L. Sanderson (New York: Norton, 1962).

1954 "Shakespeare on the New York Stage." *Shakespeare Quarterly*, 5: 311–15.

1955 "Falstaff Hackett." *Theatre Notebook*, 9: 61–67.

1955 "Shakespeare on the New York Stage." *Shakespeare Quarterly*, 6: 423–27.

1956 "Shakespeare on the New York Stage." *Shakespeare Quarterly*, 7: 393–98.

1962 "Dr. William B. Van Lennep." *Theatre Notebook*, 17: 48.

1964 "Styles in Shakespearian Acting." *Arts in Virginia*, 4: 14–25.

"In Defence of a Masterpiece: *The School for Scandal* Re-examined." *English Studies Today*. Edinburgh: University Press, Third Series, pp. 125–35.

"Edmund Kean as Othello." *A Casebook on Othello*. Ed. Leonard Dean. New York: Crowell.

1965 "Shakespeare and Melodrama." *Essays and Studies*, 18: 1–12.

"The Moments of Seriousness in Shakespearian Comedy." *Deutsche Shakespeare-Gesellschaft West Jahrbuch*, 101, 240–47. Paper first given at Wheaton College, Massachusetts, and in a revised form at the University of Basel, Switzerland.

1967 "Shakespeare's Unnecessary Characters." *Shakespeare Survey*, 20: 75–82.

1969 "Shakespeare's Characters as Parts for Players." *Festschrift: Rudolf Stamm*. Ed. Eduard Kolb and Jörg Hasler. Bern and Munich: Francke, pp. 125–33.

"Manner and Meaning in Shakespeare's Plays." *Stratford Papers*, 1965–67. Ed. B.A.W. Jackson. Toronto: McMaster University Library Press; Shannon: Irish University Press, pp. 21–28.

1971 "Dr. Hennequin and the Well-made Play." *Nineteenth Century British Theatre*. Ed. Kenneth Richards and Peter Thomson. London: Methuen & Co., pp. 145–54.

Helen D. Willard

"Shakespeare's Plays on the English Stage." *A New Companion to Shakespeare Studies.* Ed. Kenneth Muir and Samuel Schoenbaum. Cambridge: Cambridge University Press, pp. 199–210.

1973 "Robert Atkins as a Shakespearian Director." *Deutsche Shakespeare-Gesellschaft West Jahrbuch,* 109: 19–30.

Prepared by Helen D. Willard

ℜotes

NOTES–PREFACE

1. Cf. the works of Arthur Colby Sprague: his collaborative study with John C. Trewin, *Shakespeare's Plays Today* (London: Sidgwick and Jackson, 1970; Columbia: University of South Carolina Press, 1971); John C. Trewin's *Shakespeare on the English Stage, 1900–1964* (London: Barrie and Rockliff, 1964); cf. studies of individual plays such as Marvin Rosenberg's *The Masks of Othello* (Berkeley: University of California Press, 1961) and *The Masks of King Lear* (Berkeley: University of California Press, 1972); John Russell Brown's *Shakespeare's Plays in Performance* (London: Edward Arnold, 1966); Dennis Bartholomeusz's *Macbeth and the Players* (Cambridge: Cambridge University Press, 1969); and my *The Unfortunate Comedy: A Study of All's Well that Ends Well and Its Critics* (Liverpool: Liverpool University Press; Toronto: University of Toronto Press, 1968).

2. Full publication data for the quotations from his works are supplied in the appended bibliography. Specific references are *Sixteen Plays*, p. iii; "Shakespeare and William Poel," p. 37; "Gadshill Revisited," *passim*; *Shakespeare's Plays Today*, pp. 32–33; "Manner and Meaning in Shakespeare's Plays," p. 27; "Shakespeare's Unnecessary Characters," p. 78; "Manner and Meaning," p. 21; *Shakespeare and the Actors*, p. 201; "Manner and Meaning," p. 22; "Moments of Seriousness in Shakespearian Comedy," pp. 246–47.

3. Harley Granville-Barker's review of *Shakespeare and the Actors*, *Modern Language Notes*, 60 (1945): 128.

NOTES–THE ACADEMIC AND THE THEATRE

1. Arthur Colby Sprague, "Shakespeare and Melodrama," *Essays and Studies*, 18 (1965): 1–12.

2. John C. Trewin, *Shakespeare on the English Stage: 1900–1964* (London: Barrie and Rockliff, 1964).

3. *The War of the Roses*, adapted by John Barton (London: British Broadcasting Corporation, 1970).

4. Ibid., p. xxiii.

5. Ibid., p. xxv.

Notes

NOTES—DRAMATIC INTENTION AND THEATRICAL REALIZATION

1. T.S. Eliot, "The Aims of Poetic Drama—II," *Time & Tide* (London), 17 June 1950.

2. Cf. below, p. 34.

3. Lascelles Abercrombie, *A Plea for the Liberty of Interpreting*, The British Academy Annual Shakespeare Lecture (London: Humphrey Milford, 1930), p. 29.

4. Nor is an outline of the plot the same as a statement of "what the author meant."

5. Vernon Lee [Violet Paget], *The Handling of Words and Other Studies in Literary Psychology* (London: John Lane, 1923).

6. Gordon Craig, *The Art of the Theatre* (Edinburgh and London: T. H. Foulis, 1905), pp. 149 ff., and Ashley Dukes, *The World to Play With* (London: Oxford University Press, 1928), p. 108.

7. Dukes, *The World to Play With*, p. 108.

8. At which point this author's stage direction to the reader is, consult the works of Arthur Colby Sprague, *passim*.

9. The New Theatre, produced by Alec Guinness and Frank Hauser, 17 May 1951.

10. Upon which I commented in "The Shakespeare Season at The Old Vic, 1958–59 and Stratford-upon-Avon, 1959," *Shakespeare Quarterly*, 10 (1959): 545–67, when I was able to say of the Old Vic's Michael Hordern-Beatrix Lehmann *Macbeth* that I had never seen a better *paired* performance or a better rendering of this vital scene which marks the turn of the play. "The gorgeous poetry and the sheer pace and excitement which have sustained us are over, and we meet the full horror of his crimes in their naked, repulsive truth as Macbeth the murderer drives his knife savagely into the table, where it sticks, quivering, as the scene ends" (p. 548).

11. Abercrombie, *Liberty of Interpreting*, p. 29.

12. James Spedding, "Who Wrote Shakspere's *Henry VIII*," *Gentleman's Magazine*, n.s. 34 (1850): 115–24, 381–82.

13. Cf. also *The Atheist's Tragedy* (1611), *The Tragedy of Chabot* (c. 1613) with "the furious eloquence of my accuser" (act III), and *Appius and Virginia* (c. 1608), "I undertake a desperate combat." But here, theatrically, trial scene excitement is promised, no trial takes place, and "excitement" vanishes with Katherine.

14. Muriel St. Clare Byrne, "A Stratford Production: *Henry VIII*," *Shakespeare Survey*, (1950): 120–29.

15. As originally performed at Stratford-upon-Avon. It had fallen off by the time it was put on at the Old Vic.

16. For example, John M. Berdan and C.F. Tucker Brooke (eds.), *The Life of King Henry the Eighth* (New Haven: Yale University Press, 1925).

17. Even Spedding let himself go over this entrancing game and mapped out some alternative scenarios, including one which would take us on to the birth of Anne Boleyn's stillborn son and her own execution, which he considered would give us a great tragedy of retributive justice;

Notes

and when forced back upon the play itself he could only conjecture that Shakespeare had originally projected a grand historical piece which must have culminated in the final separation of the English from the Romish Church, "which being the one great historical event of the reign would naturally be chosen as the focus of poetic interest." Cf. Spedding, "Who Wrote *Henry VIII*," pp. 117, 123.

18. To which, as to the succession theme, Sir J.A.R. Marriott draws attention in *English History in Shakespeare* (London: Chapman & Hall, 1918).

19. Charles Kean, in 1855, did his best to cut, without losing the whole value of the author's structural pause, by providing a brief composite scene, including some of Henry's interview with Cranmer and the Old Lady's announcement of the birth. It was, however, omitted after the first night, when the performance ran from 8:30 to 12:00, and will be found only in the first edition, *Shakespeare's Historical Play of King Henry the Eighth . . .* First Performed on Wednesday, 16th May, 1855 (London: John K. Chapman & Co., 1855), V.i.

20. For Shakespeare's authorship I was proposing to cite Marjorie Nicolson, "The Authorship of Henry the Eighth," *PMLA*, 37 (1922):484–502; Baldwin Maxwell, "Fletcher and Henry VIII," *The Manly Anniversary Studies in Language and Literature* (Chicago: University of Chicago Press, 1923), pp. 104–12; and Peter Alexander, "Conjectural History, or Shakespeare's *Henry VIII*," *Essays and Studies*, 16 (1930): 85–120.

21. Cf. my paper on "Bibliographical Clues in Collaborate Plays," *The Library* (June 1932): 21–48 and also Baldwin Maxwell's conclusion that "in a strict sense Spedding cannot be said to have made any test whatsoever," as he did not show that the characteristics of style upon which he based his argument were peculiar to Fletcher ("Fletcher and Henry VIII," p. 104).

22. G. Wilson Knight, *Principles of Shakespearian Production* (London: Faber and Faber, 1936), and "A Note on Henry VIII," *Criterion*, 15 (1936): 228–36.

23. King Henry VIII, *The Arden Shakespeare*, ed. R.A. Foakes (London: Methuen, 1957).

24. Ibid., p. lxii.

25. Edmund K. Chambers, *William Shakespeare: A Study of Facts and Problems* (Oxford: Clarendon Press, 1930), 1:497.

26. Harley Granville-Barker, *Prefaces to Shakespeare: Hamlet* (London: Sidgwick and Jackson, 1936), p. 7.

27. Abercrombie, *Liberty of Interpreting*, p. 29.

28. Arthur Colby Sprague, *Shakespeare's Histories: Plays for the Stage* (London: The Society for Theatre Research, 1964), p. 159.

NOTES—THE TRIPLE BOND

1. Dates are taken from Alfred Harbage and Samuel Schoenbaum, *Annals of English Drama, 975–1700* (London: Methuen, 1964). Cambises asks the audience to "accept this simple deed."

2. Charles T. Prouty, "An Early Elizabethan Playhouse," *Shakespeare Survey*, 6 (1953): 64–68.

Notes

3. O.L. Brownstein, "A Record of London Inn-Playhouses, 1565–1580," *Shakespeare Quarterly*, 22 (1971): 17–24.

4. Charles T. Prouty (ed.), *Studies in the Elizabethan Theatre* (Hamden, Conn.: Shoe String Press, 1961), p. 44.

5. William Ingram, "The Playhouse at Newington Butts: A New Proposal," *Shakespeare Quarterly*, 21 (1970): 385–98.

6. Marie Axton, "Robert Dudley and the Inner Temple Revels," *Historical Journal*, 13 (1970): 365–75.

7. W.R. Gair, "La Compagnie des Enfants de St. Paul Londres (1599–1606)," *Dramaturgie et Societe*, ed. J. Jacquot (Paris: Editions du centre national de la recherche scientifique, 1968), 2: 655–74.

8. Cf. Gabriel Harvey, *Letter Book*, ed. Edward J.L. Scott (Westminster: Printed for the Camden Society by Nichols & Sons, 1884), pp. 67–68; and *The Works of Thomas Nashe*, ed. R.B. McKerrow and F.P. Wilson (Oxford: Blackwell, 1958), 3: 46.

9. Norman Rabkin, "The Double Plot," *Renaissance Drama*, ed. Samuel Schoenbaum (1964), 7: 55.

10. F.P. Wilson, *Marlowe and the Early Shakespeare* (Oxford: Clarendon Press, 1953), pp. 105–8; for prefiguration, cf. V.A. Kolve, *The Play Called Corpus Christi* (Palo Alto: Stanford University Press, 1966), ch. IV.

11. "And so they said, these matters be king's games, as it were stage plays, and for the most part played upon scaffolds, in which poor men be but lookers on, and they that wise be, will meddle no further, for they that step up with them when they cannot play their parts, they disorder the play and do themselves no good." Quoted by Philip Brockbank in *English Drama to 1710*, ed. Christopher Ricks (London: Barrie & Jenkins in association with Sphere Books, 1971, *History of Literature in the English Language*, vol. 3), p. 174.

12. C.L. Barber, *Shakespeare's Festive Comedy* (Princeton: Princeton University Press, 1959), p. 83. This is the best commentary on Nashe.

13. Gabriel Harvey, *Foure Letters, and certaine sonnets . . .* (London, 1592), letter 3.

14. Anne Righter [Barton], *Shakespeare and the Idea of the Play* (London: Chatto & Windus, 1962), a work which deals with the audience on a much wider scale than the title would suggest.

15. I.A. Shapiro, "The Significance of a Date," *Shakespeare Survey*, 8 (1955): 101.

16. L.G. Salingar, Gerald Harrison, and Bruce Cochane, "Les comediens et leur public en Angleterre de 1520 à 1640," *Dramaturgie et Societe*, p. 531. The article provides a graph of known visits to the provinces which shows a spectacular rise about the year 1560 and a spectacular drop in the year 1600. Thereafter players were increasingly refused permission to act.

17. Philip J. Finkelpearl, *John Marston of the Middle Temple* (Cambridge, Mass.: Harvard University Press, 1969), pp. 119–24.

18. Prologue, *Jack Drum's Entertainment* (1601). Cf. Gair, "La Compagnie des Enfants. . . ."

19. Jarold W. Ramsey, "The Provenance of *Troilus and Cressida*,"

Notes

Shakespeare Quarterly, 21 (1970): 223–40. I do not find this case very plausible.

20. Muriel C. Bradbrook, *Shakespeare, the Craftsman* (London: Chatto & Windus, 1969), ch. 5.

21. G.K. Hunter, "The Heroism of Hamlet," *Hamlet*, ed. John Russell Brown and Bernard Harris (Stratford-upon-Avon Studies, vol. 5, 1963), p. 108.

22. Brian Gibbons, *The Jacobean City Comedy* (Cambridge, Mass.: Harvard University Press, 1968), ch. 1 and app. A.

23. The point is taken from H.S. Bennett, *Shakespeare's Audience*, British Academy Annual Shakespeare Lecture (London: H. Milford, 1944), to whom I am also indebted for the passage from Middleton.

24. Inga-Stina Ekeblad [Ewbank], "The 'Impure Art' of John Webster," *Review of English Studies*, n.s., 9 (1958): 253, 267.

25. Ibid., pp. 253–67.

NOTES–SHAKESPEARE'S SONGS AND THE DOUBLE RESPONSE

1. Giles Lytton Strachey, *Books and Characters* (London: Chatto & Windus, 1922), p. 60.

2. On this subject there is some comment in chapter IV of my *The Dramatist's Experience With Other Essays in Literary Theory* (London, 1970). See also G.R. Hibbard's "The Forced Gait of a Shuffling Nag," *Shakespeare 1971*, ed. Clifford Leech and J.M.R. Margeson (Toronto: University of Toronto Press, 1972), pp. 76–88.

3. As suggested in my edition of *Two Gentlemen of Verona*, The Arden Shakespeare (London: Methuen, 1969), pp. xxxiv–xxxv.

4. Quotations from Shakespeare are from the New Arden editions except where otherwise noted.

5. Richmond Noble, *Shakespeare's Use of Song* (London: Oxford University Press, 1923), pp. 39ff.

6. See, e.g., T.J. King, *Shakespearean Staging, 1599–1642* (Cambridge: Harvard University Press, 1971), pp. 19, 29, 57, 77, 86–87. Here Professor King seems in general agreement with the findings of Professor Richard Hosley in numerous articles.

7. I have discussed the matter of the playwright's imagining of an "ideal" performance, with an "ideal" audience, in *The Dramatist's Experience*, pp. 238–39. For a verbal echo of *1 Henry IV* in *2 Henry IV*, see my article, "The Unity of *2 Henry IV*," *Shakespeare Survey*, 6 (1953): 21.

8. "For what human ill does not dawn seem to be an alleviation?" Thornton Wilder, *The Bridge of San Luis Rey* (New York: A. & C. Boni, 1928), p. 119.

9. I offered brief comment on this production in "More than our brother is our chastity," *Critical Quarterly*, 12 (1970): 73–74.

10. John Russell Brown (ed.), *The Merchant of Venice*, The Arden Shakespeare (London: Methuen, 1955), p. 80.

11. W.C. Clark and W.A. Wright (eds.), *Twelfth Night*, The Globe Edition (Cambridge and London: Macmillan Co., 1865).

Notes

12. J.M. Nosworthy (ed.), *Cymbeline*, The Arden Shakespeare (London: Methuen, 1955), p. 138.

13. J.C. Maxwell (ed.), *Cymbeline*, The New Cambridge Edition (Cambridge: Cambridge University Press, 1960), p. 193.

14. R.L. Brett and A.R. Jones (eds.), *Lyrical Ballads* (New York: Barnes and Noble, 1963), pp. 257–59.

15. This is something I had occasion to notice in *Twelfth Night and Shakespearian Comedy* (Toronto: University of Toronto Press, 1965), p. 55.

16. Thomas Mann, *Doctor Faustus*, translated by Helen Tracy Lowe-Porter (New York: Knopf, 1948), p. 498.

NOTES—THE KING DISGUISED

1. Quoted in Geoffrey Bullough, *Narrative and Dramatic Sources of Shakespeare* (London: Routledge and Kegan Paul, 1962), 4:362.

2. Ibid.

3. "George a Greene," *The Life and Complete Works in Prose and Verse of Robert Greene*, ed. Alexander B. Grosart, (London: Hazell, Watson, and Viney for the Huth Library, 1881–83), vol. 14, l. 940.

4. Frank Hook (ed.), "Edward I," *The Dramatic Works of George Peele*, ed. Charles T. Prouty, II (New Haven: Yale University Press, 1961), scene vii, ll. 1199–1201.

5. *The History of King Leir.* 1605 (London: Oxford University Press, printed for the Malone Society by H. Hart, 1908), l. 691.

6. "The First and Second Parts of King Edward IV," ed. Barron Field, *The Dramatic Works of Thomas Heywood* (London: Shakespeare Society, 1842), 1: act III, scene i.

7. Maurice Keen, *The Outlaws of Medieval Legend* (London: Routledge and Kegan Paul, 1961), p. 156.

8. Edward Hall, *The Union of the Two Noble and Illustrious Families of Lancaster and York*, ed. Sir Henry Ellis (London: Printed for J. Johnson, 1809), pp. 513, 582.

9. "The Lady of May," *The Complete Works of Philip Sydney*, ed. Albert Feuillerat (Cambridge: Cambridge University Press, 1922), 2: 330.

10. "The Shoemaker's Holiday," *The Dramatic Works of Thomas Dekker*, ed. Fredson Bowers (Cambridge: Cambridge University Press, 1953), V.v.104–7.

11. Leslie Hotson, "Ancient Pistol," *Shakespeare's Sonnets Dated, and Other Essays* (London: R. Hart-Davis, 1949).

12. Ernst Kantorowicz, *The King's Two Bodies* (Princeton: Princeton University Press, 1957).

13. Leslie Hotson, "Two Shakespearean Firsts—The Earl of Essex and Falstaff," *Shakespeare's Sonnets Dated.*

14. *Henslowe's Diary*, ed. R.A. Foakes and R.T. Rickert (Cambridge: Cambridge University Press, 1961), p. 126.

Notes

15. "Sir John Oldcastle," *The Shakespeare Apocrypha*, ed. C.F. Tucker Brooke (Oxford: Oxford University Press, 1918), Prologue.

16. *Henry V*, ed. John H. Walter, The New Arden Shakespeare (London: Methuen, 1954), p. xi.

17. A. P. Rossiter, *English Drama From Earliest Times to the Elizabethans* (London: Hutchinson's University Library, 1950), p. 113.

NOTES—SHAKESPEARE'S USE OF OATHS

1. *1 Henry IV*, II.iv.75. Unless otherwise noted, all line references and quotations are taken from *The Complete Works of Shakespeare*, ed. George Lyman Kittredge (Boston: Ginn & Co., 1936).

2. 3 Jac. l.c.21. Since there is no consistent policy, with *1 Henry IV* far more carefully cut than *Henry V* or *King John*, it seems probable that the changes were made before Heminge and Condell assembled the texts.

3. 21 Jac. l.c.20, which defined and set penalties for swearing, although it did not list specific words.

4. One later instance points up the range of interpretations. D'Avenant asked Charles I to overrule the censor, and Sir Henry Herbert acceded protestingly: "The king is pleased to take faith, death, 'slight for asseverations and no oaths, to which I do humbly submit as my master's judgement; but under favor conceive them to be oaths." Quoted in Virginia Gildersleeve, *Government Regulation of the Elizabethan Drama* (New York: Columbia University Press, 1908), pp. 127–28.

5. British Museum, Lansdowne MS 807, f. 54.

6. Stephen Hawes, *The Conversyon of Swerers* (London, 1540), St. 19.

7. James Peller Malcolm, *Anecdotes of the Manners and Customs of London from the Roman Invasion to the year 1700* (London: Longman, Hurst, Rees, Orme and Brown, 1811), p. 75.

8. Joannes Ferrarius, *A Woork of Joannes Ferrarius Montanus touchynge the good orderynge of a Commonweale* (London, 1559), ff. 136ᵥ–37.

9. Robert Boyle, *A Free Discourse Against Customary Swearing and A Dissuasive from Cursing* (London, 1695), pp. 8–9.

10. Gervaise Babington, *A Verie fruitefull Exposition of the Commandements by Way of Questions and Answers* (London, 1590), p. 115.

11. Ibid., p. 117.

12. Malcolm, *Anecdotes*, p. 123.

13. Julian Sharman, *A Cursory History of Swearing* (London: J.C. Nimmo and Bain, 1884), pp. 125–26.

14. David Lindsay, approved by Puritans as a devout writer, uses "forsooth" when he wishes to underline a point in *Satyre of the Three Estates*, ed. George Chalmers (London: Longman, Hurst, Rees, Orme and Brown, 1806).

15. Frederick Chamberlin, *The Sayings of Queen Elizabeth* (London: J. Lane, 1923), p. 5.

16. This usage of "protest" is dated from 1587 in the *OED*.

Notes

17. Sir Thomas Elyot, *The Booked Named The Governor*, ed. S.E. Lehmberg (London: Dent, 1962), p. 89.

18. Suffolk (*1 Henry IV*, V.v.30–34), Salisbury (*2 Henry IV*, V.i. 177ff.), and Fluellen on the necessity of keeping an oath (*Henry V*, IV.vii.137ff) show a variety of arguments.

19. Holinshed speaks of articles sent to King Henry "which articles in effect charged him with manifest periurie in that (contrarie to his oth receiued vpon the evangelists at Doncaster . . .) he had taken vpon him the crowne and roiall dignitie." *Holinshed's Chronicles as Used in Shakespeare's Plays*, ed. Allardyce and Josephine Nicoll (London: J.M. Dent, 1927), pp. 58–59.

20. Alexander Nowell, *A Sword Against Swearers* (London, 1611), B3ᵥ-B4; Ferrarius, *Good orderynge*, f. 136.

21. William Aldis Wright (ed.), *King Henry IV, Part I* (London: The Cambridge Shakespeare, 1897), note to II.iv.415–17.

22. Boyle, *A Free Discourse*, B8ᵥ.

23. In the two plays, Poins has a mere six oaths, though "zounds" is among them, while Falstaff utters about four dozen. Falstaff and his group have roughly four times as many as the King and his party in *2 Henry IV*, even when formal vows are included.

24. Sharman, *Cursory History*, p. 161.

25. Robert Crowley, *Select Works*, ed. J.M. Cowper (London: published for the Early English Text Society by N. Trübner & Co., 1872), pp. 18–19.

26. Nowell, *Sword*, E2ᵥ.

27. Edward H. Bates [Harbin] (ed.), *Quarter Session Records for the County of Somerset* (London: Somerset Record Society, 1907), I, 3 (July 16, 1607).

28. Ferrarius, *Good orderynge*, f. 136.

29. William Richardson, *Essays on Shakespeare's Dramatic Characters of Sir John Falstaff, and on his Imitation of Female Characters* (London: J. Murray, 1784).

30. Thomas Dekker, *The Honest Whore, Part I*, ii. 170–71, in *Elizabethan Plays*, ed. Arthur H. Nethercott, Charles R. Baskervill, and Virgil B. Heltzel (New York: Holt, Rinehart & Winston, 1971). Fustigo will swear like a gentleman with a £400 income.

31. Philip Stubbes, *Anatomy of the Abuses in England in Shakespeare's Youth*, ed. Frederick J. Furnivall (London: published for the New Shakspere Society by N. Trübner & Co., 1877–79), p. 294.

32. Roger Ascham, *The Scholemaster*, ed. Edward Arber (Westminster: A. Constable & Co., 1895), pp. 53–54.

33. Richard Brathwait, *A Strappado for the Diuell* (London: 1615), p. 52.

34. R.G. White, quoted in *The Tragedy of Richard the Third*, A New Variorum Edition, ed. H.H. Furness, Jr. (Philadelphia: Lippincott, 1909).

35. The longest footnote on oaths seems to be the series of comments explaining these passages, quoted in *The Life and Death of King John*, A New Variorum Edition, ed. H.H. Furness, Jr. (Philadelphia: Lippincott, 1919).

Notes

36. *The Troublesome Raigne of John, King of England,* in *King John* Variorum.

37. Boyle, *A Free Discourse,* pp. 3, 11.

38. Charles Wordsworth, *On Shakespeare's Knowledge and Use of the Bible* (London: Smith, Elder & Co., 1864), p. 84. In the *Richard III* Variorum, Wordsworth is listed as the first to comment on the uniqueness of this phrase, never again used by Shakespeare.

39. Richard Brathwait, *The English Gentlewoman* (London, 1631), L3ᵥ. Frequently a man will be listed as a "common drunkard, swearer, and blasphemer"; see *Quarter Sessions Records, North Riding Record Society,* ed. John C. Atkinson (London: Printed for the Society, 1884), I, 65.

NOTES—IN THE MARGIN

1. Arthur Colby Sprague and J.C. Trewin, *Shakespeare's Plays Today* (London: Sidgwick and Jackson, 1970), pp. 59–61.

2. Peter Bull, *I Know the Face, But . . .* (London: P. Davies, 1959).

3. Sprague and Trewin, *Shakespeare's Plays Today,* pp. 61–65.

NOTES—THE DUKE AND ISABELLA ON THE MODERN STAGE

1. Ernest Schanzer, *The Problem Plays of Shakespeare* (London: Routledge and Kegan Paul, 1963), p. 71.

2. J.M. Nosworthy (ed.), *Measure for Measure* (Harmondsworth: Penguin Books, 1969), p. 50. Mr. Nosworthy does direct his readers to Richard David's article, "Shakespeare's Comedies and the Modern Stage," *Shakespeare Survey,* 4 (1951), which offers an excellent discussion of the 1950 Stratford-upon-Avon production of *Measure for Measure.*

3. Richard David, "Shakespeare's Comedies and the Modern Stage," *Shakespeare Survey,* 4 (1951): 137.

4. Ibid., p. 136.

5. *The Stage,* 16 March 1950.

6. The Birmingham papers of 10 March 1950, the *Mail, Evening Dispatch, Gazette,* and *Post,* all took this stand.

7. See, for example, the *Warwick County News,* 17 March 1950, and *The Tribune,* 17 March 1950.

8. *Manchester Guardian,* 11 March 1950.

9. Isabella's business is indicated in stage directions in the promptbook at the Shakespeare Centre Library.

10. Alice Venezky, "The 1950 Season at Straford upon Avon—a Memorable Achievement in Stage History," *Shakespeare Quarterly,* 2 (1951): 75.

11. David, "Shakespeare's Comedies," p. 137.

12. Ibid.

13. *The Tribune,* 17 March 1950.

14. David, "Shakespeare's Comedies," p. 137. Interestingly, the prompt-

book indicates that Brook rearranged the text here so that Isabella's plea for mercy was followed by Angelo's second speech of repentance craving "death more willingly than mercy." Consequently the Duke's subsequent line, "Your suit's unprofitable," became a verdict on Angelo's rather than Isabella's plea.

15. *Sunday Times,* 19 March 1950.

16. David, "Shakespeare's Comedies," p. 137.

17. Venezky, "The 1950 Season," p. 75.

18. *The Tribune,* 17 March 1950.

19. *Leamington Spa Courier,* 10 March 1950. The omissions in the scene are indicated in the promptbook at the Shakespeare Centre Library.

20. Jack Karr, *Toronto Star,* 29 June 1954.

21. Ibid.

22. *Toronto Globe,* 30 June 1954.

23. *New York Herald Tribune,* 30 June 1954.

24. Brooks Atkinson, *New York Times,* 30 June 1954.

25. Herbert Whittaker, *Toronto Globe,* 30 June 1954.

26. Herbert Whittaker, "Introduction," *The Stratford Festival, 1953–1957* (Toronto: Clarke, Irwin and Co., 1958), p. lvi.

27. Jack Karr, *Toronto Star,* 29 June 1954.

28. *Ottawa Citizen,* 29 June 1954.

29. *New York Herald Tribune,* 30 June 1954.

30. The stage business of the novices is indicated by notations in the promptbook in the Festival Theatre archives.

31. The production which was given at the summer Festival at Stratford, Connecticut, was taken, with a few changes in cast, to the Phoenix Theatre in New York the following winter.

32. *New York Herald Tribune,* 29 June 1956.

33. *Montreal Star,* 10 July 1956.

34. *Toronto Globe and Mail,* 29 June 1956.

35. Ibid.

36. *Birmingham Mail,* 15 August 1956.

37. *The Times* (London), 15 August 1956.

38. These cuts are indicated in the promptbook at the Shakespeare Centre Library.

39. See Nevill Coghill, "Comic Form in *Measure for Measure,*" *Shakespeare Survey,* 8 (1955): 14–27. Professor Coghill himself directed a production of the play by the Bristol University Drama Department the following October. A reviewer for the *Bristol Evening Post* (16 October 1956) called special attention to Professor Coghill's treatment of the Duke's soliloquy beginning "He who the sword of heaven will bear": "As the first part of this production . . . draws to a close, dim light plays upon the Duke in the centre of the stage. He is alone, and in a soliloquy in which he explains how Angelo is to be trapped he hints at those overtones of charity and mercy which the producer, Mr. Nevill Coghill, was at pains to explain earlier in the evening. It was a most effective device, and in

my experience, an original device. Certainly no attempt has been made, either at Stratford or the Old Vic, to give this important speech the prominence it deserves."

40. This notation of stage business is indicated in the promptbook at the Shakespeare Centre Library.

41. The reviewer for *Theatre World* (26 September 1956) joined the reporters for the *Daily Telegraph* and *Leamington Spa Courier* in seeing a very human figure in Nicholls's Duke—"all ideas of forgiving father figure are banished"—but at least some sense of spirituality was caught by the reporter for the *Western Daily Press* (16 August 1956), who referred to the Duke as "an almost disciple-like figure."

42. *Manchester Guardian,* 21 November 1957.

43. Margaret Webster, *Shakespeare Without Tears* (New York: World Publishing Company, 1955), p. 249.

44. In 1908, in one of the earliest productions of *Measure for Measure* in the twentieth century, William Poel called for a lively, spirited, and witty Duke to preside over the play and recast the part in an attempt to get a more sprightly Vincentio. He probably did not achieve his goal, however. [See Robert Speaight, *William Poel and the Elizabethan Revival* (London: Heinemann, 1954), pp. 93–95.] Dukes who, to some extent, seem to have brought out the lighter and whimsical side of the Duke include Henry Oscar at the Fortune in 1931 and David King-Wood at Stratford-upon-Avon in 1946. J.C. Trewin notes that John Neville had wanted to endow Vincentio with a sense of humor, but director Basil Coleman had insisted upon his being presented with aloof dignity in the Bristol Old Vic production in 1952. See J.C. Trewin, *John Neville* (London: Barrie and Rockliff, 1961), pp. 40–41.

45. *Manchester Guardian,* 21 November 1957.

46. *Birmingham Post,* 21 November 1957.

47. Philip Squire, *Plays and Players* (January 1958).

48. *The Times* (London), 15 August 1956.

49. *The Stage,* 16 August 1956.

50. *London Daily Mail,* 15 August 1956.

51. *The Times* (London), 15 August 1956.

52. Ibid.

53. *New Statesman and Nation,* 25 August 1956.

54. Harold Hobson, "Introduction," *Measure for Measure: with Introduction by Harold Hobson, Designs by Alex Stone* (London: The Folio Society, 1964), p. 4.

55. Ibid., p. 3.

56. Ibid., p. 4.

57. Ibid., pp. 4, 5.

58. Coghill, "Comic Form in *Measure for Measure.*"

59. *Newport South Wales Evening Argus,* 1 May 1963.

60. *Manchester Guardian,* 4 April 1963.

61. The Bristol Old Vic had presented *Measure for Measure* once before in 1952 under the direction of Basil Coleman.

62. Tyrone Guthrie, Program Note, *Measure for Measure*, Bristol Old Vic, 2 March 1966.

63. *The Scotsman*, 19 March 1966.

64. Ibid.

65. *New York Times*, 15 February 1967.

66. Norman Nadel, *New York World Journal Tribune*, 15 February 1967.

67. In twentieth-century presentations of *Measure for Measure* the matter of Isabella's dress has been a subject of some discussion and disagreement among directors ever since the production of 1908 by William Poel who explained in a program note that "Isabella, who has not yet taken her vows as one of the Sisterhood of Saint Claire, is in the dress of an Elizabethan Gentlewoman." The predominant practice in twentieth-century professional productions has been for Isabella to wear some kind of religious habit.

68. *Manchester Guardian*, 11 April 1962.

69. *Warwick and Warwickshire Advertiser*, 14 April 1962.

70. *The Times* (London), 11 April 1962.

71. Ibid.

72. Ibid.

73. J.C. Trewin, *Birmingham Post*, 11 April 1962.

74. Philip Hope-Wallace, *Manchester Guardian*, 4 April 1963.

75. See, for example, *London Financial Times*, 4 April 1963; *London Daily Mail*, 4 April 1963; *London Sunday Telegraph*, 14 April 1963; *The Times* (London), 4 April 1963.

76. *Manchester Guardian*, 4 April 1963.

77. *London Daily Telegraph*, 4 April 1963.

78. *London Sunday Telegraph*, 14 April 1963.

79. *The Scotsman*, 19 March 1966.

80. *Bristol Western Daily Press*, 3 March 1966.

81. Ibid.

82. *New York Times*, 15 February 1967.

83. Giles's remarks are quoted by the *Calgary Alberton*, 12 June 1969.

84. *Victoria Times*, 12 June 1969.

85. Lewis Funke, *New York Times*, 13 June 1969.

86. Clifford Leech, "More than our brother is our chastity," *Critical Quarterly*, 12 (1970): 73.

87. Arnold Edinborough, "The Director's Role at Canada's Stratford," *Shakespeare Quarterly*, 20 (1969): 445.

88. *New York Times*, 22 June 1969.

89. Leech, "More than our brother," p. 73.

90. Walter Kerr, *New York Times*, 22 June 1969.

91. Leech, "More than our brother," p. 73.

92. Ibid., p. 74.

Notes

93. See, for example, Walter Kerr, *New York Times*, 22 June 1969, and Nathan Cohen, *Toronto Daily Star*, 12 June 1969.

94. Irving Wardle, *The Times* (London), 2 April 1970.

95. Ibid.

96. Ibid.

97. *The Observer*, 5 April 1970.

98. Robert Speaight, "Shakespeare in Britain," *Shakespeare Quarterly*, 21 (1970): 444.

NOTES–REALISM VERSUS NIGHTMARE

1. Inga-Stina Ekeblad [Ewbank], "The 'Impure Art' of John Webster," *Review of English Studies*, n.s., 9 (1958), reprinted in *John Webster: A Critical Anthology*, ed. G.K. Hunter and S.K. Hunter (Harmondsworth: Penguin Books, 1969), p. 220.

2. Hunter, *John Webster*, p. 109.

3. See Roger Warren, *"The Duchess of Malfi* on the Stage," *John Webster*, ed. Brian Morris, Mermaid Critical Commentaries (London: Benn, 1970), p. 66.

4. Ronald Bryden, *The Observer*, 18 July 1971.

5. John Russell Brown (ed.), *The Duchess of Malfi*, The Revels Plays (Cambridge: Harvard University Press, 1964), I.i.401–2. All *Duchess of Malfi* quotations are from this edition.

6. George Henry Lewes, *Dramatic Essays* (London: W. Scott, 1896), p. 121.

7. Inga-Stina Ewbank, "Webster's Realism or, 'A Cunning Piece Wrought Perspective,'" *John Webster*, ed. Morris, pp. 157–78.

8. William Bridges-Adams, *The Irresistible Theatre* (Cleveland: World Publishing Co., 1957), p. 313.

9. I did not see this production in performance but attended a late rehearsal through the courtesy of Mr. Shelton, who also let me read the notes on the play which he had sent to the actors before the start of rehearsals.

10. For information about the 1960 *Duchess* I am indebted to the Stratford promptbook and to the article by Roger Warren (*Webster*, ed. Morris); for the production at Stratford, Ontario, to a full and intelligent account written by Mrs. R.A. Vernon.

11. Cf. W.A. Darlington, *The Daily Telegraph*, 15 December 1960, and Robert Speaight, *The Tablet*, 23 December 1960.

12. John Francis Lane, *The Times* (London), 21 August 1971. The production was directed by Edmo Fenoglio.

13. *Plays and Players*, March 1971, p. 31.

14. F.L. Lucas (ed.), *The Duchess of Malfi* (New York: Macmillan, 1959), p. 14.

15. Brown, *Duchess*, pp. xlii, 39.

16. This contrast between the corrupt court and the healthy atmosphere

of battle is a commonplace of the period; it is interesting, however, that Webster, unlike most other dramatists, seems not to take Ferdinand's point of view—except perhaps by providing the figure of Count Maletesti for him to laugh at.

17. Preface to *The White Devil*.

18. Everyone knows that no human being ever reacted to a stab wound by inquiring, as Flamineo does, "O, what blade is't?" Yet Frank Dunlop, who directed *The White Devil* at the Old Vic in 1970, spent some time consulting with doctors as to realistic methods of killing which would allow Vittoria and Flamineo to go on talking up to the end. (See interview in *Plays and Players*, January 1970, p. 52.)

19. *Sunday Times*, 24 January 1971.

20. This was cut in the 1971 productions at both Stratford, England, and Stratford, Ontario, although both retained the Cardinal's earlier instructions to the courtiers not to disturb him. The directors must have been bothered by the double problem here: how to handle the changing tones of the scene and how to freeze the action on the main stage so as to allow for the conversation of the characters above.

21. One can understand why this apparently gratuitous addition to the general carnage was cut at the Royal Court and Stratford, Ontario, but Webster probably wanted as many bodies as possible onstage, both to emphasize the awful absurdity of the repeated deaths and to provide a counterpart to the play's background of war (cf. Fortinbras's comments at the end of *Hamlet*).

22. Robert Parsons, *First Booke of the Christian Exercise* (1582), as quoted in R.W. Dent, *John Webster's Borrowing* (Berkeley: University of California Press, 1960), p. 248.

23. Webster uses this as a term of praise in the Preface to *The White Devil*.

24. Brown, *Duchess*, p. 62.

25. At least, I take this to be the meaning of "I'll suffer your retreat to Julia's chamber, / But no further" (V.v. 118–19). One might, however, interpret the line differently in the light of his description of the Duchess's coffin as her "last presence-chamber" (IV.ii.171).

26. There is also the fact that Antonio remains onstage, unseen and unrecognized, during the episode involving Julia and Pescara. However, this can be sufficiently accounted for by the convention of the unobserved observer.

27. For example, in Shakespeare, "the mirror of all Christian kings," "Thou art thy mother's glass," and the striking description of Octavius thinking about the dead Antony: "When such a spacious mirror's set before him, / He needs must see himself."

28. F.L. Lucas and John Russell Brown in their editions of *The Duchess* give only the direction, "Turns and sees Ferdinand," but I feel sure that George Rylands's suggestion, which Elizabeth Brennan mentions in her New Mermaids Edition of the play (London: Benn, 1964), p. 109, is the right one. Professor P.A.W. Collins, who played the Cardinal in a student production directed by Rylands at Cambridge in 1942, tells me that this bit of business was used both then and in the 1945 Haymarket production.

Notes

The only time I have seen this done was in the operatic *Duchess* at Oxford. In the 1971 Stratford production, a different kind of eeriness was provided by having Ferdinand wear jingling spurs which, both here and in the "dead man's hand" scene, warned the Duchess of his presence even before he spoke.

29. The Stratford production of 1971 brought this out by having the two brothers die in each other's arms. It might also be noted that the Cardinal's murder of Julia parallels Ferdinand's murder of his sister. Penelope Mortimer, reviewing the 1960 Aldwych *Duchess*, observed that Julia had the same flaming red hair as the Duchess and concluded that the Cardinal, like his brother, was "full of dark and unadmitted sibling desire" (*Queen*, 4 January 1961).

30. Middleton admired Webster, as we can see from his commendatory verses to *The Duchess*. It seems to me that in his two greatest tragedies he has clarified and simplified many of Webster's methods. The same can be said of his use of imagery: there is far less of it than in Webster, and it has fewer cross-references, but it gives the same impression of being consciously worked out.

31. See above, p. 177. Robert Ornstein also points out this parallel though with different conclusions as regards Antonio's character; cf. his *The Moral Vision of Jacobean Tragedy* (Madison: University of Wisconsin Press, 1960), p. 142.

32. Brown, *Duchess*, p. xxiii.

33. Ian Jack, "The Case of John Webster," *Scrutiny*, 16 (1949); reprinted in *John Webster*, ed. Hunter, p. 158.

34. Una Ellis-Fermor, *The Jacobean Drama: An Interpretation* (London: Methuen, 1936; rev. ed., 1958), pp. 43–44.

NOTES–THE DARKENED STAGE

1. I have discussed this elsewhere in my article, "The Modernity of *Troilus and Cressida*: The Case for Theatrical Criticism," *Harvard Library Bulletin*, 17 (1969): 353–73.

2. The promptbook is located in The Folger Shakespeare Library and is identified in Shattuck, *Shakespeare Promptbooks*, as *Troilus and Cressida*, no. 1. Further evidence of Kemble's interest in the play is his personal copy of the 1609 Quarto, annotated "Collated & Perfect. 1798," and with his initials. This copy is in the Huntington Library.

3. A satirical pamphlet taunts Kemble for his management of his company and particularly for financial problems by referring to his interest in *Troilus and Cressida* and other troublesome productions. Cf. *Kembliana: being a Collection of the Jeu d'esprits, etc. that have appeared respecting King John; including the Preternatural Appearances of the Ghost of Covent Garden* (London, 1804).

4. Francis Gentleman (ed.), *Troilus and Cressida, a Tragedy, by Shakespeare: An Introduction and notes critical and illustrative, are added by the authors of the Dramatic Censor, Bell's Edition of Shakespeare's plays as they are now performed at the Theatres Royal in London*, Vol. VI (London: for John Bell, 1774), p. 156.

Notes

NOTES–THE TAMING OF THE SHREW–WITH "ADDITIONAL DIALOGUE"?

1. The following timetable derives from interviews with Mary Pickford and the late Sam Taylor, and from trade papers, especially the *Exhibitors Herald-World*, from which I quote. Additional information is from Miss Pickford's book, *Sunshine and Shadow* (Garden City, N.Y.: Doubleday, 1955), pp. 311–12. I am indebted to Lois M. Jones of the Los Angeles Public Library for the dates of the stage performances. Mr. Taylor, shortly before his death, rediscovered his mislaid shooting script, later to be analyzed, and kindly sent it to me.

2. *Catharine and Petruchio* is in *Bell's British Theatre*, (London, 1780), 14: 290–317.

3. The turnabout ending might conceivably have sprung from John Fletcher's sequel to Shakespeare, *The Woman's Prize, or The Tamer Tam'd*, but the plot there is quite different, and there is no evidence for any such influence. That the Sothern-Marlowe performances and the interpretation of Katherine in Ellen Terry's lectures provided hints is possible. See Edward Wagenknecht, *The Movies in the Age of Innocence* (Norman: University of Oklahoma Press, 1962), p. 155; Charles Edward Russell, *Julia Marlowe: Her Life and Art* (New York: Appleton & Co., 1926), pp. 333–34; Betty Bandel, "Ellen Terry's Foul Papers," *Theatre Survey*, 10 (1969): 46. However, it seems more probable that Taylor adopted his well-foreshadowed ending to conform to the qualities he found in his stars and to a reluctance to offend modern sensibilities by making Petruchio utterly triumphant over his bride.

4. The copyright entry might have confused the uninitiated. It reads: "based on the comedy by Shakespeare. Adapted and directed: Sam Taylor. The Pickford and the Elton Corporation (Sam Taylor, author)." "Author" refers to the arranger of the story for filming and implies no necessarily additional dialogue by Taylor.

Roger Manvell's *Shakespeare and the Film* (New York: Praeger, 1971), which appeared after this essay was written, repeats on p. 23 the "additional dialogue by Sam Taylor" story and on p. 25 adds: "Laurence Irving [one of the designers] did his best to persuade Sam Taylor not to make himself a laughing-stock by insisting on his credit for 'additional dialogue,' but in vain. 'Well, I did the stuff, didn't I?' was all Sam Taylor would say in reply." This evidence does not vitiate my argument, since the persuasion occurred before the film was released, and I do not deny the possibility of an "in joke" at that time nor that the "additional dialogue" might have appeared in some advertising. In *The New York Times* of 2 December 1934, in connection with the pending *Midsummer Night's Dream*, William Dieterle said, "Hollywood still laughs over the billboards of 'The Taming of the Shrew.'" Personally I think Taylor, who was quite capable of it, was pulling Irving's leg, and I still find no evidence that the credit appeared *on the film itself*.

5. It was Mr. Taylor of course who gave me the clue. He thought, mistakenly, that the paragraph had been written by E.B. White, a former schoolfellow of his in Mount Vernon, New York, who was indeed doing portions of "The Talk of the Town" for *The New Yorker* at the time of publication. Mr. White, to whom my thanks, located the piece for me and sent me a copy but informed me that he did not write it and had no

Notes

knowledge of the source of information. He guessed that it had stemmed from a wandering staff writer who heard the story on the West Coast, or that it was submitted by a contributor.

NOTES—*MACBETH* AT THE GLOBE

1. My dear Arthur,
A present should be kept a secret, so that it may at least give the pleasure of a surprise; but this one is, I fear, already familiar to you, since you have twice heard me struggle in public to give it form, and have afterwards talked my questions over with me in private, with your habitual kindness and learning, and have encouraged me to think they were worth asking; and so I offer them to you a third time together with my best wishes and congratulations, most cordially,

Yours,
Nevill

2. Reginald Scott, *The Discoverie of Witchcraft* (London, 1584), book III, ch. 3; book X, ch. 8; book XIII, ch. 6, and elsewhere.

3. King James I, *Daemonologie* (Edinburgh, 1597), book II, ch. 3.

4. Arthur Colby Sprague, *Shakespeare and the Actors* (Cambridge: Harvard University Press, 1944), p. 225.

5. *Pericles*, IV.iv.22.

6. *Hamlet*, III.ii.19–20.

7. Thomas Middleton, *The Witch*, III.iii.1331–61.

8. *The Masque of Queens*, ll. 51–67; see *Ben Jonson*, ed. C.H. Herford and Percy and Evelyn Simpson (Oxford: Clarendon Press, 1941), 7: 283–84.

9. Glynne Wickham, *Early English Stages* (London: Routledge and Paul, 1959), 1: 165–66.

10. Reprinted in Robert Ashton's *James I by his Contemporaries* (London: Hutchinson, 1969), p. 17.

11. Marc Bloch, *Les Rois Thaumaturges* (Paris: Armand Colin, 1961), pp. 331, 369; see also p. 339. I quote from his transcript of the letter of the papal spy: "Il Re s'abbia questi giorni intricato in quello ch'haveva di fare intorno di certo usanza anticha delli Rè d'Inghilterra di sanare gl'infermi del morbo regio, et cosi essendogli presentati detti infermi nella sua antecamera, feci prima fare una predicha per un ministro calvinista sopra quel fatto, et poi lui stesso disse che se trovava perplesso in quello ch'haveva di fare rispetto, che dell'una parte non vedeva come potessero guarire l'infermi senza miracolo, et gia li miracoli erano cessati et non se facevano piu; et cosi haveva paura di commettere qualche superstitione; dell'altra parte essendo quella usanza anticha et in beneficio delli suai sudditi, se risoleva di provarlo, ma solamente per via d'oratione la quale pregava a tutti volessero fare insiemi con lui; et con questo toccava alli infermi. Vederemo presto l'effeto che seguitara. Si notava che il Re faceva il suo discorso spesse volte girava l'occhi alli ministri Scozzesi che stavano appresso, com'aspettando la loro approbatione à quel che diceva, havendolo prima conferito con loro."

Notes

12. Allardyce Nicoll, "Passing over the Stage," *Shakespeare Survey*, 12 (1959): 47–55.
13. Emrys Jones, *Scenic Form in Shakespeare* (Oxford: Clarendon Press, 1971).

NOTE–HEAVENLY MINGLE

1. Thomas Beard, *The Theatre of Gods Iudgements* (London, 1597), pp. 352–53.

NOTES–THE ALPHABET OF SPEECHLESS COMPLAINT

1. Rudolf Stamm, "Der Gebrauch der Spiegeltechnik in *Titus Andronicus*," *Sprachkunst: Beitrage zur Literaturwissenschaft*, 1 (1970): 331–57. This article appeared in modified form in *English Studies*, 55 (1974): 325–39.
2. The quotations are taken from Peter Alexander (ed.), *The Complete Works of William Shakespeare*, The Tudor Shakespeare (London and Glasgow: Collins, 1951). Departures from his text are accounted for where they occur.
3. Here we come close to a reaction of Professor G.R. Hibbard, who confessed in his paper, "The Forced Gait of a Shuffling Nag," read at the World Shakespeare Congress at Vancouver, that, on hearing lines 29–32 of our soliloquy, he feels tempted to yell at Marcus: "For God's sake, man, get her to a doctor before she bleeds to death, instead of standing there talking." The paper has been published in *Shakespeare 1971*, ed. Clifford Leech and J.M.R. Margeson (Toronto: University of Toronto Press, 1972), pp. 76–88.
4. B.L. Joseph's remark in his *Elizabethan Acting* (London: Oxford University Press, 1951), p. 73, on what he believes to be the normal meaning of the "wreathed arms" (melancholy) is not applicable to the passage before us. It leads him to his unhelpful comment quoted by J.C. Maxwell in the notes of his New Arden Edition (London: Methuen, 1953), p. 70: "whilst they [Titus and Lavinia] feel more than a dull grief, their mutilations do not allow the expression of what is really within."
5. This is the solution of Capell, Dover Wilson, and Peter Alexander; it recommends itself again in the case of the "See, see!" of line 55. To follow Dyce and print "Help her" as a (quite superfluous) stage direction creates more difficulties than it solves.

NOTES–HUBERT HERKOMER'S THEATRICAL THEORIES

1. Report of his lecture on "Scenic Art" at the Avenue Theatre, 1892, in *Magazine of Art*, 15 (1892): 259–64, 316–20.
2. Hubert Herkomer, *My School and My Gospel* (London: A. Constable & Co., 1908).
3. "The Pictorial Music-Play: An Idyl," *Magazine of Art*, 12 (1889): 316.
4. Alice Corkran, "Professor Herkomer's Pictorial Music-Play," *Scottish Art Review*, 2 (1889): 14.

5. Ibid.

6. "The Pictorial Music-Play," p. 316.

7. Herkomer, *My School*, pp. 198–99.

8. Walter René Fuerst and S.J. Hume, in *Twentieth Century Stage Decoration* (London: A.A. Knopf, 1928), p. 3, quote from Giambattista Pasquali, *Del Teatro in Venezia* (Venice, 1773).

9. *The Builder*, 69 (14 December 1895): 433–34.

10. William L. Telbin, "Art in the Theatre: the Question of Reform," *Magazine of Art*, 17 (1894): 44–48.

11. *Building News*, 69 (13 December 1895): 844–45.

12. Charles Shattuck, *Mr. Macready Produces "As You Like It"* (Urbana: University of Illinois Press, 1962).

13. Telbin, "Art in the Theatre," pp. 44–48.

14. Edward Craig, "Gordon Craig and Hubert von Herkomer," *Theatre Research*, 10 (1969): 7–16.

15. This article was submitted before the publication of a chapter on "Professor Herkomer's Pictorial-Music Plays," in *Resistible Theatres* by John Stokes (London: ELEK, 1972). Readers are referred to this work for pictures of his productions and for other aspects of his work.

Index of Plays

Alchemist, The, 65
All's Well that Ends Well, x, 47–48, 137, 139, 142, 144, 145
Antonio and Mellida, 62, 65
Antonio's Revenge, 65, 90
Antony and Cleopatra, xii, 49, 144, 240–54
Arraignement of Paris, The, 53
As You Like It, 8, 27, 127, 140–41, 145

Book of Sir Thomas More, The, 52, 59–60
Broken Heart, The, 45, 185

Cambises, 50, 116
Casanovas Heimfahrt, 84
Case is Altered, The, 60, 63
Catharine and Petruchio, 206–7
Changeling, The, 185
Cherry Orchard, The, 12, 240
Contention between Liberality and Prodigality, 52
Contention Betwixt the Two Famous Houses of York and Lancaster, The, 118, 124
Coriolanus, 17, 143
Cymbeline, xi, xiii, 10, 26, 48, 67, 73, 77–83, 85–91, 137, 145, 228, 229
Cymbeline Refinished, 83

Dido and Aeneas, 279
Doll's House, A, 46
Duchess of Malfi, The, xi, 68–69, 170–88

Edward I, 54, 93–94, 99, 114
Edward II, 93, 116

Edward IV, The First Part, 95–96, 99, 100, 101
End Game, 21
Epicoene, 63–64
Every Man in His Humour, 127

Fair Em, 94–95, 106
Family Reunion, The, 30
Famous Victories of Henry V, The, 11, 106, 114, 118, 124
Fillipo, 278
Four 'Prentices of London, The, 66
Fulgens and Lucres, 51–52, 239

Game at Chess, 52
Gammer Gurton's Needle, 135
George a Greene, 93, 96, 99, 100, 110, 114
Ghosts, 30
Gorboduc, 51

Hamlet, xiii, 8, 15–16, 17, 22, 23, 39, 59–60, 64, 65, 78, 81, 137, 139, 140, 145, 146, 186, 232, 243, 247, 252–54
Helena of Troas, 274
Henry IV, 1, 61, 102, 104, 107, 110, 117, 118, 120–24, 251
Henry IV, 2, 61, 62, 102–4, 107, 110, 117, 120, 123–30, 143
Henry V, xi, 62, 64, 92–117, 125, 128–30, 190, 237–38
Henry VI, 1, 11, 22, 55–56, 61, 102, 130, 190
Henry VI, 2, 11, 22, 55–56, 61, 102, 127, 131, 135
Henry VI, 3, 11, 22, 55–56, 61, 68, 93, 102, 112, 122–23, 131, 133

Henry VIII, x, 41–49, 102, 135
Histriomastix, 60
Honest Whore, 127

Idyl, An, 275, 277, 279
Isle of Dogs, The, 58

James IV, 114
Jew of Malta, The, 178
John a Kent and John a Cumber, 60
Julius Caesar, xiii, 145
Justice, 45

King John, 56, 102, 123, 131–32, 136
King Lear, xiii, 9, 18, 20–23, 26–27, 29, 42, 65, 69, 144, 183, 241, 243, 247, 252, 253
Kig Lear (Tate's), 25
Knight of the Burning Pestle, The, 65–66, 239

Locrine, 116
Love of King David and Fair Bethsabe with the Tragedy of Absalom, The, 54
Love's Labour's Lost, 8, 24–25, 27, 49, 58, 145–46

Macbeth, xi, 10, 13, 29, 38–40, 223–39, 252
Magnetic Lady, The, 64, 120
Malcontent, The, 65
Masque of Queens, 227, 229
Measure for Measure, xi, 14, 22–23, 28, 47–48, 83–85, 139, 142, 144–45, 149–69, 252
Merchant of Venice, The, 8, 11, 22, 27, 28, 41, 85, 143–45, 234–36
Merry Wives of Windsor, The, 64, 107, 125, 127
Midsummer Night's Dream, A, 14, 23, 38, 56, 66, 139, 142, 145, 275
Mother Bombey, 53
Much Ado About Nothing, 27, 139, 144–45
Mystère des Trois Doms, 228

No Wit, No Help, Like a Woman's, 67

Othello, xiii, 8, 10, 21–22, 27, 49, 69, 81, 83, 137, 143, 146, 187

Pericles, 12, 67
Peril, 276
Pillars of Society, 46
Poetaster, 66

Revenger's Tragedy, The, 178
Richard II, 27, 59, 62 102–3, 114, 121, 123, 130, 132–33, 142
Richard III, 11, 55, 102, 127, 130, 133–35, 138–39, 185
Romeo and Juliet, 25, 27, 38, 140, 144–45
Romeo and Juliet (Garrick's), 25

Saint Joan, 45
Saints Day, 30
Satiromastix, 66
Second Maiden's Tragedy, 119
Selimus, 54–55, 116
Shoemaker's Holiday, The, 98
Sir John Oldcastle, 107–15, 117
Sorceress, The, 275
Spanish Tragedy, The, 54–55, 59, 66, 185
Speculum, 61–62
Staple of News, The, 64
Summer's Last Will and Testament, 56–57

Tamburlaine, 54–55, 61, 116
Taming of the Shrew, The, xi, 10, 22, 54, 142, 145, 203–20
Tempest, The, 14, 67, 144, 229
Terminus et Non Terminus, 58
Times Revenge, 278
Timon of Athens, 42
Titus Andronicus, xii, 24, 141, 190, 255–73
Tristan and Isolde, 278
Troilus and Cressida, xi, 20, 24, 27, 29, 42, 47–48, 59, 64, 83, 90, 138–39, 145, 190–202, 243, 252, 254
Troublesome Reign of King John, The, 132
True Chronicle History of King Leir, 54–55, 94–95, 106

Twelfth Night, 13, 16, 22, 27, 28, 58, 85–86, 89, 127–28, 137–38, 144–45

Two Gentlemen of Verona, xi, 10, 12–13, 73–76, 78, 80–81, 83, 85, 141–44

Warning for Fair Women, A, 61

Wars of the Roses, 9, 11

What You Will, 63

When Thou Art King, 11

White Devil, The, 41, 68, 172–73, 178, 183

Wily Beguiled, 61–62

Winter's Tale, The, 41, 67, 83, 87, 137, 228–29

Winter's Tale, The (Garrick's), 25–26

Witch, The, 226–27, 229

Women Beware Women, 180

General Index

Abercrombie, Lascelles, 22, 31, 40
Agate, James, 205
Aldwych Theatre, 172
Alexander, Peter, 49
American Shakespeare Theatre (Stratford, Conn.), 149, 154
Amfiteatro Michelangelo (Rome), 172
Andrews, Harry, 150, 152–53
Annan, Noel, 27
Appia, Adolph, 274, 276–77, 279
Artaud, Antonin, 24
Ashcroft, Peggy, 27
Atienza, Edward, 141
Aubrey, John, 66

Ball, Robert, xi
Bannister, John, 196
Barrie, J.M., 37
Barton, Anne, ix–xi, 59, 176–78
Barton, John, 6, 9, 11–13, 16, 167
Baynton, Henry, 143
Beaumont, Francis, 65
Beckerman, Bernard, x
Bell, The, 51
Bell Savage, The, 51
Belmont Theatre (Hollywood), 205
Benson, Frank, 4
Benthall, Michael, 144
Berlyn, Alfred, 278
Birmingham Repertory Company, 3
Blackfriars, 186–87
Blatchley, John, 159–61
Bochner, Lloyd, 153
Boleslavsky, Richard, 219
Bottomley, Gordon, 27
Boucicault, Dion, 246
Bowdler, Thomas, 127

Bradbrook, Muriel C., ix–x
Bradley, A.C., xiii
Bridges-Adams, W., 140, 171–72
Bristol Old Vic, 149, 161–62
Brook, Peter, 6, 14, 21–22, 24, 141–42, 146, 150, 152, 155–56, 158, 167
Brown, John Russell, 22, 85, 176, 180, 186
Brown, Pamela, 139
Bryden, Ronald, 173
Büchner, Georg, 89
Bull, Peter, 139
Bull, The, 51
Bullough, Geoffrey, 92
Burbage, Richard, 68, 183
Burrell, John, 139
Bury, John, 275
Byrne, Muriel St. Clare, x

Cawthorn, Joseph, 204
Chambers, E.K., 24, 47
Chettle, Henry, 115
Chew, Samuel, xii
Chichester Company, The, 8
Cibber, Theophilus, 8
Clarke, Cecil, 153–54
Clements, John, 143
Cochran, C.B., 205
Coghill, Nevill, x–xi, 5, 7, 156, 160
Coleridge, Samuel T., 22–23, 240–41, 254
Collier, Constance, 204–5
Collier, John Payne, 228
Condell, Henry, 119, 183
Cook, Clyde, 204
Courtney, W.L., 278
Covent Garden, 191

Index

Craig, Gordon, 36, 274, 276, 279
Craig, John, 204–5
Craven, Frank, 219

Darlington, W.A., 163
David, Richard, 151–52
De La Mare, Walter, 23
De Witt, J., 235–37
Dekker, Thomas, 63, 66, 98, 116, 127
Dench, Judi, 13, 163–64
Digges, Dudley, 219
Downer, Alan, xii
Drayton, Michael, 107, 112, 117
Drury Lane, 278
Dryden, John, 190, 194
Dukes, Ashley, 37–38
Dunlop, Frank, 8, 172

Edinborough, Arnold, 166
Eliot, T.S., 23, 31–32, 170, 188
Elliot, Michael, 160–61
Ellis-Fermor, Una, 188
Evans, Edith, 24, 27
Ewbank, Inga-Stina, 68, 170–71

Fairbanks, Douglas, xi, 203–20
Fernald, Karen, 166–67
Fleming, Tom, 159–60
Fletcher, John, 47
Foakes, R.A., 46
Foch, Nina, 155
Forbes-Robertson, Jean, 27
Ford, John, 45, 185
Forman, Simon, 228
Freehold Company, The, 173–74

Galsworthy, John, 45
Garrick, David, 3, 8, 25–26, 190–91,
    205–8, 212, 214
Gentleman, Francis, 191–202
George, Colin, 171
Gielgud, John, 27, 150–51, 154
Giles, David, 165–66
Gill, Desmond, 173
Gill, Peter, 173
Globe Theatre, 26, 30, 93, 138–39,
    186–87, 223–39
Godwin, E.W., 274
Goethe, J.W. von, 23

Goring, Marius, 160
Granville-Barker, Harley, xiv, 5, 8–9,
    18, 24, 26, 37
Greene, Robert, 53, 93, 115–16
Greenhill Street Cinema (Stratford-
    upon-Avon), 140
Guinness, Alec, 39, 146
Guthrie, Tyrone, 24–25, 42, 46, 145–
    46, 150, 161–62, 164–65

Hall, Mordaunt, 206
Hall, Peter, 6, 13
Hamlett, Dilys, 163–64
Hands, Terry, 6
Hathway, Richard, 107, 112, 117
Hazlitt, William, 4
Helpmann, Robert, 144
Heminge, John, 119
Hengler's Circus, 274
Henslowe, Philip, 107
Herben, S.J., xii
Herkomer, Hubert, xii, 274–79
Heywood, Thomas, 62, 95, 99, 101,
    116, 246
Hibbard, George, 90
Hobson, Harold, 152, 159–60
Hodges, Douglas, 205
Honigmann, E.A.J., 232
Hope, Julian, 174
Hope-Wallace, Philip, 157, 163
Hotson, Leslie, 100
Houseman, John, 154
Howard, Sidney, 219
Huftel, Sheila, 162, 164
Hunt, Leigh, 4
Hutt, William, 166
Hyland, Frances, 153–54

Ibsen, Henryk, 46, 48–49
Irving, Henry, 9, 26, 140, 276–77, 279
Irving, Laurence, 204

Jack, Ian, 188
Jackson, Barry, 3, 5
Jefford, Barbara, 150–53, 158
Johnson, Samuel, xiv, 24, 240
Johnston, Margaret, 158–59
Jones, Emrys, 238
Jones, Henry Arthur, 137

Index

Jonson, Ben, ix, 58, 60, 63–64, 66–67, 69, 115, 119–20, 127, 227, 229
Jordan, Dorothy, 204

Kean, Charles, 4, 11–12
Kean, Edmund, 4
Keen, Maurice, 97
Kemble, John Philip, xi, 191–202
Kemp, William, 58
Kerr, Walter, 153–55, 162, 165–66
Kittredge, G.L., xii–xiii, 20
Knight, G. Wilson, 13, 16, 23–24, 46, 49
Knights, L.C., 23
Kohler, Estelle, 167–68
Kott, Jan, 21–22, 29
Kozintsev, Gregori, 20–22, 29
Kyd, Thomas, 51, 53, 55, 115, 255

Lamb, Charles, 4, 25
Landau, Jack, 154
Laughton, Charles, 23, 150, 161
Leavis, F.R., 22
Lee, Vernon, 34
Leech, Clifford, x–xi, 165–67
Leigh-Hunt, Barbara, 164–65
Lennox, Charlotte, 25
Lewes, G.H., 171
Liverpool Playhouse, 28
Loew's State Theatre (Boston), 205
London Pavilion, 205
Lowin, John, 241
Lucas, F.L., 175
Lyly, John, 53

Macready, W., 3
Madariaga, Salvador de, 23
Marlowe, Christopher, ix, 53–55, 66, 93, 99–100, 115–16, 255
Marston, John, 60, 62–63, 65, 68, 90, 115
Martin, Quinn, 206
Mason, James, 153–54
Maxwell, Baldwin, 49
Maxwell, Edwin, 204
Maxwell, J.C., 21, 269
Maxwell, James, 160–61
Medwall, Henry, 239
Menzies, William Cameron, 204

Middleton, Thomas, 52, 67, 180, 185, 226–27, 229
Miller, Jonathan, 8
Morgan, Charles, 145
Morgan, Gareth, 12
Morgann, Maurice, xiii
Morley, Henry, 4
Mosher, John C., 206, 220
Moss, Arnold, 154–55
Muir, Kenneth, x
Munday (Mundy), Anthony, 60–61, 107, 112, 117
Murray, J.M., 23

Nashe, Thomas, 53, 55, 57–59, 61
National Theatre, The, 7–8, 172
Neville, John, 158
New Temple, The, 9
New Theatre, The, 139, 142–43
Newington Butts, 51
Newlin, Jeanne, xi
Ney, Marie, 161, 163
Nicholls, Anthony, 155–58
Nicoll, Alardyce, 234
Nicolson, Marjorie, 49
Nosworthy, J.M., 88, 149
Nunn, Trevor, 6, 15–16

Old Vic, The, 7, 27, 143–44, 146, 149, 150, 155–56, 158, 160–63, 167
Oliver, Stephen, 174–75
Olivier, Laurence, 4, 8, 21, 27, 139, 145–46
Opera House, The (Bayreuth), 274
Oxford Playhouse, The, 174

Parfitt, Judy, 173
Pasquali, Giambattista, 277
Patton, Thomas, 205
Peele, George, 53–54, 93, 99, 114, 116
Phelps, Samuel, 4
Pickford, Mary, xi, 203–20
Poel, William, xiii, 5, 8, 26, 274
Pollard, A.W., 45
Porter, Eric, 172
Potter, Lois, xi
Preston, Thomas, 116
Princess's Theatre, The (London), 4
Prospect Players, The, 8
Pushkin, Aleksandr, 22

Index

Quayle, Anthony, 6, 155, 159

Regent's Park Outdoor Theatre, 8
Reicher, Frank, 219
Rialto Theatre, The (New York), 206
Richardson, William, 127
Robbins, John Franklyn, 162
Robinson, Richard, 183
Robson, Flora, 23, 150, 161, 163
Rosenfeld, Sybil, xii
Rossiter, A.P., 116
Rowley, William, 61
Royal Court, The, 173–74, 176, 178
Royal Shakespeare Company, 6–8, 11
Royal Shakespeare Theatre (Stratford-
    upon-Avon), 3–4, 6–8, 13, 23, 28,
    42, 138, 141–42, 146, 149, 150,
    155–56, 158–59, 162, 165, 167–68,
    170–73, 183, 228
Rylands, George, 5, 7

Sadler's Wells, 4, 23
St. James's Theatre, 144
St. Paul's, 51
Sardou, Victorien, 276
Savoy Theatre, The, 9
Schanzer, Ernest, 149
Schenck, Joseph, 219
Schnitzler, Arthur, 84
Scribe, Eugène, 246
Sharman, Julian, 125
Sharpe, R., 183
Shaw, George Bernard, 24, 26, 29, 37,
    45, 83, 190
Shaw, Glen Byam, 6
Shaw, Sebastian, 168–69
Sheffield Playhouse, The, 171
Shelton, Brian, 172
Sheridan, Richard, 39
Shirley, Frances, xi
Siddons, Sarah, 23, 38–39
Silverman, Sime, 206
Sisson, Charles, 143
Skillan, George, 9
Smith, Derek, 13
Speaight, Robert, 167
Spedding, James, 41, 43
Spencer, T.J.B., 10
Spencer, Theodore, 24

Sprague, Arthur Colby, ix–xiv, 3, 49,
    50, 73, 138–39, 224, 281–83, 301
Spurgeon, Caroline, 45
Stamm, Rudolf, xii
Strachey, Lyton, 73
Stratford Festival Company, 204
Stratford Festival Theatre (Ontario),
    73, 81, 84, 149, 153, 165, 172, 176

Tarlton, Richard, 50, 58
Taylor, Sam, 203–20
Telbin, William, L., 277–78
Theatre, The, 51
Theatregoround, 11–12
Tillyard, E.M.W., x
Traversi, Derek, 24
Tree, Beerbohm, 4, 275, 277
Trewin, J.C., xi, 7, 158
Tynan, Kenneth, 158

Van Dine, S.S., 219
Vega, Lope de, 246
Verity, A.W., 5
Vischer, Peter, 206

Wagner, Richard, 274, 279
Wagner, Siegfried, 274
Wait, R.J.C., 233
Walker, Roy, 23
Wardle, Irving, 167
Wardwell, Geoffrey, 204
Watteau, Jean, 27
Watts, Richard, Jr., 165, 206
Webster, John, ix, 68–69, 170–88
Webster, Margaret, 28, 155–57, 159
Wells, Stanley, x
West, Rebecca, 23
Whittaker, Herbert, 153
Wickham, Glynne, 228
Williams, Clifford, 8, 171
Williams, Emlyn, 158, 161
Williamson, Jane, xi
Wilson, F.P., 55
Wilson, John Dover, xiii, 23, 25, 139
Wilson, Robert, 107, 112, 117
Wolfit, Donald, 4, 26
Wright, William Aldis, 125
Wynn, Pauline, 138–39

Young Vic, The, 173

312